China in
Indian Ocean Region

China in
Indian Ocean Region

Editors

Prof. R. Sidda Goud
Manisha Mookherjee

ALLIED PUBLISHERS PVT. LTD.

New Delhi • Mumbai • Kolkata • Lucknow • Chennai
Nagpur • Bangalore • Hyderabad • Ahmedabad

ALLIED PUBLISHERS PRIVATE LIMITED

Regd. Off.: 15 J.N. Heredia Marg, Ballard Estate, **Mumbai**–400001
Ph.: 022-22626476 • E-mail: mumbai.books@alliedpublishers.com

1/13-14 Asaf Ali Road, **New Delhi**–110002
Ph.: 011-23239001 • E-mail: delhi.books@alliedpublishers.com

17 Chittaranjan Avenue, **Kolkata**–700072
Ph.: 033-22129618 • E-mail: cal.books@alliedpublishers.com

751 Anna Salai, **Chennai**–600002
Ph.: 044-28523938 • E-mail: chennai.books@alliedpublishers.com

5th Main Road, Gandhinagar, **Bangalore**–560009
Ph.: 080-22262081 • E-mail: bngl.books@alliedpublishers.com

3-2-844/6 & 7 Kachiguda Station Road, **Hyderabad**–500027
Ph.: 040-24619079 • E-mail: hyd.books@alliedpublishers.com

60 Shiv Sunder Apartments (Ground Floor), Central Bazar Road,
Bajaj Nagar, **Nagpur**–440010

F-1 Sun House (First Floor), C.G. Road, Navrangpura,
Ellisbridge P.O., **Ahmedabad**–380006
Ph.: 079-26465916 • E-mail: ahmbd.books@alliedpublishers.com

Khasra No. 168, Plot No. 12-A, Opp. Wisdom Academy School,
Kamta, Surendra Nagar, **Lucknow**–227105
Ph.: 09335202549 • E-mail: lko.books@alliedpublishers.com

Website: www.alliedpublishers.com

ISBN: 978-81-8424-977-4

Published by Sunil Sachdev and printed by Ravi Sachdev at Allied Publishers Pvt. Ltd. (Printing Division), A-104 Mayapuri Phase II, New Delhi-110064

Foreword

Fall of the Cold War system and its impact on Asia carried serious geo-political implications for India. India lost her close and dependable friend, the Soviet Union. India's relations with the sole super power, the US, were never warm, as also with the Asian powers like China, Japan and the ASEAN countries. India hence had thoroughly revised her foreign policy objectives and strategic framework. Her redefined foreign and strategic objectives aimed moving close to the USA and building equally closer relations with the ASEAN countries whom she neglected long. A 'strategic partnership' agreement was signed with the United States which led to build close bilateral military, economic, technological and energy relations between the two countries. Similarly India 'Look East' policy aimed at engaging closely with the Southeast and East Asian countries as these countries represented Asian dynamism.

India's strategic aspiration is to emerge as an Asian power and play active role in the Asian power balance. A major objective of India's Asian strategy is to counter the growing power and role of China in the Asian geopolitics. Since the United States too is worried about the rise of China as an Asian and global giant, a strategic partnership exists between New Delhi and Washington. To build her strategic power, India is upgrading and building her military capabilities, and projecting power in Asia. She is adopting a dual strategy which aims at bolstering the hard military power and promoting close political, economic, energy and cultural synergies with the Asian countries. A number of bilateral and multilateral agreements are signed with the Asian countries so much that today is hardly an Asian regional group in which India is not a member.

India's geographical location at the centre of east-west highway across the Indian Ocean—linking Asia-Pacific with Europe—imposes greater security burdens on her. Large number of military, cargo and oil ships crisscross the sea lanes of Indian Ocean. Several regional and extra-regional powers who depend on the oil and resources of the Indian Ocean region, have regular military presence in the ocean. India has reasons to be concerned with such military developments and regional conflicts like the Iraq and Afghan wars. India's major worry is China's increasing naval presence in the region, especially in India's neighbourhood.

India's defence preparedness is determined by the two-front threat to nation's security from Pakistan and China. Pakistan has been the traditional friend of China and US. Both the countries had built the military strength and nuclear capabilities of India's traditional rival. Having been defeated in all the four wars with India, Pakistan has been encouraging cross-border terrorism (proxy war) across Punjab and Kashmir. Terrorism is the major threat to India's national security. India faces cross-border militancy and criminal activities through Bangladesh, Nepal and Sri Lanka, apart from Pakistan. So managing the borders is the country's major security task. India's growing economy requires regular and uninterrupted oil supplies. About 70% of energy requirements are imported from foreign countries, especially the gulf. Ensuring adequate supplies of oil should be the major goal of national security planning. In the overall interest of her growing security and economic interests, India has to safeguard the IO's sealanes which China is trying to bring under its influence.

China as is well known is trying to contain Indian role and influence in the Indian Ocean through active bilateral and multilateral strategies. Its so-called 'String of Pearls' is a much debated one at the conference organized by the UGC Centre for Indian Ocean Studies. It should however be noted that this strategy need not overly worry India, given its own multi-layered linkages with the Indian Ocean littorals and strong naval presence in the Indian Ocean. As a former Indian foreign secretary rightly commented the string of pearls is like 'a weak man's murder weapon.' Recently Beijing has proposed another doctrine called Maritime Silk Route (MSR). Its objective is to link China's east coast in the Pacific Ocean with the Indian Ocean through the South China Sea, Malacca Straits, Bay of Bengal, central Indian Ocean, Africa, Red Sea and the Mediterranean Sea. This ambitious maritime scheme proposes to link almost all the major littoral countries by developing their maritime infrastructure with the Chinese assistance. Reportedly some Indian Ocean littorals like Maldives and Sri Lanka have welcomed the Maritime Silk Route. How far this Chinese latest transoceanic doctrine is going to have impact on India that needs to be seriously examined. In any case, the fallout of the Maritime Silk Route cannot be ignored by India whose survival and destiny, by virtue of the peninsula's critical location on the east-west maritime highway of the Indian Ocean is conditioned by the geo-politics of the Indian Ocean.

P.V. Rao
Emeritus Professor of Political Science-UGC

Contributors

1. **Prof. Srikanth Kondapalli**, Professor in Chinese Studies, Jawaharlal Nehru University, New Delhi. Educated in Chinese Studies in India and China with a Ph.D. in Chinese Studies. A Post-Doctoral Visiting Fellow at People's University, Beijing, a Visiting Professor at National Chengchi University, Taipei, an Honorary Professor at Shandong University, Jinan in 2009, 2011 and 2013. A Non-Resident Senior fellow at People's University since 2014. Author of two books *China's Military: The PLA in Transition*, published in 1999 and *China's Naval Power*, published in 2001, co-edited three volumes on: *Asian Security and China* in 2004; *China and its Neighbours* in 2010 and *China's Military and India* in 2012. He received the *K. Subramanyam Award* in 2010 for *Excellence in Research in Strategic and Security Studies*.

2. **Prof. G.V.C. Naidu**, Professor in the Centre for Indo-Pacific Studies, School of International Studies, JNU, New Delhi. He specializes in Asia-Pacific issues, Southeast Asian affairs, Japanese foreign and security policies, maritime security, and the Indian Ocean. Visiting Professor at the Daito Bunka University, Japan, Gakushuin University Tokyo; National Chengchi University, Taipei, a visiting fellow at the East-West Center, Honolulu; at the Japan Institute of International Affairs, and a Research Fellow at the Institute of Southeast Asian Studies, Singapore.

3. **Dr. M. Mayilvaganan**, Assistant Professor, International Strategic and Security Studies, National Institute of Advanced Studies (NIAS), Indian Institute of Science (IISc) Campus, Bangalore.
   *P.S. Ramya, Research Assistant at International Strategic and Security Studies, National Institute of Advanced Studies (NIAS), Indian Institute of Science (IISc) Campus, Bangalore.

4. **Seshadri Vasan**, Commodore, Indian Navy (Retd) Head, Strategy and Security Studies, Centre for Asia Studies, India, Director, Asian Secretariat World Boderpol (WBO), An alumnus of the Defence Services Staff College and the College of Naval Warfare, India. A Director at the Naval Aviation Staff, Aviation Planning, Operations and Training. He was as a faculty at the prestigious Naval War College that trains senior level officers from all the three services. He is a member of the Maritime Security Programme at the Observer

Research Foundation, a major think tank in India. Director of the Asian Secretariat of the World Borderpol (WBO). Presently the Director, Chennai Centre for China Studies.

5. **Sylvia Mishra**, A Researcher with the ICRIER-Wadhwani Chair in India-US Policy Studies, ICRIER, New Delhi. He was a member of an Expedition to Central Asia to promote Track II Diplomacy supported by Ministry of External Affairs and India Central Asia Foundation. Research interests include Foreign Policy, Security and Defense Studies and South Asian and Middle Eastern Politics. Co-authored the ICRIER-Wadhwani Report 'India-US Defence Industrial Cooperation: The Way Forward' Edited 'Studies on Iran' and 'Studies on Pakistan', published by Foreign Policy Research Centre, New Delhi.

6. **Dr. Jasbir Pal Singh Rakhra**, Assistant Professor in Security Studies with Ministery of External Affairs Division at Centre for Research in Rural and Industrial Development (CRRID), Chandigarh, India.

7. **Prof. Mohammed Khalid**, Professor of Political Science, Department of Evening Studies Panjab University Chandigarh. His primary interest is geopolitics of Indian Ocean and Indian Diasporas in the Indian Ocean Region. He was Assistant Director Academic Staff College Panjab University Chandigarh, member of University Senate, Syndicate, Academic Council and Board of Finance. A teacher activist, was Treasurer, General Secretary and President of Panjab University Teachers' Association.

8. **Prof. Yagama Reddy**, Professor (Retd.), Centre for Southeast Asian and Pacific Studies, Sri Venkateshwara University, Tirupati. Authored 8 books and edited 5 books.

9. **Dr. R. Sidda Goud**, Director and Professor of Economics, UGC Centre for Indian Ocean Studies, Osmania University, Hyderabad. Ex-Member, Executive Council and Acamedic Senate, Osmania University, Hyderabad. Authored the book 'Agriculture, Trade Economic Development' and three occasional papers (i) 'India Needs a Comprehensive Inflation Index', (ii) 'Impact of Global Warming on Indian Ocean Countries', (iii) 'Micro Finance (MFs) Impact in India: A Study in Andhra Pradesh'. Editor of "India-Sri Lanka Relations: Strengthening SAARC", Allied Publishers, New Delhi (2013), "India and Iran in Contemporary Relations" Allied Publishers, New Delhi (2014), and the Editor of the Bi-annual Journal; *Indian Ocean Digest*, published by the UGC Centre for Indian Ocean Studies, Osmania University, Hyderabad.

Prof. Manisha Mookherjee, Associate Professor of Sociology, UGC Centre for Indian Ocean Studies, Osmania University, Hyderabad. She has authored two country monographs (i) 'Population Growth and Structure of Zambia and Zimbabwe (1997). (ii) 'Demographic Profile of South Africa' (1998). (iii) Co-editor of the book "India-Sri Lanka Relations: Strengthening SAARC" published by Allied Publishers, New Delhi (iv) Co-editor of the book "India and Iran in Contemporary Relations" published by Allied Publishers, New Delhi and (iv) Associate Editor of the Bi-annual Journal *Indian Ocean Digest* published by the UGC Centre for Indian Ocean Studies, Osmania University, Hyderabad.

10. **Dr. Sujata Ashwarya Cheema**, Assistant Professor, Centre for West Asian Studies, Jamia Millia Islamia New Delhi. She was awarded the Government of Israel Graduate Fellowship (2002–03) and Visiting Research Fellow (2011–12) at Hebrew University of Jerusalem. A awarded Post-Doctoral Fellow under the Indo-French Cultural Exchange Programme, a visiting Researcher at the Department of Indian Studies, Faculty of World Studies, University of Tehran. Her research interests are on West Asia, India's West Asia policy, and issues relating to democratization in the region.

    Suruchi Aggarwal is currently pursuing her MPhil in West Asian Studies from Jamia Millia Islamia, New Delhi.

11. **Vignesh Ram**, Doctoral Candidate, Department of Geopolitics and International Relations, Manipal University, Karnataka.

12. **Vivek Mishra**, Doctoral Candidate, US Studies Programme, School of International Studies Jawaharlal Nehru University, New Delhi.

13. **Dr. Durga Bhavani**, Researcher of International Relations. Member, Board of Studies, Andhra Mahila Sabha Arts and Science College for Women, Hyderabad.

14. **J.I.A. Haitao**, Professor and Director of the Institute for Chindian Studies, Jinan University, Guangzhou, China.

15. **Dr. V. Srilatha**, Assistant Professor of Political Science, UGC Centre for Indian Ocean Studies, Osmania University, Hyderabad. Her Areas of research interests are Maritime Affairs in Indian Ocean Region, South Asian Politics, Defense and Strategic Studies, Indian Naval Issues, Indo-US relations.

16. **Dr. Murali Manohar Gogulamudi**, Department of Political Science, University of Hyderabad.

17. **Dr. Sukalpa Chakrabarti**, Associate Professor (IR and Public Policy) Deputy Director, Symbiosis School of Economics, Symbiosis

International University, Pune. Her research interests include conflicts in West Asia, India's West Asia policy, politics and foreign policy of Iran, Iraq and Israel, and issues relating to democratization in the region. She has published *West Asia: Civil Society, Democracy and State* (New Delhi, 2010), several research papers, book and articles.

18. **Amrita Jash,** Doctoral Research Scholar, Chinese Division, Centre for East Asian Studies, School of International Studies, Jawaharlal Nehru University, New Delhi.

Preface

Indian Ocean, third largest ocean in the world surpasses the Atlantic and Pacific Oceans as the world's largest and most strategically significant trade corridor. Indian Ocean Region (IOR) which is surrounded by Africa, Asia and Australia serves as a maritime highway linking trans-continental human and economic relationships. Being the world's most populated region, one third of the world's bulk cargo and around two thirds of world oil shipmates pass through it. The Strait of Hormuz, located between Iran and Oman, the world's most important 'oil chokepoint', has a daily oil flow of approximately 40% of global seaborne trade and 90% of oil exported from the Persian Gulf is destined for Asia, Western Europe and the United States. The Strait of Malacca, located between Indonesia, Malaysia and Singapore, accounts for about 35% of global seaborne trade, and is the shortest sea route between China, Japan and South Korea and Persian Gulf oil suppliers. If this Strait is choked for any reason, almost half the world's fleet would need rerouting thus aggravating the oil and other transactional burden for the importing countries.

China's interest in the Indian Ocean Region (IOR) can be traced back to the early 1960s when it began expressing solidarity with some of the beleaguered Afro-Asian states through economic and military aid. Ever since Beijing has been increasingly deepening its presence in the IOR for a variety of reasons—oil, trade, security, etc., has over thirty per cent of China's seaborne trade worth above US $300 billion transits across IOR. Sharing a quarter of the world's population, China faces ever increasing demand for energy. According to a recent OPEC report while it consumed 10.1 million barrels of oil a day last year—one-ninth of the world's total—the country produced only 4.2 million barrels a day. China used only half as much energy as the United States in 2000. Nine years later, it surpassed the United States as the world's biggest energy user and last year it leapfrogged the United States as the No. 1 oil importer. China has little choice but to look beyond its borders for its energy needs. About 77 per cent of its oil imports are sourced from West Asia and Africa and these are transported through the Indian Ocean. Thus China's dependence on the Indian Ocean continues to grow for energy imports from the Gulf, to import resources from Africa and trade with Europe. China has been employing several soft power strategies, in extreme cases, even force to satisfy its growing hunger for energy to fuel its economic growth.

Sea Lanes of Communication (SLOCs) in the IOR are not only vital for the world's economy, but for India too. According to K.M. Panikkar "while to other countries the Indian Ocean is only one of the important oceanic areas, to India it is a vital sea. Her lifelines are concentrated in that area, her freedom is dependent on the freedom of that water surface." India imports about 70 percent of its oil through the Indian Ocean Region to its various ports. As a consequence, it has been enhancing its strategic influence through the use of soft power, by becoming a major foreign investor in regional mining, oil, gas and infrastructure projects. As the ability of China's navy to project power in the Indian Ocean Region grows, India is likely to feel even more vulnerable despite enjoying distinct geographical advantages in the region. China's growing naval presence around the Indian Ocean Region restricts India's freedom to manoeuvre. Of particular note is what has been termed China's 'string of pearls' strategy, which has significantly expanded China's strategic depth in India's backyard. China to protect its strategic sea lane has a 'string of pearls' strategy of bases and diplomatic ties that include the Gwadar port in Pakistan, naval and electronic intelligence-gathering facilities on the Burmese islands in the Bay of Bengal, port access and modernization of Chittagong in Bangladesh, construction of Sri Lanka's harbor like Hambantota and serious plans for a canal across the Kra Isthmus in Thailand.

With China's maritime presence in the Indian Ocean set to expand along with its economic interests, the question for India is how to cope up with this new geo-political reality. Indian is deeply apprehensive about the Chinese assertive or even aggressive attitude towards its neighbors and India. China has territorial disputes with all nations it shares border with and eight other nations [Afghanistan, Bhutan, Burma, Brunei, Tajikistan, Cambodia, Indonesia, Taiwan, Kazakhstan, Laos, Kyrgyzstan, India, Malaysia, Mongolia, Nepal, Philippines, North Korea, Russia, Singapore, South Korea, Japan and Vietnam]. Some of these countries however do not belong to the IOR. India being a strong advocate of 'freedom of navigation in the sea' has made known its 'concerns' over China's aggressive postures in the South China Sea.

In view such of Chinese assertive policies, India is compelled to carefully devise its own strategic responses. In existing situation one can't build a cordon against China's maritime presence nor its growing influence in the Indian Ocean for free navigational rights to ensure energy security.

But many Indian strategists view that the Indian Ocean is India's 'rightful domain' and India has to play a mammoth role for ensuring prospects for peace and cooperation in the IOR. Thus maritime friction is likely to grow as the Indian Navy tries to expand its footprint in the South China Sea and the western Pacific even as the Chinese Navy increases its presence in the Indian Ocean.

China recently announced 10 billion Yuan ($1.6bn) fund to take forward its ambitious "Maritime Silk Road Plan" to build ports and to boost maritime connectivity with Southeast Asian and Indian Ocean littoral countries, in support of infrastructure projects under the umbrella of the silk road plan. The Maritime Silk Road plan has become a key initiative of Chinese president after a high-profile trip to Southeast Asia in October 2013. Hence, China is keen to set-up free-trade zones to link its coastal areas with countries in Southeast Asia and in the Indian Ocean, attempting to revive the ancient maritime 'silk road' that connected China with the region. India, Sri Lanka, Malaysia, Singapore and Gulf countries have been sounded out about the initiative. The new Chinese plan focuses on 'infrastructure constructions' in Pakistan, Sri Lanka, and Bangladesh, where China is already involved in the port projects, clearly indicates Chinese intent to establish its footprints in the Indian Ocean Region.

With China steadily spreading its foot prints in the Indian Ocean Region with increasing military presence and with the rapidly growing Navy being equipped with warships, destroyers and nuclear submarines. On September 15th 2014, Changzheng2, a nuclear powered submarine was docked at the Colombo International Container Terminal Ltd. Followed by the docking of a second one in October 2014. The presence of these Chinese submarines across Palk Straits has deeply disturbed the Indian government. Now China can strike deep in the US with nuclear empowered cluster of 12 JL-2 missiles, with a range of around 7350 km being mounted on its JIN class of submarines, China so far has three JIN-class nuclear—powered submarines. The JL-2 missiles will have an array of strike option depending on whether the subs choose to fire its weapons close to Chinese shores or from areas deeper in the sea. Alaska will fall within their ambit if the missiles are fired from waters near China. Hawaii can be targeted if these weapons are launched from waters South of Japan. Western continental US and all the 50 states are endangered if waters, West or East of Hawaii are chosen as the launch pads.

Many Chinese scholars are of the view that, the acquisition of a sea based deterent has finally insulated China from a US nuclear strike. Despite going up the nuclear ladder, Chinese acquisition of sea based deterent essentially defensive and its accelerated weaponisation is largely a response to Washington's 'Asia Pivot' strategy of China's containment policy. Therefore, China going up weapons like—DF-SA missiles a liquidfuelled, which, can be fired from fixed silos, and China's nuclear armoury was beefed up in 2007 with a mobile solid fuelled D-31A missile and D-31A was a significant improvement, now China had also invested heavily in the CJ-10 a land attack cruise missiles, capable of striking the US forces in South Korea and Japan. China anxieties are fuelled by the presence of 3,60,000 personal in the theatre under the US Pacific Command (PACOM), besides PACOM has positioned 200 ships, which includes 5 aircrafts carriers strike groups which projecting power in the region—China and North Korea as the prime concerns nearly 60 percent of US forces will be deployed under the PACOM wings, on the 'Asia Pivot' strategy. Hence, China relentlessly is pursuing the development of 'Silk Road Economic Belt', a land corridor that would establish trade linkages with Europe in order to lessen dependence on the more vulnerable sea routes for its energy security from Strait of Malacca, where the Americans can still block the sea lanes and create problems to China.

While China and India are potential competitors for power and influence in IOR, they also share common interests in maintaining regional stability by combating the growing Islamic fundamentalist menace like the recent interception by the Indian Coast Guard of a so-called suspicious Pakistani fishing boat which blew itself up in the Arabia Sea shows that India's coastal surveillance system, put in place in protecting the maritime security and of 'rising threats', through the sea routes from terrorists and non-state actors, exploiting economic opportunities, maintaining access to energy sources and markets and enhancing regional co-operation. Bilateral cooperation on the above challenges can enable the two Asian powers to balance US influence and increase their negotiating positions with the sole superpower. On economic, environmental and cultural issues, they may have far more reasons to build synergies. Improvement in China-India relations will also depend upon Beijing's assessment of India's evolving political cohesion, economic growth, and military potential. China doesn't see India as a serious nuclear threat, but resulting change in the India's stature as a rising power and its improved ties with USA is a new variable in China's geo-political calculations. 'Freedom of navigation' is vital for China's and India's economic development as they both depend on the sea for trade and transportation. Thus China and India's Indian Ocean strategies can mutually promote shared objectives, underpinning thus greater cooperation, rather than competition in the IOR.

In view of the above circumstances, the relevance and growing influence of China in the Indian Ocean Region and South China Sea, the UGC Centre for Indian Ocean Studies felt the need for an academic discourse, thereby organized an International Conference in November 2014 on: "China in Indian Ocean Region."

Editor
R. Sidda Goud
Manisha Mookherjee

Acknowledgements

This book is the outcome of the International Conference on 'China in Indian Ocean Region', held on 13th–14th November 2014, organized by UGC Centre for Indian Ocean Studies, Osmania University, Hyderabad.

While we would like to thank a number of people who have encouraged and supported us in bringing out this volume, a few deserve special mention. First and foremost our deepest gratitude to Prof S. Satyanarayana, former Vice-Chancellor, Osmania University, Hyderabad for promptly accepting and giving permission to conduct the International Conference on 'China in Indian Ocean Region', when he was in the office, otherwise the conference could not have materialised. A special mention of gratitude to the Advisory Committee Members of the UGC Centre for Indian Ocean Studies for their support and encouragement to conduct the conference and for their keen interest and participation.

We express our sincere thanks and gratitude to a host of dignitaries who graced the occasion. We are grateful to Prof. Srikanth Kondapally, Professor in Chinese Studies, Centre for East Asian Studies, School of International Studies, Jawaharlal Nehru University, New Delhi, who has graciously accepted our invitation to deliver the Keynote Address of the conference, Prof. K. Pratap Reddy, Registrar Osmania University, Hyderabad for being the Guest of Honour for the Inaugural Session. Dr. D.N. Reddy, Chairman, Recruitment and Assessment Centre, DRDO and Member UGC, New Delhi, Chief Guest of the Valedictory Function. We also express our gratitude to Prof. G.V.C. Naidu, Centre for Indo-Pacific Studies, School of International Studies, Jawaharlal Nehru University, New Delhi, for his insightful Valedictory Address, Prof. A. Ravinder Nath, Dean, Development and UGC Affairs, Osmania University, Hyderabad for presiding over the function. We also express our thanks to Prof. P.V. Rao, former Director, UGC Centre for Indian Ocean Studies for his constant support, guidance and participation in the conference. We feel honoured and privileged to have one of our long standing well-wisher Prof. Yagama Reddy (Retd.) Centre for Southeast Asian and Pacific Studies, Sri Venkateshwara University, Tirupati for accepting as Guest of Honour for Valedictory Session, Commodore (Retd.) Seshadri Vasan, Head, Strategy and Security Studies, Centre for Asian Studies, Chennai, Alok Bansal, Professor, Institute of Management and Director of Centre for Security and Strategy (CSS), India Foundation, New Delhi and to all the distinguished delegates from home and abroad - China, Bangladesh, Bhutan and Sri Lanka.

We deeply appreciate the contributors for their sincere academic support by participating in the International Conference and subsequently submitting the revised papers for publication. The freedom of expression of the contributors have been taken care of and not subdued in the process of editing their papers; thereby the views expressed in these papers are essentially of those of the authors and not of the editors.

We would also like to place on record our acknowledgements to UGC, Osmania University, Indian Council of Social Science Research (ICSSR), New Delhi and Andhra Pradesh State Council of Higher Education (APSCHE), Government of Andhra Pradesh. We also express our thanks to Osmania University authorities, faculty members and the non-teaching staff of UGC Centre for Indian Ocean Studies, Osmania University, Hyderabad.

Prof. R. Sidda Goud
Manisha Mookherjee

Contents

New Dynamics of the
Indian Ocean Region and Indian Role

Srikanth Kondapalli*

The significance of the Indian Ocean Region (IOR) is loud and clear to the international community, specifically in the recent times of globalisation where maritime trade in resources, communications and interactions have become all too frequent. There are also some other new developments in the region, including the emerging contest for power between the United States and a rising resource-hungry China as reflected in the Obama Administration's "rebalance" strategy and the idea of Indo-Pacific and Xi Jinping's "maritime silk road" initiative, apart from non-traditional challenges such as piracy and natural disasters. China sending two submarines in as many months recently to Sri Lanka thus is no surprise in this backdrop. As a resident country, India has several challenges to face as well as some prospects in the region. With the new government led by Modi, there is already a keen interest evinced on the region as reflected in the Prime Minister's visits—unprecedented so far—to the commissioning of two new naval vessels in his first hundred days of assuming office.

THE CONTEXT

The traditional parameters of the IOR remain the same, although fast changing due to new actors and recent dynamics. Firstly, in terms of humanity, the IOR consists of nearly a third of the world population living in nearly 56 contiguous countries (including 1286 islands) with wide dissimilarities in national territories, population, political systems, incomes, etc. Secondly, geographically, the IOR is about 74 million square km in area (about 20 percent of the earth's surface) and thus constitutes the third largest ocean in the world, after the Pacific and the Atlantic. Thirdly, in terms of resources, the IOR is estimated to contain more than half of global strategic resources and one-third of gas reserves. Large deposits of uranium, gold, diamonds, coal, iron ore, tea, jute and

---

*Professor in Chinese Studies, Jawaharlal Nehru University, New Delhi.

other resources are available in the counties of the IOR. No rising or established power can afford to ignore these parameters.

One-fifth of the global energy resources passes through the region and hence can be termed as a major strategic pass. Besides, several Asian manufacturing units also utilize the region for transporting goods to Europe and beyond and hence economically and commercially a major hub in the world.[1] For instance, Asian imports increased from 18 percent to 26 percent between 1991 and 2001 and contributed to nearly 19 percent of global share of exports by 2001. Overall, maritime trade is expected to be doubled to about $42 billion tonne-miles in 2014. Given Asian countries economic resurgence in the recent period, their dependence on exports and imports through the seas is expected to increase in future. Also, for fuelling their industrial rise, energy consumption (mainly oil and gas) is expected to increase in future. As the IOR holds significant strategic raw minerals and gas reserves of the world, global dependence on such resources is expected to be intact for a long time to come. Intensifying winds of globalisation is expected to further enhance dependence of several countries—including in the IOR—on maritime trade.[2] However, in comparison to the Pacific and the Atlantic Oceans, the outward trade flows from the IOR constitutes nearly 80 percent (overwhelmingly composed of crude oil exports) and intra-IOR trade a mere 20 percent.[3]

Because of the narrow land outlets to other continents, the significance of the sea lines of communications and choke points became prominent in this region. This feature distinguishes the IOR with that of the Atlantic and the Pacific Oceans. Indian Ocean is home to nine major choke points, viz., the Straits of Malacca's, Lombok and Sundas in the eastern flank, while Hormuz, Red Sea corridor, Suez Canal form the western flanks, with Cape of Good Hope forming its south-western flank. Of these five routes are frequented by the energy resources carrying shipping. Nearly a tenth of the global crude oil is transported through the Gulf of Aden as this forms the shortest maritime route between Europe and Asia. It is estimated that more than 15.5 million barrels of oil, which constitutes about 40 percent of the global oil commerce passes through the Strait of Hormuz, as compared to 11 million barrels through the Straits of Malaccas.[4] Nearly 20,000 ships navigate the Gulf of Aden passing through the Suez Canal, as against 33,000 ships through the Horn of Africa every year, while 55,000 ships have to pass through the Straits of Malacca's.[5] On an average more than 60,000 ships pass through the IOR annually. One-tenth of global crude oil is transported through the Gulf of Aden, while over $200 billion worth of oil makes its way through Straits of Hormuz—half of it eastwards.[6] Because of these narrow passes, their vulnerability has become a major security issue recently, while during the Cold War period, they were kept under check partly due to the Superpower rivalry and partly due to the presence of western troops at Djibouti, Diego Garcia, Somalia and Comoros Islands and Soviets in Ethiopia and South Yemen.[7] As no single overarching security architecture prevails in the IOR, this situation breeds insecurities. The IOR, according to some estimates, constitutes to nearly 70 percent of the various forms of global disasters and hence from the point of view of security, this region is likely to be the global focus. This suggests that any disruptions to the maritime trade either through human made (piracy, terrorism, illegal migration, drug trafficking, gun running, conflict, war, oil slicks, etc.) or nature-made (tsunamis, typhoons, etc) could jeopardise international maritime trade and have drastic impact on insurance and other business interests. Indeed, IOR is notorious also to be home to international and regional terrorism in Southwest Asia and also witnessed over two-thirds of natural disasters. The *USS Cole* in the Gulf of Aden in October 2000, *Limburg* in October 2002, piracy attacks off Somalia, 2004/05 tsunami and November 2008 Mumbai terror attacks are reminders of the uncertainties in the IOR.

RESPONSES

With the above profile of the region, many a power had attempted to influence the region through unilateral, bilateral or multilateral efforts. Foremost of these is the United States which has a major base in the IOR with Diego Garcia. This had been extensively used through the Cold War and as recently as for global war on terrorism in Afghanistan and for Iraq operations. There is also the new idea—coinciding with the rebalance strategy—the Indo-Pacific region to explain the new dynamics of the IOR and contiguous regions.

The US is the largest importer of energy resources from West Asia and Africa (although declining with the shale gas finds), besides over $1 trillion in trade transiting the Straits of Malacca's every year. The US also needs to consider the interests of its allies like Japan and South Korea. The attacks on the US and its allies ships were wake-up calls. A number of US-destined ships/tankers were also attacked by pirates for ransom, affecting the commerce. The US Fifth Fleet established the Combined Task Force (CTF) 151 in January 2009. Other task forces include CTF-152 with operational focus on the central and south Gulf region; CTF

150 for the southern Red Sea, the Gulf of Aden, Gulf of Oman, north-western IOR; CTF 158 for protecting Iraqi oil platforms. Naval ships from 20 countries including the US, Germany, Australia, Italy, Japan, South Korea, Netherlands, Spain, Pakistan, etc. Additionally the US helped enforce the Maritime Security Patrol Area in the Gulf of Aden from August 2008.

Secondly, China had been knocking at the doors of the IOR in the last decade and had been contesting the US rebalance by selling its recent idea of Maritime Silk Road to its emerging allies and friends in the region or making bilateral and multilateral efforts. From around 2009, China had initiated a "two ocean strategy" with Pacific and Indian oceans as the focus. China's naval forces were deployed 14 times by 2013 for counter-piracy missions in the Gulf of Aden[8] and had sent rescue ships and aircraft for evacuation of thousands of Chinese citizens in Libya, Egypt and Syria and gained dual-use experience in out of area operations in the region. President Xi Jinping had suggested the Maritime Silk Road idea in a speech to the Indonesian Senate in October 2013 (and followed this by naval exercises in Straits of Lombok) and got endorsements in Maldives and Sri Lanka in September 2014.

The context for China's new found enthusiasm in the IOR is domestic demands, specifically in its south-western regions, apart from securing its bourgeoning energy and raw material needs passing through the IOR. China's south-western Yunnan Provincial leaders have been pushing through these ideas in the recent past. Yunnan intends to connect to the Bay of Bengal and then to the IOR through a series of networks connecting with the Salween, Mekong and Irrawaddy Rivers. While China has been an active participant in the revival of the Asian Highway and Railway concepts and has made efforts to open up the country for expanding transportation corridors linking it with Southeast Asia, Central Asia and South Asia, China has been active only recently in expanding the sea routes. In May 2014, officials in Fujian Province-one of the three key regions tasked with the maritime Silk Road initiative-announced setting up of a fund of nearly $1.6 billion to be channelized from the China Development Bank and China-Africa Development Fund.[9] This fund is to further the port developments and other infrastructure projects in the IOR in the future.

To pursue these interests, China had been setting up dual use maritime facilities in the IOR. One of the major projects is the Gwadar Port. Indeed, collaboration between China and Pakistan on the Gwadar port is termed as a landmark in the bilateral relations similar to the Karakoram

Highway project officially opened in 1978. Gwadar naval port in the western Makran coast of Pakistan was built with Chinese assistance by the China Harbour Engineering Company, a subsidiary of China Communications Construction. The first phase of the project, conceived in 1964 but started only in 2002, saw China spending $198 million as against the Pakistani share of about $50 million in a project estimated at over $1 billion and was completed by 2006. In January 2013 Pakistan transferred the port to Chinese Overseas Port Holdings Limited.

Another project undertaken with active Chinese assistance is the Hambantota project in Sri Lanka which includes a port as well as an airport. China Harbour Engineering Company and the Sino Hydro Corporation are involved in the Hambantota project. Originally offered to India, one phase of this port was opened—after cost escalation (with an estimated $40 million in additional costs out of a total $400 million for this phase) and time overruns (by one year)—for international shipping in June 2012. China also offered to construct another port at Colombo with reports of possible investments from China amounting to $50 billion. Besides, the Chinese have long expressed interest in the building of the Trincomali port—the 5th largest natural harbour in the world.

In addition to expanding its interests in the South China Sea, China had also been making significant inroads in the region with implications to the IOR. China is reportedly planning to build an artificial island military base of five-square-kilometer with an airstrip and sea port at the Fiery Cross Reef (Kagitingan/Da Chu Thap/Yongshu) with a cost of $5 billion in the next ten years. This is meant for forward power projection and enforcement of a proposed Air Defence Identification Zone in the region. In the long-term this is also meant to control the Straits of Malacca's. China is also reclaiming areas at the Johnson South Reef, Gavin Reef (Gaven Reef) and Calderon Reef (Cuarteron Reef) contested by the Philippines. These above projects are intended to back up China's objectives in the IOR in the near future.

INDIAN EFFORTS

As a major country in the IOR, with a vast coastline, vital national interests (in terms of commerce, energy imports, 4.2 million diaspora in the Gulf, etc.) and blue water ambitions,[10] India is an important factor in the IOR.[11] In 2001 the Ministry of Defence in its annual report outlined the defence parameters and responsibilities. It stated:

India's parameters of security clearly extend well beyond the confines of its conventional geographical land borders. Given its size, location, trade links and extensive Exclusive Economic Zone (EEZ), India's security environment extends from the Persian Gulf in the west to the Straits of Malacca in the east... to the Equator in the south."[12]

Later, the 2004 Indian Maritime Doctrine reiterated the above sphere of interest. It stated:

India's primary maritime interest is to assure national security. This is not restricted to just guarding the coastline and island territories, but also extends to safeguarding our interests in the [exclusive economic zone] as well as protecting our trade. This creates an environment that is conducive to rapid economic growth of the country. Since trade is the lifeblood of India, keeping our SLOCs open in times of peace, tension or hostilities is a primary national maritime interest (p. 63).

Further, in the 2007 *Freedom to Use the Seas: India's Maritime Military Strategy*, the Indian Navy identified the following tasks:

- Conflict with a state in our immediate neighbourhood or clash of interest with an extra-regional power.
- Operations in the extended and or strategic neighbourhood in response to a request for assistance from a friendly nation.
- Anti-terrorist operations—conducted multilaterally or unilaterally.
- Actions to fulfil international bilateral strategic partnership obligations.
- Ensure good order at sea which includes Low Intensity Maritime Operations (LIMO), to combat asymmetric warfare, poaching, piracy, and trafficking in arms/drugs.
- Ensuring safety and security of ISLs through the Indian Ocean.
- Actions to assist the Indian diaspora and Indian interests abroad.
- Peacekeeping operations, under the aegis of the United Nations (UN), independently or as part of a multinational force.
- Humanitarian Assistance and Disaster Relief (HADR) in our extended neighbourhood, or in response to a request for assistance from a friendly nation.[13]

As a victim of November 2008 Mumbai terror attacks through the Arabian Sea, India is in the forefront in tackling such issues. There have been several attempts by the Indian Coast Guard and the Indian Navy to combat such activities, unilaterally, bilaterally and multilaterally. India also played a significant role in conducting useful seminars and workshops to bring the coast guards and navies from different countries and had initiated several measures in this regard. To curb maritime security issues, specifically in the coastal regions, India planned to commission 204 interceptor boats, 73 coastal security police stations, 97 check-posts and 58 outposts, although progress in this regard had been tardy.[14] In 2008, India's navy chief announced that 'by 2022, we plan to have a 160-plus ship navy, including three aircraft carriers, 60 major combatants, including submarines and close to 400 aircraft of different types', constituting 'a formidable three dimensional force with satellite surveillance and networking'.[15]

Specific Indian examples in regional maritime activities are notable. In 1987, India sent troops to Sri Lanka at the latter's request to counter Tamil Tigers. Later in 1988, the Indian forces rescued and restored the Maldivian political leader from mercenaries. Indian navy sent destroyers to Madagascar for the smooth conduct of the Organization of African Union meeting. In 1999, India rescued Japanese ship *Alondra Rainbow*, plying under the Panamanian flag and carrying $14 million worth of cargo, from Indonesian pirates. In the same year of July, Indian Coast Guard seized a North Korean vessel *Ku Wol San* off Kandla port. It was carrying several tonnes of missile parts to Pakistan and Libya. This is perhaps the first instance of anti-proliferation efforts against trading in surface-to surface missile parts in 148 boxes. Later, in 2002, North Korean ship *So San*, which was carrying ballistic missile parts to Yemen was inspected. Even as the "core group" (US, Japan, Australia and India) were discussing measures to provide relief for the December 2004 Tsunami are being conducted, the Indian navy mobilised more than 25,000 sailors and scores of ships within a few hours for Tsunami relief measures in the IOR. Indian naval vessel *INS Tabar* rescued a Thai ship from the pirates on November 19, 2008, although some were critical of the handling of the "fishermen" by the Indian navy personnel in this incident.[16] In November 2009, the Indian Navy deployed *INS Savitri*, an offshore patrol vessel with a helicopter and marine commandos for surveillance of the EEZs of Seychelles and Mauritius till January 2010.[17]

India had joined several bilateral/multilateral efforts in countering piracy. India is one of the 16-members of the ReCAAP. India had hosted the first Indian Ocean Naval Symposium (IONS)—a conclave of naval chiefs from more than 30 Indian Ocean states met on February 18–19, 2008 at New Delhi. This is a more broad-based multilateral organization that includes all major regional naves, while US, UK and Japan have applied for "observer" status.[18] In 2006, India and the United States agreed to the "Indo-US Framework for Maritime Security Cooperation" which included joint efforts at countering piracy.[19] In October 2008, 8,500 naval personnel from India and the United States participated in a week-long maritime exercise "Malabar" in the Arabian Gulf. Such exercises—to enhance interoperability between the two naval forces—are being conducted for nearly two decades now. 18 such engagements took place by July 2014, when Japan was also invited for this Malabar Exercise.

MULTILATERAL INITIATIVES

Apart from the above efforts made by the US, China and India, there are also multilateral efforts to address emerging issues in the IOR. Among these, the non-security related multilateral grouping Indian Ocean Rim Association for Regional Cooperation (IOR-ARC, now IORA) formed in March 1997 in Mauritius is notable.[20] Others include Bangladesh, India, Myanmar, Sri Lanka and Thailand (BIMST-EC), Indian Ocean Rim Business Forum (IORBF), Indian Ocean Rim Academic Group (IORAG), Indian Ocean Marine Affairs Cooperation (IOMAC) established in the 1980s with 35 member states, etc. However, the mandate of these institutions is focused more on expanding economic cooperation rather than tackling pirates. A Regional Cooperation Agreement on Combating Piracy and Armed Robbery against ships in Asia (ReCAAP) was concluded in November 2004 by 16 countries in Asia—mainly to resolve issues of piracy in the Straits of Malacca's. Some suggest to the inclusive and comprehensive measures that regional organizations and institutions can carry out in the counter-piracy operations. For instance the work of the following regional organizations is noteworthy:

- Coalition of the Southeast Asian countries to control piracy—MALSINDO (Malaysia, Singapore and Indonesia) created in July 2004 to monitor the Straits of Malacca's (Thailand had also shown interest in joining the grouping, while India offered security assistance)
- South West Indian Ocean Fisheries Commission established in 2004 and headquartered in Kenya for managing fishery resources
- Regional Organization for the Protection of the Marine Environment established in 1981 and based at Kuwait for anti-pollution measures
- Port security and control mechanism through the Riyadh MoU in 2004 and based in Oman.[21]

Other initiatives include European Union's NAVFORCE, and Pakistan's seminars by National Centre for Maritime Policy Research and naval exercises, Sri Lanka helped form the Indian Ocean Marine Affairs Cooperation (IOMAC) Network, Singapore has been holding International Maritime Defense Exhibition (IMDEX) Asia biannually.

ASSESSMENT

The above brief outline of the emerging trends in the IOR indicates that these are of long-term consequences to the international and the IOR orders. Ensuring sustainable energy supplies, counter-terrorism, protection of shipping and communications, preparing pro-actively for natural disaster relief, crafting a favourable maritime and security environment in the IOR are all major tasks for a resident and rising state like India. Clearly, however, India apart from protecting its interests has to factor in the emerging contest between the US and China in the IOR, although a trend in the US—that of the Group-2 (i.e., US condominium with Beijing)—is also visible. China has been making concerted efforts to enter and sustain operations in the IOR. This is likely to be realised by China, with its naval modernisation and power projection, in the medium to long term even as it is making clear moves in the short term. While India had made several efforts to strengthen maritime security environment in the IOR, and also worked with several multilateral institutions in this regard, it has to be wary of the new dynamics emerging in the IOR. India had also recently concluded a trilateral maritime cooperation agreement with Maldives and Sri Lanka. Although Indian leaders have accepted, in their speeches, the US idea of Indo-Pacific, Indian debates have not yet coalesced towards this idea in the backdrop of the penchant for the successive new US Administrations to alter such initiatives and to the vagaries of the US politics as well as for the connotations of the Indo-Pacific, specifically in the use of force without the UN authorisation. These suggest that India need to make efforts to securing its interests in the IOR.

REFERENCES

1. See for some studies on the subject Robert D. Kaplan, Monsoon: The Indian Ocean and the Future of American Power (Random House, 2010); Ellen Laipson, "The Indian Ocean: A Critical Arena for 21st Century Threats and Challenges" at <http://www.stimson.org/pub.cfm?id=733>; Dennis Rumley, ed. "The Indian Ocean Region: Security, Stability and Sustainability in the 21st Century" Australia India Institute March 2013 accessed at <http://www.aii.unimelb.edu.au/sites/default/files/IOTF_0.pdf>; "Maritime

Security Challenges in the Indian Ocean Region—A Workshop Report" Center for the National Interest February 23–24, 2011 accessed at <http://www.cftni.org/2011.7.18fullworkshopsummary.pdf>; Colin Geraghty, "India in the Indian Ocean Region-Re-calibrating U.S. Expectations" October 2012 accessed at <https://americansecurityproject.org/ASP%20Reports/Ref% 200091%20-%20India%20in%20the%20Indian%20Ocean%20Region.pdf>; Thean Potgieter, "Maritime security in the Indian Ocean: strategic setting and features" Institute for Security Studies Paper No. 236 August 2012 accessed at <http://dspace.africaportal.org/jspui/bitstream/123456789/ 33169/1/Paper236.pdf?1>; Carlo Kopp, "Strategic importance of the Indian Ocean" Defence Today accessed at <http://www.ausairpower.net/PDF-A/DT-Indian-Ocean-Dec-2011.pdf>

2. Panikkar, K.M., India and the Indian Ocean: An Essay on the Influence of Sea Power on Indian History (London: Allen and Unwin, 1951); M.N. Pearson, The Indian Ocean (London: Routledge, 2003); P.V. Rao (ed) India and Indian Ocean (South Asian Publishers, New Delhi, 2003); Sergei DeSilva-Ranasinghe, "India's Strategic Objectives in the Indian Ocean Region" Future Directions International October 20, 2011 accessed at <http://www.futuredirections.org.au/files/Workshop%20Report%20-%20India's %20Strategic%20Objectives%20in%20the%20Indian%20Ocean%20Region .pdf>

3. Lehr, Peter, "The Challenge of Security in the Indian Ocean in the 21st Century: Plus ça change…?" Working Paper No. 13 (November 2002) Heidelberg Papers in South Asian and Comparative Politics University of Heidelberg.

4. The rate of increase of oil flows through the Straits of Malacca's is estimated to be above 3 percent annually till 2025.

5. The vulnerability of the Malacca's can be seen from the fact that its length is about 1,000 km, width is 2.4 km (at the closest Phillips Channel) and only 25 meters deep at its shallowest point. If by any man-made or natural disasters this Strait is closed, global shipping would be hit.

6. Khalid, Nazery, "Veni, Vidi, VLCC: Some reflections on combating piracy in the Gulf Aden" December 8, 2008 at <http://www.maritimeindia.org/ modules.php?name=Content&pa=showpage&pid=155>

7. Harrison, Selig S. et al. Super Power Rivalry in Indian Ocean (Oxford University Press 1989).

8. Ji, You and Kia, Lim Chee, "China's Naval Deployment to Somalia and its Implications" EAI Background Brief No. 454 May 29, 2009.

9. See Krishnan, Ananth, "China: billion dollar fund of maritime silk road" The Hindu May 20, 2014.

10. According to David Scott, while the Nehruvian focus was largely continental, recent Indian focus is on expending its blue water capability and protect interests in the IOR region and beyond. See David Scott, "India's "Grand Strategy" for the Indian Ocean: Mahanian Visions" Asia-Pacific Review, Vol. 13, No. 2, 2006 pp. 97–129. Scott argued that Mahanian vision of power projection, access and control of the SLOCs is becoming prominent in the

Indian strategic thinking and preparations in the naval sphere and is reflected in the doctrine, acquisitions, budgetary allocations, deployments, etc.

11. As India becomes the fourth largest energy importer after China, the US and Japan, India's oil imports increased to nearly 80 percent in 2010 and to about 91 percent by 2020 as its annual consumption is expected to increase from 85 million tonnes in 2006 to 300 million tonnes by 2020. This necessitates increase in the number of tanker traffic from 4,000 to 8,000 in 2020 into the Indian ports. For other South Asian countries as well energy dependence is expected to increase to about 96 percent. On the overall importance of the subject see Rahul Roy-Chaudhury, India's Maritime Security(New Delhi: Knowledge World, 2000); Donald L. Berlin, "India in the Indian Ocean" Naval War College Review Spring 2006, Vol. 59, No. 2, pp. 58–89.

12. Government of India, Ministry of Defence Annual Report 2000–2001, accessed at <http://mod.nic.in/samachar/july15–01/html/ch1.htm>

13. Integrated Headquarters Ministry of Defence (Navy), Freedom to Use the Seas: India's Maritime Military Strategy (New Delhi: 2007 (p.61). See also Integrated Headquarters of the Ministry of Defence (Navy), Vision Statement, ST/3001, May 25, 2006, http://www.indiannavy.gov.in/vision.pdf

14. Verma, B.K., "Coastal security: Where are we headed?" February 16, 2009 at <http://www.maritimeindia.org/modules.php?name=Content&pa=showpage &pid=167>

15. Joshi, Shashank, "Sixty-five thousand tonnes of ambition," *Royal United Services Institute*, December 2009 at <http://www.rusi.org/analysis/com mentary/ref:C4B20EF703EDFF>

16. These were highlighted by Nikolas K. Gvosdev, "Problems in Fighting Piracy in the Indian Ocean", May 6, 2010 at <http://sitrep.globalsecurity.org/ articles/100506578-problems-in-fighting-piracy-in.htm>

17. "India deploys warship in Indian Ocean to fight piracy" Indian Express November 23, 2009 at <http://www.indianexpress.com/news/india-deploys-warship-in-indian-ocean-to-fight-piracy/545147/>

18. "Navies from Indian Ocean Region to chalk out anti-piracy plan" The Times of India May 7, 2010 at <http://timesofindia.indiatimes.com/india/Navies-from-Indian-Ocean-Region-to-chalk-out-anti-piracy-plan/articleshow/5899314. cms#ixzz0xEamCYiP>

19. Wilson, Brian, "Indo-US Maritime Partnering: Time for the Next Step" January 23, 2009 at <http://www.maritimeindia.org/modules.php?name= Content&pa=showpage&pid=165> See also "U.S to Make India a World Power" Washington Post March 30, 2005; James R. Holmes and Toshi Yoshihara, "China and the United States in the Indian Ocean—An Emerging Strategic Triangle?" Naval War College Review, Summer 2008, Vol. 61, No. 3, pp. 41–60.

20. IOR-ARC (rechristened recently as IORA) members include Australia, Bangladesh Indonesia, Iran, India, Thailand, Malaysia, Mozambique, Tanzania, South Africa and Sri Lanka.

21. This is based on Ellen Laipson, "The Indian Ocean: A Critical Arena for 21st Century Threats and Challenges", at <http://www.stimson.org/pub.cfm?id= 733>

India, China and the Indian Ocean

G.V.C. Naidu*

For India, the Indian Ocean not merely its backyard but is also the main link to the rest of the world for the last more than 2500 years and thus its destiny inexorably tied to this ocean. Nevertheless, amazingly the discourse in India on the Indian Ocean and the developments in the rim region are so limited and sadly very little serious research output is coming out that can objectively assess the remarkable transformation that is taking place in and around this ocean and offer ideas on how best India can position itself to take full advantage of its extremely vantage geostrategic location. It is a pity that instead of Indians setting the agenda and direction of debate, they seem to be following others' lead. Unfortunately, much of the debate on the Indian Ocean tends to focus on China after having stuck to unworkable and unrealistic idea of converting it into a zone of peace. Given its strategic location connecting East Asia with South Asia, much of Africa, the Middle East and Europe, it has always attracted extra-regional powers and that is something India will have to take into its maritime strategy.

It took Robert Kaplan's seminal work *"Monsoon—the Indian Ocean and the Future of American Power"*, published in 2010 to sit up and take note of its rapidly growing geostrategic and geo-economic significance and the emerging challenges for all those that have stakes in the ocean, especially to India. His prognosis that "The Greater Indian Ocean region stretching eastward from the Horn of Africa past the Arabian Peninsula, the Iranian plateau and the Indian subcontinent, all the way to the Indonesian archipelago and beyond, will be the centre of global conflicts, because most international business supply will be conducted through this route. Most important of all, it is in this region the interests and influence of India, China and the United States are beginning to overlap and intersect. It is here the 21st century's global power dynamics will be revealed....... two key players in this region are India and China-India moving east and west while China to the South" could not have been more apt. India is looking east because it sees its future there, while is

---

*Professor in the Centre for Indo-Pacific Studies, School of International Studies, JNU, New Delhi.

China looking south because its rise depends on what happens in that region. And the entire Indo-Pacific region is critical to US interests and hence its military presence is unlikely to diminish.

As noted, sadly much of the discussion in India on the Indian Ocean is still stuck on the merits or lack of it of the 'string of pearls' thesis and as a result the discourse mostly centres on China, its long-term goals, its interactions with India's neighbours and the security challenges it poses to India rather than focusing on India's growing maritime interests, the opportunities a rising Indian Ocean offers to advance diplomatic, economic and strategic interests, and how best to deal with emerging challenges, especially in the non-conventional domain. Unfortunately, the narrative on the Indian Ocean consequently lacks what is called objectivity and thus a realistic assessment.

The issue is what has made the Indian Ocean so vital now, what kind of role major stakeholders seek to chart and what strategy India wants to pursue to regain the predominance it enjoyed historically. To do that it becomes necessary to briefly understand the changing maritime environment in general, India's growing focus on its sea power, and the China factor in India's maritime strategy.

Before analysing India's evolving Indian Ocean strategy, we need to pay attention to four issues, among others, to understand the emerging dynamics in the Indian Ocean. One, the emergence of the Indo-Pacific as a reference point for geostrategic as well as geo-economic analyses, and why it is becoming a more appropriate framework to understand the current realities. As a well known Indian strategic thinker K.M. Panikkar back in 1947 averred, "Millenniums before Columbus sailed the Atlantic and Magellan crossed the Pacific, the Indian Ocean had become a thoroughfare of commercial and cultural traffic."Skills and knowledge were transmitted through this region and civilisations, cultures, languages, religions, ideas and economic interactions flowed back and forth from one end to the other. The interface, interdependence and close links that are emerging between the Indian and Pacific Oceans are so critical that an Asian century cannot be visualised unless the Indo-Pacific concept is employed.

Two, the other most visible and significant dimension is the rise of China and India as new maritime powers. Both had traditionally been continental powers but they are now emerging as maritime powers of enormous consequence with acquisition of capabilities that would enable them to be able project power well beyond their immediate vicinity, be able to operate in far away regions and influence developments significantly. Even Japan, which had been highly defensive power with little power projection capabilities since the end of the Second World War, is likely to witness fundamental shifts in its security policies now that it is planning to revise Article 9 of the constitution and the intensifying territorial dispute over the Senkakus with China.

Three, the inexorable rise of the Indian Ocean itself and its likely impact on the rest of the world is a major development. Apart from being home huge natural resources and critical trade routes, the combined GDP of the rim countries has gone up to $6.5 trillion in 2011 from $5.7 trillion in 2010. This region is economically the most dynamic after East Asia. Indeed, East Asia's economic development and prosperity to a large extent is dependent on the Indian Ocean.

Finally, while oceans and seas have always played a key role in shaping global history, the geostrategic shift to the maritime sphere has never been as palpable as it is today. Thanks to intense globalization, the dependence on sea lines for commerce has been growing and will continue to grow in the coming years. In fact, for most countries in the Indo-Pacific trade is a major propeller of growth and prosperity. Hence, what happens on the high seas, especially along the trade routes, would be of immense and direct relevance to their economic development as well as domestic politics and thus to regional security. It would have been unimaginable even a decade back that Japan, China, Malaysia and South Korea would send their naval ships to the east coast of Africa, quite often working with their counterparts from India, US, and the EU countries, in patrolling and in taking part in counter-piracy operations but for the fact that their stakes in the Indian Ocean sea lines of communication have become so vital.

Instead, New Delhi should be looking at the opportunities a rising Indian Ocean offers since it is not merely a resident power but the most powerful too and hence it is about time it fundamentally reoriented its Indian Ocean policy. The British Empire would not have been the largest and greatest without its domination in the Indian Ocean. Today India is presented with a historic opportunity to regain its predominant status that it enjoyed for over two millennia before colonialism. India can now play a crucial role in moulding a new security and economic order in the region. Nonetheless, one should bear in mind that India faces certain limitations. Even as the overall significance of the Indian Ocean increases, it is bound to attract extra-regional great powers. Secondly, the non-security threats are becoming far more serious and many of them can only be tackled by undertaking joint multilateral efforts. A case in point is the piracy menace off the east coast of Africa. India certainly took the lead and played a key role but international cooperation proved to be far more effective in curbing it.

Not many recognise the cooperative elements between India and China in the Indian Ocean especially in dealing with a host of non-traditional security threats, which have made the navies of India and China to cooperate on a regular basis in counter-piracy operation off Africa's east coast. Beijing has offered to share technology knowhow on seabed resource exploitation. Importantly, these two have also started a maritime security dialogue in March 2012. The fact of the matter is that, given India's location and the sea power at its disposal, China has to depend on Indian security guarantees in the protection of trade routes and non-conventional challenges. Similarly, as its trade grows with the Indian Ocean rim region, Beijing will continue to be wary of India's pre-eminent position in the Indian Ocean. China has come out with the Maritime Silk Road idea to build infrastructure and improve connectivity, but details are still sketchy. India has been noncommittal so far waiting for more information from China. The idea could be to allay the concerns the 'string of pearls' has generated, which has forced it to be on defensive, by developing the facilities as multinational joint venture. Instead of looking at Chinese proposal with extreme suspicion, India should consider it positively so that they can work together in making the Indo-Pacific region more secure.

In order to consolidate its position in the Indian Ocean, India has begun to qualitatively increase the engagement with its neighbours and the island states in the Indian Ocean such as Maldives, Mauritius and Seychelles though bilateral and multilateral cooperation. Secondly, it is also trying to enhance its political, economic and strategic leverages over these countries so that they would not do anything that might undermine Indian interests.

In any case, management of the Indian Ocean security will be problematic since there are no mechanisms military or non-military, track-I or track-II, or tangible regimes or CBMs. The only multilateral institution that is exists, the Indian Ocean Regional Association (IORA), is moribund and ineffectual although security issues have been included in its agenda. The Indian Ocean region will likely see jockeying for power by major stakeholders even as its overall significance rises.

CHINA AND THE INDIAN OCEAN

The rise of the Indian Ocean in many ways is linked to the rise of India and the rise of East Asia and hence no discourse on Indian Ocean security is complete without a reference to China. For instance, bulk of China crude oil requirements imports are met from the Middle East and Africa and more than 80 percent of its trade flows through the sea lines of the Indian Ocean. So, Beijing naturally would be concerned for the security of these trade routes.

Among all the countries, China and its forays into the Indian Ocean expectedly has attracted a lot of attention especially in India ever since the American consulting firm Booze Allen and Hamilton came out with a report in 2005 called *Energy Futures in Asia* to the Net Assessment Office of the US Department of Defense, which coined the phrase 'string of pearls', according to which China was purportedly building a network of port facilities spread around India. I am not an apologist for China nor understate its potential threat, however, as scholars we need to take an objective view, otherwise we end up with wrong inferences and with grave consequences. It appears there is considerable hyperbole about China establishing forward military bases in India's vicinity since at present there is no hard evidence to suggest that China is actively involved either in building military facilities or attempting to 'encircle' India through a string of bases. As New Delhi was unwilling to develop some of these ports, Beijing stepped in. In any case these are civilian ports and to convert them into military facilities not only requires enormous structural changes but also political will by the host countries.

While the rhetoric of impending China threat premised on the 'string of pearls' thesis has subsided, many believe that it is matter of time before China pushes its security perimeter from western Pacific deep into the Indian Ocean in tandem with its rapidly growing interests. China's critical dependence is not merely limited to oil from the Gulf but its economic stakes in Africa are also mounting.[1] Its huge natural resources are going to be critical driver of Asian economic dynamism. Already all the major economies—China, India, Japan and the US—are jockeying for resources and influence with China leading the charge. China-Africa trade has gone up from $10 bn. in 2000 to 165 bn. by 2011 and expected to reach 300 bn. by 2015. Aside from US$20 bn. aid pledge, China's direct investments are growing by leaps and bounds. According to the Chinese Ministry of Commerce, by the end of 2011 Chinese investments in Africa had reached $14.7 bn., up 60 percent compared to

2009. Even a cursory look reveals that the supply routes that China uses to trade with Europe and the Indian Ocean region can be vulnerable.

China is involved in building several ports around India stretching from Gwadar (Pakistan), Hambantota (Sri Lanka), Chittagong (Bangladesh) up to Sittwe and Kyaukpyu (Myanmar), however, in order for China to use these facilities for effective military purposes, it should build a navy which can project power far from its shores and be able to undermine the existing strategic equilibrium by openly challenging India's dominant position, an unlikely proposition for the foreseeable future especially because of serious maritime disputes it is involved in East and South China Seas, the Taiwan issue, and a long gestation time and huge investments required to build a truly blue-water navy besides huge political costs of open confrontation with India. As Ashley S. Townshend rightly contends, "As the prevailing Indian Ocean power balance is tilted in favor of Washington and New Delhi, Beijing's capacity to influence international sea lanes remains grossly inferior." The Indian government too does not seem to share the concerns of the string of pearls theory. Mr. Shivshankar Menon, former Foreign Secretary and current National Security Advisor, dismissed it in a speech at the National Maritime Foundation, New Delhi:

> Let us look at the facts. There are no Chinese bases in the Indian Ocean today despite talk of the "string of pearls", (which, by the way, is a pretty ineffective murder weapon as any "Clue" aficionado will tell you). There is, however, extensive Chinese port development activity in Myanmar, Bangladesh, Sri Lanka, and Pakistan, and active weapons supply programmes to the same states.

Where would these two countries draw the redlines to avoid stepping on each other's toes is a moot question despite China's assurances that it has no plans to build a military base in the Indian Ocean[2] and India making clear that it does not intend to permanently deploy naval forces in the Pacific in general and the South China Sea in particular.

INDIA'S INDIAN OCEAN STRATEGY

Against the above backdrop, what is India's Indian Ocean strategy? It is well known that India's maritime interests are vast and expansive and defending them require considerable sea power. Besides a long coastline of about 7,600 km and numerous major and minor ports, nearly 96 percent of India's trade (about US$ 800 bn) is sea-borne, including bulk of its energy imports. Additionally, the two archipelagos of Andaman and

Nicobar in the Bay of Bengal and Lakshadweep in the Arabian Sea, numbering around 400 islands, are situated far away from the mainland but astride some of the most important sea trade routes in the Indian Ocean. India has also acquired an area of 2.2 million sq. km of ocean space as its EEZ.

Concomitantly, the Indian Navy's force structure is also undergoing a fundamental shift. It is receiving a lot more attention both in terms of funding and political support. Since the mid-2000s it on a course that would make it a blue-water capable if the ambitious plans it has set were to be realised. Three aircraft carriers, several nuclear submarines complemented by advanced conventional submarines, and a large number of ocean-going ships, greater strategic sealift capabilities and dedicated satellites will make India a formidable force in the Indian Ocean. According to Adm. Nirmal Verma, former naval chief, by 2027 the Indian Navy will wear a brand new look with some 150 principal combatant ships and another 500-odd aircraft fleet. The share of the navy from defence budget has also been steadily increasing: from 12.7 percent in 1990–91 it has risen to about 19 percent by 2012–13, excluding allocations for the coastguard.

Along with a new force structure, an entirely new maritime strategy is also taking shape. The earlier defensive and basically centred on coastal protection is being replaced by a strategy under which the navy would be able to undertake what is called 'out of area operations'. With continental threats becoming less severe and the Indian Ocean environment that is favourable, there has been a greater appreciation of the unique role the navy can perform in advancing diplomatic and strategic interests and to deal with a variety of maritime security challenges. Indeed, the central role of the navy as the third and probably the most important leg in the Indian doctrine of minimum deterrent has catapulted its role in a big way.

Contrary to the past practice, between 2009 and 2012, the Indian Navy to its credit has come out with several documents on maritime doctrine (*Indian Maritime Doctrine* 2004 and a revised one in 2009) and strategy (*Freedom to Use the Seas: India's Maritime Military Strategy*, 2007). The *Strategy* paper clearly delineates the regions of primary and secondary interest in the Indian Ocean and beyond. This is emphatically underscored by the former naval chief: "Our vision encompasses an arc extending from the Persian Gulf to the Malacca Straits as India's legitimate area of interests." The documents also clearly spell a range of activities India seeks to undertake for ensuring peace and stability by countering non-traditional security threats and deter moves that undermine its interests. Since the Indian Navy is gearing to emerge as a force that can embark on operations in far off parts, in addition to equipping itself with sufficient capability, increasingly the emphasis is on creating a sophisticated communication network: what is called shift from "platform-centric to network-centric operation". As the Maritime Military Strategy clearly enunciates, the principal components of the current strategy are "prevention of the destruction of major coastal and offshore assets and disruption of coastal mercantile traffic..." coupled with limited sea control capabilities but "sea denial over larger areas in the Indian Ocean" and the "use of maritime power in support of land operations" as a "subsidiary and not a primary role."

The force modernisation and the new strategy clearly suggest that India is aiming to emerge as the predominant power in the Indian Ocean. No question that China's potential role in the Indian Ocean would figure in India's strategic calculations, however it would be imprudent to take an unrealistic view of the threat it may pose. While keeping a watchful eye on China's emergence as a maritime power and its navy evolving into blue-water capable and its activities in the Indian Ocean, India is unlikely to do anything that would undermine a qualitatively different kind of partnership that is taking shape with China.

CONCLUSION

The maritime domain is under intense focus for several reasons. The huge international trade, which is playing a critical role in economic development, triggered by unprecedented globalisation is overwhelmingly dependent on sea for transportation of merchandise. The Indo-Pacific region that has immensely benefitted from growing trade is a case in point. This region is also witnessing momentous changes in the maritime sector. It is home to numerous territorial and maritime boundary disputes, which had remained dormant have now become major source of tension and instability. There is also relative decline of traditional maritime powers while giving rise to newer ones. The dependence on living and non-living sea resources has been rapidly increasing. In the emerging maritime equation, the Indian Ocean is once again becoming a critical factor.

Many concerns that India had harboured during the cold war have dissipated, however a variety of new challenges have surfaced. New Delhi would certainly be wary of China's presence in the Indian Ocean although it is a different issue to what extent China has either the capabilities or the urgency for the foreseeable future to make such forays by way of military bases. China certainly is involved in building several port facilities in countries around India and is actively courting island states such as Maldives, Seychelles and Mauritius with generous aid. To what extent China would be able to make use of these facilities for military actions is a moot question given its preoccupation with maritime issues in its neighbourhood and a lack of power projection capabilities. For the time being, it appears the Indian government does not seem to be terribly concerned about China's activities but would keep a close tab on them.

In order to consolidate its position in the Indian Ocean, India has begun to qualitatively increase the engagement with its neighbours and the island states in the Indian Ocean such as Maldives, Mauritius and Seychelles through bilateral and multilateral cooperation. Secondly, it is also trying to enhance its political, economic and strategic leverages over these countries so that they would not do anything that might undermine Indian interests.

In any case, management of the Indian Ocean security will be problematic since there are no mechanisms military or non-military, track-I or track-II, or tangible regimes or CBMs. The only multilateral institution that is exists, the Indian Ocean Regional Association (IORA), is moribund and ineffectual although security issues have been included in its agenda. The Indian Ocean region will likely see jockeying for power by major stakeholders as its overall significance rises. India certainly harbours the ambition of emerging as a predominant power but it cannot ignore the reality that there are many security challenges that need concerted multilateral efforts as demonstrated in the counter-piracy operations in the Gulf of Aden. India has emerged as a net security provider by ensuring the security of sea lines of communication and for the foreseeable future China will have to depend on India to safeguard its trade in much of the Indian Ocean.

Yet, given growing stakes of great powers in the region, they would strive to be present in one form or the other. The U.S. has a huge military presence in Diego Garcia and China too in the longer run may like to explore ways to protect its interests. Even Japan has opened its first overseas military base in Djibouti in 2001.[3] Given the Indian Ocean's growing security complexity, there is an urgent need to create certain maritime regimes and promote maritime dialogues besides confidence building measures and greater maritime cooperation in an inclusive fashion so that any misunderstanding that may arise is addressed and common interests are protected.

REFERENCES

1. The "Chinese are coming...to Africa", Apr 22 2011, *The Economist* online, http://www.economist.com/blogs/dailychart/2011/04/chinese_africa

2. According to the State Councillor and Minister of National Defence of China, Liang Guanglie, the "logistic supply activities do not have any connection with establishing military bases overseas." "China has no plan for Indian Ocean military bases', *The Hindu*, 4 September 2012, http://www.thehindu.com/opinion/interview/article3855313.ece

3. Martin, Alex, "First overseas military base since WWII to open in Djibouti", *Japan Times*, July 2, 2011, http://www.japantimes.co.jp/news/2011/07/02/national/first-overseas-military-base-since-wwii-to-open-in-djibouti/#.VF2jATRwlvA

China in the Indian Ocean Region: Changing Geopolitics and Challenges

M. Mayilvaganan* and P.S. Ramya**

With the booming economy, China is emerging as the key player in the Indian Ocean Region (IOR) and possibly as the dominant superpower in Asia-Pacific. The rise of strong, aggressive China has changed the geopolitics in the region as well the international order. Today China has become the most important economic partners of Asian countries and their footprints are growing 'by leaps and bounds,' transforming international relations in a dramatic way. Indian Ocean or say, Asia-Pacific have become the center-field for power play or power balance between rising powers and external powers such as the US. In turn the evolving geopolitics of Indian Ocean region with Chinese power projection has posed major challenges to the status quo in the region with consequences for its neighbours and other powers such as the US. Indeed, this heighten endeavours of both regional and external power like US, Japan and India to reposition themselves to protect their national interest whose maritime interests are linked with the sea-lanes of this ocean. Significantly, the rise of China has led India with its geographic advantage in the IOR to enhance its own capabilities and power projection to meet the challenges in the strategic arena.

In light of these developments the paper seeks to assess how the rise of China has impacted the geopolitics of the Indian Ocean Region and the challenges these changes pose to India. The paper first outlines the significance of the maritime domain which represents a 'confluence of interests' ranging from economic to strategic followed by the historic relevance of the Indian Ocean. In this context, an attempt is made to analyse the current strategic setting of the India Ocean and the challenges posed by China's rise in the region.

---

* Assistant Professor, International Strategic and Security Studies, National Institute of Advanced Studies (NIAS), Indian Institute of Science (IISc) Campus, Bangalore.
**Research Assistant at International Strategic and Security Studies, National Institute of Advanced Studies (NIAS), Indian Institute of Science (IISc) Campus, Bangalore.

MARITIME DOMAIN: CONFLUENCE OF INTERESTS

The maritime domain in the recent years has grown in its relevance as a field of study within international relations. Several factors have contributed towards the increasing relevance of the study of the maritime sphere and how it impacts the power of nations. Firstly, the oceans have been used for centuries as carries of trade and enabled economic engagement between regions. Secondly and significantly, along with carrying trade, cultural exchanges occurred simultaneously. Thirdly, the oceans formed the roadways for expedition and later paved way for colonial powers to establish and consolidate their supremacy. Apart from these aspects, the oceans also became key pathways for energy transport. Therefore, the maritime domain when considered in its entirety depicts a 'confluence of interests' wherein economic interests are intertwined with security concerns ranging from naval interests to energy security. Seen from these multiple dimensions, the waterways became crucial links for trade, commerce, and a platform for militaries to fight wars.

Therefore, the multiple roles played by maritime sphere are abundant. From the theoretical standpoint, the significance of the waterways was communicated in the work of Alfred Thayer Mahan's 'The Influence of Sea Power upon History: 1660-17-83.' The conceptualisation of the opportunities of maritime domain from the prism of power by Mahan formed a turning point in how nations perceived the oceans. Mahan provided a framework for nations to not only comprehend the power of the seas but, to use this potential for outward expansion.

The supremacy of naval power in safeguarding economic and strategic interests of nations was articulated before Mahan as well. For instance, the US Secretary of State William Seward understood the power held by the maritime sphere. He sought to expand the US interests by purchasing islands and form bases. In this regard Seward tried to improve the US commercial interests in Asia by purchasing Alaska in 1867. Similarly, Seward attempted to purchase islands in the Caribbean wherein naval bases could be built.[1] Therefore, Seward tried to use the potential of the maritime domain in expanding the US influence. When the two cases of Mahan and Seward are considered it becomes apparent how the utility of the sea for commercial purposes was deemed as significant. Moreover, both stress on exploiting commercial interests and expand that into strategic interests through sea power.

It must be noted that, Mahan's work has been interpreted mostly in context to naval strategies and propagating the need for stronger naval forces to protect maritime interests. However, for a large part he presents the need for a strong navy by first conceiving the sea as a 'highway' or a 'wide-common'. He then builds the case for expansion of naval capabilities by calling for 'far-sightedness' as it is essential for military preparedness.[2] Therefore, the significance of protecting interests at sea is enumerated through various elements of sea power by Mahan. He articulates the need for sea power by first indicating the diversity of interests that the maritime domain inherently possesses. Although, the concept of sea-power has been interpreted narrowly with specific attention to the navy and its build up/capabilities the maritime domain connotes the wider access to 'sea and its resources' for economic and strategic interests.[3] Despite the growth in the ambit the maritime power the relevance of Mahan's work, even today, stems from the attention he paid to the significance of sea power during peace time. This aspect of his work aptly depicts the diverse role the navy plays and the myriad of interests a nation can seek to obtain from the maritime domain. This 'confluence of interests' of the maritime domain has therefore, made it significant even in the contemporary context wherein nations are devoting attention to protect economic and strategic interests by actively using the potential of the oceans.

MARITIME POWER IN THE IOR: HISTORIC SETTING

As outlined the maritime landscape knits trade, commerce, energy security, etc. while urging nations to develop naval capabilities to economic and strategic interests. Moreover, it provides a useful platform for diplomatic signalling and offers a gambit of opportunities for nations to integrate military and non-military interests. Therefore, the maritime landscape which represents a plethora of interests becomes crucial in the current scenario wherein nation-states rely on the maritime sphere to expand their influence and grow.

Reflections of history consistently showcase the significance of maritime trade routes and the overarching strategic interests it serves. The success of the colonial powers such as the British, Dutch, and Portuguese was credited to the investments these powers made to consolidate their maritime power. Tracing back to the Minoans, Phoenicians, Greeks and Romans 'exhibited a strong proclivity' for maritime power which later provided a precursor to the European maritime trade patterns.[4] In context to the growth of the powers of the colonial nations the maritime route through of the Indian Ocean becomes crucial.

The Indian Ocean is the third largest water body in the world. The Indian Ocean Region (IOR) forms one of the most important sea lanes for trade and commerce. Geographically, the west of Indian Ocean lays Africa where it stretches to the Cape of Agulhas. To the north of the Indian Ocean is bounded by the Indian sub-continent and Iran. Here it stretches from the Suez Canal to the Malay Peninsula and Singapore straits going up to Australia encapsulating the most significant sea lanes of communications in the world. While, Tasmania lies to the east of the Indian Ocean and it stretches to the latitude 60 degree south as per the Antarctic Treaty of 1959.[5] Therefore, the Indian Ocean covers crucial continents and hence became significant trade route.

Many have argued that a historical analysis of the trading patterns of the IOR indicates that over a period of time the Indian Ocean became integrally tied to the Mediterranean region.[6] This historic linkage between the two water bodies provides an insight into the presence of the colonial powers and their eventual domination of Asian region. The Indian Ocean hence became a link in connecting the West to the East. Significantly, it has been noted the Portuguese established a stronghold in the trade route through the Indian Ocean that in turn led to monopoly. However, there was constant conflict between the Portuguese and the Dutch, French and British. Interestingly, the withdrawal of the Portuguese from the Indian Ocean not only led extra-regional colonial powers to try and dominate the strategic ocean but revived the maritime interests of the indigenous littoral states within IOR. This was seen in how Oman emerged as regional naval power and boasted of deep-sea penetration capability.[7] While, the Mughals emerged as a dominant force in the Bay of Bengal and also developed naval bases at Janjira and Cambay.[8] Furthermore the Marathas have also been credited with maintain strong naval forces. However, these were limited to territorial waters lacking capability to enter the deep seas.[9]

Although, the littoral states of the IOR were reinvigorating their maritime capabilities, they would remain outflanked by the maritime prowess of the colonial powers specifically, the British who attained maritime pre-eminence after defeating the Spanish Armada in 1588.[10] This pre-eminence to a large extent has been attributed to the control the British Royal Navy exerted on the Indian Ocean. The strategic significance of the Indian Ocean which connects the West to the East led to European rivalry to claim control of these waters. Therefore, with the growth of the British Empire the Indian Ocean was described as a 'British Lake' with Britain being called the 'Colossus' of the world.[11]

However, with growing unrest in colonies the maritime supremacy that the British had created that had lasted for a century began to wane.

The Indian Ocean has been a significant theatre for extra-regional powers. Particularly, with the waning influence of the British following the World Wars saw rising competition between the US and the Soviet Union. These developments at the international level were witnessed in the Indian Ocean Theater as well. Particularly, the Cold War rivalry between the US and the Soviet Union was witnessed in the Indian Ocean. For instance, the purchase of Diego Garcia by the US from the British was seen as a significant move by the US to establish a naval base in the center of the strategic Indian Ocean. Moreover, the presence of the extra-regional powers in the Indian Ocean was opposed by the littorals given the colonial history and the past supremacy of the British in these waters. Through course of the negotiations for installing a naval base in Diego Garcia the Indian Government opposed the idea on the grounds that it introduced "big-power competition into the Indian Ocean area."[12]

In a conversation between Indian External Affairs Minister Dinesh Singh and British Foreign Secretary Stewart the latter stated that the Indian Government was "very unhappy' with the increasing presence of the extra-regional powers in the IOR and outlined how the Chinese 'showed interest in the Indian Ocean' while, the Russians were seeking refuelling facilities and the American's seeking to establish a naval base in Diego Garcia made the IOR central to unwanted rivalries of the big-powers.[13] The Soviet Union in light of the Cold War politics also, began to view IOR as an important theatre to increase their presence. The naval presence of the Soviet can be traced to 1968 with a good will visit by four ships from Vladivostok to Kenya, India, Sri Lanka, Somalia, Pakistan and South Yemen.[14] In this regard, Afro-Asian nations of the IOR led by India began their 'tryst with destiny' opposing the growing presence of big-power rivalries in the Indian Ocean.[15]

The India-Pakistan war of 1971 particularly became a significant instance for the direct involvement of the big-powers—the US and the Soviet Union in the Indian Ocean. The entry of S of the US aircraft carrier Enterprise into the Indian Ocean coupled with presence of Soviet warships led to augmenting the presence of the big-powers in the strategic waters. However, the disintegration of the Soviet Union the US emerged as the dominant power in the Indian Ocean. It has a considerable presence in the Western region of the Indian Ocean specifically in the Persian Gulf and Arabian Sea which is directly linked to the dependence of oil and gas coming from region. While, the naval base in Diego Garcia depicts its presence in the Central Indian Ocean region while, in the Eastern Indian Ocean region the US continues to maintain its presence through its allies such as Singapore and Australia.[16] Therefore, through the centuries the Indian Ocean became a central trading route, significant to energy politics and its strategic location made it a playfield for extra-regional powers.

INDIAN OCEAN: STRATEGIC SETTING

In the contemporary context the Indian Ocean has become highly significant especially with the rise of Asia and was has been dubbed the 'Asian Century'. The industrialisation of Asia is traced to the 1920s with the growth of the Japanese economy followed the growing economies of South Korea and Taiwan.[17] However, in the present setting the growth of China and the rising economy of India have captured the attention of the international community. The growth of these Asian nations has been attributed to multiple factors such as ship building, high level service sector, manufacturing of high density microelectronics, etc.

Nations with growing economies become voracious consumers of energy and raw materials. The first wave of industrialisation in Europe led to competition among the colonial powers to obtain raw materials and energy. Currently the burgeoning economies of the Asia have led to a similar pattern with China and India's increasing appetite for energy and materials. As outlined earlier, the use of sea-ways to meet the demands of a growing economy becomes inevitable. The 'confluence of interests' in terms of the economic benefits, trade routes and strategic advantages possessed by the maritime domain become intrinsically used by growing economies. Contexualising this aspect to the Asian landscape, the significance of the Indian Ocean becomes manifold.

The Indian Ocean has be described as more than just a 'geographic feature' stating the it is an 'idea' which combines its vast geographic extent with growing energy politics of rising powers in the Asian region to depict a 'multilayered, multipolar world'.[18] The strategic setting of the Indian Ocean in the current context can be understood by first assessing the use of the ocean waters for trade and transport, the energy politics played out and how these factors are intrinsically linked to the rise of China and India. Also, to be noted is how the economic growth of the Asian nations has also intensified the military modernisation drives specifically in context to the maritime domain. These factors in turn have made the Indian Ocean central to the power politics unfolding in the 21st century as noted by Kaplan.

In a global context the maritime traffic has risen by 300 per cent since 1992 showcasing the growing dependence of nation-states on the maritime domain.[19] In such a scenario the rise of Asian nations has catapulted the Indian Ocean region as an important conduit of trade, commerce and also a platform to project power. Firstly, the Indian Ocean is said to carry 50 per cent of the world's container traffic while the ports of the IOR handle about 30 per cent of the global trade. Furthermore, nearly 66 per cent of the world's oil seaborne trade traverses through the Indian Ocean and significantly, the IOR is said to have 55 per cent of known oil reserves and 40 per cent gas reserves.[20] This strategic significance of the Indian Ocean can be further assessed by considering the seven key choke-points present which includes the Mozambique Channel, the Bab el Mandeb, the Suez Canal, the Strait of Hormuz, the Malacca Straits, the Sunda Strait and the Lombok Strait.[21] Significantly, the Strait of Hormuz and the Straits of Malacca have been described as the world's most important strategic chokepoints based on the volume of oil transit.[22]

The strategic significance of the Indian Ocean in terms of the energy sea-routes became a tangible reality with the oil crisis of the 1970s. With the Organisation of Petroleum Exporting Countries (OPEC) deciding to increase the price of oil deeply impacted the West and the US which depended on the hydrocarbons of the Persian Gulf.[23] Significantly, in the current context the passage of energy trade through the Strait of Hormuz and the Strait of Malacca are dubbed as 'dilemmas' for the China and India. The 'dilemma' was outlined by former Chinese President Hu Jintao in 2003 stressing on the need to find alternatives to overcome China's dependence on the Strait of Malacca wherein nearly 70 to 80 per cent of its oil imports through these straits.[24] Similarly, India is presented with the 'Hormuz Dilemma' wherein a large of number of crucial imports of India passes through the Hormuz strait which is located close to the Pakistan's Makran coast.[25] Therefore, the growing economies of Asia depend significantly on the trade routes of the Indian Ocean which in turn has made the significant chokepoints into strategic vulnerabilities. Apart from the strategic significance of the energy routes and high level of marine traffic treading through the Indian Ocean the presence of extra-regional powers especially the US lends another dimension to the strategic setting. A case in point of this complex interaction of strategic interests of China, the US and India was recently when Iran threatened to block the Strait of Hormuz. With increasing US pressure over Iran to shut down the latter's nuclear programme, Iran threatened to block the strategic chokepoint of Hormuz. The threat from Iran came in response to oil embargos being levied against it by Europe and US.[26] Significantly, the dependence of China and India who depend on the straits for their economic and energy imports Iran's threat could prove fatal. Although, China was friendly towards Iran in light of the sanctions imposed by US and the West the threat of such a blockade could result in China isolating Iran further. India too needed careful diplomatic treading in light of the threat of the blockade. Therefore, this incident depicts how the delicate the confluence of interests in the Indian Ocean is and the presence of extra-regional powers coupled with growing powers of the Asian nation-states, the strategic setting of the Indian Ocean is bound to become more complex.

CHINA'S RISE AND THE CHANGING GEOPOLITICS

The paper thus far has outlined the historic significance of the Indian Ocean and described the strategic setting in the current context. However, the theatre of the Indian Ocean is witnessing changes in its geopolitical dimensions especially in light of the rise of China. Interestingly, it must be noted that the rise of China began with a strong economic dimension which still persists but, with such a rise, China has sought to enhance its military and technology capabilities to attain great power status. This aspect of China's rise has had a significant impact on the geopolitical landscape of the IOR.

The booming of economy of China resulted in increased demand of energy and materials which led to growing dependence of China on the IOR and its trade routes. Coupled with this economic rise in the post-Deng era, Jiang Zemin and high-ranking military officers have stressed on China's naval modernization 'through the acquisition of sophisticated weapons and equipment and the development of a blue-water naval strategy.'[27] The national objectives of the Peoples Liberation Army-Navy (PLAN) seem to focus on unification of Taiwan, control of South China Sea and expansion of China's maritime influence in the Indian Ocean and Western Pacific.

Outlined in a recent 'blue-book' policy document prepared by the Yunnan University of Finance and Social Sciences Research Centre Documentation Publishing House stressed on the need for China to advocate a 'pro-active' approach in the Indian Ocean Region.[28] Furthermore, the blue-book emphasised on the need for China to deepen its economic engagements with littoral states in the IOR and warned that the India Ocean could become 'an ocean of conflict and trouble' if India, China and the US did not constructively engage each other despite overlapping strategic interests.[29] The need for China to engage more proactively with the IOR as detailed in the blue-book is manifest in close cooperation China is striving to establish with Myanmar, Pakistan and Iran in order to protect the formers crucial sea-lines of communication (SLCOs) in the Indian Ocean and in South East Asia.[30]

The uniqueness of increasing Chinese presence in the Indian Ocean rests in how China is strengthening its maritime ties with littoral states through engagements of land. This has been dubbed as the 'aggressive soft power diplomacy' that China has adopted by providing loans, offering military assistance, construction of infrastructure, providing political support in the UN Security Council through its veto power etc. China has earned the goodwill of a number of littorals in the IOR such as Pakistan, Sri Lanka, Bangladesh and Iran and as far as Western region of the Indian Ocean with increasing engagement with African nation-states such as Kenya.[31]

The Chinese influence and projects in these littorals in IOR although, motivated by economic interests has a strong military overtures. In fact, the notion of Beijing using economic means for military ends gained attention following the "String of Pearls" hypothesis proposed by the US consulting firm Booz Allen Hamilton in 2005. Although, much speculation exists over how real the suspicions posed the 'string of pearls' hypothesis one cannot ignore the increasing presence of the Chinese in the Indian Ocean. Furthermore, the PLAN began expanding its South Sea Fleet by increasing the warships to this fleet and re-allocating nuclear submarines to the South Fleet from the North Sea Fleet in 2008.[32] This move was seen as significant as it allowed the PLAN to keep its option open in the event of war with either Japan or Taiwan and possible US intervention. By expanding the South Sea Fleet China retains its ability to send its navy farther into the Indian Ocean which can be used as significant tool to project power.[33]

Another important feature of the growing Chinese presence in the Indian Ocean stems from the anti-piracy exercises the PLAN has been part of especially in the Gulf of Aden. This has been interpreted as a possible precursor to future PLAN presence in the IOR. The notion behind such an analysis stems from the strategic stakes that China has in the Indian Ocean coupled with the need for power projection by a rising power. In this context the recent naval drill conducted by PLAN in the Strait of Lombok in 2014 near Indonesia indicates that China is playing close attention and seeks to expand operations in the East Indian Ocean.[34] The drill was seen as significant because of the use of the largest amphibious landing ship, the Changbaishan accompanied by two destroyers.[35] The use of such a squadron and the location of the exercise depicted the increasing priority the Chinese were giving to the Indian Ocean specifically to secure the SLOCs.

Therefore, the rise of China has altered the strategic environment in the Indian Ocean. The change in the geopolitics in the IOR accompanied have China's rise both economically and militarily have impacted the strategic outlook of India towards the India Ocean. India has been considered the 'future dominant' in the region while, former Indian Foreign Secretary Nirupama Rao stated that 'as the main resident power in the India Ocean Region, India is well poised to play a leadership role'.[36] In such a context, the rising presence of the China in the region would in a sense lead to competing interests. Furthermore, the presence of the US as an existing power in the India Ocean has led to an 'uncomfortable status quo' between China and the US which is manifest in the IOR strategic setting as well. With the US propounding the 'pivot' to Asia policy that rests on rebalancing its attention toward the IOR region the changing geopolitical dimensions gains traction. Moreover, with China pushing for increasing presence in the IOR coupled with its focus on the Western Pacific indicates a possible 'two-ocean strategy' as outlined by Kaplan.[37]

Incidentally, the expansion of naval capabilities by China doesn't set with its narrative of 'peaceful rise' though Beijing sought to expand its influence in the IOR for multiple reasons ranging from protection of SLOCs for its energy and trade routes and also improve its ability to project power. This has in turn unfolded change—geo-economic, geo-political and geo-strategic—in the region and global power structure. Major challenges to the neighbours and other impacted the geopolitical dynamics in the IOR. While, India is posed with challenges in this regard, the US has been seen to implement its rebalancing strategy.

IMPLICATIONS AND MAJOR CHALLENGES

The real question throughout the world today is what does this changing geopolitics and the rise of China means for the region and in particular for India. The rise of China impacts the region directly. It also shapes the geopolitics of global order.

The rapid growth of Beijing has played a part in reshuffling the relationship among the regional powers and major actors. Noticeably, some of them have shown an inclination to accommodate China by recognising its significance while others like India have enhanced multilateral partnership with other powers like Japan and Australia in the region in order to protect its interest. The US, dominant power, has rebalanced its strategy to Asia-Pacific from its current focus on the Middle East. In fact, the China's inexorable rise has forced countries such as Vietnam, Japan and Australia too to look beyond their traditional partners like the US. India's strategic partnership with Vietnam, Japan, and Australia emphasise the potential of greater cooperation in IOR that can mutually advance shared objectives and interest.

As India's strategic and security interests go beyond the Malacca strait with the New Delhi's dependent on access to vital offshore natural resources and economic prospect in Asia-Pacific markets, it becomes inevitable for India to adapt to the changing geopolitical. Today India's economic and political interests are more widely dispersed beyond its own perimeter. India is focusing on strengthening its ties with Japan and Australia, who are considered as 'natural and indispensable partners' in Asia-Pacific. Through these partnerships New Delhi wants to show that it has a legitimate interest and strategic presence beyond South China.

Rising maritime interest and for which building substantive naval capabilities has created new challenges for New Delhi who have traditionally followed a principle of 'non-alignment' and 'strategic autonomy' in its international relations. India like other powers in the region was compelled to act tactically in order to cope with the Chinese ability to project power in the IOR. Indian policy makers began to formulate new maritime strategy that is in tune with its two decades old Look East Policy. India's new strategy was aimed to secure its interest in South China and ASEAN where it becomes essential for New Delhi to protect freedom of navigation in high sea and sea lines of communication. As the economic growth and prosperity of India is tied with the resources and market outside its territorial waters it becomes essential for New Delhi to act swiftly at the same time tactically to counter any threat that emerge from the assertive and aggressive Beijing in the seas. The Chinese expanding territorial claims and development of anti-access and anti-denial strategies are cases in point.

However, the major challenges that New Delhi faces in the maritime domain in IOR is to maintain its 'strategic autonomy' and at the same time pleasing the expectation of the other littoral who see the India as a 'net security provider' in the region. Even though India assists littorals like Vietnam in building their own capacities, it does not really want to take a clear stand on many of the issues in IOR related to China. For instance, though it is concerned at the developments in South China Sea it does not consider it as their own turf. This predicament in fact shows inhibition of Delhi in taking responsibility and being proactive player in the region. As a desiring global player, New Delhi needs to show more courage and take responsibility in standing by the smaller littorals that are inclined to India.

Another major challenge that India and other powers like Japan and Australia, faces is their commitment to stand by each other during the time of crisis in the future. While they have worked out a bilateral partnership aimed at protecting their mutual maritime interest in IOR but the question is can they work to form a great power concert? Since there is a perception that the Washington cannot be expected and trusted in standing by their side in any eventuality against China the above concern remains significant.

Thus, New Delhi should deepen its engagement—defence and economic—with the littorals in Asia-Pacific and utilise its advantage as here lies India's strategic and security interests and the only way to deal with the emerging geopolitical implications.

REFERENCES

1. Milestones: 1866–1898, *Office of the Historian*, US State Department, 12 November, 2014, at https://history.state.gov/milestones/1866-1898/mahan.
2. Mahan, A.T., *The Influence of Sea Power Upon History: 1660–1783*, The Project Gutenberg E-book, p. 25, at http://www.gutenberg.org/files/13529/13529-h/13529-h.htm#Page_25.
3. Sakhuja, Vijay, *Asia Maritime Power in the 21ˢᵗ Century: Strategic Transactions: China, India and Southeast Asia*, Institute of Southeast Asian Studies, Singapore, 2011, p. 4.
4. Ibid, p. 3.
5. Khalid, Iram, "Indian Ocean: Global and Regional Strategies", *Journal of Political Studies*, Vol. 20, Issue 2, November 2013, p. 22, at http://pu.edu.pk/images/journal/pols/pdf-files/Indian%20Ocean%20-%20Iram_VOLUME20_2_13.pdf.
6. Beaujard, Philippe and Fee, S., "The Indian Ocean in Eurasian and African World-Systems before the Sixteenth Century", *Journal of World History* (University of Hawai'i: USA, 2005), Vol. 16, No. 4, November 6, 2014, p. 412.
7. Rais, Rasul Bux, *Indian Ocean and the Superpowers: Economic, Political and Strategic Perspectives,* Rowman and Littlefield: USA, 1987, pp. 22–23.
8. Ibid, p. 22.

9. Ibid, p. 22.

10. Sakhuja, n. 3, p. 7.

11. Jayaramu, P.S., "Indian Ocean as a Zone of Peace: Problems and Perspectives", *The Indian Journal of Political Science* (Indian Political Science Association: Delhi, 1986), Vol. 47, No. 2, November 6, 2014, p. 237.

12. Indian Ocean: Memorandum From the Assistant Secretary of State for Near Eastern and South Asian Affairs to Secretary of State Rogers, *US Department of State Archive*, November 6, 2014, p. 123, at http://2001-2009.state.gov/documents/organization/113358.pdf.

13. Telegram from the Embassy in the United Kingdom to the Departments of State and Defense, *US Department of State Archive*, November 6, 2014, p. 125 at http://2001-2009.state.gov/documents/organization/113358.pdf.

14. Soviet Naval Presence in the Indian Ocean, *Central Intelligence Agency*, November 8, 2014, p. 1, at http://www.foia.cia.gov/sites/default/files/document_conversions/5829/CIA-RDP80R01731R002200020002-8.pdf.

15. Jayaramu, n. 11, p. 238.

16. Roy-Chaudhury, Rahul, "US Naval Policy in the Indian Ocean", *Strategic Analysis* (Routledge: Delhi, 1998), Vol. 22, No. 9, November 3, 2014, pp. 1314–1318 at http://www.tandfonline.com/doi/abs/10.1080/09700169808458885?journalCode=rsan20#.VJXuPP8LAA.

17. Kopp, Carlo, "Strategic Importance of the Indian Ocean," *Defence Today*, November 2, 2014, at http://www.ausairpower.net/PDF-A/DT-Indian-Ocean-Dec-2011.pdf.

18. Kaplan, Robert D., "Center Stage for the Twenty-first Century: Power Plays in the Indian Ocean", *Foreign Affairs* (Council on Foreign Relations: USA, 2009), Vol. 88, No. 2, November 6, 2014, p. 17.

19. "Worldwide ship traffic up 300 percent since 1992: New satellite data reveals whopping boost in shipping," *American Geophysical Union*, November 17, 2014, at http://news.agu.org/press-release/worldwide-ship-traffic-up-300-percent-since-1992.

20. Khurshid, Salman; Bishop, Julie and Natalegawa, Marty, "Putting out to sea a new vision", *The Hindu*, November 11, 2014, at http://www.thehindu.com/opinion/op-ed/putting-out-to-sea-a-new-vision/article5305845.ece.

21. Michel, David and Sticklor, Russell, "Indian Ocean Rising: Maritime and Security Policy Challenges", in David Michel and Russell Sticklor (eds.), *Indian Ocean Rising: Maritime and Security Policy Challenges*, Stimson, USA, 2012, p. 9, at http://www.stimson.org/images/uploads/research-pdfs/Book_IOR_2.pdf.

22. World Oil Transit Chokepoints, *US Energy Information Administration*, November 4, 2014, at http://www.eia.gov/countries/regions-topics.cfm?fips=wotc&trk=p3.

23. Jayaramu, n. 11, p. 239.

24. Storey, Ian, "China's Malacca Dilemma", *China Brief*, Jamestown Foundation, USA, 2006, Vol. 6, No. 8, November 3, 2014, at http://www.jamestown.org/single/?no_cache=1&tx_ttnews[tt_news]=3943#.VJZsd_8LAA.

25. Kaplan, n. 18, p. 21.

26. "Iran will 'block' Strait of Hormuz if pressed," *Aljazeera*, October 16, 2014, at http://www.aljazeera.com/news/middleeast/2012/07/2012789645779519.html

27. Jae-Hyung, Lee, "China's Expanding Maritime Ambitions in the Western Pacific and the Indian Ocean", *Contemporary Southeast Asia* (Institute of Southeast Asian Studies: Singapore, 2002), Vol. 24, No. 3, November 6, 2014, pp. 549–550.

28. "China Reveals its Grand Strategy for Indian Ocean Region," *Defence Express*, November 2, 2014, at http://www.defenceexpress.com/index.php/navy/item/279-china-reveals-its-grand-strategy-for-indian-ocean-region.

29. Krishnan, Ananth, "China details Indian Ocean Strategy and Interests," *The Hindu*, November 2, 2014, at http://www.thehindu.com/news/international/world/china-details-indian-ocean-strategy-and-interests/article4795550.ece.

30. Jae-Hyung, n. 27, p. 553.

31. DeSilva-Ranasinghe, Sergei, "Why the Indian Ocean Matters," *The Diplomat*, October 3, 2014, at http://thediplomat.com/2011/03/why-the-indian-ocean-matters.

32. See Khurana, Gurpreet S., China's South Sea Fleet Gains Strength: Indicators, Intentions and Implications, India Strategic, October 2008 at http://www.indiastrategic.in/topstories183.htm

33. Mahadevan, Prem, "China in the Indian Ocean: Part of a Larger PLAN", *CSS Analyses in Security Policy*, No. 156, November 2, 2014, at www.css.ethz.ch/publications/DetailansichtPubDB_EN?rec_id=3022.

34. Rajan, D.S., "China in the Indian Ocean: Competing Priorities," *IPCS Articles*, November 2, 2014, athttp://www.ipcs.org/article/india/china-in-the-indian-ocean-competing-priorities-4302.html.

35. Ibid.

36. Brewster, David, *India's Ocean: The Story of India's Bid for Regional Leadership*, Routledge, USA, 2014, p. 36.

37. Kaplan, Robert D., "China's Two Ocean Strategy", in Abraham Denmark and Nirav Patel (eds.), *China's Arrival: A Strategic Framework for a Global Relationship*, CNAS, USA, 2009, p. 55, at http://www.cnas.org/files/documents/publications/CNAS%20China%27s%20Arrival_Final%20Report.pdf

Maritime Power Play in the Indian Ocean in the Century of the Seas: China and India—Equations and Prospects

R. Seshadri Vasan*

INTRODUCTION

No discussions today are complete without a mention of China in global affairs. There are no doubts that the economic growth and prowess of China is of immense proportions that could tilt the scale in its favour on many counts. What is of concern is the intransigent behaviour particularly with respect to settling its claims both at sea and over land. The incidences in East China Sea and South China Sea portend an aggressive nation that would like to settle issues by force on its terms.

While there are no direct claims or counter claims in the Indian Ocean Region, there are issues of common interest to both China and the Indian Ocean Countries. The Chinese interests hinge on its dependency on the Sea Lines of Communication (SLOCs) and the need to protect its seaborne interests. The incidents of piracy off Somalia and now the resurgence of this act even in Malacca Straits have raised the concerns of all nations and China which uses the sea for most of its export and import would be severely affected due to any disruption of its seaborne commerce by asymmetric threats. China has a well-orchestrated agenda to befriend the maritime nations in the Indian Ocean with an eye both for the present economic engagements as well as for the future possibilities of strategic applications in the maritime domain. By its actions in the neighbourhood of India, China has set in to motion a power play in IOR that needs to be analysed.

India on its part by its geographic location and its Island outposts both in Bay of Bengal and the Arabian Sea enjoys significant strategic advantage. Both the Indian Navy and the PLA Navy have embarked on modernising their force levels. The shape and size of the Navies of these two Asian powers are impressive and need to be factored in any maritime calculus.

*Commodore, Indian Navy (Retd.) Head, Strategy and Security Studies, Centre for Asia Studies, India.

There are no conflicts in the Indian Ocean though some analysts look at the investments of China in the maritime neighbourhood with suspicion. The interests of both the countries converge when it comes to keeping the SLOCs open and in ensuring that there is unimpeded traffic for enabling trade, commerce, and people to people contact. One would therefore ask as to what are the issues which cause estrangement and what are the issues that promote engagement?

The paper seeks to examine the past, the present and the future of Chinese interests in the IOR and also look at the short term and long term prospects of such interests along with possible Strategic impact in India's backyard.

History has recorded that both China and India were great economic powers from the past and the present century will visit the ascendency of both the powers in global order. The growth of the two Asian powers has immense significance in the Asian Century. The importance of the area has been reemphasized with the reorientation of the American policy towards Indo Pacific region which earlier carried the tag of Asia Pacific. While USA is trying to slant its thrust line towards the Asia Pacific which is now being referred to as Indo Pacific, China appears to be looking west where its interests lie in terms of economy, energy security and engagement with the economies in Asia, Africa and Middle East. India on its part has always been a reluctant power despite its geographic advantage,[1] resources, technical man power and a youthful population. There are high expectations that the new Government lead by Narendra Modi would change the status quo in the Indian Ocean.

A brief examination of the past would bring out the glory of the past centuries during which both China and India occupied a high place in the comity of nations. The following paragraphs should help to lead the discussions on the current topic.

15 CENTURY: THE CENTURY OF THE SEAS FOR CHINA AND INDIA?

After all both India and China till about the 15th century did enjoy considerable advantages that accrued through the traditional silk and spice routes for trade commerce and connectivity. As per the historic records China during the 14th century Myng dynasty rule, undertook many expeditionary voyages through the Indian Ocean under Admiral Zheng He. The routes followed and the ports visited are shown in the map below. The depiction in the map makes it amply clear that the reach of China during the Myng dynasty touched the shores of Africa, Middle Eastern Countries, India, South East Asian Countries, and the Island nations in the Indian Ocean Region. China even commemorated the voyage by replicating the route by sailing through the same silk routes of great significance. It is significant that China is now trying to reinvent its past glory by revisiting the Maritime Silk Route initiative that would provide it with connectivity and leverages for the future as China aims to displace United States of America from the number One slot. There are certain similarities in the way both India and China lost their place of preeminence in the 15th century where it has been established that the combined economies of China and India was more than half the combined GDP of the entire world put together.

The collapse of the Ming dynasty including the military fall[2] due to multifarious reasons paved the way for China's decline in global affairs.

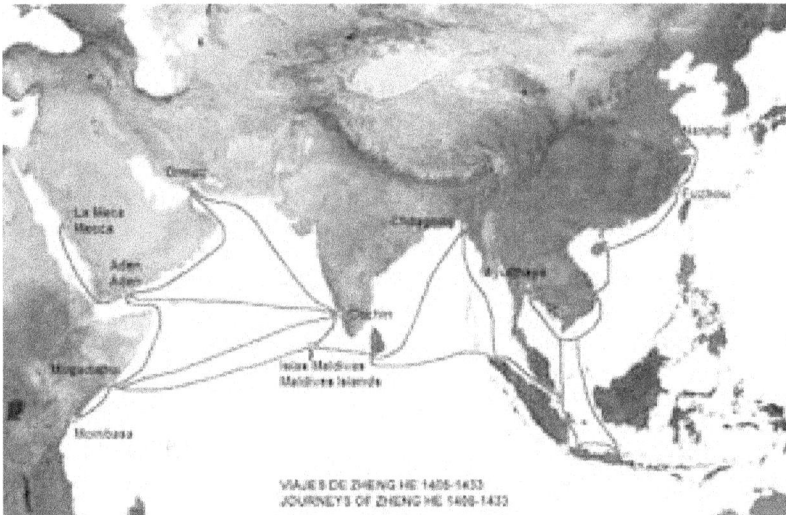

VIAJES DE ZHENG HE 1405-1433
JOURNEYS OF ZHENG HE 1405-1433

The maritime history of China is as ancient as that of India. India's maritime past is laced with the spice route[3] and the trade winds called monsoon in Arabic that provided connectivity both in the Arabian Sea and the Bay of Bengal. The spice routes predominantly covered the sea routes that reached the far corners of the world including Rome on the West and Japan and China in the east. So while India chose the Spice route for its prosperity China chose the silk route to establish connections and influence in areas of interest. The items traded included silk, porcelain and other items of interest to the west.

The story today is no different when it comes to Chinese initiatives through trade in the IOR rim countries today as China is the manufacturing hub of the world and is meeting the increasing demands of growing economies around the world. This has allowed China to reconnect to its past and engage with countries in far corners of the world. The strategy of China is to work on leverages for the future through the economic route.

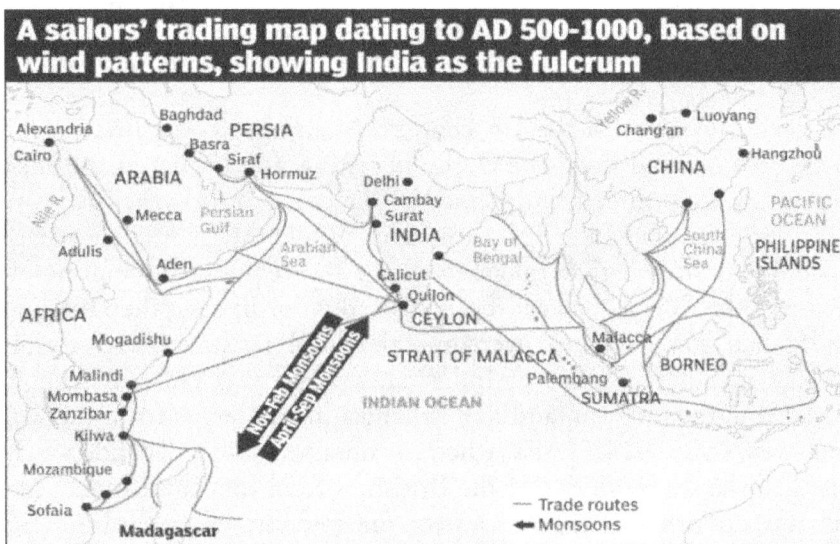

A sailors' trading map dating to AD 500-1000, based on wind patterns, showing India as the fulcrum

The Chinese maritime routes and connectivity are identified with the silk routes. The silk routes also had a complimentary route running through the land routes of countries in the north. The exploits of a Admiral Zheng He as outlined above during the Ming dynasty are illustrative of the prowers of a maritime China that wanted to look westwards by using the sea routes more than 500 years ago. The Admiral put together ships of all descriptions that included men of war, supply ships, auxiliaries and sent a signal to the countries visited about the might of the Chinese power. The combination of ships was impressive and definitely an envy of any maritime nation. This was a classic example of using trade and diplomacy along with a strong war machine for forward posturing and diplomacy. Such expedition doubtlessly demonstrated both the capability and the intent to use the Navy to support national objectives of China of that period. China even commemorated the event by sailing through the same routes in an effort to reinvent its glorious past linked to the seas. However, the face of China as a Maritime Power took a beating in the subsequent centuries leading to decline of both a land and maritime power due to changes in the global order during successive centuries till the ascendency of Great Britain as the sole power in the 19th century.

A 21ST CENTURY CHINA AS A MARITIME POWER

"If the 19th century belonged to Britain, and the 20th century to the United States. Then the 21st century will surely belong to China. My advice: Make sure your kids learn Chinese."

—**Jim Rogers**
Worth Magazine

It is acknowledged that the 19th century belonged to Great Britain which set up colonies and ruled the world by setting up colonies in the Indian Ocean. India continued to the jewel of the crown during the British rule contributing to its wealth and prosperity. While the traditional seafaring capability of the native rulers in India had equipped them to even challenge the foreign powers the British, the Portuguese, the Dutch and the French were able to overcome the local resistance and establish colonies in different parts of India. However it was Great Britain that prevailed in the long run and Pax Britanica ruled most parts of the world from 1815 to 1914. India when it obtained its independence had inherited the sea traditions of the Britishers from the Royal Indian Navy and was on firm footing to protect the interests of a maritime India though it took considerable decades for the Indian Navy to come of age. That is another story which has its origins in the successful contribution of the Indian Navy in liberating Bangladesh.

The 20th century belonged to the USA which became the dominant power post world war and by investing in a Mahanian navy was able to take on global missions in various trouble spots. It is Admiral Alfred Thayer Mahan who is credited with the entire shape and size of the US Navy that is still a global power with unlimited reach and capability. It has been analysed that Mahan influenced the leadership not just in USA but also in Germany and Japan. Of particular importance is the fact that Thedore Roosevelt came under the influence of Mahan's writings,[4] and worked assiduously to build a navy that matched the description of Mahan. The singular contribution of AT Mahan to the growth of America as a Sea Power can never be minimized. The adventures of USA in far corners of the world as a Super Cop and use of its preeminent maritime power is claimed to provide stability and security. Though not distracting from the capability of the US Navy and the military or casting aspersions on the valiant forces, the intervention is a mixed bag of results in different theatres. After all the Military option is one of the extensions of the Foreign Policy of a nation and by and large is resorted to when all other means have failed. The results therefore; whether good or bad have more to do with political processes and leadership than the maritime/ Military power potential. This has been debated and would form the topic of a separate discussion. The decline that is now being discussed in the American context is nothing unusual. This has happened through the ages and will happen again depending on the rise and fall of nations due to many nations including a natural cyclic process just as the changing seasons in a year. Even while the decline of the USA is considered inevitable in pure economic terms, it will be decades before USA can be displaced from its powerful position and this factor needs to form part of any calculus. USA as many other global powers,[5] will remain relevant for a long time. Some aspects of this dimension is also discussed in the succeeding paragraph while examining the trends in the 21st century.

The 21st century has been touted as the one that belongs to Asia and it has even been indicated that both China and India the ascending powers of the present century would be the key players in global calculus particularly in the maritime arena in the Indian Ocean Region. USA would continue to be relevant with its renewed interest in the Asia Pacific area which has been renamed as Indo Pacific area. The withdrawal of troops from Afghanistan and reorientation to the Indo Pacific area appears to be a well-planned strategy to be present in areas of interest to an assertive China which is needling the traditional allies of USA in the Pacific Ocean. While there is lot of analysis suggesting that China would surpass USA in many areas, it would be at least two to three decades before China can achieve such a status. Despite the kind of money being invested by the PLA-Navy on modernization and acquisition, China would need that kind of time before it can become a global power of the description of USA. Having realized the centrality and importance of Aircraft Carriers for global missions, China has rebuilt a carrier and will doubtlessly have more of them being produced. Considering that USA has a dozen nuclear powered carriers and the supporting elements which will all be in service for at least another 20–30 years, it is not going to be easy for China to replace US as the sole super power. There is nothing to suggest that US will stop building carriers to ensure that they still have the ability to intervene to protect perceived or actual interests. USA even if acknowledged as a declining power in the coming decades will maintain its technological lead and will continue to maintain the No. 1 position for a long time. Both its predominance in the maritime arena and its reach will not be affected as it plans to deploy larger maritime assets in the bases of its allies in the Pacific.

When one moves to the Indian Ocean, the famous quote on Indian Ocean 'Whoever controls the Indian Ocean will dominate Asia, the destiny of the world will be decided on its waters.' is attributed to AT Mahan sums up the importance of the Indian Ocean in the current century. While the major player in the Indian Ocean still continues to be the USA, the forces of China and India will be seen jostling for strategic space and influence in this area of great importance. The context of the struggle for gaining maritime influence in the region will be the notable feature of the current century.

It is abundantly clear that there would be clash of interest as USA realigns its policies to provide leverages in the hot spots in East China Sea and the South China Sea. The Indian Ocean Region is also becoming an arena for great competition in the present century and beyond. With the kind of economic growth and sustainability that is totally dependent on the safety of Sea Lines of Communication (SLOCs) and the protection of the concept of the Freedom of safe navigation, there would be greater emphasis on the maritime environment in the Indian Ocean Region which India traditionally considers as its back yard. The recent attempt by the National Security Advisor Ajit Doval,[6] during the 'Galle Dialogue' at Galle in Sri Lanka in early December for the Indian Ocean to be preserved as a zone of Peace did lead to certain analysis of the intent of the Indian Government. He recalled the appeal of Sri Lanka to "calling upon great powers not to allow escalation and expansion of military presence in the Indian Ocean." This renewed appeal by the National Security Advisor in Galle has been analysed as an attempt not just to keep the super powers but also China as upper power in the making also out of the Indian Ocean. But if both the past and the present are any indication, it is clear that this ploy will not work as it has never worked in the past. Despite the so called attempts to declare the Indian Ocean as a Zone of Peace way back in 1964, and the UNGA resolution in 1971, there was no mechanism to prevent the presence of the Extra Regional Powers during the Cold War. The proclamations and the clarion calls by regional leaders in South Asia for the Indian Ocean to be maintained as a Zone of Peace have never been heeded.

The situation is no different today as American led forces are stationed close to the Straits of Hormuz a strategic choke point. The presence of the US forces has its origin in the Carter Doctrine which was all about protecting the oil interest and providing energy security to the western powers who were dependent on the oil and gas from the region. The discovery of the Shale gas and also the expectation that US would be energy dependent by 2020 may alter the way maritime forces are positioned in the region but there would be no attempt by anyone to move out of the Indian Ocean. The Combined Maritime Force 150, the Combined Task Force 151 and 152 have carried on with their "stabilizing activities" in the west Arabian Sea both on their own and also with the combined forces from NATO and the regional navies including Pakistan. Both Indian and Chinese war vessels have operated in the adjacent areas but have not under any one flag for anti-piracy missions which have been going on since 2008 in the Gulf of Aden and off the Somali coast.

The territorial interests of China and the contested claims in the East China Sea and the South China Sea have everything to do with energy dependence,[7] and sea line security. The expectation of huge gas and oil reserve in ECS and SCS have spurred the maritime nations in the adjoining area to lay their claims based either on historical assumptions or based on the UNCLOS. With this in the background, it would be worthwhile to examine the maritime initiatives of China in areas of interest in the IOR. There is an obvious pattern to what China intends to do in the present to reap rich dividends in the future. The measures are also aimed at securing the long time interests of a country that is heavily dependent on the sea routes for trade commerce and most importantly for bringing in the energy products from around the world.

That China has a lead of at least two decades over India in terms of its initiatives has never been disputed. An energy hungry China started scouting for energy resources in far corners of the world including Africa, Siberia, Middle East and even South Eastern countries. The fact that more than eighty percent of China's energy imports are through the sea routes brings in an inbuilt vulnerability of the elongated supply chain. China is conscious of this vulnerability and has not left any stone unturned to ensure that its future transportation security is not compromised. The investments in the maritime neighbourhood of India stretching from Bangaladesh, Myanmar, Sri Lanka, Maldives and Pakistan is an exercise to find markets, investments and opportunities in the Indian Ocean that has been assessed as the ocean that holds the key to prosperity of nations in the present century. It is through these engagements both in Bay of Bengal and the Arabian Sea that China seeks to obtain political and strategic leverages that could be used for contingencies when its shipping routes or the exit and entry through the Choke points are threatened.

There are clear indications about how this can be achieved. With the heightened threat of piracy which started peaking 2005 onwards, both India and China started deploying their naval vessels,[8] in the Gulf of Aden and the waters off Somalia. The two ship patrol has been sustained since 2008,[9] and it has provided a great opportunity for the PLA-Navy to build data bases on the traffic patterns along the Sea Lines of Communication and in areas of operation. Factors such as weather, characteristics of regional navies and maritime forces, assessment of deployment patterns and force levels of extra regional players, bathymetric conditions that enable future anti-submarine operations, communication grids in the areas of operation, efficacy of multi-lateral action against piracy, terrorism etc., PLA Navy by sustaining its forward presence is able to test many of the concepts that would require PLA-Navy to protect its sea borne and commercial interests in the Indian Ocean. The data bases generated during the deployment would be of immense use to the planners in China who would need to factor all these inputs to craft their maritime responses to the possible scenarios in the Indian Ocean.

On the part of India, India has done fairly well in terms of building its maritime potential by designing and building its own arsenal.[10] There are gaps due to certain delays in bridging the gap of the most modern and dominant navy in the region. There have been efforts of late to overcome these limitations in a big way with heavy funding support for some of the delayed projects such as the submarine programmes and other projects.

Ominous Signs

The berthing of the Song class conventional submarine in Colombo on the eve of the visit of President Xi Jinping to Sri Lanka and Maldives prior to visiting India signals the intention of the PLA Navy to put to test the concept of operations (CONOPS) of its underwater arsenal in the IOR to further its strategic objectives. This was to demonstrate a resolve to protect its commercial and strategic interests in the Indian Ocean. As per the recent newspaper reports, India has expressed concerns at the allowing of submarines to operate from Colombo. From the point of India's southern neighbour, it is not in a position to say no to China as it is a major recipient of investments, aid and assistance from China. Also,

India too is not in a position to prevent China from exercising its seaborne options in any part of the world as long as it complies with the provisions of the United Convention on the Laws of the Seas and International conventions for transits through the oceans to any area/port of interest. From the point of view of Indian Navy, since it is not in a position to prevent the operation of the Chinese war ships or submarines in its back yard, at best, it could use the opportunity to track the units and obtain maximum data about the unit's operating in its areas of interest which could well be the areas of conflict /cooperation in the future. There is nothing new in this method as every navy uses such opportunity offered to track and record the movement of all vessels of interest and also record the parameters that could be stored, analysed and used at a later date.

PLA Navy has made phenomenal investments to modernize its navy and also add punch to the capability of its naval assets by introducing modern weapon systems. The combination of Anti-Ship Ballistic Missiles, Nuclear submarines, The new found capability to operate an aircraft carrier, stealth ships, submarines and aircraft have enhanced the capacity and capability of the PLA Navy not just to protect its interests in the Pacific but also beyond the Malacca Straits in the Indian Ocean.

By deploying its naval assets from Colombo and off the Gulf of Aden, China has tested the utility of its economic leverages by testing the concept of operations in the Indian Ocean Region. Whether it is the nuclear submarine or the conventional submarine, it is now confident that any future operations requiring deployment of submarines or a turnaround would not pose any problem due to the 'dependency ports'[11] in the IOR which will readily accommodate the turn round and logistic requirements of such deployment at extended ranges from the main land. Thus the concept of 'dependency ports' along with forward presence and posturing in the Indian Ocean has been validated much to the chagrin of Indian leadership. In this context, it has been brought out that it is the lack of decision making process and the bureaucratic bungling,[12] that led to Hambanthota project being given away on a silver platter to the Chinese. Unfortunately, Indian leadership and the bureaucracy failed to capitalize on an opportunity to be relevant in the southernmost strategic post at Hambanthota. Along with the Andaman and Nicobar group of Islands which serves as the forward post of India close to the Malacca Straits, Hambanthota would have served the strategic maritime interests of India well in to the next coming decades of intense competition.

It must also be noted that the nuclear submarine of the strategic forces of PLA have made their declared presence in the Indian Ocean and these signs are indeed ominous. While China has adhered to international norms of declaring the passage of the nuclear submarine through the Malacca Straits, it is clear that the intention was to make it public and to declare its big entry in to the IOR which sends a message to its potential adversaries whether US or India that it means business and is willing to go the extra mile to protect its interests. With the presence, deployment and possibility of regular forays of the Chinese submarines in Indian Exclusive Economic Zone, the importance of building adequate Anti-Submarine Capability by the Indian Navy cannot be overstated.[13]

The assessment of what China would do in the next century is not totally in the realm of speculation. The analysis of current day trends provides very good indications on that count. The Chinese have been actively pursuing the Maritime Silk Routes[14] to reestablish maritime linkages through trade and investment along the sea routes. The MSR was launched in October 2013 by Xi Jinping with the stated objectives of connectivity and trade with the countries in Asia, Middle East and Africa. However, the Maritime Silk Route also appears to have a hidden agenda of protecting the Chinese interests in the Indian Ocean. The ambitious plan that has given a very high priority by the Chinese leadership has not left any stone unturned to make this a success. The recent visit of the Chinese President Xi Jinping to Sri Lanka and Maldives prior to visiting India is also a part of this grand plan to obtain leverages through the maritime connectivity and trade. Very recently, China and Qatar have pledged to enhance the strategic relations. China by its engagement with the Middle Eastern and GCC countries plans to promote its energy security. China was also indeed very enthusiastic about getting India onboard the MSR initiative. However, India has not been particularly enthusiastic about the scheme that would provide enormous advantage and leadership role to China.

On a comparative note, when it comes to India, Not to be left behind as China is looking west; India in its continuation of look east policy has proposed Mausam which likewise conceptualized to revisit the cultural and trade routes enabled by the North East and South West monsoons. In the century of the seas where two dominant players are vying with one another for wielding influence, both the MSR and the Mausam appear to have a common objective of engaging with the countries in the Indian Ocean Rim. China has recently acknowledged that it does not want to be seen as playing in the back yard of India.[15] What is not left in doubt is that the MSR and the Mausam could either play a complementary role or could be seen as a competition of the big two in the Indian Ocean. With the kind of lead that China has in launching its MSR initiative backed by its economic investments, it will take plenty of thinking out of the box from the Indian side to make Mausam relevant and workable.

CONCLUSION

While the Asian century is synonymous with the growth of the two Asian neighbours, it is clear that China has a clear road map on how it wants to establish presence and wield influence in different parts of the world. The silk routes have all the makings of a resurgent China that has economic investments in all most all countries of interest particularly in the Indian Ocean Region. The investments in the maritime neighbourhood has caused great anxiety in Indian minds as India finds itself not in a position to match either the huge investments or the decision making processes that give a clear edge to China in strategic space.

China just as USA or any other western power is an Extra Regional Power and the leadership has not shown any hesitation in operationalizing the plans for being present where there interests lie whether it is in the Pacific or in the Indian Ocean or in the Atlantic. The presence of the Chinese Navy in the neighbouring nations of India would become more frequent as China aims to become a de facto Indian Ocean Power. From the Indian point of view, it is hardly in a position to contest this development as it has not been able to manage the maritime neighbourhood for various reasons including lack of vision and flaws in the decision making processes. India has a lot of ground to cover to be able to protect its maritime and national interests. There are huge gaps in capacity and capability that are prerequisites to remain as the most powerful navy in the region. The nation has lost out more than ten years during the UPA rule in which stalling the processes and defence procurement was the order of the day. The shortages of modern submarines, Integral Helicopters and modern weapons and sensors have stymied the growth of the Indian Navy. While the commencement of the sea trials of Arihant the only nuclear submarine is good news, it still has miles to go before it can be fully integrated in the scheme of strategic deterrence architecture of the nation.

China is conscious of its vulnerability,[16] in the Indian Ocean when exposed to the might of the Indian Navy and is taking measured steps to protect its interests should there be a fall out of the border conflict in to the maritime arena where India clearly has a lead both due to geography and also due to the training and sophistication levels of its navy. While numerically, it appears that China has an edge, the vintage and also the type of the vessels that add to the numbers is not exactly mesmerizing. The only assets that are of concern from the point of view of Indian Navy operations is the possession of six nuclear submarines in the arsenal which post both strategic and tactical challenge to the Indian Navy units operating in pursuit of their missions.

While acknowledging the legitimacy of China to protect its sea borne interests at all costs, India cannot be a silent spectator when it is challenged in its own back yard. This is not to say that war is imminent in the coming decade, but there should be no mistake in reading the signs that are obvious. India remains challenged today in the Indian Ocean and cannot just depend on the advantages conferred on it by geography. There is a lot more that needs to be done to protect the legitimate interests of a maritime India that is growing and will have an important role not only in the Indian Ocean littoral abut also in global affairs. There is an immediate need to introspect on India's failures in the neighbourhood be it in Sri Lanka, or Maldives, or Myanmar or Bangladesh who are all our immediate maritime neighbours. Whatever happens in these countries would affect the strategy and security equations in the region. By inaction and proactivity, India has conceded strategic space to China which has outwitted India by its aggressive and assertive action with the smaller neighbours who are quite happy to play the Indian card in China and vice versa to gain advantages on their respective home turfs.

REFERENCES

1. Adem, Seifudein and Afrasia, Ali A. Mazrui, A Tale of Two Continents, University Press of America, Plymouth UK, p. vii.
2. Swope, Kenneth M., The Military Collapse of China's Ming Dynasty, 1618–44, Rourledge, New York 2014, p. 4.
3. Pamela D. Toler. Mankind: The Story of All of Us, Running Press Philadelphia 2012, p. 183.
4. Jones, Howard, Crucible of Power: A History of U.S. Foreign Relations Since 1897, SR Books Oxford 2001, p. 3.
5. Brown, Stuart S., The Future of US Global Power: Delusions of Decline, Palgrave Mcmillon, New York 2013.
6. http://www.thehindu.com/news/international/south-asia/indian-ocean-has-to-remain-a-zone-of-peace-ajit-doval/article6651325.ece

7. Eberling, George, Chinese Energy Futures and their Implications for the United States, Lexington Books 2011, Plymouth UK, p. 3.

8. Brewster, David, India's Ocean: The Story of India's Bid for Regional Leadership Routledge, New York 2014, p. 185.

9. David L. Shambaugh Tangled Titans: The United States and China, Rowman and Littlefield Publishers Plymouth UK 248.

10. Gordon, Sandy, India's Rise as an Asian Power: Nation, Neighborhood, and Region, George Town University Press, USA, 2014, pp. 128–129.

11. A term used to connote the use of commercial ports for future use in times of hostilities. The dependency ports would be used to turn round and provide logistic support to men of war engaged in operations in the areas of interest.

12. 'Indo Sri Lanka Maritime Issues: Challenges and Responses' the full paper by Commodore RS Vasan is available at http://www.asiastudies.org/index.php?option=com_content&view=article&id=124&Itemid=91

13. As brought out by the author in Times of India article. Full article is accessible at https://www.academia.edu/9128842/Chinese_Subs_challenge_Indias_Sea_control

14. Sandy Gordon India's Rise as an Asian Power: Nation, Neighborhood, and Region, George Town University Press, USA, 2014, p. 125.

15. Jonathan Holslag, China and India: Prospects for Peace, Columbia University Press New York 2010, p. 136.

Great Game in the Indian Ocean Region: Revising the Legacy of Mahan

Sylvia Mishra*

The Indian Ocean Region is witnessing unprecedented flux in its security complexion and recently there has been a flurry of events in the region which has both regional and global implications. In recent times, in spite of strong warning from India's National Security Advisor Ajit Doval, a Chinese submarine, Changzheng 2 was docked at Colombo, along with warship Chang Xing Dao. This incident has geopolitical implications and portends to China's growing naval profile in the region. Similarly, several other incidents such as sinking of a naval vessel off Vishakhapatnam and the loss of life of Navy personnel, airports and seaports in Kolkata receiving series of intelligence warnings of a serious threat of an attack exemplify the myriad complexities of maritime security. These events highlight the importance of maritime security and throw light to the varied aspects of maritime security challenges that needs to be addressed. The Indian Ocean is of strategic significance to India as it covers about 20 per cent of water on the world's surface and it is the third largest of the world's five oceans. The Indian Ocean Rim countries have a population of approximately 2.6 billion, or 39 per cent of the world's people. The Indian Ocean accounts for 50 per cent of the world's container traffic and Indian Ocean ports handle about 30 per cent of global trade. Around 66 per cent of the world's seaborne trade in oil transits the Indian Ocean. Roughly 55 per cent of known oil reserves, and around 40 per cent of gas reserves, are in the Indian Ocean region.[1]

Successive governments have underscored the strategic importance of securing the Indian Ocean and have given credence to the need of a maritime security agenda. Coastal and maritime security assumed greater importance after Mumbai terrorist attacks. Following the 26/11 terrorist attack, policymakers in New Delhi realized that India needs a more focused maritime approach to national strategic planning. Simultaneously, policy pundits also began exploring potential alternatives to prevailing policy thinking. A robust maritime strategy is one which is multi-

---

*Researcher with the ICRIER-Wadhwani Chair in India-US Policy Studies, ICRIER, New Delhi.

dimensional, that takes into consideration aspects of both traditional defence security issues and also covers non-traditional issues such as rising sea levels, oil spill-overs, fishery depletion, piracy and management of living and non-living marine resources. Maritime security has an important bearing on a country's security as seas play a pivotal role in maintaining the power and greatness of a nation. To an extent, it could be stated that a country's economic wellbeing is directly proportional to a strong navy and comprehensive infrastructure, and vice versa. Capabilities to utilize naval power to harness the strength of a state have lent a country the edge to militarily defend itself and strengthen maritime security. India, by the virtue of its 7,500-km long coastline which juts out in the Indian Ocean with two strategic outposts of Lakshadweep and Andaman, is a maritime power with naval ambitions and vulnerabilities.

This paper argues central to Mahan's thesis that a nation's greatness is achieved through the control of the seas, the Indian Ocean would become the epicenter of hard power projection as India, China and the United States would each attempt to carve a sphere of influence. Taking into cognizance China's legitimate interest in the Indian Ocean, both India and China would face competition and security challenges from each other. The paper further argues that due to common political values and growing convergences India need to closely cooperate with the US in the Indo-Pacific region. The paper is thematically arranged into three parts: In the first part, Mahan's theory in the backdrop of centrality of the Indian Ocean is discussed whilst in the second part competition and rivalry between India and China is discussed and analyzed. The third part of the paper deals with the US Rebalance to Asia and Cooperation and Possibilities in the Indo-Pacific.

Several recent developments vindicate India's thrust towards expansion of hard power and the protection of territorial waters and sea lines. The expansion of hard power in the maritime domain has also become a necessity for India as it is a major trading nation which is dependent on the import of energy resources by the sea. During her recent visit to Mauritius, External Affairs Minister Sushma Swaraj said presciently: "Maritime security is of vital significance for an island nation like Mauritius as well as for a country with a vast coastline like India. A large part of our trade passes through the vast expanse of the Indian Ocean. Safety and security of the sea-lines is thus indispensable for our territorial, economic and energy security." Thus, the Indian Navy is committed to ensuring continued smooth access of energy resources from the Persian Gulf to the Malacca Straits. Along with securing sea lines of communication in the Indian Ocean, the Indian government is also investing in the development of maritime infrastructure, world class ports, ship-building capacity and maintaining India's littoral interests in the Indo-Pacific.[2]

MAHAN'S THEORY IN THE BACKDROP OF CENTRALITY OF THE INDIAN OCEAN

Assessing the 21st century Indian Ocean through the prism of maritime thinkers like Mahan may appear quixotic but eminently fits the posture and power projection of India, the United States and China in the Indian Ocean. American naval strategist Alfred Thayer Mahan in his seminal work *The Influence of Sea Power upon History (1660–1783)*—a theoretical treatise argued that American national greatness could be achieved through control of the seas. He *stated:*

> The history of Sea Power is largely, though by no means solely, a narrative of contests between nations, of mutual rivalries, of violence frequently culminating in war.

Thayer offered intellectual argument that if there is a profound shift of power in the Pacific; the US would stand to lose both economically and militarily. Mahan identified six elements of sea power namely— Geographical Position; Physical Conformation; Extent of Territory; Population; Character of People and Character of Government (including national institutions). And further argued that seas are great means of communication between nations: the best defence is to crush the enemy by depriving enemy the use of the sea.[3] In the struggle to carve a sphere for influence and project power in the Indian Ocean, one can find a striking relevance between maritime strategy reorientation and naval power reinforcement by India, China and the US in the Indian Ocean Region. Mahan's thesis strikes a chord among naval strategist and is relevant till date as his promulgated theory hinges on the idea that key to economic and military supremacy is not only a strong navy but also promotion of commercial interests, protection of trade and control of what is today known as 'strategic chokepoints'. One could argue that the context in which Mahan based his work is completely different due to the changed geopolitical complexion and multipolarity in Indian Ocean and Asia-Pacific. However, geography just provides the setting within which regional dynamics play out. As Clausewitz teaches, competitive human endeavours will invariably involve an interactive clash of wills and manifests from time to time.

INDIA AND CHINA: RIVALRIES AND COOPERITION IN THE INDIAN OCEAN

As China celebrated its 65th anniversary on September 30, 2014, President Xi Jinping stated that China would continue to *give priority to development, adhere to reform and innovation and remain committed to the path of peaceful development.*[4] There is and have been continuous discussions, debate and speculations whether China would rise peacefully or will China flex its military muscle. While there is no single structural realist answer to these questions, some realist theorists predict that China's ascent will lead to serious instability. The unchanging nature of geographical proximity that mandates two countries which inhabit a contested space would continue to be confronted with competition from each other. With China's forays in the Indian Ocean Region (IOR) which India considers its own strategic backyard, IOR has become one such contested space which has become a theatre of both competition for influence and power projection.

On September 7, 2013, President Xi in a speech at Kazakhstan's Nazarbayev University announced a new foreign policy initiative called "Silk Road Economic Belt" to intensify international cooperation and undertake joint development through Eurasia. Elaborating on this new foreign policy directive, he stated that China with overall regional cooperation would strengthen economic collaboration, improve road connectivity, promote trade and investment, facilitate currency conversion and bolster people-to-people exchanges.[5] Following the enunciation of China's Silk Road Economic Belt, Chinese President in a speech addressing Indonesia's Parliament extended the Silk Road policy to the maritime domain. He called for a re-establishment of the old sea networks to create a "Maritime Silk Road" to foster international connectivity, scientific and environmental research and fishery activities.[6] The idea of a maritime silk road has evolved into a foreign and security policy of China as the country envisions constructing a maritime silk road that connects the waters of the Pacific and the Indian Ocean Region through a route of inter-state commercial activities. The Maritime Silk Road is aimed at connecting China in the east to Iran and the Mediterranean in the West and is expected to strengthen maritime economy, environment, technical and scientific cooperation.

Indian government is also gearing up to undertake initiatives that restore strategic balance in the IOR. India has close defence ties with almost all important countries in the region, particularly Mauritius, Maldives,

Seychelles, Sri Lanka, Singapore, Vietnam and Malaysia. India started
Maritime Security Cooperation in October 2011 with Sri Lanka and
Maldives to intensify trilateral cooperation on maritime security which
included initiatives to enhance Maritime Domain Awareness (MDA)
which training and capacity building in the areas of MDA and joint
activities including trilateral exercises.[7] India cannot prevent Maldives
and Sri Lanka from joining Xi's Silk Road, however it could take another
look at the existing cooperation agenda and improvise on short to long
term agenda for the three countries in the IOR. Recently, India's
External Affairs Minister, Sushma Swaraj traveled to two key neighbours
in the IOR, Mauritius, where three ships from the Western Fleet of the
Indian Navy namely, INS Mumbai, INS Deepak and INS Talwar were
docked, and to Maldives, to enhance and deepen security ties. This
underscored the importance of India's bilateral ties aimed at multi-
faceted cooperation in ensuring peace, stability and maritime security
with these countries.[8] Along with regional neighbours, India has sought
to deepen military ties with Vietnam. India has offered a $100 million
concessional credit line to Vietnam for purchasing patrol boats and is
focusing on enhancing naval cooperation through joint naval exercises
and working on issues of maritime security.[9]

Element of trust deficit between India and China has shaped security
dilemma leading to a gradual arms race in the region. Regarding frequent
appearances of Chinese submarines and ships at Sri Lankan ports, Indian
strategic studies expert, C. Raja Mohan has stated that explanation often
is worse than the presumed offence as statements from Colombo and
Beijing are likely to worsen New Delhi's security concerns rather than
blunt them.[10] China has been actively involved in building strategic ports
such as Chittagong in Bangladesh, Sittwe and Cocos in Myanmar,
Hambantota in Sri Lanka, Karachi and Gwadar in Pakistan. While many
security experts worry about Chinese presence in IOR, some see no
reason for alarm. They point out that ports cannot be quickly converted
into naval facilities. Expert Bharat Karnad has noted that rising Chinese
naval profile in the IOR is more of a shadow play. He offers reasons that
during war time, no port in the Indian Ocean is going to be available to
the Chinese navy because none of these countries can afford to alienate
India. All of India's neighbours have relied heavily substantively on
Indian security for their protection both in the past and the present.[11]
China's assertive stance in the South and East China Seas has been met
with apprehensions from neighbours including Japan, Vietnam, the
Philippines and Singapore. Chinese project of Maritime Silk Road which
aims to connect the waters of the Pacific and the Indian Ocean have been

accompanied by a profound shift in Chinese naval power's presence in the Indian Ocean Region. The fundamental problem with President Xi's enunciated Maritime Silk Route project (MSR) is the opaque nature of its proposal. On the face of it, the project boasts of the development of massive maritime infrastructure and connectivity in the Indian Ocean and the Western Pacific. Beijing has been smart enough to project the MSR as a purely commercial venture and has invited India to join the project. Significantly, China has released no details whatsoever about the project and this abject lack of specifics have added to concerns of New Delhi.

Central to Mahan's thesis is a narrative of contests between nations to gain influence of sea commerce, culminating into mutual rivalries and clash of interests. Borrowing from Mahan's premise to take a stock of developments in the IOR provides ground of analysis that expansion of Chinese footprints in the IOR is likely to clash with Indian interests. Indian government is also gearing up to undertake initiatives that restore strategic balance in the IOR. On the multi-lateral front, one of the key initiatives launched by the present government to retain Indian influence in the IOR is 'Project Mausam'. Project Mausam is a multi-disciplinary, trans-national project which would endeavor to position itself at two levels: at the macro level it would reconnect and re-establish communications between countries of the Indian Ocean while at the micro level, the focus would be to understand national cultures in their regional maritime milieu.

PROJECT MAUSAM

The Ministry of External Affairs has enunciated a new foreign policy initiative 'Project Mausam'. "Mausam" which is Arabic for "Mawsin" refers to the season in ancient times when ships could sail safely. Project Mausam launched by India is a multi-disciplinary, trans-national project which would endeavor to position itself at two levels: at the macro level it would reconnect and re-establish communications between countries of the Indian Ocean while at the micro level, the focus would be to understand national cultures in their regional maritime milieu. Project Mausam would link cultural route and maritime landscape across the multi-faceted Indian Ocean "world"—extending from East Africa, the Arabian Peninsula, the Indian subcontinent and Sri Lanka to the Southeast Asian archipelago coastal centres to their hinterland. The aim of this project is to enhance and multiply the movement of people, goods and ideas across the Indian Ocean enabling multi-cultural and multi-ethnic interaction and exchange. Of particular interest is the undertaking of joint collaborative research studies on the knowledge and manipulation of the monsoon wind which impacted ancient and historical trades, local economies, politics and cultural identities. Thus, along with rekindling long lost ties across the Indian Ocean Littoral and forging new avenues of cooperation and exchanges between India and states of the Indian Ocean, Project Mausam would also contribute to the dissemination of culture and civilization along the IOR.[12]

Perhaps Indian Navy could consider developing the Andaman and Nicobar Islands as a bastion of trade and security. An interesting article titled 'From Outpost to Springboard' by the Economist reported that Andamans islands are of strategic importance as the islands stretch 750 km-long above the entrance to the Malacca Strait, which connects the Indian and Pacific Oceans. The strait is one of the world's busiest sea routes, with more than 1,000 ships running through it each week. The Economist article reported that the Andamans could be treated as a "chokepoint", a place to disrupt Chinese trade in the event of any future confrontation as four-fifth of Chinese oil imports goes through the strait.[13] Borrowing from the defensive realist strand of thought, in spite of the scramble for security competition, it is likely that the international system would create a strong incentive for China to be able to co-exist with neighbours peacefully.[14]

Competition however, does not mean confrontation. Since India and China remain locked in the traditional security dilemmas, faces similar security challenges and share common interests in the IOR, it is necessary that both the countries compete to a reasonable extent while pushing forward functional cooperation. Because of the existence of an inter-dependent relationship and common security challenges, the future scenario will be one of a dynamic and a manageable competition instead of an inevitable conflict and rivalry. Robert Kaplan in his book Monsoon explained the civilizational and political connections and players in the Indian Ocean Region focusing on the Indian-Chinese competition and the US interests in the region. He opines as a solution, the US should act like a broker to mitigate the likelihood of conflict in the IOR. Kaplan expects that with greater economic rise of India and China, US power and influence in the region to counter balance will be welcomed. According to Kaplan, China and India will compete more with soft power than with hard power since territorial expansion is an option for neither and the US Navy can engineer an elegant decline from hegemony by fostering cooperation with other navies to protect the maritime commons.[15] It is encouraged that India and China resorts to more liberal cooperative frameworks since both the countries are key players in Asia's maritime security architecture and should combine efforts to constructively counter non-traditional security challenges such as piracy and maritime terrorism. This would also offset the possibilities of an arms race in the Indian Ocean and dilute concerns emanating from traditional security dilemmas as maritime economics and security of international shipping lanes is critical for both. The navies of India and China have operated together in the Gulf of Aden to tackle the threat of the Somali pirates and their ships have escorted each other's commercial ships, as also other flag vessels passing through the IRTC (International Recommended Transit Corridor).

THE US RLBALANCE TO ASIA: COOPERATION AND POSSIBILITIES IN THE INDO-PACIFIC

The end of the Cold War marked a major shift in world politics and fundamentally structured a number of relationships around the world, including that of India and the United States. The post-1990 story of India-US relations is one about rediscovering common political values which also provided space for India and the US to explore the possibility of defence cooperation. The first military-to-military cooperation started between India and the United States in 1991 which included joint naval exercise, staff exchange and shared participation in United Nations peacekeeping operations. India's Army Chief, the late General B.C. Joshi, visited the US at the end of September 1994 and held discussions with Defense Secretary Perry, Chairman of the Joint Chiefs of Staff General John Shalikkashvili, and the Deputy Secretary of State Strobe Talbot. This was symbolic of developing new military-to-military links between the two countries. In October 2002, India and the United States started the joint military exercise known as the 'Geronimo Thrust', which took place in Alaska and was one more step towards enhancing "inter-operability" between the defence forces of the two sides. This was the first time that India was taking part in a military exercise in North America.[16] In February 2004, the Air Force of both the countries took part in 'Operation Cope India 04' at Gwalior and in the same year in June, took part in 'Co-operative Cope Thunder' in Alaska.[17] The Navies conducted anti-submarine warfare in April 2004 and Malabar 04 exercises off Goa.[18] The India and US Armies organised peace-keeping operations workshop and continued the special forces 'Iroquois' series of exercises, and 'Operation Yudh Abhyas 04' (in Mizoram again).[19] India-

US Defence relations in the recent past have witnessed a significant upward swing. The New Framework of Defence for US-India Defence Relationship, signed in 2005 by the then Indian Defence Minister, Pranab Mukherjee and US Defense Secretary Donald Rumsfeld had set the tone for a new era which transformed the complexion of India-US defence and security ties.[20] Following the New Framework of Defence agreement, India-US Defence relations in the maritime domain have witnessed a significant upward swing and strategic convergence on the Indo-Pacific has expanded military-to-military cooperation between the two countries

Three clear and abiding U.S. interests in the Indian Ocean that seems to remain the focus of U.S. strategy are:

1. To maintain the Indian Ocean as a secure highway for international commerce, particularly between the oil-rich Gulf States and an economically dynamic East Asia.
2. To maintain freedom of navigation through the strategic choke-points of the Indian Ocean highway in the Strait of Hormuz on one end and the Strait of Malacca and the South China Sea on the other.
3. To maintain a stable equilibrium in the region and partner with major maritime powers within the region that aligns sufficiently with the US interests.[21]

To quote a Center for Strategic and International Studies report which states that the U.S. strategy should focus on supporting Indian pre-eminence in the Indian Ocean and closer U.S.—India strategic cooperation. In addition, the U.S. strategy should encourage and support closer alignment and enhanced strategic consultation among the major maritime democracies in the region, reviving the U.S.—Japan—Australia—India "Quad" concept.[22]

India and the US for the first time mentioned in a joint statement that maritime territorial disputes have to be resolved in accordance with the United Nations Convention on the Law of the Sea.[23] The reference says more about India's changing political attitude of New Delhi's policy towards the maritime territorial disputes in the South and East China Seas between Beijing and its Asian neighbours, especially Japan, Vietnam and the Philippines. According to the joint statement, Prime Minister Modi and President Obama reaffirmed their shared interest in preserving regional peace and stability, which are critical to the Asia-Pacific region's continued prosperity. "The leaders expressed concern about rising tensions over maritime territorial disputes, and affirmed the importance of safeguarding maritime security and ensuring freedom of navigation and over flight throughout the region, especially in the South China Sea," it said. This is significant because so far India has not gone beyond recognizing the US rebalance or pivot to Asia."[24] However, there are uncertainties about the US posture due to continued high level US attention in the Middle East as well as at home. The challenge to Pivot to Asia policy is not the absence of military resources but of demonstrable political commitment. A recent article by Fareed Zakaria suggested that Obama's biggest foreign policy initiative—Pivot to Asia—is powerful, intelligent but incomplete. He writes that the greatest threat to global peace and prosperity over the next decade comes not from a band of assassins in Syria but from the rise of China and the manner in which that will reshape the geopolitics of Asia and the world.[25] If Washington can provide balance and reassurance in Asia, it will help ensure that the continent does not become the flashpoint for a new Cold War.

In conclusion, it is highlighted that New Delhi intends to expand India's maritime presence, culturally, strategically and psychologically in the region. Project Mausam is a positive step in that direction and has been generally well-received in the democratic world. It is to be hoped, however, that the project is meaningful and does not lack teeth. One cannot simply overlook maritime turbulence in South East Asia. China's positioning of an exploration rig in Vietnam's EEZ, its skirmishes with Philippines over the Scarborough reef, its aggressive patrols off the Senkaku islands and the recent covert visits of its submarines to Sri Lanka raises concerns regarding Chinese maritime intentions. Drawing from the realist tradition, balance of power is considered to be a function of tangible assets—such as armored divisions and nuclear weapons that each power controls. A Chinese nuclear submarine like hunter-killer in the Indian Ocean is only escalating concerns and creating security dilemma. In spite of rhetoric of China's 'peaceful rise', a competing narrative of unilateral action as seen when the Ministry of National Defence of the PRC announced the establishment of an Air Defence Identification (ADIZ) in the East China Sea.[26] These unilateral actions have only added to uncertainty about intentions and have now rather become unavoidable due to Chinese forays in the Indian Ocean. No single country can shape and sustain the security architecture in the Indian Ocean Region. There is a need for strengthening regional forum like the Indian Ocean Rim Association (IORA) architecture. As Mahan wrote, naval power often proves "more silent than the clash of arms—as influential as it is quiet", India needs to ensure that the "Great Game" in the Indian Ocean does bolster a dynamic and a strong multipolarity. A strong regional security framework would incorporate China in a multipolar order in which it is not dominant and ensure a dynamic equilibrium on the guiding principles on which a regional security framework could be charted are: No Containment; No Hegemony; No Condominium.

REFERENCES

1. Khurshid, Salman, http://www.thehindu.com/opinion/op-ed/putting-out-to-sea-a-new-vision/article5305845.ece

2. Mishra, Sylvia, 'India's Maritime Security: Strategy, Choices and Imperatives', India Writes, December 1, 2014, available at http://www.indiawrites.org/diplomacy/indias-maritime-security-strategy-choices-and-imperatives

3. Mahan, Alfred Thayer, the Influence of Sea Power upon History 1660–1783.

4. 'China celebrates 65th anniversary', Xinhua, September 30, 2014, available at http://www.china.org.cn/china/2014-09/30/content_33664454.htm

5. Ministry of Foreign Affairs of the People's Republic of China, 'President Xi Jinping Delivers Important Speech and Proposes to Build a Silk Road Economic Belt with Central Asian Countries', September 7, 2013, available at http://www.fmprc.gov.cn/mfa_eng/topics_665678/xjpfwzysiesgjtfhshzzfh_66 5686/t1076334.shtml

6. 'President Xi gives speech to Indonesia's Parliament', China Daily, October 2, 2013, available at http://www.chinadaily.com.cn/china/2013xiapec/2013-10/02/content_17007915_2.htm

7. NSA Level Meeting on Trilateral Maritime Security Cooperation between India, Sri Lanka and Maldives, Ministry of External Affairs, March 6, 2014, available at http://www.mea.gov.in/in-focus-article.htm?23037/NSA+level+meeting+on+trilateral+Maritime+Security+Cooperation+between+India+Sri+Lanka+and+Maldives

8. "India to cooperate with Mauritius to safeguard Indian Ocean: Sushma Swaraj", IBNLive, November 2, 2014, available at http://ibnlive.in.com/news/india-to-cooperate-with-mauritius-to-safeguard-indian-ocean-sushma-swaraj/510188-3.html

9. "India to Supply Naval Vessels to Vietnam", Wall Street Journal, October 28, 2014, available at http://online.wsj.com/articles/india-to-supply-naval-vessels-to-vietnam-1414507972

10. Mohan, C. Raja, "Lanka pit-stop', Indian Express, November 5, 2014, available at http://indianexpress.com/article/opinion/columns/chinese-takeaway-lanka-pit-stop

11. "India concerned about Chinese subs at Sri Lankan port", Voice of America, November 5, 2014, available at http://www.voanews.com/content/india-concerned-about-chinese-subs-in-sri-lankan-ports-/2509079.html

12. Mukherjee, Ambassador Bhaswati, "International Recognition of India's World Heritage; New Exciting Projects on the Anvil', Ministry of External

Affairs, July 10, 2014, available at http://www.mea.gov.in/in-focus-article.htm?23601/International+recognition+of+Indias+world+heritage++New+exciting+projects+on+anvil

13. 'From outpost to springboard', The Economist, September 13, 2014, available at http://www.economist.com/news/asia/21617000-india-eyes-strategic-opportunity-bay-bengal-outpost-springboard

14. Waltz, Kenneth, Theory of International Politics, 1979.

15. Kaplan, Robert D., 'Center Stage for the 21ˢᵗ Century: Power Plays in the Indian Ocean', Foreign Affairs, March/April Issue, 2009, available at http://www.foreignaffairs.com/articles/64832/robert-d-kaplan/center-stage-for-the-21st-century

16. 'India- US Joint Military Exercise Begins', Times of India, October 4, 2002, also available at http://articles.timesofindia.indiatimes.com/2002-10-04/india/27298408_1_military-exercise-paratroopers-and-iaf-personnel-transport-plane

17. 'Exercise Cope India 04', Indian Air Force, also available at http://indianairforce.nic.in/show_page.php?pg_id=144

18. 'Malabar 04 Exercises Conclude Successfully off Indian Coast', America's Navy, October 4, 2004, also available at http://www.navy.mil/submit/display.asp?story_id=15512

19. 'Indo-US Forces Conduct Joint Exercise', Rediff News, May 2, 2003, also available at http://www.rediff.com/news/2003/may/02josy1.htm

20. Krishnaswami, Sridhar, 'India US sign framework for defence cooperation', Hindu, June 30, 2005, available at http://www.thehindu.com/2005/06/30/stories/2005063004261200.htm

21. Green, Micheal J. and Shearer, Andrew, 'Defining US Indian Ocean Strategy', Center for Strategic and International Studies, March 19, 2012, available at http://csis.org/publication/twq-defining-us-indian-ocean-strategy-spring-2012

22. Green, Micheal J. and Shearer, Andrew, 'Defining US Indian Ocean Strategy', Center for Strategic and International Studies, March 19, 2012, available at http://csis.org/publication/twq-defining-us-indian-ocean-strategy-spring-2012

23. 'US-India Joint Statement', The White House, Statements and Releases, September 30, 2014, available at http://www.whitehouse.gov/the-press-office/2014/09/30/us-india-joint-statement

24. 'In a first, India-US joint statement mentions South China Sea', Times of India, October 2, 2014, available at http://timesofindia.indiatimes.com/india/In-a-first-India-US-joint-statement-mentions-South-China-Sea/articleshow/44028687.cms

25. Zakaria, Fareed, 'Will Obama become a foreign policy President?' The Washington Post, November 6, 2014, available at http://www.washingtonpost.com/opinions/fareed-zakaria-will-obama-finally-become-a-foreign-policy-president/2014/11/06/91984644-65fa-11e4-836c-83bc4f26eb67_story.html

26. 'Announcement of the Aircraft Identification Rules for the East China Sea Air Defense Identification Zone of the P.R.C.', Xinhua, November 23, 2013, available at http://eng.mod.gov.cn/Press/2013-11/23/content_4476143.htm

Asian Gaints in the Indian Ocean Region: Détente or Entente

Jasbir Pal Singh Rakhra*

INTRODUCTION—INDIAN OCEAN AS A ZONE OF STRATEGIC COMPETITION

Indian Ocean Region has been described as a "Centre Stage for Twenty-First Century" (Kaplan, 2009) which never lost its strategic sheen since ancient times. It has seen the birth of civilisations around its periphery and has benefited the peoples from its rich trade being a centre-point of cultural and religious interactions. The traditional patterns of interaction were greatly influenced by European powers sailing around the Cape of Good Hope to establish trade links and build empires in the East. Portuguese were the first to arrive as traders discovering potential lands but the Britishers utilising their sea power created a large Indian Ocean empire and established its hegemony. Post-World War II witnessed decolonisation process thus marking an end of British hegemony and Indian Ocean emerged as an area of contest between the super-powers during the Cold War era.

Since then Indian Ocean had been a zone of intense super-power rivalry. Both the United States and Soviet Union were engaged securing the naval bases and refuelling facilities for their nuclear-armed flotilla thus initiating nuclear race in the region. The super-powers were seen as interlopers by the Indian Ocean states and the efforts were started to declare it a 'Zone of Peace' (Berlin 2002). Sri Lanka introduced the proposal to declare Indian Ocean as a 'Zone of Peace' which was unanimously adopted by the United Nations General Assembly through Resolution 2832 (XXVI) (Geethangani 2009). By the end of Cold War many scholars and observers hoped for less confrontations and competitions in IOR. To their utter dismay, the 'New World Order' comprising of emerging regional and extra-regional powers showed no signs of conciliation thus fuelling strategic rivalry turning IOR into a 'Zone of

---

*Assistant Professor in Security Studies with Ministry of External Affairs Division at Centre for Research in Rural and Industrial Development (CRRID), Chandigarh, India.

Strategic Competition'. It completely altered the power dynamics of the region with growing maritime ambitions of China and counter-efforts by India, being sensitive about its security owing to border conflicts with China and its geo-strategic affinity with Indian Ocean.

India and China have shown their economic prowess to the world and consolidated their economic rise through diplomatic as well as military vigour. The rise of these Asian Giants, in particular China's ambitions of control over IOR in fulfilling its growing demand for raw materials, energy resources and finished goods prioritize the discourses on regional maritime security. In the regional context, maritime security envisages the freedom of Sea Lines of Communication (SLOCs) and increasing importance of vital choke points of Malacca Straits, Straits of Homruz or Bab-el-Mandeb which serve as strategic links between the regions. Given the presence of western naval powers and increasing interests of China in the region there is a need to explore and put regional security architecture in place to deal with growing naval competition. Therefore, this paper centres on the strategic value of Indian Ocean to China and India, both being major naval powers in the region and key competitors exploring the future of their relations.

STRATEGIC SIGNIFICANCE OF INDIAN OCEAN

The geographic proximity of Indian Ocean with resource rich region along its periphery enhanced its strategic importance and eminence. Indian Ocean is the third largest ocean of the world that covers 14 per cent of the earth's surface touching the coastlines of 37 independent nations. On the west it borders with continental Africa to a longitude of 20°E, stretching south from Cape Agulhas. Continental Asia forms its northern border from Suez to Malay Peninsula. In the East it touches Australia till longitude 147°E and Tasmania along with Singapore and Indonesian archipelago (Forbes 1995). Looking through the political, cultural and economic kaleidoscope, it is a highly diverse region with approximately 39 per cent of the global population and traditionally benefits around 50 Indian Ocean countries including 20 Indian Ocean Rim Association (IORA) states along with 6 dialogue partners of IORA (IORA Website). Indian Ocean Region also serves as a life-line to number of land-locked states of Central Asia and Africa for trade and commerce across the globe. Half of the world's container traffic traverses through Indian Ocean where its ports handle around 30 per cent of the global trade. Straits of Homruz, Malacca and Bab-el-Mandeb are world's most important chokepoints in Indian Ocean which are strategically valuable for global trade and energy flow and a rationale for extra-regional naval presence. Strait of Homruz alone accounted for an oil flow of 17 million barrels per day in 2013 which is about 30 per cent of seaborne-traded oil, whereas, Strait of Malacca accounted for 15.2 million barrels (EIA 2014). The Middle East alone has produced 24.1 million barrels of crude oil in 2012 (EIA 2013) and fulfils the world's energy demands through these vital choke points. Apart from oil resources the region is rich in flora and fauna and possesses abundance of mineral resources ranging from uranium, gold, nickel, cadmium, cobalt, tin etc.

The economic bounty offered by Indian Ocean Region (IOR) resulted into conflicts ranging from regional to global. According to a recent analysis of Heidelberg Institute for International Conflict Research, the countries of Asia and Oceania, Middle-East/Maghreb and East Africa, most of which are associated with IOR region, accounts for world's highest number of conflicts. The region accounts for 129 conflicts in Asia/Oceania, 71 in Middle-East/Maghreb and 97 in Sub-Saharan Africa revolving around system/ideology, sub-national predominance and resources and secession (Conflict Barometer 2013, p. 92). The list is capacious but the most notable conflict areas include Middle-East, Somalia and Pakistan extending up to Afghanistan. Most of these conflicts are the outcomes of failed state structure, corruption, competition for scarce resources, foreign interference and Global War on Terror turning Indian Ocean as a hot spot for conflicts (Potgeiter 2010). These conflicts made way for multilateral initiatives—from eliminating piracy to counter-terrorism efforts paving the way for countries to measure their stakes in the IOR and consolidate their naval power.

Therefore, the economic gains and risks of instability in the IOR have raised the international interest in the region manifold. The significant rise in the international interest on the pretext of energy trade and commerce and the rise of regional powers and their military capabilities have raised the stakes in the IOR where India and China emerged as major players in this strategic arena. India sees itself traditionally connected to Indian Ocean which serves as its strategic backyard whereas China has major strategic interests connected to its economic rise. Given this background of engagements in IOR both the countries at times were at loggerheads. To understand the dimensions of Sino-Indian engagements in Indian Ocean, it is important to understand the course of their relations.

SINO-INDIAN EQUATIONS:
BETWEEN AMITY AND EUMITY

India and China are world's oldest civilisations which created pathways for the humanity through the ancient knowledge and wisdom. Today both the countries are emerging as powerful economies with ample human resources, both being world's most populous countries. The relationship between both the countries started evolving soon after the end of Colonial rule in India and incipience of Communist rule in China. The advent of Sino-Indian relations started with an initiative of peaceful co-existence through Non-Align Movement and entered a bitter phase of rivalry on border issues which culminated into Sino-Indian War of 1962.

The Asian giants have massively expanded their militaries with an added nuclear factor, thus making claims for the regional as well as the global supremacy. With the expansion of their economies and geopolitical sphere, the bilateral relationship between both the countries could well be characterised more as a competition than cooperation. In the last few years, both the countries have shown some rapprochement to stabilise the relationships based on economic progress and growing sensitivity on bilateral security. The initiatives are backed by high-level visits but seem to be lacking the spirit of friendship. From time and again the Chinese policy of rapprochement is being negated by confrontation in the disputed territories. The recent face-off between People Liberation Army's (PLA) troops with Indian Army in Chumar sector of Ladakh region just ahead of President Xi Jinping's India visit raises concern on the intentions and motivations of China. Though the visit claimed to be highly successful but does this act of *détente will ever lead to entente cordiale, it is yet to be seen.*

The border confrontations during past few months are endorsing the claims of long time observers that the relations between India and China will remain fragile and are vulnerable to a slightest instigation. Specifically looking at IOR, there are several external factors effecting constructive Sino-Indian engagements.

The Pakistan Factor

China maintains a special relation with Pakistan to counter India's growing dominance in the region. Though India's status as a dominant South Asian power is recognised by China, but its special relation with Pakistan is an act of maintaining regional equilibrium. The growing military alliance between China and Pakistan in terms of missile technology, nuclear weapons programme and military aviation aims at counter-weighing India's military power. The Sino-Pakistan nexus also points out their trust-deficit against India as both the countries are suspicious of India's growing strategic ambitions of forming regional and extra-regional alliances. More or less it seems to be China's grand strategy to militarily engage India with Pakistan so as to divert its attention from its strategic manoeuvres in India's near neighbourhood as well as IOR.

Sino-Pakistan 'special relationship' also holds political and strategic advantages for China due to Pakistan's geostrategic location where it forms a corridor for China felicitating alliances in West Asia and the Gulf region. Further it serves as its key to security of its Muslim majority province of Xinjiang where ETIM (East Turkmenistan Islamic Movement) is highly active and have linkages with militant groups based in tribal areas in Af-Pak region.

Above all China wants to protect its SLOCs in the Indian Ocean to ensure uninterrupted supply of energy resources but the major concern is India's geo-strategic advantage in IOR. India is best located to take action against Chinese interests in Indian Ocean to compensate the drawbacks in case of any mainland border conflicts. Other than India, China is seeking its bases in the Persian Gulf region as a palisade against United States. In this scenario, given its geographical location, Pakistan is best suited for the purpose.

Myanmar—China's Gateway to Bay of Bengal

Bay of Bengal is gaining importance in Chinese strategic thinking as a gateway to Indian Ocean. It is emerging as a new locus of strategic competition in Asia, in particular the IOR like South China Sea in the Pacific Ocean (Brewster 2014). Therefore, Myanmar is gaining a strategic importance for China as its key transit zone in Bay of Bengal with an access to Indian Ocean, making China a generous contributor of economic and military aid in Myanmar. Myanmar, which is at the forefront owing to the dysfunctional military junta rule and persistent human rights abuses together with host of insurgency related security problems, has a long history of playing India and China card to get economic aid in exchange for its mineral resources.

China is investing heavily in Myanmar to achieve its strategic aim. Most notable is the construction of large scale oil terminal and a gas terminal on Ma Dan Island adjacent to Rakhine and Shwe offshore gas fields where oil and gas is to be pumped to Kunming in China through a high capacity dual pipeline across Myanmar into Southern China (Kopp 2012). It is well known that China has emerged as a biggest importer of oil since 2013 and most of its oil is imported from Middle East and Africa through Straits of Malacca and reaches its ports but the pipeline will shorten the distance of energy supply to its land-locked southern provinces thus reducing the dependence on Straits of Malacca (BBC 2013). The creation of new transit points in Myanmar also requires the security of newly created hubs and SLOCs in Bay of Bengal making the deployment of PLAN's (Peoples' Liberation Army-Navy) assets inevitable. It is evident from the Chinese investments in infrastructure development which also comprises building of the military air bases at Mingalodon, Shante, Nampong and Namsang and hence PLA might need to protect its energy infrastructure in case of conflict (Kopp 2012).

Geo-strategic Interests of United States

United States always considered Indian Ocean Region as an important facet of its national security policies. Indian Ocean has gained far more importance today than the Cold War era. It is an important theatre for United States owing to incessant conflict in the Middle East and Global War on Terror (GWOT). Moreover it is imperative for United States to maintain its influence in the IOR to fulfil its energy requirements from the Middle East as well as to safeguard its trade routes. In the wake of changing global security environment it is the priority of United States government and as well reflected in Department of Defense report titled, "Global Leadership: Priorities of 21st Century Defense". According to the report:

> U.S. economic and security interests are inextricably linked to developments in the arc extending from the Western Pacific and East Asia into the Indian Ocean region and South Asia, creating a mix of evolving challenges and opportunities. Accordingly, while the U.S. military will continue to contribute to security globally, we will out of necessity rebalance toward the Asia-Pacific region (DoD 2012).

Indian Ocean is no more a unipolar domain after the emergence of China and India as major naval and economic powers. The economic and strategic concerns of the trio turned IOR into a zone of competition, especially in the wake of U.S.-India strategic partnership to nail the Chinese advancement in the region. Moreover, U.S. views India as a major stakeholder in the Indian Ocean. The 2010 Quadrennial Defense Review (QDR) of United States' Department of Defence notes; India as the largest power in the Indian Ocean Region and net exporter of security in the future (Green and Shearer 2012, p.176). India's bilateral security and political engagements with United States have started very recently and India does not see itself under U.S. security umbrella but as a strategic partner with mutually beneficial relationship. The rise of China as a major regional challenge in the Indian Ocean brought both the countries together.

Ashley J. Tellis' (2012) notion of Indian Ocean as a commercial highway for the United States is turning hazy due to Chinese continuous efforts to control and turn Indian Ocean as its freeway to energy hubs. In the wake of U.S. engagement in Afghanistan; its trade with Asian nations; and China's strategic interest in the IOR, the 2014 QDR of Department of Defence clearly reflects its Indian Ocean policies. It proposes to deepen United States' engagement in the IOR to bolster its rebalance to Asia and support India's rise as an increasingly capable actor in the region and increase strategic partnership between the two nations through defence trade and technology initiative (QDR 2014)—much to China's annoyance.

UNDERSTANDING CHINA'S STRATEGIES AND INDIA'S SECURITY CONCERNS

India's major concern is China's growing ambitions in Indian Ocean Region through the visible presence of its military assets and supporting infrastructure in the region. The power-projection capability of China in the region is perceived as a threat by India's security establishment. In this direction the most important is China's notion of "String of Pearls", a term coined by the consultants of Booze-Allen-Hamilton in 2003. This might be a frivolous term for many scholars but holds significant strategic agenda for the need of overseas bases in the IOR advocated by many Chinese intellectuals. Professor Shen Dingli from Fudan University Shanghai asserts, "China have every right to establish its military bases overseas to protect its interest and fulfil its four major responsibilities of protection of the people and fortune overseas; the guarantee of smooth trading; the prevention of the overseas intervention which harms the unity of the country and the defence against foreign invasion" (Dingli 2010). The statement is also reinforced through the diplomatic wrapping of 'cutting of supply cost through overseas military bases' and to 'promote regional and global stability' (Dingli 2010). India's major security concern is an extension of China's military footprint with expansion of its naval capabilities in manifestation of its great power status. The U.S. Department of Defense's annual report to Congress on military and security developments involving China in 2014 asserts:

> Chinese leadership has described initial two decades of 21st century as "period of strategic opportunity" where they anticipate that a successful expansion of "comprehensive national power" will serve China's overriding strategic objectives, which include perpetuating Chinese Communist Party (CCP) rule, sustaining economic growth and development, maintaining domestic political stability, defend-ing national sovereignty and territorial integrity, and securing China's status as a great power (DoD 2014).

In this direction, China's new strategic discourse envisages control of its periphery—the land and maritime regions adjacent to China through 'Silk Road' strategy and to augment its naval influence through the strategy of 'Far Sea Defence' with long range capabilities.

China's Silk Road Strategy

As per China's strategic discourse, its rise and harmonious growth could be assured through control and influence over China's internal and external periphery. The Chinese leadership sensible to this strategic thinking, if not actually eternalizing it, held the first ever conference on "periphery diplomacy" just prior to its *Third Plenum* (Third meeting of Communist Party's Central Committee) in the last week of October 2013. Apart from the members of Central Committee, the meeting was attended by a small group of leading members responsible for foreign affairs along with Chinese ambassadors to important countries. At the meeting China's need for stable external environment conducive for its domestic economic reforms was emphasized by President Xi Jinping (Glaser and Pal 2013). Looking at China's strategic discourses the underlying objectives revolves around China's policy to exercise an influence along its periphery and to counter the U.S. rebalancing towards Asia.

Therefore the Chinese proposal of continental or maritime Silk Routes is a grand strategy of extending peripheral influence and regional integration to enhance Chinese political and economic influence. From Indian perspective the entire proposal is viewed in context of broader geo-strategic implications, particularly the Indian Ocean Region. Though the initiative will bring economic integration and benefit the region at large but the strategic pitfalls cannot be neglected.

The proposals of Silk Route are excellent, given the economic opportunities involved but suspicions revolve around China's intentions. Therefore, the major concerns emanate from the architecture of Land Silk Routes which straddle India from West to East highlighting China's *String of Pearls* strategy. In the West is the proposed China-Pakistan corridor connecting restive Xinjiang province in China and Gwadar port in Pakistan passing through Pakistan occupied Kashmir (PoK)—a disputed territory which is against international norms. The maritime security aspects related to Gwadar are equally important. In the East is the Bangladesh, China, Myanmar and India (also referred to as BCIM) corridor connecting India's North-Eastern region with Kunming province of China. It is an acceptable idea for the economic development of India's North-Eastern region and its connectivity with Southeast Asia but the strategic concerns hover around the securitisation of Bay of Bengal. Bangladesh and Myanmar being major energy transhipment hubs for China may create a strategic challenge on India's eastern seaboard given the obvious presence of PLAN (People Liberation Army-Navy).

China's Strategy of 'Far Sea Defence'

Chinese military strategy and capabilities evolved alongside its power aspirations over a period of time. The consolidation of its naval power is highly desirable to accomplish the task to control the SLOC in the Indian Ocean Region. The future of Chinese naval development has far reaching effects on the security of IOR. The Chinese naval strategy went through major changes over a period of time—from 'near-coast defence' (*jin'an fangyu*) strategy prior to mid-1980s to the 'near-sea active defence (*jinhai jiji fangyu*) after the mid-1980s followed by the advancement to 'far-seas defence' (*yuanhai zuozhan*) strategy by mid-2000s which may have major implications for the future development of PLAN capabilities (Li 2011). The naval strategy was designed for coastal defence of China during the Cold War era from the time of its founding in 1949 to 1980s primarily for the security of its waters upto 12 nautical miles (NM) that extend seawards from China's coastline or land territories where its political and economical cities are located (Li 2011, p. 110). The strategy was adopted for the security of important straits and water ways which could be used by the enemy to capture China's strategically important land targets. The "near-seas defence" strategy was adopted close in late-1970s which covered the near seas of the inner-rim of first island chain covering islands of Japan, Taiwan, Philippines to Borneo and seas adjacent to the outer-rim covering North Pacific. This does not include South Pacific and Indian Ocean. The strategy was mainly adopted to deter United States and aimed to reunify Taiwan and claim the lost territories.

The Chinese Strategy of "Far-Seas Defence" gained prominence during Jiang Zemin's regime who advocated enhancing far-seas defence and operation capabilities to preserve China's maritime security and protection of its maritime interests vital for its economic rise in the territories away from Chinese mainland and to protect its major sea lanes. The far-seas naval strategy is aimed at control over Indian Ocean region for the security of its transport routes as all its energy requirements are catered through here. The most important aspect of naval operations in the far-flung regions is the requirement of continuous logistical support for which overseas naval bases are highly desirable. Therefore the notion of 'String of Pearls' seems to be closely related to far-seas defence strategy given the Chinese infrastructure investments in Pakistan, Sri Lanka, Bangladesh and Myanmar. Construction of these facilities may have economic and commercial motivations but military connotations are also attached to it. Incidentally, the bases around India appear to be 'String of Pearls' but as a matter of fact the locations are most ideal to control China's SLOCs extending from Straits of Homruz to Malacca entering into Pacific Ocean. China has now moved beyond these theories with projection of its military assets in the region through its continuous naval manoeuvres from submarine patrols to counter-piracy operations and undertaking search and rescue missions in the Indian Ocean. Strategically, Indian Ocean also serves as China's backdoor in event of any confrontation with United States or Japan in the Pacific, thus, extending its theatre for naval operations to safeguard its lines of communication.

Apart from securing vantage points around India, China is looking forward to control the access points to Indian Ocean. China reportedly built an underground nuclear submarine base at Hainan Islands around 1200 NM from Malacca Straits. Named as Yulin (Sanya) Naval Base, it reportedly houses nuclear submarine fleet for both expeditionary and defensive operations and pose a threat to the security of Asian states as well as U.S. presence in the region (Telegraph 2008).

To sum up, China is consolidating its political, economic and military interests in IOR by gaining access to IOR through land routes while maintaining its naval credibility at sea. Given the presence of Chinese military in the near vicinity and its strategic backyard, India suffers the strategic depth problem.

CONCLUSION: DÉTENTE OR ENTENTE

The Sino-Indian relations can be characterised as détente with an undertone of strategic competition which is reflected by a desire to reduce tensions through negotiations with enhanced diplomatic, economic and cultural contacts but at the same time countering each other's influence in the region. The missing element of trust along with a viable solution to amicably resolve the land border issue is a major stumble block in building partnerships and cooperation.

Both the countries are engaged in diplomatic manoeuvres to cease opportunities with Indian Ocean littoral states. Though China has frictions in South-East Asia but it remained successful to consolidate the region through its booming economy and trade partnership with ASEAN. Given the strategic importance of South-East Asian region India too felt the need of enhanced engagements in the region both economically and militarily. India is responding to the China's strategic initiatives in the Indian Ocean through its engagements with Vietnam and its naval presence in the South China Sea, much to the annoyance of China. Further India has modified its "Look-East Policy" to "Act East" under Prime Minister Narendra Modi's regime to deepen its economic and strategic links in the South-East Asian region specifically with Myanmar and Vietnam. Like China's economic interests in the Indian Ocean, India has several interests in the South China Sea which includes secure movement of its merchant fleet and joint oil exploration ventures with Vietnam. At the same time China has embarked upon its "Look-West Policy" which seems to be giving primacy to Sino-Indian relations but tilted more towards countering American influence in Pakistan and involves geopolitics of energy.

The friction between both the countries is more on strategic front but at economic front the Sino-India relations are highly successful with estimation of bilateral trade reaching $100 billion by 2015. Combining their population, the Sino-India bilateral relations will impact the international order to address the transnational threats of pandemics, climate change and global terrorism. Both the countries came forward to establish BRICS Development Bank on the lines of World Bank and Asian Development Bank. Therefore, Sino-Indian bilateral economic relations can be well characterised as entente through mutual cooperation but both differ when it comes to gaining a strategic edge over other.

As a matter of fact, India's engagements in IOR are more like an act of balancing China than to contest it. The usage of the phrase 'strategic rivalry' seems less appropriate here as both India and China are still retraining themselves from a fully-fledged contest. India's engagements to counter China are based on the fact that India wants to protect its sovereignty and interests from the influence of a stronger neighbour both in terms of economy and military. It seems that both the countries are following the theme of 'peaceful co-existence' which holds the foundation of their relationship from the very outset which virtually turned into 'competitive co-existence'. Jeff M. Smith has nicely termed the Sino-Indian relations as 'Cold Peace' which seems to be turning warm after the beginning of fresh initiatives by both the governments towards cooperation—a likelihood from Détente to Entente.

REFERENCES

1. Ashly, Tellis J. (2012). The Indian Ocean and the US. Grand strategy. Lecture at the National Maritime Foundation, Carnegie Endowments for International Peace. https://www.google.co.in/webhp?sourceid=chrome-instant&ion=ashley%20tellis%20and%20.

2. British Broadcasting Corporation (2013). 'China Overtakes US as the Biggest Importer of Oil,' London.
   http://www.bbc.co.uk/news/business-24475934. Accessed 18 November 2014.

3. Brewsterm, David (2014). 'The Bay of Bengal: A New Locus for Strategic Competition in Asia,' East West Center, Number-263.

4. Berlin, Donald (2002). 'Neglected No Longer: Strategic Rivalry in the Indian Ocean,' Harvard International Review, Vol. 24, No. 2 (Summer 2002), pp. 26–31.

5. Department of Defense (2012). 'Sustaining U.S. Global Leadership: Priorities of 21st Century,' United States of America, Washington DC.

6. Department of Defence (2014). 'Annual Report to Congress: Military and Security Developments Involving the Peoples' Republic of China 2014,' United States of America, Washington DC.

7. Dingli, Shen (2010). 'Don't shun the idea of setting up overseas military bases,' China Internet Information Centre, Beijing.
   http://www.china.org.cn/opinion/2010-01/28/content_19324522.htm. Accessed 18 November 2014.

8. Forbes, Vivian Louis (1994). 'The Maritime Boundaries of the Indian Ocean Region,' Singapore University Press, Singapore.

9. Fillingham, Zachary (2013). 'China-India Relations: Cooperation and Conflict,' Geopolitical Monitor.
    http://www.geopoliticalmonitor.com/china-india-relations-cooperation-and-conflict-4798. Accessed 22 November 2014.

10. Glaser, Bonnie and Deep Pal (2013). 'China's Periphery Diplomacy Initiative: Implication for China's Neighbors and the United States,' China-US Focus.
    http://www.chinausfocus.com/foreign-policy/chinas-periphery-diplomacy-initiative-implications-for-china-neighbors-and-the-united-states. Accessed 22 November 2014.

11. Green, Michach J. and Andrew, Shearer (2012). Defining U.S. Indian Ocean Strategy, the Washington Quarterly, Spring 35.2, p. 176.

12. Harding, Thomas (2008). 'Chinese Nuclear Submarine Base,' The Telegraph.
    http://www.telegraph.co.uk/news/worldnews/asia/china/1917167/Chinese-nuclear-submarine-base.html. Accessed on 22 November 2014.

13. Kopp, Carlo (2012). 'Sino-Indian Strategic Competition in the Indian Ocean Region,' Defence Today.
    http://www.ausairpower.net/PDF-A/DT-Sino-Indian-June-2012.pdf. Accessed 23 November 2014.

14. Li, Nan (2011). 'The evolution of China's Naval Evolution and Capabilities: From "Near-Coast" and "Near-Seas" to "Far Seas",' in Saunders *et al.*, ed. *The Chinese Navy: Expanding Capabilities, Evolving Role.* Institute for national Strategic Studies (INSS), Washington DC, p. 109.

15. Smith, Jeff M. (2013). 'Cold Peace: China-India Rivalry in the Twenty-first Century,' Lexington Books, Lanham.

16. U.S. Energy Information Administration (EIA) (2014). 'World Oil Transit Chokepoints,' U.S. Department of Energy, Washington DC.

China in the Indian Ocean:
From Junk Ships to Effective Naval Presence

Mohammed Khalid*

Indian Ocean had been a centre of vibrant trade and commerce from the time immemorial and has seen nurturing of great civilizations in the past. China, though touching the shores of North Pacific Ocean, has been deeply interested in the Indian Ocean. China has shown its presence in the Indian Ocean in myriad ways for a couple of centuries. After 1403 China sent its fleets consisting of trading ships, warships, and support vessels, to embark on major voyages to the Indian Ocean. These voyages continued till 1431 and traversed the waters of Bay of Bengal and Arabian Sea. During this time Chinese fleets visited all the major ports of India, the African continent, Persian Gulf and the Red Sea. After the death of Emperor Zhu in 1424 and admiral Zheng in 1431, Chinese forays in the Indian Ocean receded and China lost track of the waters of the Indian Ocean. During the Colonial period, Chinese rulers surrendered their powers and responsibilities to the colonial masters. After the Second World War as the Cold War set in, China remained busy and confined to itself and its immediate vicinity and could not show any kind of effective presence in or around the Indian Ocean littoral.

Economic reforms were introduced in China in December 1978 by Deng Xiaoping. Its thrust in the beginning was decollectivization of agriculture, the opening up of the country to foreign investment, and permission for entrepreneurs to start-up businesses. In the late 1980s and early 1990s China privatised and contracted out the state-owned industry, lifted price controls, protectionist policies, and regulations which led to the remarkable growth of private sector. China's economy surpassed that of Japan in 2010 as Asia's largest economy and became the second largest after the United States and is projected to become the world's largest economy by 2025.

The rapid industrialization has forced China to ensure uninterrupted supplies of raw materials especially oil which come from the littoral of

---

*Professor of Political Science, Department of Evening Studies Panjab University Chandigarh.

Indian Ocean. With 28 littoral states and six island republics Indian Ocean region offers coveted markets for Chinese products. To protect its interests, China is steadily spreading its presence in the Indian Ocean Region on two fronts—economic and strategic. It has sought and successfully established economic-diplomatic relations with the countries of the Indian Ocean region especially from Africa. China has set up its network of military and commercial facilities and relationships—referred as the String of Pearls—along its sea lines of communication which extend from the Chinese mainland to Port Sudan. The sea lines run through several major maritime choke points such as the Bab al-Mandeb, the Strait of Malacca, the Strait of Hormuz and the Lombok Strait, as well as other strategic maritime centers in Pakistan, Sri Lanka, Bangladesh, the Maldives and Somalia. This is indicative of China's growing geopolitical influence to increase access to ports and airfields, expand and modernize military forces, and foster stronger diplomatic relationships with the countries of Indian Ocean. India has reasons to worry and has to counter pose as the presence of China is detrimental to its economic and strategic interests. The paper is an attempt to elaborate on the issue of increasing Chinese presence in the Indian Ocean region and Indian response to it.

China is geopolitically so located that on the east it has vast Pacific Ocean. Historically, its lands on the Pacific littoral were barren, sparsely populated, and without any commercial activity. China considered the China South Sea and countries of Southeast Asia as its natural sphere of influence and the area was devoid of any noticeable trade and commerce.[1] On the other hand, Indian Ocean had been a centre of vibrant trade and commerce from the time immemorial. Some of the world's great civilizations—the Babylonian, the Egyptian and the Indus—had developed on its coasts. Apart from the commercial activity, the migrations of the people generating a cultural amalgam has been a significant trait of the lands and peoples of the Indian Ocean region.

HISTORY OF CHINESE VOYAGES IN THE INDIAN OCEAN

Annals of history indicate that Chinese envoys sailed into the Indian Ocean from the late 2nd century BC, reaching Kanchipuram (Tamil Nadu), even up to Ethiopia. During the late 4th and early 5th centuries, Chinese pilgrims and monks travelled by sea to India. In 674 the private Chinese explorer Daxi Hongtong was among the first to end his journey at the southern tip of the Arabian Peninsula, after traveling through 36 countries west of the South China Sea. China had never been a maritime power but to consolidate the tributary system it extended its maritime thrust towards Southeast Asia and the Indian Ocean. Chinese junk ships were even described by the Moroccan geographer Al-Idrisi in his Geography of 1154, along with the usual goods they traded and carried aboard their vessels.[2] As China became internally week, it had to suffer many internal wars and it gradually became overly dominated by the outside powers, it did not think of having presence in the Indian Ocean for a long time.

To explore new territories and expand commercial and diplomatic relations with the states of South and Southeast Asia and to demonstrate the power of the Ming Empire, China sent its fleets consisting of trading ships, warships, and support vessels in 1403 onwards. In 1414–15 a Chinese fleet called at the ports of Champa (now part of Vietnam), Java and Sumatra (Indonesia), reached the Strait of Hormuz and entered the Persian Gulf. Chinese voyage went to Bengal, coast of Malay, Sri Lanka, and the Maldives. This voyage marked the height of Chinese presence in the Indian Ocean. From 1417 to 1419 Chinese sent another massive voyage which sailed to the Indian Ocean and called at the ports of Indonesia, India, Malacca Straits, Sri Lanka and Maldives. Ships from this fleet explored further the Arabian coast from Strait of Hormuz to Aden and the east coast of Africa. Similarly a voyage was sent in 1421–22 to explore more of the coast of Africa. In 1424 Emperor Zhu died and was succeeded by Zhu Zhanji. Continuing the tradition, the new Emperor too sent voyages—the seventh voyage—in 1431 which remained at sea for two years when admiral Zheng—the main architect of these voyages—died in 1433.[3] After his death China lost track of the waters of the Indian Ocean. By the time Vasco da Gama arrived at Calicut on May 20, 1498—the most important turning points in the history of the Indian Ocean region—the Chinese had already retreated from the Indian Ocean.

CHINESE ABSENCE FROM INDIAN OCEAN TILL THE END OF COLD WAR

In the 15th century the Europeans armed with new tool and techniques of sea faring, escaped their medieval "prison"—that Christian Europe was in the Middle Ages—by adventuring out upon the trackless oceans. Subsequently, the nations of Western Europe, with their superior ships and guns, opened the new "Oceanic Age" by their daring and ingenuity.[4] Before the arrival of the Portuguese in the Indian Ocean no littoral power had attempted to monopolize the sea lanes that connect the ports of the Indian sub-continent with the Middle East and East Africa on the West, and the ports of Southeast Asia and China to the east. The British East India Company entered the Indian Ocean and initially sent two small ships in December 1602 to the port of Bantam (Java, Indonesia). Slowly under a design, first the Company and later the British established trading posts around the Ocean followed by occupation of many littoral lands including India. Though other European powers, the Dutch, and the French followed but could not be as successful as the British who effectively converted Indian Ocean into a 'British Lake'.[5] To maintain its trade links with China the East India Company fought three wars— called the Opium Wars—and after the victory in Opium War of 1842, Chinese imperial power declined and was forced to cede the barren island of Hong Kong. The British also opened Guangzhou (Canton) and four other ports for trade in China. Then on, trade in the Indian Ocean and from the Chinese ports became exclusive domain of the British till the Second World War.

After the war with Japan in 1937 till the end of Second World War and a four year long civil war till October 1949, the Communist forces emerged triumphant and Mao Tse-tung declared the People's Republic of China on October 1, 1949. China at that time was week, had little industry, with high population growth, and was facing high unemploy- ment and food shortages. As the Cold War set in and manifested itself in Korean Crises in 1950, China faced formidable challenges. United States military presence in the region, challenge of US protected Taiwan, denial of membership of United Nations thus Veto Power in the United Nations Security Council, presence of other colonial powers in Southeast Asia and build up of US backed military alliances like SEATO and ANZUS were a headache for China's Communist establishment. A closed economy, China had neither intention nor capacity or capability to show its presence in the Indian Ocean and its littoral.

ECONOMIC UPSURGE OF CHINA

After the death of Mao in 1976, his successor Deng Xiaoping decided to build the Country's economy on the lines of its Asian neighbours. In China "Reform and Opening up" also referred to as the "Socialism with Chinese characteristics", were initiated in December 1978.[6] In 1979 foreign investment was legalised and China began to set up Special Economic Zones (SEZ) along the south-east coast and Yangzi (Yangtse) River. During this period government controls in the industrial sector were decentralized. As power passed to third generation of leadership under Jiang Zemin in 1989, first Stock exchange was opened in 1990 in Shanghai. Fast economic growth took place in mid-1990s. State owned industries were phased out committing to liberalization in every sector of industry and in 2001 China became a member of WTO. China did not venture into the Indian Ocean and did not show any naval presence in the region, in the better part of the Cold War. Indian Ocean was a theatre to demonstrate the strength of US and Soviet naval fleets.[7] Trade and commerce was conducted primarily in the North Atlantic and the Pacific during this period and the Indian Ocean Region was a peripheral backwater in this regard.

After the end of Cold War, as the globalisation and liberalisation made their way, China began to increase its sphere of influence in the Indian Ocean Region. It coincided with fast economic growth in the country. Industrial growth and increased production made China increasingly dependent on resources and markets accessible only via maritime routes. Markets to its products and source of raw material especially oil, have been on the Indian Ocean shores. Safeguarding its trade routes and to ensure the flow of resources made China to show more than the normal interest in Indian Ocean affairs. Chinese naval planners devised the ways to secure Sea Lines of Communication (SLOCS). To meet these demands, China started naval modernization in 1980's, and launched an ambitious futuristic weapons development programme including high energy microwave beam-weapons, ship-based laser cannon and space-based weaponry to destroy communication and reconnaissance satellites. Ever since, China is trying to give its Navy a greater visibility, operability and rapid action capability in the Indian Ocean Region.

CHINESE EXPANSION IN INDIAN OCEAN AFTER THE END OF COLD WAR

China's expansion towards Indian Ocean had two aspects—economic and military. In the recent years China has steadily spread its wings in the Indian Ocean Region with its rapidly-growing well equipped Navy with all logistic support. China has established several access points through a series of arrangements for refueling, replenishment, crew rest and low-level maintenance facilities. By doing so, China is mainly trying to ensure protection of its sea lanes for critical energy needs. To assume a role beyond its natural geographic and historical maritime boundaries; China began to set up a series of bases in order to project its power. Its secure land borders helped to build a strong navy and increasingly concentrate on South China Sea and Indian Ocean where supplies of oil, natural gas, and other commodities critical to China's economic growth pass through. China has developed naval out-posts in Bangladesh, Maldives, Pakistan, Sri Lanka and other countries of the Ocean littoral.[8]

China has made serious attempts to wean Bangladesh and has supplied it arms and other defence equipment. Bangladesh's Armed Forces today are predominantly equipped with Chinese military hardware. China signed Defence Co-operation Agreement with Bangladesh in December 2002— first such agreement ever signed by Bangladesh in its history. China sold missiles, missile guided frigate in 1988 and later torpedo boats to enhance striking capability of Bangladesh Navy. China is building port in Chittagong by funding the transformation of its coastline at an estimated cost of $8.7 billion.[9]

China is the most important supplier of military aid and maintains extensive strategic and military cooperation with Myanmar. Since 1989, China has supplied Myanmar with jet fighters, armoured vehicles and naval vessels and has trained its army, air force and naval personnel. China has access to Burma's ports and naval installations providing it with strategic influence in the Bay of Bengal. China has developed a deep-water port of Kyaukpyu (western Myanmar) in the Bay of Bengal. It has also built an 85-metre jetty, naval facilities and major reconnaissance and electronic intelligence systems on the Great Coco Island, located 40 km off the northern tip of the Andaman Islands, giving China capabilities to monitor India's military activities, including missile tests at Wheeler Island off the Odisha coast on the Bay of Bengal.[10] China has assisted in construction of a naval base in Sittwe (Akyab), a strategically important sea port of Myanmar just 542 km flight distance away from port of Kolkata. China has funded the construction of China-Burma road to the ports of Yangon and Sittwe, providing the shortest route to the Indian Ocean from southern China.[11]

Sri Lanka's geographical location in the Indian Ocean has prompted China to develop strategic relationship with Colombo. China intends to use the partnership with Sri Lanka to enhance its influence over strategic sea lanes from Europe to East Asia and oil tanker routes from the Middle East to the Malacca Straits. China has entered into the oil exploration business in Sri Lanka, and has built bunker facilities creating an oil tank farm at Hambantota, Chinese insist is a purely commercial move.[12] Or that it is being created—as Sri Lanka claims—to develop its impoverished southern region. China's help is likely to boost Sri Lanka's annual cargo handling capacity from 6 million containers to some 23 million. Hambantota also will have factories producing cement and fertilizer for export. This makes Sri Lanka welcome the Chinese investment. Sri Lanka has also allocated a block in the Mannar Basin to China for petroleum exploration.[13] This provides presence to China just a few kilometers from India's southern tip. These new initiatives are aimed to augment its power projection in the Indian Ocean.

Marao is one of the largest of the 1192 coral islands grouped into atolls that comprise Maldives and lies 40 km south of Male, the capital. In May 2011, Wu Bangguo, Chairman of the Standing Committee of the National People's Congress visited Maldives. That underscored the increasing importance of the Maldives to China's regional strategic calculations. Though there is no evidence that suggests a Chinese military presence of any kind in Marao but the Atoll is regarded as a potential Chinese military base of operations.[14] Two years back, Maldivian government had cancelled a $511 million contract to expand Male airport signed with India's GMR Infrastructure. The contract has now been given to a Chinese firm and the agreement was signed on September 15, 2014, as Chinese President Xi Jinping toured Maldives. It should be a matter of great concern for India.

In Pakistan's western province of Balochistan, Gwadar is located about 533 km from Karachi and 120 km from the Iranian border and 380 km northeast of the nearest point in Oman across the Arabian Sea. Gwadar Port is located at the mouth of the Persian Gulf, about 600 km outside the Strait of Hormuz, near the key shipping routes in and out of the Persian Gulf. China is developing the port as its military-commercial base.[15] For both Pakistan and China, the Gwadar port offers a number of key benefits. For the Pakistani government, the Gwadar port is seen as having the potential of hedging against a possible Indian blockade of the port of Karachi, which currently handles 90 percent of Pakistani seaborne trade. For the Chinese, who have funded much of the US$1.2 billion construction, Gwadar represents an important strategic foothold. China has set up electronic eavesdropping posts at Gwadar to monitor ship traffic through the Strait of Hormuz.

Chinese companies have also constructed a railway link between Khartoum, the capital of Sudan, and Port Sudan—country's major port on the Red Sea. It has invested over $10 billion in infrastructure projects in the country to take advantage of its substantial oil reserves. China has also financed to build a US$10 billion port in Bagamoyo, Tanzania, which is expected to be completed in 2017 to handle 20 million shipping containers annually.[16] Some analysts suggest that Chinese Indian Ocean bases are purely commercial because they would be nearly indefensible in wartime. It is also argued that a large component of China's efforts to establish ports and bases in the Indian Ocean is the result of a need to formalize logistics support agreements for Chinese naval forces conducting anti-piracy operations off of the Horn of Africa.

CHINESE NAVAL OUTREACH IN INDIAN OCEAN

Chinese naval presence though not substantial or threatening has increased into the Indian Ocean Region in the recent times. It is understood that China aims at building a stronger Navy which is able to project power across the greater Asia-Pacific and the Indian Ocean region. China is focusing heavily on its navy, and building an increasingly sophisticated submarine fleet. With its 26 shipyards, it has emerged as the world's fourth largest shipbuilder and its naval expansion is aimed at assured access and control over its adjacent oceans, especially the Indian Ocean. This has given roots to China's naval diplomacy from Suez down the east coast of Africa. China's naval build up is not only because of its phenomenal economic growth and military power but also because of its ambitious and determined drive towards achieving global power status.[17] The Chinese, however, argue that their initiatives towards the Indian Ocean are guided by both strategic and economic compulsions and capabilities, as about 85 percent of its sea borne trade passes through the Indian Ocean.

Rise of China as a sea power is one of the biggest developments after the end of Cold War. Dominance of South China Sea and the East Sea makes China a great regional power but its presence in the Indian Ocean makes it a great naval power. Being a state from outside the region, it is difficult for China to deploy its naval forces permanently in the Indian Ocean. To meet this difficulty it has made Pakistan, Myanmar and other countries in the Region its allies. By increasing its presence in the Indian Ocean, China can also control its supplies and threaten to disrupt supplies, if need be, to its economic rivals such as India, Japan, South Korea and Taiwan, etc. To expand its pangs in the Region through naval presence, China has pumped massive economic aid and assistance to many littoral states of the Indian Ocean.

Of late Chinese nuclear submarines have made "frequent forays into the Indian Ocean". By doing so Chinese submarines probably also try to determine the Indian Navy's ability to detect undersea objects. United States Naval Institute has warned that these operations are going to pose a sub-surface (undersea) challenge to India in future. These submarines are believed to be from the South Sea Fleet based at Sanya on Hainan Island, off China's southern coast. These forays can be seen in the context of the proposal made by President Xi Jinping during his visit to Southeast Asia in October 2013, to create a Maritime Silk Route (MSR) to foster cooperation and goodwill between China and the ASEAN countries.[18] It was further extended to the entire Indo-Pacific region as China's outreach subsequently expanded to Sri Lanka, India and even to Africa. Though its finer details are still unclear, the Maritime Silk Route is said to involve the construction of ports, logistical stations, storage facilities, and free-trade zones. The rationale behind it is the leveraging of Chinese soft power and its 'legitimate interests' in the Indian Ocean region. It was reflected recently when following the MH370 incident in March 2014, China was the most active participant in the rescue effort, with more than eleven naval and Coast Guard ships scouring vast tracts of the Southern Indian Ocean.

To curb piracy in the Gulf of Aden, China has been deploying its Task Forces since 26 December 2008 each force comprising at least three ships including destroyers, frigates and replenishment ships. Till December, 2013, the Chinese Task Forces had escorted 5460 ships including 2765 foreign ships and 7 ships of World Food Program in cooperation with the European Union EU's counter piracy mission and Command Maritime Force 'Team CTF-465'.[19] These counter-piracy operations are helping PLA Navy to familiarize with the uncharted waters in the Indian Ocean which is getting increasingly important for China's maritime trade.

CHINA AND SEABED RESOURCES OF INDIAN OCEAN

In August 2011, the China Ocean Mineral Resources Research and Development Association announced that the Country has obtained approval to explore a 10,000 sq km poly-metallic sulphide ore deposit in an international seabed region of the southwest Indian Ocean. Subsequently, Chinese research vessels surveyed poly-metallic deposits in the Indian Ocean and stepped up efforts to extract minerals from the seabed. It has deployed research vessel "Dayang-1" under China's State Oceanic Administration (SOA) which has discovered four hydrothermal anomaly areas. China has made successful attempts to explore for hydrothermal sulfide a seabed deposit containing copper, zinc and precious metals such as gold and silver. Approval from International Sea Bed Authority (ISA) in 2012 to explore poly-metallic sulphide ore deposit in the international seabed region of the southwest Indian Ocean ridge is an important Chinese inroad in the Indian Ocean.[20] Apart from this China has also got exclusive rights for exploration of poly-metallic nodules over 75,000 sq km area in the east Pacific Ocean in 2001.

CHINA'S TRADE AND COMMERCE WITH INDIAN OCEAN REGION

Apart from the naval presence, China has substantially expanded its trade with the countries of the Indian Ocean. It is estimated that trade between China and African countries, reached US$166.3 billion in 2011, an increase of 31 per cent compared with the 2010. Exports from China to Africa were 73.1 billion (an increase of 22 per cent), and imports from Africa were 93.2 billion (an increase of 39 per cent). Similarly, China invested in 2013 more than US$40 billion in Africa, where more than 2,000 Chinese companies are operating and providing countless job opportunities to the local population.

Among the African littoral states of the Indian Ocean, China is South Africa's largest trading partner, making up over 14 percent of all imports (excluding gold) and almost 12 percent of all product exports. China's trade with Mozambique was almost a billion dollars in 2011, which was a 37 per cent increase on the 2010. Mozambique was China's 23rd most important trade partner. Trade between China and Tanzania reached over US$ 2.5 billion at the end of 2012 making China as Tanzania's single biggest trading partner accounting for 15 percent of its trade. China is second largest trade partner of Kenya with bilateral trade amounting to US$2.8 billion in 2013. China had good trading relations with Somalia that have suffered due to continuous violence in that country. In 2009, the volume of trade between China and Djibouti reached US$197 million, an increase of 55 percent over the same period of 2008. In 2002, the value of trade between China and Eritrea came to US$ 6.029 million, of which the export from China was US$ 6.025 million. China is Sudan's largest trading partner mainly due to its oil imports from Sudan. China's bilateral trade with Egypt reached from US$4 billion in 2007 to 7 billion in 2010. In 2011 Egypt was the 5th largest trading partner of China in Africa and in the first 8 months of 2012 it was the 4th.[21]

China's is aware that its future depends on the capacity of the Gulf Cooperation Council (GCC) countries to provide a steady flow of oil for the coming decades. Among the countries of Arabian Peninsula, China considers Jordan as its gateway to Middle East and in 2013, organized its 10th annual China Fair the "Largest China Fair in the Near East." The exhibition featured over a thousand Chinese suppliers displaying 12,000 made-in-China products for customers from across the Middle East. In June 2014 China organized China-Arab States Cooperation Forum in Beijing and called upon its Arab counterparts to upgrade their strategic relationships, by deepening bilateral cooperation in areas ranging from finance and energy to space technology. China's trade volume with Arab countries has been growing stronger for more than a decade. Trade has increased from US$25.5 billion in 2004 to 238.9 billion in 2013. China is now the Arab world's second-largest trading partner, and within ten years, the volume of China-Arab trade is expected to reach US$600 billion.[22] China's "march west" into the Arab world is a bold effort to translate its economic might into enduring regional—and, ultimately, global influence.

Among the countries of South Asia on Indian Ocean littoral, China's trade with Pakistan has reached about US$15 billion; with India it has crossed 49.5 billion and both have pledged to increase bilateral trade to 100 billion dollars by 2015. Trade between China and Sri Lanka reached US$3.6 billion in 2013 from US$1.1 billion in 2006. China-Bangladesh trade reached US$6.778 billion in 2012–13. Bangladesh imported US$6.32 billion of goods from China and exported goods worth $458.12 million in that period. In Southeast Asia China had US$4.46 billion trade with Myanmar in 2013–2014 and was largest trading partner of Singapore and Malaysia in 2013 with bilateral trade of US$91.4 billion and US$106 billion respectively. It is second largest trading partner of Indonesia with bilateral trade standing at $66.2 billion in 2014, four times that of 2005. China's trade with Australia reached AUD$150.9 billion in 2013. China has free trade agreements with Pakistan, Thailand and Singapore and its companies have heavily invested in almost all the countries of the Indian Ocean Region. To develop close relations with these countries, China has funded many welfare projects including building parliament houses, super markets, school buildings, stadiums, railway lines and other infrastructure in these countries.

China has been working for quite long to ensure it is not left out of the regional equations in the Indian Ocean. It intends to be a major player in the Indian Ocean, alongside India and the US. There are deep worries in India over increasing Chinese presence in the Indian Ocean, where India's geographical edge is being chipped away by billions of dollars in aid from China and big Chinese construction projects. China's initiative expressed by its Prime Minister during his recent visit is creation of the maritime Silk Road through a series of agreements that would link China to Europe by sea. But if China heralds the Silk Road as a vision of international cooperation, many in India think it is a Trojan Horse to hide Beijing's expanding influence in the Indian Ocean region.

CONCLUSION

India needs to focus more on the littoral countries of the Indian Ocean region by way of promoting trade and commerce with these countries. India needs to realize that it not only has geographical advantage due to its location centrality but also has huge benefit of connectivity with each one of the littoral states through its Diasporas. This must be encashed through cultural diplomacy. India needs to make special efforts to attract tourism, including religious tourism from these countries in a big way. India may not be able to invest in these countries but can export affordable intermediate technologies for various infrastructure projects, IT connectivity and by helping them process their resources. Indian companies governmental or private need to further increase their presence in the littoral states. With fifth largest navy is fifth largest in the world, India needs to flex its naval muscle across the Indian Ocean by more port calls, offering training to the naval personnel from these countries and play a pro-active role in fight against piracy, protect SLOCS and frequently organize naval exercises with the navies of these countries. India must broaden and sharpen its look east policy to rope in the countries of Southeast Asia. India needs to build economic alliances involving Japan, the United States and Australia to counter Chinese growing economic might in the region. India has strong challenges ahead and needs to take a host of such measures to checkmate China's growing naval presence in the Indian Ocean Region.

REFERENCES

1. For details see, Wang, Gungwu (2003). The Nanhai Trade: Early Chinese Trade in the South China Sea, Hong Kong, Marshall Cavendish International. ISBN 9789812102416.
2. Ahmad, S. Maqbul, ed. and translators (1960). India and the neighbouring territories in the *"Kitab nuzhat al-mushtaq fi'khtiraq al-'afaq"* of al-Sharif al-Idrisi, Leiden, E.J. Brill; Ubayd Allāh ibn •Abd Allāh Ibn Khurradādhbih *et al.* (1989): Arabic Classical Account of India and China, Indian Institute of Advanced Study in association with Ṛddhi-India, Calcutta.

3. Deng, Gang (2005). Chinese Maritime Activities and Socioeconomic Development, c. 2100 BC-1900 AD, Santa Barbara, Greenwood Press. ISBN 0-313-29212-4; Dreyer, Edward L. (2007): Zheng He: China and the Oceans in the Early Ming, 1405–1433, London, Longman. ISBN 0-321-08443-8.

4. See, Headrick, Daniel R. (1981). The Tools of Empire, New York, OUP, pp. 17–42 and 83–95.

5. Abraham, Saji, "Maritime Strategy and Indian Ocean", April 9, 2014, available at http://www.security-risks.com/security-trends-south-asia/indian-ocean/maritime-strategy-and-indian-ocean-2605.html; Robert D. Kaplan (2010): Monsoon: The Indian Ocean and the Future of American Power, Random House, New York, 2010.

6. Allen, Franklin *et al.*, "China's Financial system: Past, present and future", in Brandt, Loren (2008): Rawski, G. Thomas, China's Great Transformation, Cambridge: Cambridge University Press.

7. Harrison, Selig S. and Subrahmanyam, K. (1989). Superpower Rivalry in the Indian Ocean: Indian and American Perspectives, OUP; Rasul B. Rais (1987): The Indian Ocean and the Superpowers, New Delhi, Barnes and Noble Books-Imports (Division of Rowman and Littlefield Pubs.).

8. Pehrson, Christopher J., "String of Pearls: Meeting the Challenge of China's Rising Power across the Asian Littoral", Carlisle Papers in Security Strategy, Washington, July 2006. Consulted on 20 October 2014; Eshel, David, "'String of Pearls' is Securing China's Sea Lanes." Defense Update, 20 December 2010.

9. Devichand, Mukul, "Is Chittagong one of China's 'string of pearls", Indian Defense Forum; "China offers to develop Chittagong port", The Hindu, March 15, 2010.

10. "India's lone missile test-firing range Wheeler Island face sand erosion", Times of India, May 11, 2013; "India test-fires nuclear-capable strategic missile Agni-IV", Times of India, Sep 19, 2012.

11. Geng, Lixin, "Sino-Myanmar Relations: Analysis and Prospects", The Culture Mandala, Vol. 7, no. 2, December 2006; "Myanmar shows India the road to Southeast Asia", Asuia Times, February 21, 2001.

12. Sirimane, Shirajiv, "Hambantota port, gateway to world". Sunday Observer, 21 February, 2010; Namini Wijedasa, "China gets controlling stake at Hambantota port", The Sunday Times, available at, http://www.sundaytimes.lk/141019/news/china-gets-controlling-stake-at-hambantota-port-123262.html

13. Srilatha, V., India-Sri Lanka maritime Cooperation in Indian Ocean—Prospects", in, Sidda Goud, R. and Mookherjee, Manisha ed. (2013): India-Sri Lanka Relations Strengthening SAARC, Hyderabad, Allied Publishers, pp. 102–122.

14. "China-India rivalry in the Maldives", Jakarta Post, 17 June, 2011.

15. Bhutta, Zafar, "Gwadar Port: Pakistan, China all set to develop master plan", The Express Tribune, February 15, 2014; "China Confirms Takeover of Pakistan's Gwadar Port", The Times of India. September 4, 2012.

16. "With $11bn Bagamoyo port, Tanzania prepares to take on EA hub Mombasa", The East African, May 11, 2013, retrieved on 18.10.2014 from, http://www.theeastafrican.co.ke/news/Tanzania

17. See, Daniel M., Kliman, "Is China the Fastest-Rising Power in History? dated May 16, 2014, retrieved from http://www.foreignpolicy.com/articles; Dingding Chen, "China Is a Different Kind of Global Power", available at, thediplomat.com/2014/06/china-is-a-different-kind-of-global-power

18. Abhijit, Singh, "China's Maritime Silk Route: Implications for India", Institute of Defence Studies and Analysis (IDSA), posted on July 16, 2014, see at, http://www.idsa.in/idsacomments; "China subs 'pose worry' for India", The Tribune Chandigarh, 23.10.2014.

19. Bo, Zhou, "Counter-piracy in the Gulf of Aden: Implications for PLA Navy", posted on December 30, 2013. Available at www.chinausfocus.com/peace-security

20. Dasgupta, Saibal, "China gets first-ever chance to enter Indian Ocean for exploration", Times of India, August 2, 2011; "China speeds up Indian Ocean exploration for minerals", The Economic Times, February 26, 2014.

21. Collected from different sources from official and non-official and media websites.

22. Zhao, Minghao, "China's Arab March", Project Syndicate, The World's opinion page, available at, http://www.project-syndicate.org/commentary/minghao-zhao-lauds-china-s-efforts-to-deepen-its-ties-to-arab-countries

China's Foray into Indian Ocean: A Catalyst or an Impediment to the Emergence of Indian Ocean Community

Yagama Reddy*

INTRODUCTION

Jawaharlal Nehru's well-expressed appreciation of the "deeper urge of the mind and spirit of Asia" bears testimony to his vision of Asia as an integrated whole and Asian solidarity as a precondition for Asia in order to lend its legitimate weight to world politics (Acharya 2007). In his speech at the Asian Relations Conference held in New Delhi in March–April 1947 held a few months before India's independence, Nehru while explaining need for the 'Asian identity' underlined the need for regionalism and institutionalization of cooperation and mutual understanding"(Nehru 1948, p. 22; Gopal 1984, pp. 504–05). It was about the same time, Nehru was so much impressed by the millennium-long cultural contacts and fraternal friendship between India and China as to envision "a worthy model for sustenance of the Asian way of harmony and co-existence," as enshrined in the Panchsheel, the Five Principles of Peaceful Coexistence signed by Prime Minister Jawaharlal Nehru and Premier Zhou En-Lai. However, India's engagement in the past with much of Asia was built on an idealistic conception of Asian brotherhood, based on shared experiences of colonialism and cultural ties. Added to this idealism was India's much prophesied non-alignment movement (NAM) policy in the context of Cold War cleavages. Just as the NAM failed to garner the expected support from other countries, Nehru's idea of evolving 'a non-aligned' Indian Ocean region, repugnant to its glorious past of universal exposition, too got frozen.

INDIAN OCEAN TYPIFIED BY ITS FABULOUS HISTORICAL GEOGRAPHY

The Indian Ocean, described as the 'Heart of the Third World' or the 'Ocean of the South', with low per capita income and low levels of

*Professor (Retd.), Centre for Southeast Asian and Pacific Studies, Sri Venkateshwara University, Tirupati.

development in the majority of countries (Chaturvedi 1998, p. 712), is also known as Afro-Asian Ocean by virtue of its being bound by the two continents. The Indian Ocean Region (IOR) consists of 51 states, coastal and land-locked (excluding Central Asia), with a total area of 101.6 million sq km., including 33.05 million sq km of land area. The chains of mountains and expansive desert, forming something like a roof over the Indian Ocean, have got the India Ocean physically separated from the hinterland of African continent, Europe and the Asia interior. Thus, the Indian Ocean got itself insulated from the direct European influence and virtually remained as a geographical entity in isolation until the discovery of sea route circumscribing the African continent by Vasco de Gama at the turn of 15th century. The monsoon rhythm has had its indelible influence on the course of maritime history of the Indian Ocean. The commercial and cultural contacts across the Arabian Sea (between India and Arabian Peninsula and North African coast) and Bay of Bengal (between India and Southeast Asia) spanning over two millennia testify to a trading system linked by an ancient sea route from the mouth of the Red River (near modern Hanoi) through the Malacca Strait to Sri Lanka and India, and as far west as the Persian Gulf and Red Sea. At the beginning of the Ming dynasty (1368–1644), China was reported to have dispatched formidable voyages into maritime Southeast Asia and the Indian Ocean, sailing as far as the Middle East. Chinese Admiral and explorer, Cheng Ho or Zheng conducted seven voyages to the Indian Ocean in the 15th century; the Chinese fleet called at ports in Southeast Asia, India, Sri Lanka, the Middle East and East Africa. Though the subsequent Qing dynasty (1644–1911) showed little interest in maritime power, a strategic mistake which People's Republic of China decides to repel and revive the conditions at the beginning of the Ming dynasty (Yee 2010). Arab traders too dominated shipping in the Indian Ocean, even much before Vasco de Gama sailed to India. The discovery of sea routes to different parts of the Indian subcontinent and Southeast Asia and the British colonization of Australia transformed the Indian Ocean into an arena of conflict and confrontation for the European powers. Britain eventually gained almost virtual maritime control over the Indian Ocean, thanks to its colonization of vast territory of Indian Ocean littoral zone, especially of the Indian subcontinent with virtual exclusion of other colonial masters, like the Dutch, Portuguese and the French. Indian Ocean turned to become the 'British Lake', on account of its unquestionable supremacy of naval power which conferred on it the title of 'mistress of the sea lanes' (Senate Standing Committee on Foreign Affairs and Defence, 1976, p.6). Justifiably, the Indian Ocean, as the well-known historian Andre Gunder Frank pointed out, was "central in global history in all the millennia upto1800 and now is re-emerging again as central" (Saran 2013).

INDIAN OCEAN CREDITED WITH GEOSTRATEGIC SIGNIFICANCE

India's geographic position, military strength, and natural resources had won the appreciation of the former British Viceroy, Curzon, whom the former Indian Foreign Secretary, J.N. Dixit, in January 2002 described as "one among the greatest of the Indian nationalists" (Raja Mohan 2004, pp. xvii, 204). India's 'centrality in Asia' had impressed Curzon so much as to observe in his book, *The Place of India in the Empire,* that India could exert influence in many directions—on Persia, Afghanistan and China—while controlling the sea routes to Australasia and the China Seas (Curzon 1909). The British colonial power was also so much engrossed in the pursuit of ensuring security to the British India. The strategic significance of Indian Ocean had begun to be well perceived in all the geopolitical theories propounded from the beginning of 20th century. Indian Ocean littoral zone was credited with immense strategic significance through its inclusion as part of the Inner (Marginal) Crescent and the Insular (Outer) Crescent in Mackinder's Heartland theory; and it was likewise projected in the Spykman's 'Rimland' as being capable of exercising control over the Eurasian Heartland. The post-World War witnessed the withdrawal of the United Kingdom from the area lying east of Suez Canal; and there was no power capable of establishing effective control over the Indian Ocean region, although the USSR and the United States tried to establish hegemony. The US had its bases established in Diego Garcia lying about 1200 km south of the southern tip of Indian peninsula, though not intended to pose any threat to the Indian subcontinent. If the US had embarked on the policy of containing the Soviet influence, the Soviet too had begun starting deployment of its naval ships which frequented the waters of Indian Ocean on rotation basis. The presence of two super powers in the Indian Ocean was simply a contest for supremacy between a land power and sea power, as had been propounded by Mackinder in his Heartland theory. The Cold War divided the Indian Ocean in numerous ways, fermenting border disputes, mistrust and tensions, despite the vain attempts of the developing countries in the Indian Ocean rim to make the Indian Ocean a "zone of peace". In pursuance of the UN General Assembly resolution (A/RES/2832(XXVI) of 16 December 1971 at its 26th regular session, the

UN Committee held 450 meetings, yet the IOZOP was remained as a mere concept rather a sheer rhetoric than a reality. Thus, Geographical determinism and historical momentum have made the Indian Ocean an arena of geopolitical conflict and contest not merely among the littorals, but among the extra-regional powers.

POST-COLD WAR GEOPOLITICAL NUANCES

Though the termination of Cold War has to a certain extent eased off the tensions of power-contest, there was a widespread concern for many a country within and outside the region about the sea lines of communications (SLOCs) across the Indian Ocean, obviously, for reasons of energy security which remained a key component of contemporary geopolitics in the Indian Ocean region vis-à-vis geo-economic imperatives of globalization. The region has a population of about 2.6 billion (39% of the world's population) and accounts for 50% of the world's oil production, 55% of the known world oil reserves and 40% of the world's known natural gas reserves. As the resource-richness of IOR attracting the attention of both resource-surplus and resource-deficit nations, the SLOCs across the Indian Ocean have assumed paramount significance in the east-west trade, passing through the narrow choke-points of Suez Canal and Malacca straits. If 80 per cent of the world's sea-borne trade in oil passes through the Indian Ocean, Middle East being the source for nearly 36 per cent world's oil importation. As logical corollary, security for oil shipping from Middle East through the Indian Ocean is imperative for many countries as, for instance, Japan (80 per cent of its oil imports) China (39 per cent), Europe (21 per cent) and the United States (16 per cent) (Rumley *et al.*, 2013, p. 23). Security in the Indian Ocean is vital for India, with 75 per cent of India's trade in value terms and 95 per cent in volume terms moves by sea (Kitazume 2011). Further, India's geography together its interests and concerns spanning the Indian Ocean Region confers on it an inimitable position in the geopolitics of Indian Ocean. In the event of over 50,000 vessels transiting the Straits of Malacca per year, facing the prospect of blockade, nearly 50 per cent of the world's fleet need to be diverted through the Lombok Straits or the Sunda Straits, simply circumnavigating the Indonesian archipelago (Sufyan 2011). Besides the maritime terrorist attacks by the extremist groups and sea piracy, the region is equally afflicted with illegal human-trafficking and narco-terrorism, gun running and natural disasters. Though Indian Ocean littoral region has become a heavily militarized zone, historically its

SLOCs largely remained free of military intervention, inasmuch as majority of the Indian Ocean littorals pursued the Continental Strategy with minimal application of naval forces.

That "India and the Indian Ocean are inseparable" is not a mere geographical implication, but, according to the India's Foreign Secretary Nirupama Rao, it pertains to "deeper civilizational, historical, cultural, economic and political linkages (Rao 2010). Though India for long pursued Mackinder's continental strategic outlook with heavy reliance on the Army (Tellis 2002, pp.262-63), it had of late subscribed to the Curzonian maritime strategy of dominance of Indian Ocean and began maintaining the largest naval force and militarized its outlying islands. Being the third largest in Asia, Indian Navy is the most powerful maritime force in the Indian Ocean after the U.S. fleet (Sakhuja 2006, pp. 95–116; Raghuvanshi 2003). Though India's naval build-up was imperative to protect its lengthy coastline of 7500 km, island territories and Exclusive Economic Zones, the Indian Ocean littorals which were suspicious of India's naval capabilities became blind of the proven track of India's good neighbourly relations. It was about the same time that the energy security concerns had driven India to develop closer relations with the United States alongside improving naval force projection capability all along the Indian Ocean littoral, as evident from the Malabar exercises in the Bay of Bengal in 2007 along with the navies of U.S., Australia, Japan and Singapore. India is looked upon to play a major role in enlisting the support of other nations such as Japan, South Korea, Australia and New Zealand, besides the ASEAN by way of participating in joint naval operations in providing security to SLOCs and containing the hostile powers in the Indian Ocean (Gordon 2012). The Indian Ocean has become "a kind of pivot all its own, a place where the interactions among the land-based and sea-based interests of important countries are already salient and will become more so"; and the "concerns of the United States, India, China, Japan, and Australia have made the Indian Ocean strategically integral to the balance of power in the Western Pacific" (Lee and Horner 2014). The Indian Ocean thus has a long maritime history encapsulating various phases of transformation— from glorious chapter of cultural and trade relations on equal-footing (good neighbourhood), through European incursions and exploitations (imperialism) manifesting in intrusion into the indigenous societies, to a zone of power contest by super-powers during the Cold War period, and presently to an arena liable for probable conflict and offering possible regional cooperation.

CHINA'S FORAGE INTO INDIAN OCEAN

Geographical distribution of Chinese 'pearls', USA 'diamonds' and Indian 'nuggets', principally reflects concerns over energy security and secure access to SLOCs. China's maritime multilateralism with the Indian Ocean littorals from mid-1980s, by way of regular incursions into the Indian Ocean region and naval deployments in the region, has the potential to translate into strategic partnership. It was with a view to secure its access to energy from the Middle East and Africa that China has developed strong political, economic and military ties with all the Bay of Bengal littoral states, and thereby into the Indian Ocean. Through its tacit bases built in the Indian Ocean, China could emerge as a stakeholder in the Indian Ocean security architecture (Rechard 2006, p. 13; Malik 2007; Sakhuja 2009). China has its presence in four northern Indian Ocean rim locations—electronic surveillance installations in Myanmar, maritime infrastructure developments in Bangladesh (Chittagong) and Sri Lanka (Hambantota) as well as at the deep-sea port in Pakistan (at Gwadar) both for commercial and naval activities. Of all these, the Myanmar-China pipelines are the most important to China as to serve an alternative energy-supply route against the backdrop of maritime territorial disputes in the East and South China Seas (Yhome 2013).

China's "string of pearls" is intended to expand its influence aggressively by consolidating its presence through the acquisition and construction of military and naval facilities and by improving relations with the island and littoral states of the Indian Ocean, and thereby to sustain its economic development. "String of Pearls" is thus an explicit expression of Chinese growing strategic impact testifying to its determination to upsurge its way in harbours and airports combined with geopolitical association to endeavor for having a "harmonious ocean". In the context of Russia's inability to take on the reigns of the Soviet presence in the Indian Ocean consequent upon termination of Cold War, there existed a sort of "dynamic power vacuum" in the Indian Ocean henceforth making it an "arc of instability". Despite the emergence of U.S as the only super power, the space is likely to be encroached upon by China which is fast emerging as a "super power" (Malik 2013, pp. 100–111). Furthermore, China's forage into the Indian Ocean is an inevitable part of its need to develop efficient supply routes across the back of Asia for energy and resource supplies out of the Middle East and Africa, in as much as these routes on the Indian ocean are still largely secured by the US navy (Drysdale 2013). In pursuit of achieving its goal of being seen as an emerging and responsible world power, China has clandestine designs to isolate India and reduce the role of the United States which has its presence in 12 Indian Ocean locations—the centrally-located Diego Garcia, five in the Persian Gulf (Bahrain, Kuwait, Oman, Qatar and UAE), three in Africa (Egypt, Djibouti and Kenya) and a further three on the eastern rim (Australia, Indonesia and Singapore). India's presence in the Andaman Islands, Mauritius and Maldives is added to the list of 'contested spaces'; one-third of all Indian Ocean states incur a relatively high, seldom escalated, expenditure on traditional military security. Evidently, unlike sizeable passive players and regional players in the Indian Ocean region, the US, India and China are the big players with their own geo-strategic interests seeking preponderance or influence across the entire Indian Ocean, but not looking for territorial conquests (Malik 2013, pp. 100–111).

INDIA'S BELATED RESPONSE TO CHINA'S STRING OF PEARLS

In fact, the Indian government has not adopted a specific policy in the Indian Ocean region, but for ad hoc responses to the regional and global developments almost until the termination of Cold War. But, the Indian Navy's maritime perspective that dovetailed with the country's larger foreign policy objectives in the region eventually facilitated India to come out of its isolation syndrome in the Indian Ocean region. An economically vibrant and geopolitically confident India has long term plans to emerge as a major player in the evolving geopolitical map of Asia. Energy security has an embedded position in India's "extended strategic neighbourhood" concept, as could be discernible from its "Look East Policy". But, it was India's lethargic attitude that facilitated China's expansion into the Indian Ocean littoral zone; and India has apprehensions over China's "string of pearls" and its implications for energy security and SLOC's in the Indian Ocean (Evans 2011, pp. 85–113). India also remains concerned about China's overt links with Pakistan, its covert support to Pakistan on Kashmir crisis, its phenomenal economic growth and growing influence in Eurasia. Unlike China, India is constrained by geographical setting that becomes inimical to the Indian war-logistics; and therefore, India can ill-afford to have a hostile and indignant China on its borders, nor could it gain any substance by entering into an anti-Chinese alliance. Vital for the bulk of China's oil imports are the SLOCs of East Asia and the Indian Ocean, particularly the Straits of Malacca, which is thus the strategic asset for Beijing rather considered as China's maritime oil lifeline. If China is engrossed to develop a credible maritime force to deal with its 'Malacca dilemma', it is equally committed "to build a powerful navy that adapts to our military's historic mission in this new century." Evidently, "New Delhi's strategic geography", as Vijay Sakhuja, a Naval strategic analyst pointed out, " is predicated on long-range naval operations and the exercising of influence around the strategic choke points of the Straits of Hormuz, the Straits of Malacca and the Sunda Straits" (Sakhuja 2006, p. 112).

Conformed to the oft-expressed view-points on the China's encirclement of India vis-à-vis India's strategic calculus were the arguments sustained by the participants from India and China at the International Conference on *"India and the Emerging Geopolitics of the Indian Ocean Region"* organized by Asia-Pacific Center for Security Studies in August 2003. Unlike China which has often sought to tone down the fears of being 'encircled by other states', India has its security strategy centred on the fears of China's 'encirclement of India'. If India's implicit intention is 'to stop China east of Malacca Strait', China has a three-pronged strategy in the Indian Ocean explained in terms of 'trade and development, good neighborliness and friendship, and security and cooperation' in the post-Cold War globalized world. On the other hand, "the United States, unmistakably the most dominant player in the Indian Ocean in modern history", has the capability to project military power in the region and a well-defined strategy to pursue its policy of preeminence (APCSS 2003). John Hartley, Future Directions International Director and CEO, discussed in detail the two schools of thought among the analysts on China's strategic objectives in the Indian Ocean: (i) China is seeking to expand its influence aggressively by consolidating its presence through the acquisition and construction of military and naval facilities and by improving relations with Indian Ocean island and littoral states, thus isolating India and reducing the role of the United States in the region; (ii) China is simply seeking to sustain its economic development and to achieve its goal of being seen as an emerging and responsible world power (Hartley 2010, pp. 95–101).

PROMINENCE OF THE PIVOT OF INDIAN OCEAN VINDICATED

All said and done, on the face of it, the Chinese forage into the Indian Ocean and India's growing presence in the South China Sea are never clear as to whether the motives of these two Asian giants are of economic gains or creating sphere of influence or counter-balancing each other

(Wu Lin, Li Fujian and Saloni Salil 2013). Though both consciously downplay their differences, "the two may never be friends, but will not go to war and will not queer the pitch beyond a point". The maritime rivalry, likely to be intensified in the Indian and Pacific Oceans ostensibly to safeguard their respective SLOCs, will likely to intensify their mutual distrust and tensions. Whatever the reality of the limitations of the concept of "India balancing China", China seeks to play its own balancing game and to push its own agenda till opposed. Though China has neither intention nor capability to contain India or to prevent it from emerging as a major power, New Delhi should make China to recognize India's importance. With proven track of history of "good and enduring relations" with China, and as an "emerging economic power and major consumer of energy", India favours a multilateral action to meet common challenges to regional maritime security (Kitazume 2011). Chinese and Indian analysts continue to cite Mahan's supposed geopolitical comment, 'Whoever controls the Indian Ocean, controls Asia. The Indian Ocean is the gateway to the world's seven seas. The destiny of the world in the 21st century will be determined by the Indian Ocean'. The Indian Ocean Region (IOR) is becoming an important front in China's naval strategy, and India's presence at the centre creates a clear challenge with which China must deal.

LOOKING FOR INDIAN OCEAN COMMUNITY

In an environment of *détente,* consequent upon the termination of Cold War, the Indian Ocean Rim (IOR) initiative, also known as the M-7, was launched in March 1995 at Port Louis (capital of Mauritius) by seven littorals of the Indian Ocean (Australia, India, Kenya, Mauritius, Oman, Singapore and South Africa) with the 'spirit of open regionalism'. Indian Ocean Rim Association for Regional Cooperation (IOR-ARC), is established to promote regional cooperation, especially trade and investment between its member states and with the high hopes of developing it into a forum for economic and trade cooperation on the lines of APEC. But, IOR-ARC has endured stagnation in its progress towards regional cooperation or integration, largely because of divergent national interests and political economies of the member states as well as of explicit differential perceptions of the IOR-ARC. Similarly, national rivalries, the fallout of colonialism and diversity of the region have forced majority of the littoral states consider themselves as being a number of different sub-regions with the most tenuous links or commonalities; and hence the Indian Ocean region remains more of a geographical entity, rather than any kind of political community (Luke 2010).

For all the uncertainty looming large, an Indian Ocean Community is fondly hoped to create new opportunities for the economic uplift of the poorest countries through infrastructure projects like highways, railways and coastal/inter-state waterways, climate management, marine bio-reserves protection, mineral prospecting and other cooperation projects such as cold-storage for fisheries and related products, self-reliant dairy and agro-industry infrastructure. Indian Ocean Community is a "Union of Indian Ocean nations" which can, like the European Union, "transform itself into a free trade zone, and can even work towards adopting a common currency". Indian Ocean Community, as a socio-economic powerhouse of Asia, is considered as the forerunner of a United States of Asia, a vision articulated by Ban Ki Moon, UN Secretary General on November 7, 2007 in his address to the Asia Society.

Both China and India have membership in as many as 5 Asian regional organizations (ARF, JACIK, EAS, RIC and BCIM) and BRICS as well as have the benefit of observer status in some other organizations (China in SAARC and India in SCO). There is immense scope for them to evolve on to the stage of mutual benefit as, for instance, the arrangements they have put in practice for maritime cooperation and research, including joint efforts against piracy and the offer of Indian naval escorts for Chinese oil tankers (Drysdale 2013). Indeed, their cooperation would conform to the 1982 United Nations Convention on the Law of the Sea and also to the outcome of the First Conference of IOMAC-I (Economic, Scientific and Technical Cooperation in Marine Affairs in the Indian Ocean, known as IOMAC-I) held in 1987 that underscored the need for states to carry out activities in cooperation with each other. Furthermore, IOR-ARC could serve as a good platform; India is currently the Chair and China is a dialogue partner; both the Asian powers need to embark on a cooperative mechanism to address the issues and common concerns such as piracy, drug trafficking, climate change and the security of SLOCs.

REFERENCES

1. Acharya, Amitav (2007). Regional Institutions and Security Order in Asia, Centre for Peace and Development Studies, Goa.
2. Asia-Pacific Center for Security Studies, 2003, Conference on India and the Emerging Geopolitics of the Indian Ocean Region, 19–21 August 2003. Available at: http://www.apcss.org/core/Conference/CR_ES/030819-21ES.htm (Accessed 29-07-2014).

3. Chaturvedi, S. (1998). "Common security"? Geopolitics, development, South Asia and the Indian Ocean', *Third World Quarterly*, Vol. 19 (4).

4. Curzon, George N. (1909). *The Place of India in the Empire*, John Murray, London.

5. Drysdale, Peter (2013). "China's Reach in the Indian Ocean", *East Asia Forum*, 25 March. Available at: www.eastasiaforum.org/2013/03/25/chinas-reach-in-the-indian-ocean/ [Accessed 25 January 2014].

6. Evans, Michael (2011), "Power and Paradox: Asian Geopolitics and Sino-American Relations in the 21st Century", *Orbis*, Winter.

7. Gopal, S. (ed.) (1984). *Selected Works of Jawaharlal Nehru*, Second Series, Vol. II, Jawaharlal Nehru Memorial Fund, New Delhi.

8. Gordon, Sandy (2012). *'Indian Ocean: don't militarise the 'great connector',* http://www. eastasiaforum.org/, 10 April 2012 (Accessed 13 April 2012).

9. Hartley, John (2010). "Differing Perceptions of China's Role in the Indian Ocean", in Chapter Four: "China in the Indian Ocean Region and Beyond", (pp. 95–117), *Indian Ocean: A Sea of Uncertainty*, Future Directions International, 2012, West Perth, Australia, 162p.

10. Kitazume, Takashi (2011). "India bids for closer East Asia ties for regional integration", *Japan Times*, 24 October 24. Available at: http://www. japantimes.co.jp/news/2011/10/24/business/india-bids-for-closer-east-asia-ties-for-regional-integration/#.U9h6r3pMBkg (Accessed 26 September 2012).

11. Lee, John and Horner, Charles (2014). "China faces barriers in the Indian Ocean", *Asian Times*, 10 January 2014. Available at: http://www.atimes.com/atimes/China/CHIN-02-100114.html [Accessed 06-10-2014]

12. Luke, Leighton G. (2010). "United in Disunity? Pan-regional Organisations in the Indian Ocean Region", *Future Directions International Strategic Analysis Paper*, 30 April, pp. 1–6.

13. Malik, Mohan (2007). "India-China Competition Revealed in Ongoing Border Disputes," *Power and Interest News Report*, No. 695, 9 October. Available at: http://www.pinr.com (Accessed 15 June 2008).

14. Malik, Hasan Yaser (2013). "Beginning of an end in Indian Ocean*", IOSR Journal of Humanities and Social Science (IOSR-JHSS)* Vol. 14, Issue 3, July–August 2013.

15. Nehru, Jawaharlal (1948). *Asian Relations: Report of the Proceedings and Documentation of the First Asian Relations Conference, New Delhi, March-April 1947*, Asia Relations Organization, New Delhi.

16. Raghuvanshi, Vivek (2003). "India's Navy Reaches for Blue Water Goals," *Defense News*, 27 October.

17. Raja Mohan, C. (2006). "India and the Balance of Power," *Foreign Affairs*, July/August.

18. Rao, Nirupama (2010). "India as a Consensual Stakeholder in the Indian Ocean: Policy Contours," *National Maritime Foundation*, New Delhi, 19 November; at http://www.mea.gov.in/ mystart.php?id=530116701.

19. Rechard, B. (2006). "The Karakorum Highway: Opportunities and Threats", *Peace and Conflict*, 9/9.

20. Rumley, Dennis and others (2013). *The Indian Ocean Region: Security, Stability and Sustainability in the 21st Century*, Australia India Institute, Melbourne, 132p.

21. Sakhuja, Vijay (2006). "Indian Navy: Keeping Pace with Emerging Challenges," in Lawrence W. Prabhakar, Joshua H. Ho and Sam Bateman, (eds.), *The Evolving Balance of Power in the Asia-Pacific: Maritime Doctrines and Nuclear Weapons at Sea*, Institute of Defence and Strategic Studies, Singapore.

22. Sakhuja, Vijay (2009). "Maritime Multilateralism: China's Strategy for the Indian Ocean", *China Brief*, Vol. 9, Issue 22, 4 November.

23. Saran, Shyam (2013). *Towards an Indian Ocean Community: Creating a Platform for Cooperation in a Transforming Global Landscape*, Gandhi Memorial Lecture 2013, Mahatma Gandhi Institute, Mauritius, October 15.

24. Senate Standing Committee on Foreign Affairs and Defence (1976). *Australia and the Indian Ocean Region*, Australian Government Publishing Service, Canberra.

25. Sufyan, Khan A. (2011). *Greater Indian Ocean—A Peaceful Geo-political Pivot or A Contentious Source of Hedging*, athttp://pakpotpourri2.wordpress.com/2011/06/24/greater-indian-ocean-%E2%80%93-a-peaceful-geo-political-pivot

26. Tellis, Ashley J. (2002). "South Asia," in Richard J. Ellings and Aaron L. Friedberg (eds.), *Strategic Asia 2001–02 Power and Purpose*, National Research Bureau, Seattle.UKessays.com, *Neither Conflict Nor Cooperation Preordained History Essay*. Available at http://www.ukessays.com/essays/history/neither-conflict-nor-cooperation-preordained-history-essay.php

27. Wu Lin, Li Fujian and Saloni Salil (2013). India-China relations: How can they be improved? *Future Directions International*, 15 September. Available at: http://www.futuredirections.org.au/publications/indian-ocean/1305-india-china-relations-how-can-they-be-improved.html#sthash.IgRYPxic.dpuf

28. Yee, Andy (2010). "China rising: what would Mackinder do?" *Open Democracy*, 6 August. Available at: https://www.opendemocracy.net/andy-yee/china-rising-what-would-mackinder-do [Accessed 10-10-2014].

29. Yhome, K. (2013). "The geopolitics of China's new energy route", *East Asia Forum*, 19th June 2013, Available at: http://www.eastasiaforum.org/2013/06/19/the-geopolitics-of-chinas-new-energy-route

Growing China Influence in Indo-Pacific Oceans: Implications

R. Sidda Goud* and Manisha Mookherjee**

INTRODUCTION

A resolution was passed way back in 1971 by UNGA decelerating the Indian Ocean as a Zone of peace (IOZOP) in order to contribute to the prosperity of different nations by using the Indian Ocean for maritime security. The resolution was initiated by Sri Lanka, calling upon the great powers not to allow escalation and expansion of military presence in the Indian Ocean Region. In violation of the UNGA 1971 resolution, competition between the rising powers in Asia and the dominant one (USA) is still going on in Indian Ocean Region for geo-strategic interests. Though India has been status—quoist power in the region for 5000 years, never had any aggressive design or strategic reasons for dominance determental to any other country. The US on the one side, in the name of Free Trade Agreement i.e Trans Pacific Partnership (TPP) initiative aimed to forge regional Free Trade Agreement in the Asia Pacific region, wants to keep its hold in the Indo-Pacific Oceans. On the other side, the rising power, China is trying to limit the influence of the US in Indo-Pacific Oceans and wants to amplify its Maritime Silk Route initiative to South Asian and Southeast Asian nations to enhance its relationship and wants India to be part of Maritime Silk Route (MSR) to control the 'Asia Pivot'. In addition China also reached agreement with Pakistan to built an four-line-fenced Road from China to Pakistan via Pakistan—Occupied Kashmir (POK) to Gwadar port in Balochistan province to serve as a terminal for China to pump oil procurement from Persian Gulf. So, the game between the US and China in the Indian Ocean Region is still on even though there is a resolution passed in 1971, declaring it as a Zone of Peace. China with its aggressive and assertive character is having disputes with all its neighbours which share borders and in the South China Sea showing historical evidence and is trying to

---

* Director and Professor of Economics, UGC Centre for Indian Ocean Studies, Osmania University, Hyderabad.
**Associate Professor of Sociology, UGC Centre for Indian Ocean Studies, Osmania University, Hyderabad.

control the Indo-Pacific countries. This paper aims to focus on India's interest in the Indian Ocean—regional security and maritime security and to contain China in Indian Ocean Region.

The Indian Ocean was the home of the world's first urban civilization, and centre of the first sophisticated commercial and maritime activities. This Ocean was a great highway and source of food and raw materials and a vital force moulding many societies on its shores long before people maintained written records. Northern parts is surrounded by Africa, almost linked to the Mediterranean through the Red Sea; penetrates the central lands of the Middle East via the Persian Gulf, and through Bay of Bengal links up with the South China Sea, beyond which the Pacific. Asia and Australia to the extent that it tends to resemble a huge bay— and this is one of the factors contributing to its geopolitical and geostrategic significance. Ancient civilization in Egypt, Arabia, Mesopotamia, the Persian highlands, the insular South East Asia had ready access to the Indian Ocean and used it to develop their first maritime trading links. Therefore, to ensure the safety and security of these vital trade routes will become more important over coming decades.

Ranking after the Pacific and the Atlantic, the Indian Ocean is the third largest Ocean in the world, surpassing the Atlantic and Pacific Oceans as the world's biggest and most strategically significant trade corridor. One third (1/3) of the world's bulk cargo and around two thirds (2/3) of world oil shipmates now pass through the Indian Ocean.[1] The Indian Ocean is the world's most important energy route in terms of International trade, half of the global daily oil production was transported by tankers on fixed maritime routes. About 30 percent of the world's oil imports derive from the Middle East, securing interregional shipments through the Indian Ocean are vital to world prosperity. Oil import security is especially important for Japan (80% of oil import from Middle East) China (39%) Europe (21%) and USA (16%). Further, more than 80% of the world's seaborne trade in oil passed through only three Indian Ocean choke points of Strait of Hormuz, strait of Malacca and Bab-el-Mandab.[2]

The Strait of Hormuz, located between Iran and Oman, is the world's most important 'oil chokepoint', with a daily oil flow that is equivalent to approximately 40% of global seaborne trade. The Straits of Malacca, located between Indonesia, Malaysia and Singapore, account for about 35% of global seaborne trade, and is the shortest sea route between China, Japan and South Korea and Persian Gulf oil suppliers. Bab-el-

Mandab, an oil chokepoint between Djibouti, Eritrea and Yemen, is a strategic link between the Mediterranean and the Indian Ocean via the Red Sea and Suez Canal, and accounts for approximately 8% of global seaborne oil trade. The Indian Ocean and the South China Sea are recent terms created by the geographers to delineate the physical boundaries between three regions, the Indian sub-continent, Southeast Asia and China.

CHINA INFLUENCE IN SOUTH CHINA SEA

The South China Sea (SCS) one of the most important seas of the world geopolitically, economically and strategically, hence the sea attracts considerable attention in the strategic community in India. The SCS continues to be seen as one of the most difficult regional conflicts in Asia-Pacific. India has a vital maritime interests in the SCS. About 55 percent of India's trade is with Asia-Pacific, transits through the SCS region. India expresses its interests in the freedom of navigation in SCS and peaceful resolution of territorial disputes between Beijing and its maritime neighbours.[3] The SCS is an important junction for navigation between Pacific and Indian Ocean. It connects with the Indian Ocean through the Malacca Strait. The Sea lane running between the Paracel and Spartly Islands is used by oil tankers moving from the Persian Gulf to Japan as well as by warships enroute from the Indian Ocean to the Pacific. Security in SCS is concern both for regional countries such as China, Vietnam, Philippines, Malaysia, as well as extra-regional countries including India, due to their strategic and economic interests in this region. Therefore any conflict in SCS will pose a threat to regional and international security.

The SCS region possessing both oil and gas which led to speculation that, the disputed territories could hold potentially significant energy resources. According to US Energy Information Administration (EIA), estimates, that, the SCS contains 11bn barrels of oil and 100 trillion cubic feet of natural gas in possession. According to Chinese Military of Land and Resources, the SCS oil reserves are estimated to be around 23 to 30 bn tonnes and 16 trillion cubic meters of natural gas.[4] The SCS occupies important position in terms of international shipping as majority of energy shipments and raw materials have to pass through it.

China's dependence on the Indian Ocean is antedated and it will continue to grow for energy imports from the Gulf, to import resources from Africa and trade with Europe. With China's maritime presence in the Indian Ocean set to expand along with its economic interests, the question for India and its strategic community is how to engage with this new reality. In this contemporary situation one can't build a wall against China's maritime presence. In India, most of the opinion from scholars are still highlighting China's so-called 'string of pearls', referring to port projects China is involved in Pakistan, Sri Lanka, Myanmar and Bangladesh. Some of the them are apprehensive of China making them as military bases, although China has been maintaining that these are purely commercial. Chinese ships are plying through the Indian Ocean Region, for the sole purpose of securing energy supplies.

THREAT PERCEPTIONS FROM CHINA

There are four major issues identified of the two Asian giants for troubled relationship: (i) nuclear issue (ii) Tibet (iii) border problem and (iv) regional competition. India's nuclear weapons capability is quite likely not driven by the nuclear powers in the UN security council other than China. Pakistan nuclear capabilities supported and sustained by China, added to New Delhi perception. India was willing to pay the price of economic and other sanctions in order to became a nuclear weapons state. It was a major measure to change the asymmetry which allowed New Delhi to approach its bilateral problems with China in a more confident manner. China doesn't see India as a serious nuclear threat, but resulting change in the India's stature as a rising power and resultant improved ties with USA is a new variable in China's calculations.

Tibet has been a source of continuing friction between China and India,[5] China has not been able to satisfy either the Tibetan population or the global opinion on its intentions in Tibet. China's approach to the resolution of the boundary issue and its tone and tenor during the stand-off on the LAC in Ladakh in 2013, have all combined to create in India the widely held perception of hostile and inflexible China. China's economic growth, admirable in itself, when combined with massive military capabilities. The slow pace of boundary negotiations and a continuing series of irritants on the disputed border have a connection with Beijing's Tibet conundrum.

The Australia India Institute (AII) has conducted a public opinion survey in October 2012 in India with regard to India, Indian's and the World, called as 'India Poll 2013: *Facing the Future.*[6] The poll was commissioned by the Australia India Institute at the University of Melbourne and the *Lowy Institute of International Policy,* focusing the survey on India and the world-its foreign policy and security challenges.

According to the findings of the survey results, 84 percent believe there is threat from China, and 70 percent of the respondents agreed that China's aim is to dominate Asia. Over 80 percent agreed that, the threat was for few reasons—China possesses nuclear weapons, it was competing with other countries in resources; China was strengthening relations with the countries in the Indian Ocean Region and its was claiming sovereignty on parts of India territory. Almost 75 percent of respondents expressed that threat was due to China's stronger military power, its bigger economy, its military assistance to Pakistan and it doesn't show respect to India, while 88 percent believed that there could be threat of going to war with China over the next decade. Hence, 65 percent of respondents expressed that India should join with other countries to limit China's influence, to avoid threat from it.

Indians are deeply apprehensive about China's assertive or even aggressive attitude towards India. China has territorial disputes with all nations it shares border with and other nations like; Afghanistan, Bhutan, Burma, Brunei, Tajikistan, Cambodia, Indonesia, Taiwan, Kazakhstan, Laos, Kyrgyzstan, India, Malaysia, Mongolia, Nepal, Philippines, North Korea, Russia, Singapore, South Korea, Japan, Vietnam, of these, most of countries falls under South China Sea wherein India has its own maritime interest. Taking into note of the threat perception from China, the relation between India and China can't be viewed merely on the border disputes, but beyond, the behavior of China with its neighbours and its growing influence in the Indian Ocean and its territorial disputes in the South China Sea, where India's free navigational transit is important in exporting goods to East Asian countries.[7]

During the time of Chinese President Xi Jinping's recent visit to India in September 2014, China has amplified its vision of Maritime Silk Road (MSR) amid the repositioning of America forces in Asia-Pacific and an emerging trade deal, between the USA and its traditional regional allies.[8] The MSR was designed in 15th century itself by Zheng He, across the Southeast Asia, including India, Maldives, Sri Lanka in search and development of new markets and investment destinations in infrastructure bank and slew cables projects. China Silk Road ambition is to the Central Asia and Europe with Silk Road Economic Belt in order to expand its trade and strategic reach in the South China Sea and Indian Ocean all the way to East Africa with help of Maritime Silk Road.

China used to supply goods in ancient times to Central Asia traders, as well as Arabs, Persians, Indians and Malaysias, who played the Central role in the old Silk Road. In the new Silk Road of Xi Jinping's imagination, China will not only sell its domestically produced products but it also likes to create pathways to move goods and even manufacture them in the partner countries. Instead of the world coming to China as in the past, China will now would like to go out to the world, building naval and resupplying facilities along the Indian Ocean routes.

The proposed $40 billion Silk Road Fund will finance the construction of Rail Roads, Pipelines and Roadways that will link China with three continents over land and Sea. A proposed canal across the Isthmus of Kra in Thailand could provide a faster link between South China Sea and Indian Ocean. A state owned Chinese company is building a deep-water container port and industrial park in Malaysia. China has already taken over from India a $500 million airport development in Maldives, considered an integral part of MSR. Chinese President recently inaugurated one of the most ambitious of China's recent projects—$1.4 billion Colombo port city. And, further unmentioned in the Silk Road projects, is setting up facilities for China's power projection—a special transmission center in Southern Balochistan to communicate with submerged submarines: an air craft maintenance facility near China's aided Hambantota port in Sri Lanka, the recent appearance of Chinese submarines in Sri Lanka gave a peek into the steel that lies under the so called MSR.[9]

Hence, the Chinese Maritime Silk Road project is to counter Washington's Free Trade Agreement move i.e. Trans Pacific Partnership (TPP) initiate, which aimed to forge a regional free trade agreement in the Asia Pacific region—a 12 member participating countries, which began in 2005: Australia, Brunei Darussalam, Canada, Chile, Japan, Malaysia, Mexico, New Zealand, Peru, Singapore, the United States and Vietnam.[10]

CHINA SETS SILK ROAD EXTENSION INTO SOUTHEAST ASIA

The MSR is part of a string of Silk Road initiatives that Chinese are undertaking which includes Bangladesh, China, India and Myanmar (BCIM) corridor, which aspires to establish economic linkages between Southeast Asia with its 21st Century Silk Road initiative, through a railway corridor that would connect the countrie's Yunnan province with Thailand and Laos, covering 734 km and 133 respectively with dual—track, once completed, these lines will connect Bangkok with Thailand's Nong Khai and Rayang province. This new railway project will offer a new channel for bilateral trade and also help in tourist route starting from China's Yunun province to Lao's Vietnam and Thailand Bangkok. The Thailand's Prime Minister has recently declared and admitted that, the railway tie-ups with Beijing were meant to amplify China's Silk Road Economic Belt and the 21ˢᵗ Century MSR initiative.[11] The Chinese President has been relentless in pushing for a Silk Road Economic Belt—a giant project that would connect Asia with Europe along the Eurasian corridor through rail, road, fiber optic highways and energy pipelines.

India is set to launch what is probably the Narendra Modi, government's most significant foreign policy initiative to counter Beijing's growing influence in the Indian Ocean region "Project Mausam: Maritime Routes and Cultural Landscapes Across the Indian Ocean". Mausam project is a transnational initiative meant to revive its ancient maritime routes and cultural linkages with countries in the region to explore the multi-faceted Indian Ocean "World"—extending from East Africa, the Arabian Peninsula, the Indian sub-continent and Sri Lanka to Southeast Asian archipelago, which can counter—balance the MSR of China. The India government has apprehension that, the MSR project is likely to enhance China's further intensity its naval activities in the region, hence, India initiating Mausam project in Indian Ocean Region. The revival of ancient maritime routes India used earlier based on seasons and wind directions.

CHINA AN UNEASY NEIGHBOUR

India and China were not each other's immediate neighbours before 1950, Tibet was a strategic buffer between the two, their knowledge of each other was limited the Himalayas are traditionally a natural barrier in the North kept them separated. The Chinese annexation of Tibet altered the situation so much as remain an eternal source of tension in China-India relations—China accused India of trying to undermine its rule in Tibet which India charged China with suppressing Tibetan autonomy. The relation between these two countries were not stable since 1962 onwards, inspite of diplomatic visits from India to China and China to India officials and Heads of the governments respectively. Though the efforts were sincere and serious, the talks on resolving the border issue were stalled. What is more, there have been reports of increased Chinese incursions across the Line of Actual Control, and increased Chinese activity in the Northern Areas of Pakistan Occupied Kashmir (POK). Recently China and Pakistan reached an agreement called China-Pakistan Economic Corridor—a 60 km long—4 lane fenced Hazara

Motorway in Khyber Pathtunkhw a province costing $297 mn. Pakistan Prime Minister in his recent visit to China signed the agreement worth of $ 45.6 bn which included projects connected with the corridor. India has objected to this project since it is planned through Pakistan Occupied Kashmir.[12] The continuing Chinese military build-up, the growth of its infrastructure in Tibet and the nationalistic rhetoric coming out of China have raised another Sino-Indian clash in future.

INDIA FRETS OVER CHINA'S SOUTH CHINA SEA PLANS

India has joined the US in rising alarm bells over China's expansionist expeditions in the South China Sea clashing with Vietnam and the Philippines.[13] Since beginning India called for freedom of navigation in the sea. China's ships rammed Vietnam's vessels near the Parcel Islands in the South China Sea. Government of India likes to see resolution of the issue through peaceful means in accordance with universally recognized principles of international law.

China has called on Vietnam to stop disrupting its oil drilling in South China Sea days after ships from both countries clashed in disputed waters in the most serious escalation in maritime tensions between the two countries. China has justified drilling in the region by claiming the disputed Parcel Island falls within the islands exclusive economic zone. Vietnam and Philippines demanded for stronger action to confront China's aggressive behavior in the South China sea at the first Southeast Summit hosted by Myanmar in May 2014. A showdown between Chinese and Vietnamese ships near the Parcel Islands has put long standing and bitter maritime disputes. Beijing claiming sovereignty over the strategically important waters which are the world's busiest transport lanes and believed to confirm significant oil and gas recently. Several ASEAN members rejected China's claim, but few are willing to risk their political and economic relationship with regional power house. The stand-off between China and Vietnam started on May 1st, when China moved a deep sea oil into water close to the Parcel Islands in assertive move to cementing its claims of sovereignty over the area since Ming Dynasty, 1368–1644.20.[14]

China in its reply to New Delhi's apprehension about recent tensions in the South China Sea sparked by a stand-off between Chinese and Vietnamese vessels as "did not have to concern", Beijing's comments were in response to New Delhi's views on recent developments with "concern". The tensions recently were triggered by deployment of an oil rig by China in waters disputed by Vietnam. Chinese Foreign Ministry spokespersons Hua Chunying told India that, there is no reason to 'concern' about the recent development in South China Sea and assured that China and ASEAN have important consensus and confidence to uphold peace and stability in this region. However, meeting in Myanmar, ASEAN foreign Ministers called on all parties to resolve disputes peacefully. This clearly shows China's 'dominant' mindset approach towards a neighbours and downsizing India role in South China Sea.

China has also told the US not to get involved in its disputes in the South China Sea, a day after ticking—off India for the same reason.[15] China also accused Washington of provoking Vietnam and the Philippines to act against China. Chinese Foreign Minister Wang Yi asked US secretary of State John Kerry that his country must 'avoid emboldening relevant parties' provocative actions in regard to stand-off between China and Vietnamese sparked by China's deployment of an oil rig in the water of the South China Sea of the Parcel Islands, which are claimed by Beijing. Foreign Minister spokesperson Ms. Hua of China added that, the US should reflect on its own word. If the US really hopes for the Pacific Ocean to be a Pacific Ocean, what kind of role its wants to play? She repeatedly demands Vietnam to stop provocations, such as 'raming' Chinese vessels near the rig, China again maintained that it was well within its rights to deploy the $1 billion rig in the waters off the Parcel Islands.

As the consequences of a stand-off between China and Vietnam over a deployment of Chinese oil rig in a disputed South China Sea sparked protests in Vietnam on 14th May 2014, hundreds of people had torched and ransacked several Chinese factories. According to Vietnamese authorities, mob of thousands of people had attacked business in industrial zones. Many had attacked Taiwanese factories mistaking them to be companies from Mainland China. The attacks has been triggered by increasing tension between China and Vietnam, that have till recently enjoyed close relations between communists led governments, over the deployment of Chinese oil rig in the disputed water of Parcel Islands. In consequence of riots by Vietnamese, China started evacuation of its people from Vietnam by ships by evacuating 7000 people, besides 4500 Taiwanese have left the country by air.[16]

China is building a military base in the disputed waters of Spartly Islands in the South China Sea. According to a leading defence publication it is Jane's weekly, with the possible aim of turning it into an airstrip. The new island is large and the first of its kind in the South China Sea, where in Beijing is planning to convert the mineral rich archipelago into military installations, which might lead to tension over the area which is claimed by Vietnam, Malaysia, Philippines, Taiwan and Brunei. It also challenges Washington's call for a freeze in provocative activity in the South China Sea, which is one of the most intensive security problems in Asia.[17]

Indian Prime Minister Narendra Modi has sent tough messages to China during his three nation visit—Myanmar, Australia and Fiji, while attending to East Asian Summit and ASEAN—India Summit in Myanmar, the G-20 in Brisbane as well as a Summit of Pacific Nations in Fiji in November 2014. Modi clearly emphasized 'Look Act' Policy instead of merely 'Look East' Policy and asserted Indian stakes in South China Seas (SCS) and Pacific Ocean, wherein India has legitimate interests with 55% of its trade going through the South China Sea. China has been trying to push us out of here, even as it makes inroads in the Indian Ocean. Indian Prime Minister in his recent visit to Fiji has doled out financial support to Fiji and 13 other Pacific Island countries in space cooperation and defence ties. New Delhi is keen to catch up and create strategic space in Asia-Pacific by extending its expertise in democracy and capacity building.

China is steadily spreading its foot prints in the Indian Ocean Region with its increasing by military presence and with the rapidly growing Navy being equipped with warships, destroyers and nuclear submarines. On September 15th 2014, Changzheng2, a nuclear powered submarine was docked at the Colombo International Container Terminal Ltd, in Sri Lanka. Followed by the docking of a second one in October 2014. The presence of these Chinese submarines across Palk Straits has deeply disturbed the Indian government, which conveyed its displeasure to Sri Lanka over its decision to permit Chinese submarine to dock in its ports.[18] Besides this, China is also investing heavily in infrastructure projects on the Island and deepening the China-Sri Lanka strategic and defence cooperation. With China's maritime presence in the Indian Ocean set to expand along with its economic interests, India is deeply apprehensive about the Chinese assertive or even aggressive attitude towards India. In 2009, Robert D. Kaplan saw an inevitable geopolitical "great game rivalry", between India and China emerging in the Indian Ocean. As a solution, he argued that the U.S. should "act as a broker" to mitigate the likelihood of conflict between these two rising economic and military power houses even though he foresaw the superpower (US) as an unavoidable "elegant decline". Now the question for India is how to cope up with this new geo-political reality.

Modi government's most significant foreign policy initiative for countering China's growing influence on the Indian Ocean Region with China's 'Maritime Silk Road' project proposal, is the Indian project 'Mausam' a transnational initiative meant to revive its ancient maritime routes and cultural linkages with countries in the region. extending from East Africa, the Arabiab Peninsula, the Indian sub-continent and Sri Lanka to Southeast Asian archipelago, which can counter and balance the MSR of China.[19]

Another decisive step taken by the present Indian government in countering China's assertive power, is by committing to help Vietnam in defence modernization worth $100 million USD, by sharing civil nuclear cooperation and in carrying out oil exploration in the sea. Beijing strongly opposed and warned India against meddling with its disputes with Vietnam in the South China Sea which is rich in oil and natural resources with the US Energy Information Administration estimating it contains 11 billion barrels of oil and 190 trillion cubic feet of natural gas in proved and probable reserves. That would be enough to replace China's crude oil imports for five years and gas imports for the next century according to data compiled by Bloomberg. Thus, freedom of navigation is vital for China's and India's economic development as they both depend on the sea for trade and transportation.[20] Though India expects China's cooperation in realizing mutually promoted shared objectives, undermining China's incursions across the Indian border, and it not responding positively to India's offer of friendship leads to competition in the Indian Ocean Region.

Chinese experts noted that the US economy has rebounded from the 2008 crash more strongly than some analysts had expected, while China's own growth is slowing after several decades of rocked-ship acceleration. The US economy at the end of 2014 is estimated at 17.55 trillion USD, while China's economy at the same time is around only 10 trillion USD. A 5% growth of a giant $17 trillion American economy is impressive, but it will only slow down China, whose economy is half of the size of US economy, and China's regional ambitions have been complicated by its aggressive and assertive maritime security that has frightened Japan, Philippines, Vietnam and other neighbours, pushing them towards the US. All these, factors argue that China is looking towards India for greater cooperation for establishing an "Indo-Pacific Partnership" based on shared interests in developing new routes to Europe and avoiding the "Asia Pivot" doctrine of the United States.

Till date India has not yet neither a member of the Trans-Pacific Partnership (TPP) Free Trade Agreement group nor with the 21st Century Maritime Silk Road project which initiated China to a massive Asia Centred Development of Eurasia though land and water, but India was willing to be part of BCIM economic corridor initiative between Bangladesh-China-India and Myanmar.

India and Australia have shared interests in ensuring safety and freedom of navigation in key SLOC in the Asia Pacific region such as the Straits of Malacca and the South China Sea. They also have shared interests in promoting democracy, political stability and secularism in Southeast Asia. Another major challenge that Australia will need to address in the India Ocean is how to navigate its important relationship with both China and India. China is now Australia's leading economic partner and India is also rapidly become a key economic partner. India and China are also rapidly developing trade relationship, although they also have a number of bilateral security issues, that some time creates significant threat perception particularly on the India side.

Australia needs mindful of Indian concerns and differences in perceptions of China in engaging with India. In the Indian Ocean in particular, there are some important differences between Australian and Indian perception of China's security interests. Indian strategists are highly sensitive to any Chinese military presence in the Indian Ocean. Many view Chinese commercial interests in the region with suspicions and a sizeable number of Indian analysts believe that, China has long-term strategy of enriching or containing India. In contrast Australian analysts see that any Chinese commercial interests in the region in relatively benign terms and perceive any Chinese security presence in the Indian Ocean as an expression of China's interests in protecting its key trading routes. Some believe that, mutual threat perceptions of India and China in the lead to heightened naval rivalry not only in Indian Ocean but also in Pacific Ocean. As a result, in developing its strategic relationship with Australia it is forced to choose between China and India in strategic terms, whether in the Indian Ocean or in Southeast Asia.[21]

Australia in coming years may need to choose whether it should work with its security partners to limit any Chinese naval presence in the Indian Ocean or facilitate the role of China as a responsible stakeholder in the Indian Ocean security. However, the viability of any long-term understanding with China in the Indian Ocean may depend on China's willingness to recognize India's legitimate security interests in the Pacific Ocean, and for India to recognize China's interests in the Indian Ocean. But, an understanding of this nature may be difficult to reach. However, it may well be in Australia's interests if the major powers were able to reach some sort of understanding in both Indian and Pacific Ocean.

CONCLUSION

India's Indian Ocean is life line for its development therefore protecting Sea Lanes of Communication are important. India, till date has not utilized the Sea Power since long time even after post-Independence due to several problems left out by the Britishers. Hence, India did not concentrated much on maritime security issues. Till the end of cold-war Indian Ocean was a battleground for big powers, after cold-war US increased its influence in the Indian Ocean, and now in the 21st Century—China is growing its influence in the Indian Ocean, South and East China Sea of Pacific Ocean as its status has emerged to 2nd largest economy after the US. Subsequently the US and China became competitors in the Indo-Pacific Oceans for dominance. The US led—12 member countries of Trans-Pacific Partnership—a free trade regional group wants to improve its trade relations with countries in the Asian region and to extend to periphery countries of South China Sea as a part of 'Asia Pivot'.

To contain the US 'Asia Pivot' programme, China amplified its Maritime Silk Route aimed to enhance its engagements with countries of South Asia, Southeast Asian countries to do the business. China investing huge investments in Sri Lanka, Bangladesh, Maldives, Myanmar, Pakistan in the projects—construction of railways, roadways, ports, to improve the connectivity in order to improve trade. The proposed BCIM economic corridor aimed to improve the connectivity with Asian countries and to Europe. China reached an agreement recently with Pakistan, a China-Pakistan 4-line fenced road through Pakistan Occupied Kashmir (POK) to link port in Pakistan to secure energy from Gulf countries. China is planning to reach an agreement with Bangladesh in laying the road between China and Bangladesh—a Kunming project via Myanmar. Therefore, China aimed to dominate in South China Sea, and wants to create trouble to India. China has been trying to push us out of South China Sea, even as it makes inroads into the Indian Ocean. so, it is do or die situation for India. China is building networking of ports facilities spreading around India, where India's interests are very high, as 55% of India trade transits through South China Sea. All these projects clearly shows China's expansionist attitude and to have control in Indo-Pacific Oceans. China invited India to be part of Maritime Silk Route but India did not responded to the programme and China also invited India to be part of China's Indo-Pacific partnership to limit or to oppose the US 'Asia Pivot'.

India's National Security Advisor Ajit Doval emphasized recently that, the UNGA resolution of 1971—IOZOP to be honoured and implemented to maintain Indian Ocean as Peace of Zone if it has to contribute to the prosperity of different nations. The said UNGA resolution was passed in 1971 when the China was not in the picture and it was a developing country. Therefore, keeping in view of this, India should enhance relation with countries and Island states of Indian Ocean such as Maldives, Mauritius etc., to engage in bilateral and multi-lateral agreements to contain China's growing influence apart from Southeast Asian countries which will become a force so that India's position in the Indian Ocean and South China Sea will improve in containing China in the Indian Ocean Region. Therefore, the call given by the Agit Dovel keep IOZOP applies to both China and the US not to escalate military presence and tensions which hurt the interests of not only India, but also other countries, who were using the Indian Ocean and Pacific Ocean for trade and energy security. India has to enlarge its engagements with small countries and Island states in Indian Ocean Region through bilateral and multi-lateral agreements, apart from Australia and ASEAN countries to limit China's growing influence in Indian Ocean Region.

REFERENCES

1. Dieter, Braun, The Indian Ocean: Region of Conflict or Peace Zone, Oxford University Press, New Delhi, 1983, p. 1.
2. Dennis, Rumley, The Indian Ocean Region: Security, Stability and sustainability in the 21st Century, Australia India Institute, 2013, p. 92.
3. India's Maritime Gateway to the Pacific, *The Hindu*, 22nd February 2014.
4. Ibid.
5. Agarwal, Ajay B., India Tibet and China, NA Books Industrial, Mumbai, 2003.
6. Amitabh, Matto and Rory, Medcall, India, Indian's and the World: Public Opinion and Foreign Policy, Australia-India Institute Melbourne, 2013.
7. China Territorial Disputes, *The Economic Times*, 5th December 2013.
8. The Hindu 14th December, 2014.
9. The Times of India, New Silk Road, 20th December 2014.

10. The Hindu, 14th September 2014.
11. The Hindu, 20th December 2014.
12. The Hindu 1st December 2014.
13. India Frets Over China's South China Sea Plans, *The Times of India* 10th May 2014.
14. China Territorial Disputes, *The Economic Times*, 5th December 2013.
15. After India, China Ticks off US as Sea Dispute, *The Times of India*, 14th May 2014.
16. More Chinese Shipped from Vietnam, *The Times of India*, 20th May 2014.
17. The Hindu, 11th November 2014.
18. The Times of India, 4th November 2014.
19. The Hindu, 27th October 2014.
20. The Times of India, 16th September 2014.
21. Dennis, Rumley, The Indian Ocean Region: Security, Stability and sustainability in the 21st Century, Australia India Institute 2013, p. 92.

China and India in the Persian Gulf and Other Energy Theatres: Cooperation or Conflict?

Sujata Ashwarya Cheema* and Suruchi Aggarwal**

INTRODUCTION

The march of China and India on the path of rapid economic development has fuelled similar surge in demand for energy. The two countries have followed similar energy security strategy of procuring consistent and durable supply of energy. To take the similarity further, the Persian Gulf is vital for both countries' continued high growth path, in view of their huge dependence on hydrocarbons as the primary energy source. Oil constitutes 18 percent of China's energy consumption/supply and in the case of India it is 22 percent. China imports 51 percent of oil from the Gulf countries, whereas the figure for India is 62 percent. Realists tell us that states pursue international relations in the perusal of national interest and that is the raison d'etre of their existence. China and India's national interests are embedded in having a stable supply of energy from the Gulf. With parallel interests in such a vital and strategic area, the two Asian economic powers are more likely to cooperate in the Gulf region. However, conflicting interests vis-à-vis energy could emerge over questions of who gets what, when and how. As a matter of fact, they have, in several other energy theatres.

ENERGY TRENDS OF CHINA AND INDIA

The International Energy Outlook of the EIA summarizes the energy demand and consumption of China and India, thus:

> Since 1990, energy consumption in both countries as a share of total world energy use has increased significantly, and together they accounted for about 10 percent of total world energy consumption in 1990 and 21 percent in 2008. Although energy demand faltered in many parts of the world during the recession, robust growth continued in China and India, whose economies expanded by

---

  * Assistant Professor, Centre for West Asian Studies, Jamia Millia Islamia New Delhi.
** M.Phil in West Asian Studies from Jamia Millia Islamia, New Delhi.

12.4 percent and 6.9 percent, respectively, in 2009. U.S. energy consumption declined by 5.3 percent in 2009, and energy use in China is estimated to have surpassed that of the United States for the first time. ... Strong economic growth [is projected] in both China and India, and their combined energy use [would] more than double, accounting for 31 percent of total world energy consumption in 2035. In 2035, China's energy demand is 68 percent higher than U.S. energy demand. Energy use in non-OECD Asia (led by China and India) shows the most robust growth of all the non-OECD regions, rising by 117 percent from 2008 to 2035.[1]

CHINA

As far as China is concerned, coal constitutes the dominant fuel in the energy mix, accounting for 69 percent of the total energy use, followed by oil at 18 percent. Much less than coal, the share of oil in the total energy consumption basket is critical to energy requirements of the country and will remain so in the near future. The share of natural gas in China's energy consumption has not been so important. Constituting only 4 per cent of the energy mix in the current scenario, China has been planning to propel the consumption of natural gas, by reinforcing domestic reserves with imports via pipeline and as liquefied natural gas (LNG) (See Table 1). China has designated natural gas a fuel of choice, intending to substitute this fuel for environmentally burdensome coal and oil.

The share of oil in China's energy consumption has been increasing steadily. China is the world's second-largest oil consumer behind the United States. The country was a net oil exporter until the early 1990s and became the world's second-largest net importer of crude oil and petroleum products in 2009, as economic development increased domestic demand. China is expected to surpass the United States in terms of largest net oil import in 2014, according to an EIA projection.[2] China's oil consumption growth accounted for one-third of the world's oil consumption growth in 2013, and EIA projects the same share in 2014.[3]

To maintain consistent economic growth, energy flow must be un-interrupted. For China, this scenario is critical for social and political stability. Indeed, it is crucial to the continued legitimacy and survival of the Communist Party. Therefore, energy security is the most significant aspect of China's international relations. China's efforts at energy security has several dimensions: maximizing domestic production, increasing energy efficiency, creating an energy reserve, concluding contracts with exporting countries, gaining exploration rights and production control i.e. equity in oil and gas resources, and building infrastructure to handle imported energy. The nation has been forging broad-based energy relationship—'energy diplomacy' or 'oil diplomacy'—with oil and gas producing nations in Asia, Africa and Latin America, by investing in infrastructural development in return for shares in their energy sector.

Many OPEC (Organization of Petroleum Exporting Countries) members are focusing on China as a key buyer of their oil output. Saudi Arabia, the world's biggest crude exporter, has long looked towards oil consumption by Western countries as indicator for addition of new pumping capacity, but that yardstick has shifted to Asia, with the emergence of giant consumers, such as, China and India. In 2013, more than 50 percent of China's total crude oil imports came from the Persian Gulf region (Figure 1), and therefore, the country is keen to secure this region, which it regards as politically unstable.

Table 1: Total Energy Consumption in China by Type, 2011

Type of Energy	% of Consumption
Coal	69
Oil	18
Hydroelectric power	6
Natural gas	4
Nuclear	<1
Other renewable	1

Source: "China", *EIA*, February 4, 2014.

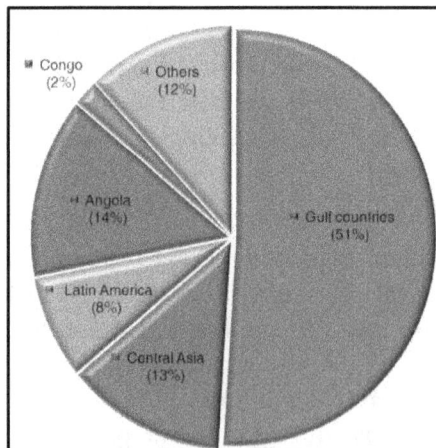

Fig. 1: China's Crude Oil Imports by Source, 2013
(*Source:* "China", *EIA*, February 4, 2014)

INDIA

India was the fourth largest energy consumer in the world after the United States, China, and Russia in 2011, and also the fourth largest consumer of oil and petroleum products after the United States, China, and Japan in 2013. As in China, the dominant fuel in India's energy mix is coal, followed by oil. The share of oil in India's energy consumption at 23 percent is higher than that of China but comparable in terms of the criticality of the resource to the current energy needs. India's natural gas consumption is slightly higher than that of China (Table 2). New Delhi began importing LNG from Qatar in 2004 and relies on imports to meet domestic natural gas requirement. Gas consumption has grown at an annual rate of 10 percent from 2001–2011, although supply disruptions in 2011 arrested consumption levels. In 2011, India consumed 2.3 trillion cubic feet (Tcf), and LNG imports accounted for about a quarter of total gas demand. The Indian Oil Ministry projects this trend to continue, with the country's gas demand more than doubling in the next five years.[4] LNG will account for an increasing portion of that use.

The gap between India's oil demand and supply is widening, as demand reached nearly 3.7 million barrels per day (mbd) in 2013 compared to less than 1 mbd of total liquids production. EIA projects India's demand will more than double to 8.2 mbd by 2040, while domestic production will remain relatively flat, hovering around 1 mbd. With production projected to flatten out, there will be a huge gap between production and consumption of crude oil in the coming years.[5] Being a net importer of oil and gas, energy security naturally figures prominently in India's foreign policy. How does India tackle high degree of dependence on imported crude oil and gas? Through increasing domestic exploration and production; building strategic oil stocks; diversifying fuel use; and encouraging diversification of supply source through purchase of equity stakes in overseas oil and gas fields, the country has been taking measures to reduce vulnerability on the energy front. The majority of imports continue to come from the West Asian region (Figure 2), where Indian companies have little direct access to investment, although, the Indian national oil companies (NOCs) have purchased equity stakes in overseas oil and gas fields in other oil-rich regions of the world, to ensure security to supply.

Table 2: Total Energy Consumption in India by Type, 2012

Type of Energy	% of Consumption
Coal	44
Petroleum and the liquids	22
Biomass and waste	22
Hydroelectric power	3
Natural gas	7
Nuclear	1
Other renewables	1

Source: India," *EIA*, June 26, 2014.

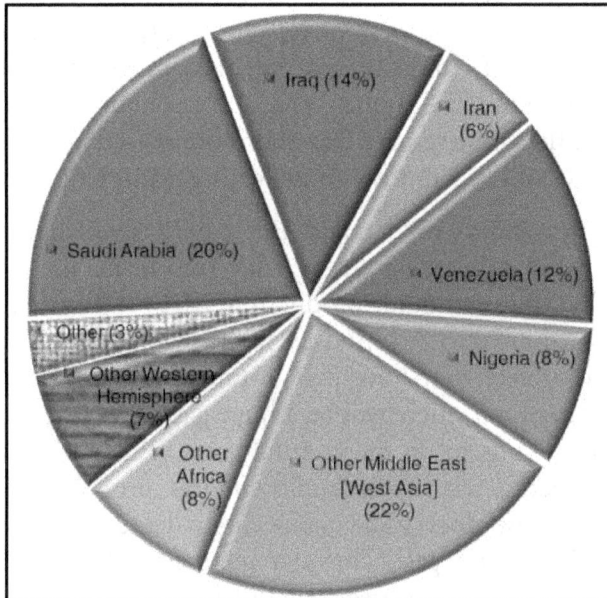

Fig. 2: India's Petroleum and Other Liquids Imports by Source, 2013
(*Source:* "India", *EIA*, June 26, 2014)

CHINA AND INDIA: THE IMPERATIVES OF ENERGY SECURITY

Energy security is emerging as a strategic issue for China and India, as their oil consumption increases and natural gas becomes a fuel of substitution. Heavy dependence on imported energy is a point of immediate commonality between the two countries. Their 'going-out' strategy in quest for energy equity is also quite similar. As both countries rely heavily on Gulf oil (and gas in case of India), they are seeking to diversify both the source and type of fuel. To reduce reliance on oil, the fuel of choice for India and China is natural gas, although both need to import gas as well. In their quest for energy source diversification, they have met in every energy theatre on the globe: Middle East, Russia, Central, South and Southeast Asia, Africa, Latin America and Australia.

To secure the supply source, China and India have embarked on similar strategies: purchases in the open market (through supply contract and spot purchases) and acquisition of stakes in overseas exploration and production of energy through state-owned companies. In all these efforts, China is far ahead of India, a source of great alarm in New Delhi and one of the compelling reasons for increasing emphasis on energy security. More to this point, Indian oil companies lost to their Chinese counterparts in the competitive bidding for production contracts in Angola (2004) and Kazakhstan (2005), Nigeria (2006).

It was the intensely competed Kazakhstan bid that made Indian policymakers realize that energy cooperation with China was a better option than competition. India took the initiative to institute an Indo-Chinese Dialogue in 2005 and a diplomatic agreement between New Delhi and Beijing on bidding protocol was reached. Both countries realized that an intensely nationalistic approach to energy security was likely to harm political relations between them. The Chinese motivation for engaging in energy cooperation with India stemmed from concern over Indian naval presence in the Indian Ocean and security of energy shipments.

In the backdrop of improved Indo-American ties, and China's fearing an American-led effort at 'energy strangulation,' China has grown increasingly wary of India's ongoing plans to extend its presence in key shipping routes along the Indian Ocean by developing blue-water navy. In order to secure the Sea Lines of Communication (SLOC) and reduce its dependence on the Indian Ocean, China is pursuing a two–pronged strategy: first, building an energy transport route from the Middle East to China by overland pipelines running through Pakistan; and, second, constructing port in India's neighbouring countries in South Asia, the so-called 'string-of-pearls' strategy. It has heavily invested in the construction of the Pakistani deep-sea port of Gwadar that begun in March 2002 and took over its functioning in 2012. Gwadar is located 72 km from Iran and 400 km from the Strait of Hormuz. An EIA report highlights the importance of the Strait of Hormuz thus:

> Located between Oman and Iran, is the world's most important oil chokepoint due to its daily oil flow of about 17 million bbl/d in

2011, roughly 35% of all seaborne traded oil and almost 20% of oil traded worldwide. More than 85% of these crude oil exports went to Asian markets, with Japan, India, South Korea, and China representing the largest destinations. The blockage of the Strait of Hormuz, even temporarily, could lead to substantial increases in total energy costs.[6]

In turn, India has been assisting Iran in the construction of Chabahar port in southeastern Iran on the border of the Indian Ocean. The politics of Gwadar and Chabahar ports show that China and India have divergent and rival interests in the Indian Ocean.[7] If India's relations with its neighbours do not improve, the region will remain an area of energy competition between the Asian giants in the medium-term. China's port-building or 'pearl' strategy also extends to India's southeast neighbourhood. In Myanmar, China was able to successfully negotiate a pipeline project to import natural gas from the Shwe field to Yunnan province, in which India was clearly interested. In fact, India's failure to grant certain concessions to Bangladesh for a pipeline running from Myanmar through its territory, nixed the deal. The Chinese have been able to deal more deftly in negotiating the gas deal with Myanmar than the Indian side. Moreover, given the importance of Myanmar to China as an access point to the Indian Ocean and the Malacca Strait, the country has added strategic value in China's calculations. In this scenario, China will be less disposed to cooperation with India in Southeast Asia.[8]

Russia is another energy theatre where China and India meet in their quest to secure energy supplies. Being the world's second largest oil producer and leading gas producer, it is an attractive source of energy for both countries. India is on a stronger footing here than China because of its better political relations, secured by cooperation in the military arena. In the energy sector, Indo-Russian cooperation includes Indian investments in the Sakhalin Island projects as well as joint explorations for energy resources in the Caspian basin. The possibility of transporting energy through overland pipelines from Russia is an immensely appealing for China that would not only diversify the country's oil supply source, but also reduce its reliance on the critical SLOC. Therefore, China is increasingly paying greater attention to Russia, more so, as it encounters competition from Japan around its east. Reports of trilateral talk on Russia-China-India oil pipeline indicate that collaboration with Russia in the energy sphere could spur China and India towards cooperation.[9]

On the contrary, the Central Asian Republics appear to offer a less conducive environment for energy cooperation between China and

India. China is spurred by the convenience of importing energy via pipelines given the geographical proximity of the region and the prospects of bypassing the SLOC. India considers Central Asia an important source of oil and gas in its strategy of energy source diversification. The Chinese inroads into Central Asia have got a fillip with the creation of the Shanghai Cooperation Organisation (SCO) in June 2001. With China, Russia, Kazakhstan, Kyrgyzstan, Tajikistan and Uzbekistan as members of the organization, enhancing energy cooperation is high on their agenda. Concerned about China's involvement in the regional security through the SCO, India has been building trade routes to Central Asian republics via Afghanistan and Iran and trying hard for the membership of the SCO itself.[10] The interest and presence of the United States in Central Asia adds another competitive dimension in the Central Asian energy scenario. Being a strategic neighbourhood of China, the two Asian giants are more likely to compete than cooperate.

China and India's energy quest has taken them to distant Africa, where competition and cooperative – 'competitive cooperation' – has been the trend of their meeting. Competition took place in Angola, where the CNPC (China National Petroleum Corporation) outbid India's ONGC (Oil and Natural Gas Corporation) in 2005. In contrast, in the same year, the companies worked together on the Greater Nile Oil Project in Sudan. As a matter of fact, major oil companies from China and India collaborated for the first time in a joint venture here. The increasing interests of US and European powers and their strategies for African oil has enabled India to formulate a policy framework for energy cooperation with China in the Francophone Africa. Moreover, competition between Chinese and Indian companies has the potential to drive up energy bidding prices, which works to the detriment of both. This is another reason why the two countries are likely to cooperate on the African continent. Africa being out of the immediate neighbourhood of both China and India has less strategic value, a factor that enhances prospects for greater cooperation.[11]

Western hemisphere offers another environment conducive to Indo-Chinese energy cooperation, being low in strategic terms for the two countries. For instance, the ONGC and Sinopec (China Petroleum & Chemical Corporation) jointly won a bid for 50 percent stake in oil company Omimex de Colombia Ltd. in September 2006.[12] The relationships of the two Asian powers with the United States could also determine energy cooperation or competition, as the latter is the dominant power in the region. They could collaborate to challenge US dominance in accessing the energy resources of Latin America.

INDIA, CHINA AND THE GULF

West Asia ranks the first in terms of proven oil reserves, oil production and oil exports. In 2012 alone, proven reserves reached 795 billion barrels, making up 48.1 percent of the world's total of 1652 billion barrels; oil production operated at 27.69 mbd in 2011, accounting for 36.2 percent of the world's total of 54.5 million barrels per day. These figures explain why China and India (as well as Japan and Europe) are heavily dependent on West Asian oil. Dependence on imported oil is considered an area of strategic vulnerability by both countries, and, therefore, energy security is an issue of utmost importance to them. China and India will continue to consume Gulf oil originating from the GCC (Gulf Cooperation Council) countries as well as Iran and Iraq, a point that concurs with the producers' strategy of securing long-term and stable oil market for their energy exports.

The other significant aspect of Gulf-Asia energy commerce is the expanded business opportunities for the Gulf nations in China and India. A reciprocal relationship is gradually developing. China's export oriented growth strategy has presented Gulf business community to travel to China for cheap goods. There are increasing Gulf investments in China's downstream and refining sectors.[13] Gulf businesses have also been exploring collaboration with India in the fields of information technology and education with some urgency. India has set up University of Pune's branch campus in the United Arab Emirates (UAE) and Qatar, which is expected to help boost the higher education sector in these countries, and ultimately the economy, by training competent and highly skilled individuals.[14] The relationship of reciprocity developed through mutually beneficial bilateral ties with the Gulf's oil and gas producers, links the region intimately with the two Asian giants.

CHINA AND THE GULF

China's rapid economic growth propels energy demand, while the Gulf producers need stable energy market to earn consistent revenue through energy sales. Thus, energy cooperation is at the core of the Sino-Gulf relationship, which has also spurred cooperation in other economic areas. Ever since China and the GCC (Gulf Cooperation Council) countries signed the Framework Agreement on Economic Trade, Investment and Technology Cooperation and launched their negotiations on the China-GCC Free Trade Area in 2004, their economic ties have developed quickly in the fields of trade, investments, and project contracting. The

GCC has become China's eighth largest trading partner, which is also an emerging market that Beijing wants to explore.[15]

The GCC

China and the GCC countries are diversifying their bilateral relations beyond hydrocarbons, heralding a 'New Silk Road' with economic and possible political dimensions. The Gulf and China have an ancient economic relationship. The two were once trade partners via the Silk Road of yore. Today, the rise of Chinese economy is an accelerant for the Arab world. Its demand for oil has helped fuel the Gulf economies. In return, China's factories churn out consumer goods for these countries. Events after September 2001 have also helped to strengthen ties between China and the GCC. The Arab world's relations with America and Europe are increasingly strained and the rise of China presents an alternative strategic partner. The New Silk Road concept is a new path to enhanced bilateral trade between the two areas.[16] Charles Freeman, a former US ambassador to Saudi Arabia has commented:

> The Arabs see a partner who will buy their oil without demanding that they accept a foreign ideology, abandon their way of life or make other choices they would rather avoid. They see (in China) a country that is far away and has no imperial agenda in their region, but which is internationally influential and likely in time to be militarily powerful.[17]

China's economic ties with the Gulf have continued to grow significantly despite the global financial crisis of 2008. This bourgeoning trade could develop much faster if China concludes a free-trade agreement with the GCC states. Negotiations since 2004 have revolved around forging an agreement that would facilitate a greater flow of Chinese manufactured goods and industrial equipment to the Gulf, while lowering the cost of exporting oil and other goods to China.[18] The coming together of the two most dynamic economies, those of Gulf countries and China, could create a colossal new commercial bloc, with the potential to reshape global trade and commerce.

Kingdom of Saudi Arabia

After Iran, Saudi Arabia is the second largest oil exporter to China. China signed a major deal in 2004 to explore for oil in Rub-al-Khali (Empty Quarter) region of Saudi Arabia. The Sino-Saudi relationship has been transformed by regular high level visits in recent years. During King Abdullah's 2006 visit to China, the two countries signed an agreement on energy cooperation that called for increasing joint investment in oil and natural gas fields. China wants Saudi Arabia to open up its huge oil and gas resources to more Chinese investment. This process is already under way and was boosted by Prime Minister Wen Jiabao's Gulf tour in January 2012.[19] A number of potentially significant deals were concluded during the visit including a civil nuclear pact with Saudi Arabia for help with the Kingdom's plan for a $100 billion programme for 16 nuclear reactors by 2030.

There is a growing industrial collaboration between the Kingdom and China. In 2007, Saudi Aramco and Sinopec, and the US ExxonMobil concluded an agreement to fund a petrochemical complex and refinery in Fujian province to use Saudi heavy crude. There are now proposals for a second refinery. Yanbu on the Red Sea is to be operational by 2014. This complex, which is already under construction, will be one of the largest of its kind ever built covering a 5.2 million square metre area and designed to process 400,000 b/d of heavy crude oil. Aramco is a 62.5 percent partner in the venture with Sinopec holding 37.5 per cent of the business.

Naser Tamimi summarises the extent of trade between China and the Gulf:

> The growth in Sino-Gulf trade is the result of Beijing's soaring demand for oil and the Gulf countries' hunger for low-cost goods. The bilateral trade between China and Saudi Arabia clearly favours the latter. The value of Saudi exports into China exceeded its imports by more than US$36 billion in 2012. The bulk of Saudi exports to China comprise crude oil. China is the second largest destination (after Japan) for Saudi Arabia's exports. China also is largest supplier of goods and services to the Kingdom. While Saudi Arabia is the largest oil supplier to China, followed by Angola and Iran. Saudi Arabia became China's eighth biggest source of imports in 2012, supplying goods and services worth of almost $55 billion. The kingdom's exports to China include a growing segment of non-oil products, such as chemicals used to make plastic products. Cheap consumer goods including electronics, textile and food account for most Saudi Arabia imports from China. Furthermore, increasing participation by Chinese contractors in Saudi Arabia's construction, communication, oil, gas, and petrochemical sectors is already becoming more evident.[20]

UAE

China-UAE trade has soared by an average 35 percent every year during the past decade, surpassing $35 billion in 2012, according to the Dubai

Chamber of Commerce and Industry. It now represents 10 percent of total trade excluding oil. In 2011, Dubai's non-oil trade with China was valued at $27.2 billion.[21] China's main exports to the UAE are textile products, clothes, light industrial products, products made of the five metals (gold, silver, copper, iron and tin), handicrafts and machinery, etc. China mainly imports from the UAE aluminium ingot, chemical fertilizer, petroleum and polythene. In recent years, the labour service cooperation between the two countries is developing from service contract towards project subcontract and general contract. The fields of bilateral cooperation include construction, factories, shops, medical care centres, and sailors. In 1985, China and the UAE had signed an agreement on economic, trade, and technological cooperation, whereby a Joint Commission was established. The agreement on the Protection of Investment and the agreement on avoidance of double taxation were signed between the two countries in 1993. The UAE and China have succeeded in building stronger bilateral ties, in which trade, tourism, construction and financial services are the main sectors of mutual benefit.[22]

As of 2013, around 2,411 Chinese companies were affiliated with the Dubai Chamber, up 18 percent in only two years. The majority are in building materials, electrical, machinery, garments, gifts and novelty items. A further 1,400 are based elsewhere in the UAE. There has also been an increase in the number of Chinese firms using the emirate's onshore financial hub, Dubai International Financial Centre, as a platform to access markets in region. Large Chinese companies such as the Industrial and Commercial Bank of China and oil giant Petro China have set up there.[23]

Qatar

In 2007, bilateral trade volume between China and Qatar reached $1.21 billion, up 21 percent year-on-year, of which Chinese imports total $590 million and exports $620 million, according to the statistics of China's Ministry of Commerce. China and Qatar have strengthened cooperation in the energy sector. In March 2008, Qatar signed a memorandum promoting bilateral energy cooperation with China. China-Qatar trade reached $5 billion in 2011 boosted by sales of liquefied natural gas. Around two million tonnes of LNG a year is being sold which could rise to five million tonnes.[24]

The Chinese and Qatari economies are highly complementary. The majority of Chinese exports to Qatar include mechanical and electrical products, textiles, and high-tech products, which meet the needs of the

Gulf country, which is rich in energy resources but has a limited manufacturing industry. China and Qatar also have increasingly close cooperation in engineering projects and the labour service sector. During the first quarter of 2008, Chinese companies signed contracts worth nearly $2 billion with Qatar for undertaking engineering projects and providing labour services, according to the Economic and Commercial Counsellor's Office of the Chinese Embassy in Qatar. Investment between the two countries surged in recent years as well. In 2007, the Chinese direct investment in Qatar reached $15.48 million. At the same time, Qatari investors are increasingly turning to the Chinese market for investment opportunities, especially in the fields of finance, real estate and petrochemicals.[25]

Iran

Beijing has concluded several oil and gas contracts with Iran, making it the largest Gulf oil supplier to China and accounting for 14 percent of China's total oil imports. In 2004, Sinopec signed a $100 billion deal to buy 10 million metric tons of LNG from Iran annually over a 25 year period and secured a 51 percent stake in the giant Yadavaran oilfield in Iran's south, leaving a minority 20 percent stake for a consortium of Indian oil companies led by OVL (ONGC Videsh Limited). Another Chinese company, CNOOC (China National Offshore Oil Corporation), signed a MoU in 2006 to develop Iran's massive North Pars natural gas field. Under the $16 billion deal, CNOOC would cooperate with the National Iranian Oil Company to develop and liquefy the field's estimated 80 trillion cubic feet of natural gas. In the same year, another Chinese firm, PetroChina, inked a deal to annually import some three million tons of LNG from Iran over a quarter of a century. PetroChina's parent company, CNPC, followed suit, finalizing a $3.6 billion project to explore and exploit Iran's South Pars gas field. Geopolitically, China is keen to establish a naval presence in the Persian Gulf, through which 40 percent of global energy is transported.

China has emerged as Iran's top trading partner in the non-oil sector too. Iran's total non-oil exports to China have risen to $37 billion that accounts for 23 percent of Iran's non-oil exports. Iran's top exports to China included iron ore, petroleum products, marble, oil and mineral seals and purified copper. Iran mainly imports railroad and subway locomotives parts, oil and gas pipelines, LCD and LED modules, automobile parts, polystyrene, and cars. This accounts for 20 percent of China's exports to Iran.[26]

Iraq

China had been making its presence quietly felt in Iraq. Ten years after the American invasion, Iraq has emerged as China's important oil and trade partner. According to the UN Comtrade data, the volume of bilateral trade between China and Iraq shot up to $17.5 billion by end 2012 from small amount of $517 million in 2002. In 2012, China was the second largest purchaser of Iraqi exports, $12.6 billion, (after the US $19.6 billion) and the second-largest supplier of imports, $4.9 billion, (after Turkey $10.8 billion). In August 2008, China surprised Western and Asian oil majors by winning the first Iraqi oil service contract since the US invasion in 2003, a deal worth $3 billion. Iraq and China's CNPC renegotiated terms of an old Saddam Hussein-era deal signed in 1997 to pump oil from the Al-Ahdhab oilfield, whereby CNPC would own 75 percent of a joint venture while Iraq's Northern Oil Company would own 25 percent. In December 2009, CNPC was awarded a 50 percent stake in the development of the Halfaya oilfield located southern Iraq. CNPC currently holds a 37.5 percent stake in the Halfaya field, a 75 percent stake in the al-Ahdab field and a 37 percent stake in the Rumaila field. Beijing and Baghdad recently consolidated their trade ties with the two countries signing a cooperation deal on economic and technology and an exchange of notes on personnel training; during the Iraqi Prime Minister Nuri Al-Maliki's visit to China in July 2011.[27] "The success of Beijing's energy diplomacy in the Gulf is evidence that China today has better relations with the three largest energy suppliers- Iran, Saudi Arabia and Iraq-than does the United States (or any other major power), says Mohan Mailk.[28]

INDIA AND THE GULF

The Gulf countries wanting to decrease their dependency on the western bloc nations look towards India as an economic and strategic partner. More so, as India has never sought to dominate or forcefully intervene in the local politics of the Gulf nations. Omar Mohamed explains:

> The growing insecurity in the area surrounding India, the Gulf, Arabian and Indian oceans requires a much higher level of cooperation on important issues such as piracy, terrorism, maritime terrorism and safety of supply lines. Both the Gulf states and India need to work together; the Gulf states would be interested in an Indian presence that emphasizes stability, economic and military cooperation.[29]

The GCC

The bilateral trade between India and the GCC increased by 8 percent in 2012–13 when compared to previous year over $159 billion. While Imports of GCC from India increased by 13 percent in 2012–13 when compared to previous year to $51 billion, exports have gone up by six percent during the same time period when compared to previous year to $ 8 billion.[30] Trade intensity between the regions has also risen led by numerous bilateral trade agreements signed in the recent past. Although the trade relationship between India and the GCC remains largely concentrated around oil, other tradable items are also slowly gaining importance due to the latter's diversification drive.

Cumulative investments from the GCC in India totalled just $2.6 billion over 2001–11, despite a sharp rise in investments lately. The power, services and construction sectors continue to account for the largest share of FDI inflows from the GCC to India. On the other hand, information from individual investment agencies of GCC countries suggests that India is one of the major sources of FDI in the region. Software development and engineering services, tourism, readymade garments, chemical products, agricultural and allied services continue to generate majority of the interest from Indian corporates.[31] India and GCC have identified sectors like oil and gas, fertilizers and information technology as key areas of cooperation. In the financial year that ended in March 2013, remittances from the GCC to India rose to $24.93 billion from $16.43 billion in 2011.[32]

Kingdom of Saudi Arabia

Saudi Arabia is the world's largest oil exporter, whereas India has become the world's fourth-largest oil consumer (after US, China and Japan). Riyadh and New Delhi have trade agreements and joint ventures in energy, information technology, telecommunications, pharmaceuticals, health services, biotechnology, agriculture, infrastructure projects, financial services and educational/training opportunities. In 2012, Saudi Arabia was the fourth largest trading partner (excluding the EU) of India and the bilateral trade between the two countries reached almost $36 billion in 2012. For Saudi Arabia, India is the fifth largest market for its exports, accounting for nearly 6.3 percent of its global exports. In terms of imports by Saudi Arabia, India ranks sixth and is the source of around 8.2 percent of Saudi Arabia's total imports.[33]

The import of crude oil by India forms a major component of bilateral trade with Saudi Arabia being India's largest supplier of crude oil, accounting for almost one-fifth of its needs. Apart from seeking enhanced energy supplies to India, Saudi and Indian companies are seeking major reciprocal investment opportunities. According to Saudi Arabian General Investment Authority (SAGIA), it has issued 426 licenses to Indian companies for joint ventures/100 percent owned entities till 2010, which are expected to bring total investment of $1624.60 million in Saudi Arabia. These licenses are for projects in diverse sectors such as management and consultancy services, construction projects, tele-communications, information technology, pharmaceuticals, etc. Moreover, several Indian companies have established collaborations with Saudi companies and are working in the Kingdom in the areas of designing, consultancy, financial services and software development. On the other hand, Saudi Arabia was the 46th biggest investor in India with investments from April 2000 to June 2012 amounting to $33.81 million.[34] Saudi companies are in search of "professionals as well as experienced talent and to develop technology, applications and solutions to meet the needs of an increasingly sophisticated business environment and also address sustainability related issues."[35]

UAE

Economic and commercial cooperation is a key aspect of overall bilateral relationship between India and the UAE. The UAE is India's largest trading partner and rising trade between UAE suggests that their business relations are getting more robust. Bilateral trade between the two countries stood at $75 billion in fiscal 2012–13, up from $67 billion during 2010–2011. For UAE, too, India is the largest trading partner. The UAE's exports to India totalled $39 billion, while imports amounted to $36 billion. UAE was the fifth largest import source of crude oil for India in 2011–12 with import of 15.79 MMT of crude oil.[36]

The UAE is a significant investor in India. The country was the 10th largest investor in India in terms of FDIs during 2000–12. Cumulative FDI equity inflows from the UAE to India during the period amounted to $2.36 billion. UAE's investments in India are concentrated mainly in five sectors: Energy (19.1%); Services (9.3%); Programming (7.8%); Construction (6.8%); and, Tourism and Hotels (5.6%). Several prominent private and public sector Indian companies and banks are also operating in the UAE. Following the emergence of UAE as a major re-export centre, Indian companies have emerged as important investors in the free trade zones. A UAE-India High Level Task Force was formed in 2012 to look at new opportunities for investment between the two countries. The two countries have signed numerous agreements and

MoUs, including the Civil Aviation Agreement (1989 and 2014), Double-Taxation Avoidance Agreement (1992); MoU on Defence Cooperation (2003); Bilateral Investment Promotion and Protection Agreement, or BIPPA (2013); and a MoU on Cooperation in the Field of Renewable Energy (2014), among others.[37]

Qatar

There is a large and expanding market for Qatar's LNG, oil and petrochemical sectors in India. Bilateral trade between the two countries has been steadily growing and exceeded $16.30 billion in 2012–13.[38] "With the IPI natural gas pipeline project a casualty of US opposition and persistent mistrust between New Delhi and Islamabad, India has increasingly turned to Qatar to meet its growing natural gas requirements over the past decade. Holding the world's third-largest gas reserves after Russia and Iran, Qatar is a natural choice for such a role," opines an analyst.[39] Qatar has made significant progress in the development of its natural gas reserves in the North Dome Field. India is a large and expanding market for export of LNG from Qatar and the geographical proximity of the two countries virtually ensures mutually beneficial interaction in a long-term perspective. In addition, there are enormous opportunities for expanding bilateral trade and other economic linkages, considering the geographical proximity and historical ties between the peoples of both the countries.[40]

With annual imports of 7.5 million tonnes, India is one of the biggest buyers of Qatari gas. India imported 5.6 million tonnes of crude oil from Qatar in 2010–11 and has been asking the Gulf country to increase gas supply by at least 3 million tonnes a year. Qatari authorities are also focused on exploring investment opportunities in India. India and Qatar have agreed to increase cooperation in the areas of education, legal affairs, banking, culture and tourism.[41]

Iran

India and Iran have been working towards managing their energy and economic cooperation under the shadow of the US and European Union (EU) sanction against the latter's controversial nuclear programme. Despite the tightening of sanctions, India cannot halt the import of crude oil from Iran given that it still imports a critical six percent of Iranian oil. Iran was India's second largest supplier of oil until 2012, furnishing between 350,000 and 400,000 barrels a day or around 16 percent of India's oil needs. India was also Iran's third-largest customer after China and Japan, importing 13 percent of overall Iranian oil exports. The complex regime of sanctions targeting Iranian oil exports put major restrictions on financial transactions, crude oil insurance and transportation. That has had the effect of drastically reducing India's import of Iranian oil. India's crude oil import from Iran dropped to around 200,000 barrels a day in 2013—a drop of between 33 percent and 50 percent. India, however, increased its imports of Iranian oil in the wake of the November 2013 Geneva interim nuclear deal, which led to easing of sanctions on the Islamic Republic. In January 2014, Iranian oil exports to India reached 412,000 barrels a day, a rise from 189,000 in December 2013.[42]

India does not import any natural gas from Iran, but there have been discussions in the past about a long-term supply contract, as well as an Iran-Pakistan-India (IPI) pipeline. Yet, the prospects of Indo-Iranian natural gas trade have never reached anything substantial. Sitting on the second-largest proven natural gas reserves in the world, Iran has made many efforts to sign a deal with India. Tehran's LNG export plans to India were unsuccessful due to international sanctions and strong international pressures on the other (mainly from the United States), prevented Iran and India from reaching an agreement over natural gas trade.[43] India is also trying to expand trade in other commodities like tea, pharmaceuticals, automobile, electronics, spare parts and agricultural products. India has already approved $364 million (20 billion rupees) fund to provide reinsurance to local refineries that process Iranian crude oil.[44]

Iraq

Iraq is the second largest supplier of crude oil to India after Saudi Arabia, and ahead of Iran. Indian Oil Company (IOC) is the single largest purchaser of oil procuring around 250,000 barrels per day (bpd). In 2012, India is estimated to have imported crude oil worth more than $20 billion. The bilateral trade relations between India and Iraq slowed down after the US invasion of Iraq in March 2003. The two-way trade has been growing actively in recent times. In addition to importing crude oil in bulk, India also imports small quantities of commodities like raw wool and sulphur from Iraq. India's imports from Iraq accounted for $19247.31 million in 2013. Indian exports to Iraq in 2013 were estimated to be $1278.13 million. These exports mainly consist of agro chemicals, cosmetics, rubber manufactured products, paints, gems and jewellery, ceramics, manufactures of metals, machine tools, electrical machinery and instruments, transport equipment, electronic goods, handicrafts, cereals, sugar, tea, garments and pharmaceuticals.[45]

CHINA AND INDIA: COOPERATION ON CONFLICT?

Many analysts believe that China and India are bound to cooperate by virtue of their similarity in historical experience and developmental needs. For this reason, the portmanteau, 'Chindia,' has become popular in international diplomatic lexicon. The two countries have followed similar paths to economic development and have faced similar obstacles to that end. China and India are also perceived internationally as nation-states that might have the greatest impact on future world events. Evidently, the oil-rich countries of the Gulf consider China and India as most significant markets for their energy resources. The demands from the two Asian giants are imperative for global energy security as such, spurring vital investments needed to increase production. They are also seen as important sources of good and services. Afshin Molavi writes:

> If we look at "Chindia" as a single energy entity, we see a powerful energy consumer. Chindia's oil consumption and oil imports rank it second in the world, after the United States. Its natural gas consumption ranks it third, after the United States and Russia. Clearly, every major oil producer is fashioning a China and India strategy for the future.[46]

After decades of diplomatic passiveness between China, India and the Gulf, a new phase began in the 1980s. A change in the leaderships of both the countries and their market liberalisation efforts, led China and India to embark upon a path of massive economic development, forcing the two Asian giants to develop near identical interests in the region of the Gulf. At present India and China are interested in the Gulf as a source of oil and an oil services market. Indian and Chinese elites and businesses are keen on pursuing opportunities in investment, sale of consumer goods and tourism. Both Beijing and New Delhi are eager to enhance its ties with Saudi Arabia to improve its standing amongst its Muslim population and the Muslim world. China and India have also sought to utilise Iran and the GCC states support respectively in order to boost its power base on the international stage.[47]

Both China and India have pursued a policy of detachment from political issues in the region. Nima Assl points out that "both Beijing and New Delhi seem to have adopted a similar policy towards this region, based on the principles of neutrality and non-intervention. As such, they both have used soft power/trade diplomacy to expand ties with all the states— regardless of their domestic politics and/or their historical/sectarian rivalries with one another."[48] Therefore, the Gulf nations are more receptive to the increasing presence and involvement of China and India in their region. Having complementary interests, the Gulf states are increasingly courting the two Asian economic powerhouses. Nonetheless, China's presence in the Gulf has worried Indian policymakers of creeping Chinese influence in the region. India is keen to prevent China from becoming a major naval power in the Indian Ocean for fear of strategic encirclement and this rivalry could extend to the Gulf, where Indian influence has been an accepted fact for centuries.

That the Gulf is keeping the two Asian giants equally well supplied is having a positive impact on their ties. With security of energy assured and having little political interest in the Gulf region, energy cooperation between India and China seems to be more likely. In West Asia, where most of Chinese and Indian energy imports come from, cooperation materialized at least on two occasions. First, in Syria, a joint venture company was set up by India's OVL and China's CNPC in February 2006. In the same month, ONGC and Sinopec concluded a joint energy deal with Iran. The West Asian cooperation experience shows that cooperation is more likely to occur in places that do not constitute a part of China's geopolitical influence.

The fact that China and India have equal access to Gulf energy by virtue of long-term contracts—which mitigates their competition in this vital region—it would still not be easy for them to abandon competing strategies. The contours of their energy demand will alternate between competition and cooperation in the foreseeable future, even as both countries will make efforts to expand trade and economic ties with each other. From the discussion above it is evident that cooperation and conflict will depend upon the 'region' variable. Competition will prevail in South, Southeast and Central Asia—strategic neighbourhoods for both countries—whereas distant energy theatres will witness more cooperative arrangements. China's naval strategy in the Indian Ocean to secure energy will be an important factor in the development of conflicting or cooperative scenario between the two Asian powers. On the other hand, India's inability to resolve problems with its neighbours will see a more aggressive Chinese strategy of building ties with them, in order to limit India's ability to procure energy from proximate quarters. Moreover, if China perceives Indo-American relations as an alliance against itself, Beijing will be more inclined to follow policies aimed at restricting India's rise contingent upon developmental goals.

SOME CONCLUDING REMARKS

Growing energy intake and regional competition for increasingly scarce energy sources has the potential to transform resource competition between the two powers in Asia from its current restricted forms into open confrontation. In its pursuit of energy security, India is constantly dogged by the 'China factor'. India and China are openly competing in an energy strategy that calls for diversifying sources of supply. Chinese oil companies, led by the CNPC, have executed more than 200 oil and gas transactions in equity stakes across the globe, with a total reported value of more than $135 billion, over the period from 2006 to 2011. In comparison, OVL's cumulative investment as in 2011 is a modest $ 14.35 billion. Although China and India have joint stakes in producing fields in Syria and Sudan as well as OVL-CNPC joint gas pipeline project in Myanmar; this has not prevented them from direct competition over energy deals. In Central Asia fierce energy competition was illustrated in 2005, when China outbid India to acquire PetroKazakhstan—Kazakhstan's third-largest oil producer—with CNPC raising its bid to $4.18-billion.

The energy tussle between India and China is very visible as both look towards South Asia (Sri Lanka and Bangladesh) and South-East Asia (Vietnam) for oil and gas. OVL's oil and gas exploration activities in the South China Sea, off the coast of Vietnam, have evoked strong criticism from China, which claims that Indian operations in the region are a violation of China's sovereignty. Nonetheless, India has vociferously displayed its intent of staying on. Such incidents show that as far as energy is concerned, Sino-Indian relations will continue to be competitive.

Indo-Chinese rivalry is expected to continue in the 2020, as both India and China rush to meet their developmental goals. However, as China becomes a settled economic power with greater success on developmental indicators (poverty alleviation etc.), it would want to engage in more of cooperative arrangements with other Asian powers than come into conflict with them and fritter the gains of development. This could impel the formation of joint development zones in the disputed maritime areas with energy resources, such as the South China Sea. Currently, South China Sea is mired in dispute between China, Japan, Vietnam, South Korea and India.

A critical factor in the evolution of energy cooperation among the Asian powers in the long-term (2040 scenario) would be role of the United States. As the US has interdependent economic relations with several states in the region, it remains a significant regional player. If the US policymakers focus on keeping a regional presence and avoiding confrontation with China by increasing military-to-military contacts, a secure environment would emerge, benefitting all the players in the area. The US and China in a display of bold leadership could promote collaboration on new supplies and ensure openness on the sea-lanes of energy transport. India has the most to gain from the evolution of cooperative institutional framework in the energy sector, as it lags behind all major regional countries in terms of growth indicators. It can ill afford a conflict with China and risk disruption in energy supply.

The long-term prospect of India-China cooperation is greater than in the short-term. It is highly unlikely that India would become openly hostile to China. China is India's largest trading partner in terms of merchandise and India cannot afford losing the Chinese market. China is militarily stronger than India and India being risk averse, will not want an all-out resource war with China. In the end, the fact remains that China is far ahead of India in energy deals with different countries across the globe. Therefore, it is more in India's interest to collaborate in the energy arena than that of China.

REFERENCES

1. "International Energy Outlook," *US Energy information Administration* (EIA), September 2011, http://pbadupws.nrc.gov/docs/ML1220/ML12205A382.pdf, p. 10.
2. Today in Energy," *EIA*, August 9, 2013, http://www.eia.gov/todayinenergy/detail.cfm?id=12471.
3. "China," *EIA*, February 4, 2014, http://www.eia.gov/countries/cab.cfm?fips=CH.
4. Richa Mishra, "Between a Rock and a Hard Place," *The Hindu Business Line*, November 10, 2013, http://www.thehindubusinessline.com/industry-and-economy/between-a-rock-and-a-hard-place/article5335576.ece.
5. "India," *EIA*, June 26, 2014, http://www.eia.gov/countries/cab.cfm?fips=in.
6. "Strait of Hormuz is chokepoint for 20% of world's oil," *EIA*, September 5, 2012, http://www.eia.gov/todayinenergy/detail.cfm?id=7830.
7. Christophe Jaffrelot, "A Tale of Two Ports," January 7, 2011, *YaleGlobal Online*, http://yaleglobal.yale.edu/content/tale-two-ports.
8. See Zhao Hong, "China and India's Competitive Relations with Myanmar," Institute of China Studies (ICS) University of Malaya, *ICS Working Paper No. 2008–7*, http://ics.um.edu.my/images/ics/workingpaper/2008-7.pdf; "Chinese Pipeline Program Raises Indian Eyes," *Pipeline and Gas Journal*, Vol. 236, No. 8, August 2009, http://www.pipelineandgasjournal.com/chinese-pipeline-program-raises-indian-eyes.
9. "Rogozin says Russia-India oil pipeline project is possible," *Russian New Agency*, February 26, 2014, http://itar-tass.com/en/economy/721066; John Daly, "Russia, India Planning $30 Billion Oil Pipeline through Xinjiang, *OilPrice.com*, 23 April 2014, http://oilprice.com/Energy/Energy-General/Russia-India-Planning-30-Billion-Oil-Pipeline-Through-Xinjiang.html.

10. See "SCO membership to help India get foothold in energy-rich CAsia," *Business Standard*, September 21, 2014, http://www.business-standard.com/article/pti-stories/sco-membership-to-help-india-get-foothold-in-energy-rich-casia-114092100458_1.html; Waheed Rahimi, "India's entry into SCO to affect the regional security," *Khaama Press*, September 30, 2014, http://www.khaama.com/indias-entry-into-sco-to-affect-the-regional-security-8748;

11. Bo Kong, *China's International Petroleum Policy*, (Santa Barbara, California: Praeger Security International, 2010). pp. 133–135; Michael Chambers, "Rising China: The Search for Power and Plenty," in Ashley J. Tellis, Michael Wills (eds.), *Trade, Interdependence, and Security* (Seattle, Washington: National Bureau of Asian Research, 2006), p. 89.

12. Keun-Wook Paik, Valerie Marcel, Glada Lahn, John V. Mitchell and Erkin Adylov, "Trends in Asian Noc Investment Abroad," Chatham House, *Working Background Paper*, March 2007.

13. See Robert Bailey, "China and GCC: Growing Ties," *Gulf Business*, April 16, 2013, http://gulfbusiness.com/2013/04/china-and-gcc-growing-ties/#.VJX CincgQ.

14. See Samir Pradhan, "India's Economic and Political Presence in the Gulf: A Gulf Perspective," in *India's Growing Role in the Gulf: Implications for the Region and the United States* (Gulf Research Center Dubai, United Arab Emirates, 2009), p. 21; *The Observatory on Borderless Higher Education*, March 2009, pp. 1–3.

15. "GCC-China FTA talks on fast track," *China FTA Network*, May 11, 2005, http://fta.mofcom.gov.cn/enarticle/engcc/engccnews/200911/1636_1.html; Mahmoud Ghafouri, "China's Policy in the Persian Gulf," *Middle East Policy Council*, Vol. XVI, No. 2 (Summer 2009), http://www.mepc.org/journal/middle-east-policy-archives/chinas-policy-persian-gulf?print.

16. Lee Hudson Teslik, "China-Gulf Economic Relations," Council on Foreign Relations, June 4, 2008, http://www.cfr.org/china/china-gulf-economic-relations/p16398; Stephen Glain, "The Modern Silk Road," *Newsweek*, May 17, 2008, http://www.newsweek.com/modern-silk-road-90283.

17. Quoted in Bailey, "China And GCC: Growing Ties," *Gulf Business*, April 16, 2013.

18. Ibid.

19. Andrew White, "Year of the Dragon for Gulf oil and gas producers," *International Bar Association*, http://www.ibanet.org/Article/Detail.aspx?ArticleUid=c4584 834-e2f2-431e-baa1-58d7f627aec7.

20. Naser Al-Tamimi, "China-Saudi Relations: Booming Trade", *Al Arabiya News*, February 22, 2013, http://english.alarabiya.net/views/2013/02/22/267670.html.

21. Courtney Trenwith, "China-UAE trade: Enter the dragon," *Arabian Bussiness.com*, March 10, 2013, http://www.arabianbusiness.com/china-uae-trade-enter-dragon-492242.html.

22. "China and the United Arab Emirates", *Embassy of the People's Republic of China in the United Arab Emirates,* n.d., http://ae.china-embassy.org/eng/sbgx/t150466.htm.

23. Trenwith, "China-UAE trade: Enter the dragon", *Arabian Bussiness.com,* March 10, 2013.

24. "China-Qatar cooperation benefits both countries," *Embassy of People's Republic of China in the Republic of Liberia,* n.d., http://lr.china-embassy.org/eng/majorevents/t468200.htm; Bailey, "China and GCC: Growing Ties," *Gulf Business,* April 16, 2013.

25. "China-Qatar cooperation benefits both countries," *Embassy of People's Republic of China in the Republic of Liberia.*

26. Adam Kredo, "China Becomes Iran's Largest Trade Partner," *The Washington Free Beacon,* February 25, 2014, http://freebeacon.com/national-security/china-becomes-irans-largest-trade-partner/; Blake Hounshell, "China is now Iran's top trading partner," *Foreign Policy,* February 9, 2010, http://foreignpolicy.com/2010/02/09/china-is-now-irans-top-trading-partner/.

27. Naser Al-Tamimi, "China in Iraq: winning without a war", *Al Arabiya News,* March 16, 2013, http://english.alarabiya.net/en/views/2013/03/16/China-in-Iraq-Winning-Without-a-War.html.

28. Mohan Mailk, "The Indo-Pacific Maritime Domain: Challenges and Opportunities," in Mohan Malik (ed.), *Maritime security in the Indo-Pacific: perspectives from China, India, and the United States* (Lanham: Rowman & Littlefield, 2014), p. 16.

29. Omar Mahmood Mohamed, "India-GCC ties can boost regional stability," *Gulfnews.com,* June 6, 2014, http://gulfnews.com/opinions/columnists/india-gcc-ties-can-boost-regional-stability-1.1343841.

30. "IT, petrochemicals, healthcare to spur India-GCC trade," *Economic Times,* April 8, 2014, http://articles.economictimes.indiatimes.com/2014-04-08/news/48971111_1_gcc-countries-india-gcc-indian-healthcare.

31. "Trade and Capital Flows-GCC and India," *Alpen Capital Investment Banking,* May 2, 2012, p. 18.

32. "IT, petrochemicals, healthcare to spur India-GCC trade," *Economic Times,* April 8, 2014.

33. "India-Saudi Arabia Relations," *Ministry of External Affairs,* January 2013.

34. Ibid.

35. Naser Al- Tamimi, "Saudi-Indian energy to power the future?" *Al Arabiya News,* February 28, 2014, http://english.alarabiya.net/en/views/news/middle-east/2014/02/28/Saudi-Indian-energy-to-power-the-future-.html.

36. India-UAE Relations, *Ministry of External Affairs,* August 2012; Shailesh Dash, "UAE, India share strong friendship and trade ties," *Khaleej Times,* June 24, 2014, http://www.khaleejtimes.com/biz/inside.asp?xfile=/data/ opinion analysis/2014/June/opinionanalysis_June41.xml&section=opinionanalysis.

37. Shailesh Dash, "UAE, India share strong friendship and trade ties," *Khaleej Times,* June 24, 2014; UAE-India Relations: Economy and Trade, n.d.,

http://www.uaeembassy-newdelhi.com/uae-indiarelations_economic&trade. asp; "Brief on Trade between India and Dubai & Northern Emirates," *Consulate General of India, Dubai*, n.d., http://www.cgidubai.com/category/india-uae-trade/india-dubai-trade.

38. "India's bilateral ties with Qatar to blossom further, hopes envoy," *Gulf Times*, January 22, 2014, http://www.gulf-times.com/qatar/178/details/378613/india%E2%80%99s-bilateral-ties-with-qatar-to-blossom-further,-hopes-envoy.

39. Saurav Jha, "India, Qatar Broaden Ties beyond Energy Trade," *World Politics Review*, April 27, 2012, http://www.worldpoliticsreview.com/articles/11896/india-qatar-broaden-ties-beyond-energy-trade.

40. "India-Qatar Bilateral Economic Relations," *Indian Embassy*, Qatar, n.d., http://www.indianembassy.gov.qa/imagesOld/ec2.html.

41. Gyanendra Kumar Keshri, "India, Qatar deepen energy ties, seek to promote investments," *Indo-Asian News Service*, April 13, 2012, http://news.yahoo.com/india-qatar-deepen-energy-ties-seek-promote-investments-112827460.html.

42. Sara Vakshouri, "India-Iran energy ties may take off," *Almonitor*, March 5, 2014, http://www.al-monitor.com/pulse/originals/2014/03/india-iran-energy-ties-nuclear-accord.html#.

43. Ibid.

44. Meena Singh Roy, "India and Iran Relations: Sustaining the Momentum," *Institute for Defense Studies and Analyses*, May 20, 2013, http://www.idsa.in/issuebrief/India-IranRelations_msroy_200513.

45. "India-Iraq Relations", *Ministry of External Affairs*, November 2013.

46. Afshin Molavi, "The New Silk Road, 'Chindia,' and the Geo-Economic Ties that Bind the Middle East and Asia," in Bryce Wakefield and Susan L. Levenstein (eds.), China and the Persian Gulf: Implications for the United States (Washington D.C.: Woodrow Wilson International Center for Scholars, 2011), p. 48.

47. See Nima Khorrami Assl, "China and India: Rival Middle East strategies," *AlJazeera*, January 10, 2012, http://www.aljazeera.com/indepth/opinion/2012/01/20121811164584439.html.

48. Ibid.

The Politics of Maritime Cooperation in the Straits of Malacca: Implications for Regional Peace and Stability

Vignesh Ram*

INTRODUCTION

The Sea Lines of Communication in the Indian Ocean have been crucial for a number of countries around the world. The Sea Lines of Communication or SLOCS are crucial ocean highways that carry goods and resources across the region, thereby feeding the growing economies of the world. In this complex medley of interdependence, SLOCS have become more of a strategic necessity and a strategic opportunity or threat depending on the country that is looking at it. The main channel of trade passing from the Strait of Hormuz in the Persian Gulf through the nine degree channel and the Malacca Straits has been the crucial passageway in the Indian Ocean Region. The issues that the region confronts range from issues related to natural disasters to piracy and challenges of major power rivalries. Hence the region has always been a key ground for major powers in exercising their capabilities to control the resources.

Since historical times oceans have been the lifelines of a number of states around the world. The discovery of new sea routes to Asia from Europe firmed up the roots of colonial empires which saw a sharp decline in the capabilities of Asian economies barring that of Japan. Hence the centrality of China and India to the revival of trade in the Indian Ocean Region has remained a significant aspect. India has been a geographically key state in the Indian Ocean Region. Bound by resource rich West Asia on its western flank and the crucial East Asian economies in the East, India has a crucial geographic location to control the flow of traffic in its expansive region. Hence as the 21st century takes shape with the revival of Asia as the pivotal region the maritime expanse of the Indian and the Pacific Oceans will be central to major powers exercising their capabilities in the region.

*Doctoral Candidate, Department of Geopolitics and International Relations, Manipal University, Karnataka.

In the current context of growing geopolitical significance, the economically dynamic and geographically central Southeast Asian region will enjoy a key position in the emerging regional power play. The geographically diverse region which is often divided for ease by analysts into Maritime and Mainland is already seeing a renewed emergence of vigorous competition among major states in the region. The renewed reforms in Myanmar have restarted the race for dominance among major powers in the rich resources in the country. Moreover due to the linkages within the region, ASEAN, the main regional organisation has faced a number of challenges in terms of its mainland members to the organisations' sustenance. Hence the, maritime half of relatively developed Southeast Asian states also the founding members of ASEAN have reassessed their strategies towards containing the regional power dynamics.

The major power involvement in the region has often contributed to the notion of countries in the region being unable to handle the security of key geographic areas that are of vital importance to world trade. The SLOCS being one of the key geographical features has been a cause of concern but over the years there has been a move in the region to follow the 'regional solution to regional problems' policy much driven by the power dynamics of regional states.

SLOCS, Geopolitics and Regional Power Play

The Ocean's have been a key part of geopolitical thinking in both the western and eastern civilizations. The biggest and the greatest civilizations have turned to the sea for increasing their power and influence in other regions of the world. The European civilizations were dependent on the highways of trade focused mainly on the land routes consisting of trade with India and China which ran the length of central Asia and Europe, the route carried spices and precious commodities which were of high value in Europe. The Silk Route as it was known was a key trading route that was used in the region.[1] Though land based routes of trade were important, the Sea based routes had existed mainly in the Indian Ocean for a number of years before the first European sailors reached the shores of the Indian Ocean along the East Coast of Africa thereby connecting to the extensive trading networks of the Indian Ocean Region (IOR), Southeast Asia and China.

Powerful naval empires had existed in the region in various parts of the region such as the Martha's and Cholas on the Indian sub-continent who had extensive navies and also the Ming Empire in China and Sri Vijaya Empire in Southeast Asia. These powers had a strong history in using maritime tactics in controlling and deploying naval forces in the region. The testimony of this is the fact that the Maratha Empire once controlled vast expanses of the western coast of India and also tried to thwart the control western navies by controlling the strategic Andaman and Nicobar Islands.[2] Though the Maratha navy had limited control and was considered more of a navy that treaded on local waters there by making it defensive,[3] the Cholas of southern India who had established a vast empire had expanded maritime influence through trade and later conquest through expeditions in Southeast Asia. It has also been indicated that the Cholas had used their influence to control the Malacca Straits to establish a direct trade with the Song dynasty in China.[4] Hence it can be understood that empires of the Indian sub-continent had played a key role in trying to keep the Malacca Straits free from any threat emerging in the region.

The Chinese annals very clearly document the arrival of the Ming dynasty admiral Zheng He to Southeast Asia. According to data gathered the importance of the Malacca straits and curbing piracy in the region was a crucial factor in the advent of Ming voyages in the region. Zheng He's ouster of the famous Cantonese pirate Chen Zuyi in 1407 from the Malacca straits was one of the key acts carried out by an extra regional power in the region.[5] The voyages carried out by the treasure fleets was an important feature in understanding China's conduct of diplomacy and trade in the region and the importance that security and safety of the SLOCS played in this endeavour.

While regionally Chinese and Indian empires played a key role the prominence of colonialism led to preponderance of western maritime thought and strategies. Western powers were tasked with the control of vital waterways to control the spice trade and the resources, key battles were fought to control the maritime approaches that led to the founding of new cities and strategic ports in the region such as Singapore. Shrewd, often cut throat competition among colonial powers led to conflicts. The colonial conquests in Southeast Asia started with the Portuguese conquest of Malacca in 1511. The control of the trade in the straits was still a key feature among colonial powers in the agreements which they carried forward. The Anglo Dutch Treaty for instance signed between the Dutch and the British in 1824 was important as it transferred the possession of the city of Malacca and the Malay Peninsula to the British and with the establishment of Singapore and development of Singapore since 1819 Britain held the sway over the straits and became a predominant power in the region.[6]

The influence of one particular geopolitist has been profound on the thinking of maritime strategy in the West in particular, and the world in general. Alfred Thayer Mahan played a key role in devising early American modern naval thought. Mahan advocated that three major factors were needed by states to achieve dominance; one being, geography (location to the world's sea-lanes), second, bases (necessary for power projection and sustainability) and the third was fleet (a powerful fleet manned with trained crews that would be concentrated in an offensive action to engage the enemy's fleet).[7] Mahan's strategy focused on protecting its increasing trade with Japan and China and led to the establishment of bases in the Caribbean Islands, Hawaii, and the Philippines.[8] Though American focus was primarily in the Pacific, in the last phase of the Second World War, the US became a key nation in the maritime geopolitics of Southeast Asia and later the Indian Ocean Region.

In understanding the key geopolitical implications for major powers, projecting key geopolitical underpinnings are the basis for decisions. Strategic waterways and devising new sea routes have been crucial for holding sway in regions considered geopolitically crucial for trade and commerce and thereby security. The idea of 'choke points' was first proposed by British Admiral John Fisher as a part of restructuring of the Royal British Navy and its forces around "five keys" of the world which would be sufficient to protect British vital interests around the world.[9] While geopoliticians over the years have pondered on the prospect of application, some of the concepts have found applicability especially in conceptualization of great power projections in the region in the current context.

The Geopolitics of the SLOCS has been once again revived as the important systems of world trade are rejuvenated by the rise of China and India and the renewed economic persistence of Japan. The ASEAN economies too have shown promising signs of growth since the end of the Asian Financial Crisis in 1997. The flurry of economic activity in these regions has resulted in the rise of trade and transport through the straits. Reports have suggested that container traffic in the Malacca Straits has increased steadily posting all-time highs of 77,973 transits through the Malacca Strait in 2013 of vessels of 300 gt or more, passing the previous high of 76,381 in 2008. Though container traffic had decreased in 2008 following the world economic slowdown, the report notes that the traffic of Very Large Crude Carriers (VLCC) has seen a steady increase.[10] At the same period juxtaposing the economic growth of countries in the region it can be observed that China's recovery economically helped the rise in traffic in the region.[11]

As the competition between the US, China and other major powers increases in the region the vibrancy of the region and increased focus on the Sea lanes of Communication including the Malacca Straits will heighten leading to cooperative and at times competitive ventures among major powers. The scope for cooperation lies in countering common threats such as piracy, environmental disasters and other crisis mainly emanating from non-state sources. There are also a number of issues among major powers that adds to the trust deficit in the region. The growing military capabilities among major states particularly China has had a key impact on the outlook by other major powers such as the United States and India in the region.

THE ECONOMY OF RESOURCE FLOWS AND TRADE IN THE MALACCA STRAITS

Economies are powered by resources and the geographical position of resources and resource dependent markets in Asia have added to the increasing importance. Over the years major energy demand has been linked to developing countries and their increasing economic sizes. The impacts of new discoveries and natural resources have a scope of shifting the focus of the flow of energy between regions. Hence this also has an impact on the SLOCS and the flow of energy and resources through them. For instance, Figure 1 indicates the world flow of energy from west

Crude oil exports from the Middle East - in 1,000 b/d

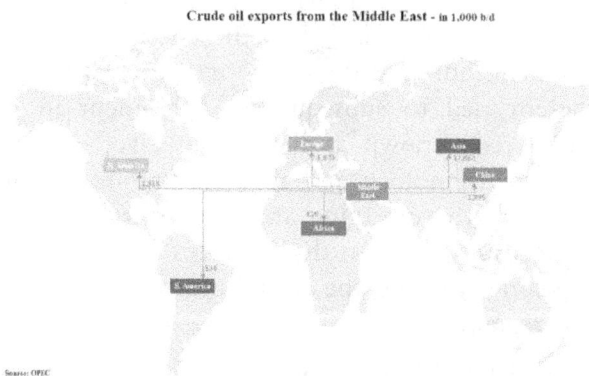

Source: OPEC

Fig. 1: Crude Oil Exports from Middle East/West Asia

Asia.[12] New energy finds have indicated that there may be a drastic shift in the world energy flow.[13] The discovery of new resources such as shale gas especially in North America and other regions such as Russia and China have shown potential to reverse the trend of energy flows in the world. Figure 2 highlights the countries which contribute maximum to China's crude oil imports (China being one of the largest importers in the world).[14]

China's crude oil imports by source, 2013

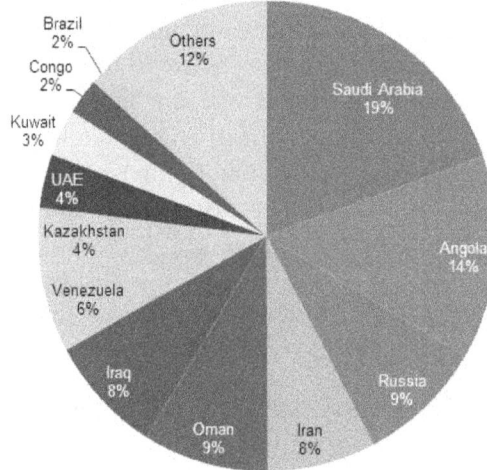

Source: FACTS Global Energy, Global Trade Information Services.

Fig. 2: China's Crude Oil Imports

The flow of resources is dominated by the economic rise of countries in the region. East Asia has dominated the realm of economic development since the end of the Second World War. The economic rise of Japan in the 1970's and the subsequent move by Japanese investment into newer markets such as Southeast Asia led to the coining of the term 'Flying Geese Model' which indicated the development in East Asia initiated by Japan and thereby, led to subsequent development in a number of countries in East Asia known as the 'Asian Tiger' economies due to inflow of Japanese technology and more importantly capital.[15] As the world's focus lay on the emerging and fast growing economies of the region, there was also a focus on the resources acquisitions subsequently leading to question regarding the safety and security of key waterways and ports in the region.

The Asian Financial Crisis was one of the key changes in the region which led to more economic degradation, there by not only reducing trade flow through the straits but also was a contributing factor for an increase of threats to the safety and security of passage of ships through the region. The crisis which occurred in 1997–98 had a deep impact on the increase in piracy in the region owing to the degradation of economic situation. For instance among the straits economies, Indonesia was the strongest hit, while Singapore was able to avert a major catastrophe through monetary intervention and management.[16] The International Maritime Bureau also confirmed that from the year 1992 to 2006 Asia was the most pirate infested region of the world and a major chuck of the attacks were attributed to various regions in Southeast Asia and in particular high numbers were reported in Indonesia and the Malacca straits. Though it is not to undermine the fact that piracy was not present in the region before the crisis struck its significance in the face of global recovery from the crisis and importance to growing powers such as China meant that the interest in tackling piracy was manifold and more urgent.

As indicated in preceding arguments the height of piracy in the Malacca Straits started at the end of the century in 1999–2000 and went to its peak in 2003–2004. According to the International Maritime Bureau the pirate attacks in the straits of Malacca jumped from nearly 2 in 1999 to 75 in 2000 and subsequently remained worrisome with nearly 17 attacks in 2001, 16 attacks in 2002, 28 attacks in 2003 and nearly 27 attacks on 2004.[17] Though the attacks decreased in subsequent years due to various measures undertaken by the three littoral states maritime security also achieved a new dimension of 'maritime terrorism' since 2001. The main concerns were the large crude carriers and the relative narrow points in the waterways could be seen as potential targets. The use of tankers as 'floating bombs' and terrorist attacks such as the bombings in Bali in 2002 were reminders of the vulnerability that Sea lanes in the region faced from terrorism.[18]

The rising security threats had a key impact on the trade and flow of goods and more over confidence of the international community on the safety of the straits and the trade in the region. The repercussions were felt and it was evident under various global indicators that the threats in the region were overshadowing the advantages that it enjoyed. The shipping insurance company Lloyds for instance, declared the Straits of Malacca as a 'war risk' region charging higher insurance premiums for insuring ship transits in the region. This also led to more pressure from extra regional states on the straits countries to step up security in the region. Due to the improved security efforts the regional situation improved vis-a-vis piracy and the 'war risk rating' was dropped in 2006.[19]

There are other factors which are responsible for the security situation in the straits. Most of the Indonesian Archipelago is placed on a geologically sensitive region prone to seismic activity such as earthquakes and volcanic eruptions which have threatened the movement of traffic through the waterways. The yearly haze which emerges mainly from forest fires in Indonesia has also been a key challenge to navigation in the Straits of Malacca. However a number of academics and policy makers have challenged the latest notion which is threatening to make the trade through the Malacca Straits smaller and less relevant. The new sea routes which have been discovered in the world along with the shifting resource bases are a great long term challenge for the countries in the region.

As of now majority of trade bound to and from East Asia uses the conventional SLOC's which pass through the Indian Ocean Region. The new proposed Sea routes which will pass through the Northern reaches of Russia mostly in the Arctic Ocean have been indicated as saving both time and thereby money for transport of goods to major markets in Europe. For instance it has been noted in Figure 3[20] that a trip from Japan's Yokohama port to Rotterdam in the Netherlands will be about one third or nearly 6947 km shorter.

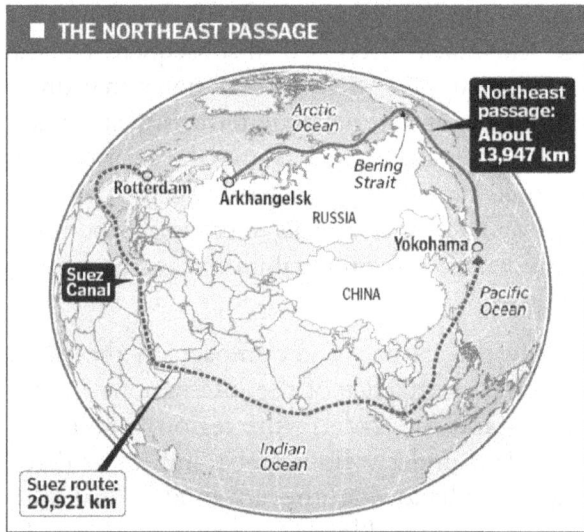

ST GRAPHICS

Fig. 3: The Alternative Route through the Arctic

The alternative sea routes would not be the only challenge that will alter the regional dynamics in the Malacca straits, the shifting energy flow into large economies such as China and their bid to acquire newer forms of energy from other countries and the prospect of lower reserves in the future in traditional areas of the world such as West Asia can also alter the fate of the countries of the straits. For instance, the Singapore economy was entirely built on due to its strategic location along the Malacca Straits there by benefiting from trade. Singapore is not only the second busiest port after Shanghai but it also contributes substantially to the GDP of the country.[21] Hence there is a gradual alteration in the geopolitics of the trade, energy flows in the region but due to the continued growth in East Asia spurred by China's economic growth and increasing demand in ASEAN countries and India, the Straits of Malacca will remain relevant for countries of the region. Therefore, security issues both traditionally causing concern such as major power rivalry and military build up of states and new issues such as cooperating in environmental disasters have put emphasis on regional and extra regional states to play a leading role in safeguarding the waterway.

REGIONAL SECURITY IN THE MALACCA STRAITS AND REGIONAL POLITICAL DYNAMICS

The political equations among the states in Southeast Asia especially Indonesia, Malaysia and Singapore were marred by mutual suspicion and distrust throughout the early part of 1960's. The equations among these key states settled following the end of Sukarno's government in Indonesia in 1965 and the bilateral understanding between Malaysia and Singapore following the later' split from the federation of Malaya in 1965.[22] One of the key regional initiatives was Association of Southeast East Asian Nations (ASEAN) which was formed in 1967. The formation of ASEAN was able to limitedly contain the security threats among member states in the region. Hence understanding the behavioural patterns of the countries of the straits will enable in understanding the reasons for a particular strategy in patrolling the straits. In trying to understand the security outlook in the region it can be said that all three states Singapore, Indonesia and Malaysia have very distinct relations within the ASEAN grouping.

INDONESIA AND REGIONAL POLICY: REGIONAL SOLUTIONS TO REGIONAL PROBLEMS

In terms of the cold war it has been seen that Indonesia has played a key role in projecting a 'regional view' of issues affecting Southeast Asia. Indonesia's stance on balancing interests in the region is very much aligned to its foreign policy outlook of balancing all major power interests in Southeast Asia. Jakarta played a key role in initiating dialogue amongst the countries during the Cambodian crisis. Indonesia's approach in using ASEAN as a base for regional issues was also a result of Indonesia's own ability to manoeuvre among major powers throughout the Cold War, though it showed signs of closeness to the United Sates, Indonesia still maintained a balanced position in the region when it came to extra regional power influence. The trend has continued, sometimes being positive and at times negative for Indonesia's interests in the region. One instance was the Indonesian initiative to use ASEAN as a forum to mediate regional conflict between Cambodia and Thailand over the Preah Vihear temple issue. Moreover, Indonesia has also played a key role in using ASEAN to suppress regional fears over China's overtures in the South China Sea.[23]

In certain cases ASEAN initiated agreements have also seen reluctance by Indonesia. The Trans Boundary Haze agreement and the ASEAN Convention on Counter Terrorism (ACCT) are important examples. The need for Indonesia to sign these agreements as Indonesia remains central to the solutions to these issues. Hence Indonesia's centrality to Southeast Asia and importantly to the security of the Malacca Straits remains very important.

INDONESIA'S STAND ON PATROLLING OF THE MALACCA STRAITS

Indonesia has been one of the countries which have objected to any extra regional presence in patrolling the Malacca Straits. At the height of piracy attacks in 2003–2004, bilateral assistance was offered to Indonesia to tackle the piracy attacks by the Indian Navy but Indonesia declined the offer.[24] Indonesia preferred a more regional approach rather than inviting major powers to contain the issues, mainly piracy in the straits. While for most of the pirate attacks took place in Indonesian waters, Indonesia has been sceptical in allowing foreign navies in Indonesian waters citing reasons of infringement of sovereignty.[25] The issue of sovereignty has been a central aspect for countries in Southeast Asia and especially Indonesia which was one of the countries which pushed for the concept of archipelagic state to be included in the UNCLOS. Hence, archipelagic sea doctrine under the UNCLOS protects Indonesian territorial integrity and the sea becomes in a sense a uniting factor among the various islands in the state.[26] Therefore, any outside positions in the straits are perceived as a potential problem for its territorial integrity and sovereignty.

MALAYSIA'S REGIONAL POLICY: DINESTUC CIMPLUSIONS AND ASEAN APPROACH

Malaysia's role in Southeast Asia has been primarily guided by its policy of trying to exercise its role as a 'large state' in maritime Southeast Asia in the region. Malaysia followed a policy of proposing a Zone of Peace, Freedom and Neutrality (ZOPFAN) in Southeast Asia and also the subsequent neutrality of Southeast Asia in the face of a growing conflict in Vietnam.[27] Malaysia has been one of the key countries in proposing ASEAN role in the region. At times the voices of both Indonesia and Malaysia have been in tandem regarding the maritime security of the straits in the region. Though Malaysia's foreign policy endures years of sticking to region viewpoints there have been domestic pressures from Malaysia's ethnic groups mainly its large Chinese entrepreneurial diaspora which has played a key role in Malaysia's development. The Chinese businesses in fact had become powerful in Malaysia so much so that there were policies such as the 'Bhumiputra' which gave more rights to the 'sons of the soil' and tougher competition to Chinese businesses in the region.[28] Though policies cannot be attributed to be 'Pro China' due to this case it was also accentuated by former Prime Minister Mahathir's policy of Looking East played a key role in developing close linkages with broader East Asia in general and more so China in particular.[29] A good example of this was the Chinese opposition and Malaysian support for the agreement to keep out India, Australia and New Zealand from the core membership of the East Asia Summit (EAS) in its formative years.[30]

MALAYSIA'S STAND ON THE PATROLLING THE MALACCA STRAITS

Malaysia has also always preferred non involvement of extra regional powers in the patrolling of the straits. The issue similar to Indonesia remains that of sovereignty of the states' waters. Geographically, Peninsula Malaysia forms the opposite side of the Malacca Strait. Malaysia along with Indonesia has been quite vocal about the opposition to the intervention of outside powers in the straits. For instance, at the height of piracy in 2004 when the United States proposed the Regional Maritime Security Initiative (RMSI), there were two components which drove Malaysian policy towards refusing to approve the initiative. One was the, issue of sovereignty and presence of external powers in its territorial waters and the other more importantly was the war on terror context under which the initiative was proposed. In this case also there was an impact of domestic constituency which Malaysia considered.[31]

While Indonesia has been firm in not admitting any major powers Malaysia had considered proposals in considering extra regional power involvement in the region. For instance the Malaysian Navy chief visited New Delhi in September, 2004 and explored a role for the Indian Navy in the region.[32] The Malaysian Navy is also a part of the 2014 set up of the Cobra Gold exercises to be held with the US and its allies in the region.

SINGAPORE AND REGIONAL POLICY: LOOKING OUT FOR A BALANCE OF POWER IN SOUTHEAST ASIA

Singapore has been one of the leading economic power houses in Southeast Asia. Due to its strategic location and its relatively small size (perceived as vulnerability) Singapore has had a very realist orientation to its foreign policy in the region. Singapore has been often viewed as a state which has been able to use its leverage to position itself a stronger level compared to its two larger neighbours Indonesia and Malaysia which have had very different policies regarding extra regional states in the region. For instance, Singapore has been a key non treaty ally of the United States in the region and has been regularly part of a number of joint exercises with multiple powers including the United States.

Singapore has also been a part of multiple exercises in the region including Cobra Gold exercises which have played a key role in projecting US power in the region. The US navy in particular has used offshore form Singapore as the destination for deploying its stealth patrol vessels. There are also regular exercises between Singapore and other major powers including India. Singapore has tried to carefully project its image so as to not align too close to the United States in the region. The Singapore navy recently concluded a joint naval exercise with China which is seen as a contentious power in the region which has had multiple issues with other ASEAN members such as Philippines and Vietnam.[33] Singapore's main focus has been sustaining its economic growth which is highly reliant on its sea borne trade driven by its strategic location. Hence Singapore's interest is twofold one being keeping the straits of Malacca open and the other being using a combination of powers in the region to balance regional extra regional conflicting interests.

Singapore has been able to play what commonly its commentators have termed as 'punching above its weight'. As S. Jayakumar notes in his book, Singapore played a key role in bringing in India into the ASEAN Regional Forum (ARF) even though there were opposition to India's inclusion into the grouping.[34] Though Singapore has used ASEAN as a platform to enhance its position in the region and used an approach of multi power engagement to balance out major powers it has also continued to increase its own individual capability to protect its own territory. The Singapore Armed forces especially the Republic of Singapore Navy has been one of the most advanced in the region. Singapore has not only been one the largest/one of the largest defence spenders in Southeast Asia, it is also the fifth largest defence spender in the world.[35]

SINGAPORE'S STAND ON THE PATROLLING THE MALACCA STRAITS

Singapore has had a very different stand compared to other countries in the region. The first issue with the countries has been the very definition of what countries make up the Malacca Straits. While it has been argued that Indonesia and Malaysia are the main countries along the Malacca Straits, the Singapore Strait which is a vital International Choke Point and the narrowest point along the journey becomes important place. Singapore has been supportive of many of the initiatives which have been proposed by a number of states in the region.

PIRACY AND TERRORISM: DUAL TRACK PROBLEMS OF MARITIME SECURITY IN THE REGION

In the face of the rising threats from piracy there was also a sharp manifestation of terror outfits such as the Jemaah Islamiyah in Indonesia which was carrying out large scale attacks in the region. Hence there was a fear among major powers that terrorism would take on the intensely maritime character of the region and may use the straits to target trade and commerce. Hence the objective of major powers was now fused in tackling both the rising piracy issues and the increasing terrorist influence and its subsequent threat to the region. In the subsequent years after the war on terror was launched Southeast Asia was considered as the 'second front'. In the face of rising tensions there were various initiatives which were proposed by extra regional powers which were designed to tackle this dynamic. Two initiatives were the Regional Maritime Security Initiative (RMSI) and the Proliferation Security Initiative (PSI).

Once again the main issue among the states were the issue of sovereignty. For instance, when the RMSI was proposed one of the clauses entitled the use of US marines in fast patrol crafts to interdict suspected vessels.[36] A similar concern was raised by Indonesia with regards to the

Proliferation Security Initiative. Jakarta's main grievance was the conflict of interest with the clause of freedom of navigation especially under the UNCLOS and issues over sovereignty in the Malacca straits.[37] While Malaysia remained silent initially and endorsed the agreement in 2014, Singapore agreed to the PSI from its inception.[38]

THE TRILATERAL 'MALSINDO' INITIATIVE
TO PATROL THE STRAITS OF MALACCA

In the face of increasing tensions in the region with regards to piracy there was increasing pressure on regional states to find a solution to the issue. While Malaysia and Indonesia favoured to keep extra regional powers out of the Malacca Straits, Singapore had favoured involvement of extra regional powers. An agreement was finally reached among the three littoral states to combat the rising threat of piracy in the region. A coordinated exercise known as 'MALSINDO' was launched which used 'coordinated' and not 'joint' initiatives to counter the threat in the region. The regional sensitivity was still reflected in the agreement where, 'MALSINDO' did not have provisions for hot pursuit or joint operations in others' territory.[39] An Ariel component was added to the exercises by including Thailand known as 'Eyes in the Sky' which is not actually a primary strait country but stands very close to the northern end of the approach to the Malacca Straits.

Over the years there have been changes in the type of cooperation that was being carried out through the initiative. The non-availability to carry out activities of hot pursuit of suspected vessels in each others' waterways caused difficulties in coordinating amongst navies. While progress was made in the realm of maritime surveillance for instance with joint monitoring straits with radars, it was also outside assistance such as that from the US which had helped.[40] While progress was made in 2008 where negotiations were underway to allow 'hot pursuit' stretching to other countries' waters, International law here has been the hurdle but possible agreements are in the pipeline among countries in the region. A strong trust deficit still exists in the region when it comes to key issues requiring intra state cooperation.

CHINA AND THE MALACCA DILEMMA:
IMPLICATIONS FOR REGIONAL RELATIONS

Southeast Asia has been an important part of China's strategy in its rise as a major power in Asia. China's rise has been marked with both the economic and the military variants. As economic development has been the chosen path for China, it has relied on resources and Sea lanes for developing its economic growth. It can be argued that China's increasing military capabilities are a result and a measure to safeguard its rise as a major power of which its rising economic growth is one of the main components. As highlighted in the preceding arguments, it can be inferred that China's reliance on the Malacca Straits for most of its energy supply has created a number of challenges. While China has been able to assert itself over the past few years in the South China Sea region, its hold over the Straits of Malacca flow remains almost nonexistent.

For instance, in 2004 former Chinese president Hu Jintao highlighted the 'Malacca Dilemma' where there was a juxtaposition of China's over reliance on resource flows through the Malacca Straits and inability to militarily deter it over larger geopolitical ambitions in the region vis-a-vis major powers such as US.[41] There have been a number of views which have emerged about China's strategies towards mitigating its maritime security threats. It has been argued by some that China has followed an offensive strategy of preventing access to its mainland form adversarial powers while continuing to expand its naval capabilities further in the region. It has also been argued that China has tried to mitigate the threat by alternatively courting neighbouring countries to have alternative access if ever access to Malacca Straits is cut off. One of the main projects has been the Chinese development of a port at Kyaukpyu in Myanmar where there will be provisions made to accommodate Malacca ships and pipelines which can transport oil and natural gas through Myanmar to Kunming. While China's policy has raised suspicion about encirclement of India there have been doubts, some analysts have argued that China has also resorted to various measures to combat the 'Malacca dilemma' which necessarily need not be military in nature.[42]

Over the years there have been a number of theories of China's expansionism and is strategy to secure its maritime approaches. In relation to its growing economic size and its geopolitical ambitions, China has been developing capabilities to supplement its strategic moves vis-a-vis its ambitions in the region. According to a report submitted to the United States Congress in 2011, China has developed various capabilities including the Anti-Ship Ballistic Missile (ASBM) capability. This allows it to target moving ships and aircraft carriers. Though this is a unique technology which is possessed by China, recent debates in the United States have suggested that there are various means by which this technological hurdle can be overcome. A Congressional Research Service report outlined that the ASBM capability could be overcome using many active and passive measures to stop the missile at various levels. The report suggested four levels including controlling electromagnetic emissions or using deception emitters, disabling or jamming China's long range maritime surveillance and targeting systems, acquisition of sea based terminal interception and development electromagnetic rail guns and development and deployment of high power free electron lasers and solid state lasers.[43]

China has been laying special focus on its submarine capabilities which encompass four new classes of domestically designed and built submarines: Jin or Type 094 (SSBN){Ballistic missile submarine}, Shang or Type 093 (SSN) {Nuclear powered attack submarine}, Yuan or Type 041/039A (SSP){non-nuclear, air-independent propulsion submarines, and Song or Type 039/039G (SSK){Diesel attack electric submarines}.[44] Moreover China has also successfully refitted and has put its new aircraft carrier into service. The aircraft carrier came into service in 2012. Though China claimed initially that the aircraft carrier would be used for research purposes it conducted a successful landing of an indigenously produced J-15 jet on the aircraft carrier in November 2012. China continues also to build on its indigenous program to build its own naval equipments.

There have been a number of reputations of China's actions in the immediate region. One has been the increasing struggle by China's neighbours to improve their defence capabilities and the other has been the lurking fear in the region about the possibility of a confrontation along key trade and waterways especially between China and other regional naval powers. The Malacca Strait is one such area which has been suggested by naval analysts as a potential place to check Chinese naval assertion. Though China has been working to develop alternatives to bypass the straits to avoid the eventual 'blockade' it has also been working to look at other possible factors that it can use to dispel fears of its rising profile in the region. China has always tried to support its image and its rise as being a positive contributing factor in Asia. For instance when the International community raised alarm over China's rising profile, China proposed the peaceful rise/peaceful development doctrine. In the current context China has proposed the concept of the Maritime Silk route allying fears of littoral states in the Indian Ocean and contributing to the development in the region.

Conceptually, the Maritime silk route has a two pronged strategy. One strategy is to exercise China's historical centrality which it currently enjoys in the world's trading architecture and the other is the strategic dimension to protect its resource flows and develop capabilities to offset any adversarial intent in denying China's its rising position in the hierarchy of powers in the region. In the speech given at the Indonesian parliament in October 2014, Xi Jinping urged ASEAN states to join in promoting maritime security cooperation. The concept was eventually expanded to include other countries in the Indian Ocean region such as Sri Lanka and Maldives.[45]

Hence China has been working to change its stance vis-a-vis Southeast Asia and its relations with the countries of the region. Though China has continued to assert its position through the conduct of its soft and hard power tactics it has to be noted that there has been a steady increase in capabilities of states in the region especially in the naval realm. Except for capabilities of countries such as Vietnam in mainland Southeast Asia, the three maritime countries led by Singapore navy have increased focusing on their naval capabilities. Due to the varying perspectives among states and complex relations between states in the region there has been a mixed if not to say a complex response to China in the region. While the Indonesian's allowed transit to Chinese naval ships to cross the Sunda straits and exercise in the eastern Indian Ocean and more passive about the maritime Silk route concept there has been growing concerns over China's claims in the South China Sea which have raised concerns about China's presence in the gas rich Natuna gas fields.[46] While Singapore was the second country to support the Maritime Silk Route idea after Sri Lanka, which has been in tune with its policy of balancing all major powers by supporting initiatives in the region,[47] Malaysia has remained supportive of the Chinese proposal despite its disputes with China in the South China Sea, as per reports Malaysian administration along with former Malaysian leaders have evinced keen interest in the proposal.[48]

CHINA-INDIA—US MARITIME TIES: IMPLICATIONS FOR SECURITY OF THE STRAITS

It is worthwhile to gauge the impact of these trilateral relations starting with changing Sino—US relations in 1972. China has benefited previously from its close cooperation with the Soviet Union until the fallout since 1960's. Maritime security issues have always been the highlight of the policy towards the Southeast Asian region. While China developed its capabilities steadily aiding Washington diplomatically to find a suitable solution through Vietnam crisis, the United States still remained a predominant power in the region. It would be a worthwhile exercise to analyse the relations in terms of naval relations among these states and their relations with Southeast Asian countries. An analysis of the military equipment will also highlight the challenges and the convergence that exists among states in the region.

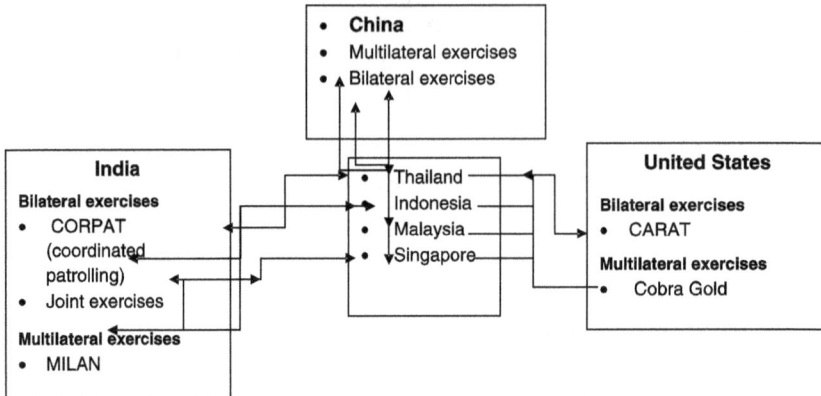

Fig. 4: Naval Exercises between Countries around Malacca Straits and Major Naval Powers in the Vicinity

The diagram in Figure 4 demonstrates the complex web of relations which the countries around the Straits of Malacca share with major naval powers in the region. It can be observed that Southeast Asian countries mainly the countries of the Malacca Straits in particular (as illustrated in the diagram) have tended to create a favourable balance of naval power in the region by engaging multiple powers. Among the countries in the region it can be observed that engagements among countries such as Malaysia and Indonesia have remained restricted to areas of cooperation which do not form part of the Malacca Straits. Comparatively India has a better position vis-a-vis countries as the maritime patrolling for instance with Indonesia takes place close to the northern approaches of the Malacca Straits. Compared to bilateral measures the countries of the Malacca Straits have been actively participating in regional maritime exercises such as MILAN hosted by the Indian navy, RIMPAC hosted by the US Navy.

Incidentally, countries in the region have developed a working relationship with China on issues regarding maritime security in the region. Thailand has been holding regular military to military contact with China while, Malaysia was mulling on the idea of conducting joint exercises with a (strong maritime element) included. Singapore and China concluded a joint exercise in 2014. Indonesia on the other hand has seen continuity in its policy towards any major powers by not engaging them in the security of the straits in the region where as Indonesia has been part of a number of pacific multilateral naval exercises.[49] While the Southeast Asian dynamic highlights the common tendency of Southeast Asian countries to balance out extra regional power influence by an all inclusive but selective engagement, the relations among the three powers still remains underdeveloped and to a large extent marred with trust deficit and diverging geopolitical ambitions.

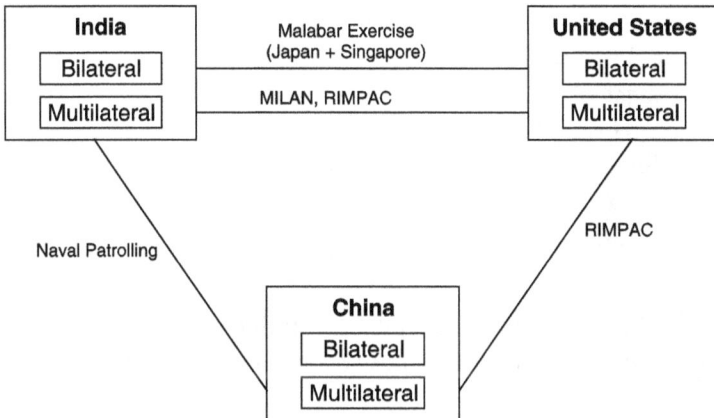

In the Asian context there has been a growing emphasis on the role of Sino-Indian naval capabilities. China remains a highly competent power in the region but albeit remains a 'controversial player' compared to India. For instance in Southeast Asia, China has been perceived as a boon in the economic sense but a troublesome problem due to its disputes and at times a posture in the region which puts economically dependent and militarily week Southeast Asian states in a difficult position. In understanding the dynamics of the trilateral relations between China, India and United States, it becomes crucial to note that finding the converging and diverging points can give an understanding of the possibilities of cooperation and finding a robust solution in securing the straits within the constraints of regional concerns. Major Powers have followed different strategies in securing the straits in the region.

Country	Issue	Approach
China	Piracy	Alternative (securing other approaches)
United States		Counter (using power projection
India		Regional (Bilateral and Multilateral)
Japan		Soft (Institutionalization)

It can be observed that both the countries i.e. China and United States have had opposite approaches in securing the waterways especially their approaches towards the Straits of Malacca. While China has resorted to a two pronged strategy of developing alternative methods of bypassing the Straits of Malacca, it has also been developing its military capability to ensure safe passage if that method fails. The United States on the other hand has not ratified the UNCLOS but has recognised the law as a codification of customary International law.[50] Hence it forms a basis for US conduct and how it perceives other states to behave in the region. Therefore at times the US has used its military positioning in the region and the prospect of non-enforceability of UNCLOS on it to use its forces in the region to signal its intent in protecting the straits. Though it gives the United States "rights" under International Law to freely navigate its forces in high seas including EEZ's sometimes the positioning of forces comes too close for comfort for regional states and extra regional powers alike.[51]

While India has indicated the Malacca Straits to be its primary areas of interest in its Naval Doctrine, it has worked with regional navies more so with Indonesia and Singapore consistently in securing the waterway. India has also worked to create multilateral understanding through naval cooperation in the region especially by holding the MILAN exercises which have not only the significance of having various large naval powers included in the exercise it also signals India's strategic reach in the northern approaches of the Straits of Malacca. Due to its constraints Japan has pursued an institutional approach in aiding countries in protecting the straits which remains a key area of its energy supply.

CONCLUSION

The Malacca Straits will continue to remain a key area of geopolitical influence in the world and for the countries of the region. The geopolitical influence of major powers will continue to put pressure on states of the region to take adequate action to combat the menace that threaten the security of the key water way. The lack of strong military capabilities and lack of ability to address developmental issues has led to the rise of piracy which is a combination of vital weakness of state apparatus to handle the domestic situation. Hence states in the region need to improve their naval capabilities and also the intra country coordination capability to counter these issues. There needs to be a case built to integrate cooperation among states in the region. The 'MALSINDO' operations proved to be a success but there needs to be more done to ensure that the security can be enhanced. The disparity in the capabilities that have been employed also vastly differ, in this case here need to be policy amendments which help in filling these gaps.

Indeed the first and foremost issue has been that of sovereignty among states which is further reaffirmed through regional institutions such as ASEAN which have enshrined non interference as one of its core principles. The rise of Trans regional challenges is altering the way in which Southeast Asian countries guard their sovereignty. Changing regional pressures form regional and extra regional forces have played a key role. In terms of transnational issues such as terrorism and the regional haze scenario there has been a strong move to include a regional solution through ASEAN indicating that ASEAN is truly advancing albeit slowly into a cohesive group of nations. Extra regional power involvement is where the real challenge for ASEAN lies.

Southeast Asia has always remained a region prone to geopolitical competition. The influence of US and China's political power play during the cold war has had one of the deepest impact on the psyche of the region, the move to remain out of the power play resulted in the primacy of rules such as 'non intervention' and multi power balancing with the region to neutralize any effect of power politics in the region. As the Asia-Pacific transforms to Indo-Pacific, Southeast Asia being the natural highway for regional economies is facing the heat from resident, regional, resurgent and rising powers alike. The main challenge is from an impending struggle between China and US to keep their tab on the region's vital waterways. The countries of the straits have tried to play the delicate balancing game between both these powers but remain stringent in including either due to their historical as well as current experiences in the region.

India which has been a time tested and reliable friend of countries in the region can be the security provider for the Malacca Straits. Not only has it proved its capabilities by escorting naval vessels at the height of piracy in 2004, India has also been able to build adequate trust and confidence among countries buy holding joint naval exercises with the Indonesian, Singaporean and Thai navies. With the dispute settlement with Bangladesh over the maritime boundary in the Bay of Bengal, India has also demonstrated that it is an adherent of International Law and subscribes to all the principles of regional accession relating to ASEAN countries such as the Treaty of Amity and Cooperation (TAC) which promoted non intervention and peaceful settlement of disputes as a core principle. It is also to note that India was able to actively deploy a strong response during the Indian Ocean Tsunami in 2006 making India not only a reliable power in the region but also a one which respects International Law regardless of a countries' size or reach.

Though there are a number of instances to build a case for including India if at all the regional dynamics change there are still issues in such an enterprise. The different defence procurements will demand for a stronger understanding and development of strong interoperability capabilities. Hence there must be a move by India to develop a stronger defence profile with the countries of the region. This can ensure a smooth increase in cooperation. Existing spheres such as the joint production efforts undertaken with Singapore should also be deepened.

It should be noted that Tome Pires, a Portuguese apothecary exclaimed in the 14th century that 'He who rules Malacca will have his hands on the throats of Venice', today the dynamics of trade may have shifted but Malacca Straits continue to remains crucial for the world, hence a concerted effort is needed to preserve the seamless flow of goods through one of the world's major super highways.

REFERENCES

1. "About the Silk Road", UNESCO available at https://en.unesco.org/silkroad/about-silk-road

2. "History of Andaman and Nicobar Islands", for more see http://www.andamanonline.in/About/profile/history/index.html

3. Sardesai, H.S., *Shivaji, the Great Maratha, Volume 3* (Cosmo publications: New Delhi, 2002) p. 625.

4. Sen, Tan, "The Military Campaigns of Rajendra Chola and the Chola-Srivijaya-China Triangle" in Hermann Kulke, K Kesavapany, Vijay Sakhuja (eds.) *Nagapattinam to Suvarnadwipa: Reflections on the Chola Naval Expeditions to Southeast Asia* (ISEAS: Singapore, 2009) p. 72.

5. Viviano, Frank, "China's Great Armada, Admiral Zheng He" *The National Geographic Magazine* (Washington D.C) July, 2005 for more see: http://ngm.nationalgeographic.com/print/features/world/asia/china/zheng-he-text

6. "History of Singapore" for more see http://www.nationsonline.org/oneworld/History/Singapore-history.htm

7. Black, Bruce, "Legacy of Mahan in the 21st century" *USAWC Strategy Research Project* (US Army War College: USA, 2006).

8. "Chronology for the Philippine Islands and Guam in the Spanish-American War" *Library of Congress* for more see: http://www.loc.gov/rr/hispanic/1898/chronphil.html

9. Ross, Angus, "Losing the Initiative in Mercantile Warfare: Great Britain's Surprising Failure to Anticipate Maritime Challenges to Her Global Trading

Network in the First World War" *International Journal of Naval History* (Naval Historical Foundation: USA, 2002).

10. Hand, Marcus, "Malacca Straits transits hit all-time high in 2013, pass 2008 peak", *Sea Trade Global* (Colchester, UK), 10th February, 2014 for more see: http://www.seatrade-global.com/news/asia/malacca-straits-transits-hit-all-time-high-in-2013-pass-2008-peak.html

11. Thompson, Mark, "China growth points to gradual recovery" *CNN Money* (online), 18th January, 2013 for more see http://money.cnn.com/2013/01/18/news/economy/china-economy

12. http://www.bqdoha.com/wp-content/uploads/2013/09/Oil-flow.png

13. "How US Shale Boom Changes the Global Energy Trade Landscape" for more see: http://www.oilgaspost.com/2013/11/12/shale-boom-global-energy-trade-landscape/

14. http://www.eia.gov/countries/analysisbriefs/China/images/crude_oil_imports_source.png

15. Schröppel, Christian and Mariko, Nakajima, "The Changing Interpretation of the Flying Geese Model of Economic Development" for more see http://www.dijtokyo.org/doc/dij-jb14-Schroeppel-Nakajima.pdf

16. The Indonesian economy contracted nearly 13.13% in the year 1998. While Singapore economy recorded -2.23% rate for the same year. Also see: "The roots of piracy in Southeast Asia", APSNet Policy Forum, October 22, 2007, http://nautilus.org/apsnet/the-roots-of-piracy-in-southeast-asia/and "International Maritime Bureau Report on piracy and armed robbery against ships available at: http://www.peacepalacelibrary.nl/ebooks/files/ICC_InternationalMaritimeBoard_Annual_Piracy_Report2004.pdf

17. Liss, Carolin, "The Maritime dimension of Energy Security" in Benjamin K Sovacool (ed.), *The Routledge Handbook of Energy Security* (Routledge, U.K, 2011).

18. Watkins, Eric, "Facing The Terrorist Threat In The Malacca Strait" *Terrorism Monitor*, Jamestown foundation, V. 2, n. 9 for more see: http://www.jamestown.org/single/?no_cache=1&tx_ttnews%5Btt_news%5D=26473#.VCPjBPmSwc8

19. Burton, John, "Lloyd's drops war rating on Malacca Strait", *The Financial Times* (Singapore), 9th August, 2006 for more see: http://www.ft.com/intl/cms/s/0/025f165e-26cc-11db-81f8-0000779e2340.html#axzz3EK6OYjfd

20. "Ice melt opens Arctic trade routes" *Strait Times* (Singapore), 5th August, 2011 for more see.

21. The shipping sector contributed about seven percent of the GDP of Singapore, which equals to about US$ 19.62 billion revenues from the shipping and related industries for more see http://www.maritime-executive.com/article/Strong-Growth-for-Singapores-Maritime-Industry-2014-01-07 also see Singapore Workforce Development Agency http://www.wda.gov.sg/content/wdawebsite/L202-SingaporeJOBSpedia/L302-010B-Marine.html

22. The konfrontasi policy initiated by Sukarno against the formation of Malaysia had a key conflict initiated among Malaysia, Singapore and Indonesia which ended following the coup in Indonesia in 1965. Other regional tensions included the post-independence problem over Sabah with the Philippines

23. The Preah Vihear issue came under moderation by ASEAN under the Indonesian chairmanship of the organisation in 2011 for more see: Sujane Kanparit, "A mediator named ASEAN: Lessons from Preah Vihear", *Sarakadee magazine* (Bangkok), 2011 for more see: http://www.aseannews. net/a-mediator-named-asean-lessons-from-preah-vihear. On Indonesian foreign policy and centrality of ASEAN see: Dewi Fortuna Anwar, "Indonesia's foreign relations: policy shaped by the ideal of 'dynamic equilibrium'" *East Asia Forum* (Australia), 4th February, 2014, Yanyan Mochamad Yani, "Change and Continuity in Indonesian Foreign Policy" available at: http://pustaka.unpad.ac.id/wp-content/uploads/2010/01/change_and_continuity_in_indonesia_foreign_policy.pdf

24. Sittnick, Tammy M., "State Responsibility And Maritime Terrorism In the Strait of Malacca: Persuading Indonesia and Malaysia to Take Additional Steps to Secure The Strait" *Pacific Rim Law and Policy Journal Association* (University of Washington, School of Law: Washington, 2005) v. 14, n. 3, p. 12.

25. Hong, Nong, *UNCLOS and Ocean Dispute Settlement: Law and Politics in the South China Sea* (Routledge: New York, USA), p. 119.

26. "1971 Zone of Peace, Freedom and Neutrality Declaration" available at: http://www.icnl.org/research/library/files/Transnational/zone.pdf

27. Chareonwongsak, Kriengsak, "The Global Chinese Diaspora-Creating Wealth, Contributing to National Development" for more see: http://www.asli.com.my/uploads/20121128045203_Full%20paper_Dr%20 Kriengsak%20Chareonwongsak_231112.pdf

28. Saravanamuttu, Johan, "Malaysia in the new Geopolitics of Southeast Asia", *IDEAS reports* (London School of Economics: London, 2012) n. 15, available at: http://www.lse.ac.uk/ideas/publications/reports/pdf/sr015/sr015-seasia-saravanamuttu-.pdf

29. Pandya, Archana and Malone, David M., "India's Asia Policy: A Late Look East", *ISAS Special Report* (ISAS: Singapore, 2010) n. 2.

30. "Malaysia says US intervention in Malacca Straits could create problems" *Associated Free Press* (online), 11th May, 2004 for more see: http://www. freerepublic.com/focus/f-news/1146912/posts

31. Dutta, Sujan, "Navy mulls joint patrol with Singapore, Malaysia", *The Telegraph* (Kolkata), 22nd September, 2004 for more see: http://www. telegraphindia.com/1040923/asp/nation/story_3791028.asp

32. Singapore and India conduct annual maritime exercises known as SIMBEX which have been held in Indian waters and in Singaporean waters since 1994. For more see: "SIMBEX 2014", Press Information Bureau, Government of India for more see: http://pib.nic.in/newsite/PrintRelease.aspx?relid=105133, on Singapore China exercises see: "Navies of Singapore and China carry out bilateral exercise in East China Sea" for more see: http://www.naval-

technology.com/news/newsnavies-of-singapore-and-china-carry-out-bilateral-exercise-in-east-china-sea-4363300

33. Jayakumar, S., *Diplomacy: A Singapore Experience* (Straits Times Press: Singapore, 2011), pp. 91–93.

34. Ranasinghe, Dhara, "Singapore, the tiny state with military clout" *CNBC news* (online), 9th February, 2014 for more see: http://www.cnbc.com/id/101393982#.

35. Cheney-Peters, Scott, "US, Japan to Boost ASEAN Maritime Security" *The Diplomat* (online), 30th April, 2014 for more see: http://thediplomat.com/2014/04/us-japan-to-boost-asean-maritime-security

36. Lieggi, Stephanie, "The Nonproliferation Tiger: Indonesia's Impact on Nonproliferation in Asia and Beyond" *Nuclear Threat Initiative* for more see: http://www.nti.org/analysis/articles/nonproliferation-tiger-indonesias-impact-nonproliferation-asia-and-beyond

37. "Malaysia Endorses the Proliferation Security Initiative", Press Release US Department of State, 29th April, 2014 for more see: http://www.state.gov/r/pa/prs/ps/2014/04/225349.htm

38. Erickson, Andrew S., "Maritime Security Cooperation in the South China Sea region" in Zou Keyuan and Shicun Wu (eds.), *Maritime Security in the South China Sea: Regional Implications and International Cooperation* (Ashgate: UK, 2009).

39. "Indonesia guarantees security in Malacca Strait", *Antara News Agency* (Jakarta), 17th January, 2011 for more see: http://antaranews.com/en/news/67096/indonesia-guarantees-security-in-malacca-strait

40. "Military and Security Developments Involving the People's Republic of China 2014" (Department of Department: USA, 2014), Christian Bedford, "The View from the West: String of Pearls: China's Maritime Strategy in India's Backyard" *Canadian Naval Review* (Centre for Foreign Policy Studies: Halifax, 2009) v. 4, n. 4, Chen Shaofeng, "China's Self-Extrication from the "Malacca Dilemma" and Implications" *International Journal of China Studies* (University of Malaya: Malaysia, 2010) v.1, n.1, pp. 1–24.

41. Rourke, O' Ronald, "China Naval Modernization: Implications for U.S. Navy Capabilities—Background and Issues for Congress" (Congressional Research Service: USA, 2012).

42. Rourke, O' Ronald, "China Naval Modernization: Implications for U.S. Navy Capabilities—Background and Issues for Congress" (Congressional Research Service: USA, 2014).

43. "Speech by Chinese President Xi Jinping to Indonesian Parliament", available at: http://www.asean-china-center.org/english/2013-10/03/c_133062675.htm, Joint statement during Xi Jinping's visit to Sri Lanka"Plan Of Action Of The Democratic Socialist Republic Of Sri Lanka And The People's Republic Of China To Deepen The Strategic Cooperative Partnership" for more see: http://www.mea.gov.lk/images/stories/Newspapers/plan%20of%20action%20-%20final.pdf

44. Shekhar, Vibhanshu, "Maritime silk route: China's foothold in the Indian Ocean?" *Jakarta post* (Jakarta), 25th February, 2014 for more see: http://www.thejakartapost.com/news/2014/02/25/maritime-silk-route-china-s-foot hold-indian-ocean.html

45. "Xi Jinping's Maritime Silk Road gets key backing ahead of South Asia visit", *The Economic Times* (Mumbai), 12th September, 2014 for more see: http://articles.economictimes.indiatimes.com/2014-09-12/news/53851018_ 1_maritime-silk-road-indian-ocean-msr

46. "Malaysia backs Maritime Silk Road in 21st century", *China Daily* (Online), 24th June, 2014 for more see: http://www.chinadaily.com.cn/business/2014-06/24/content_17612579.htm, Tho Xin Yi, "Enhancing two-way cooperation" *The Star* (Kuala Lumpur), 12th September,2014 for more see: http://www.thestar.com.my/Opinion/Columnists/Check-In-China/Profile/ Articles/2014/09/12/Enhancing-two-way-cooperation/

47. Panda, Ankit, "China and Malaysia To Hold Maritime Exercises: What Gives?" *The Diplomat*, 15th November, 2013 for more see: http:// thediplomat.com/2013/11/china-and-malaysia-to-hold-maritime-exercises-what-gives/, Adrian Lim, "Singapore and Chinese navies carry out bilateral exercise in East China Sea", *The Straits Times* (Singapore), 4th September, 2014 for more see: http://www.straitstimes.com/news/singapore/more-singapore-stories/story/singapore-and-chinese-navies-carry-out-bilateral-exercis#sthash. BgyjD3BW.dpuf

48. Beckman, Robert, "South China Sea conundrum: US and China's differing views" *Strait Times* (Singapore), 26th September, 2014 for more see: http://www.straitstimes.com/news/opinion/more-opinion-stories/story/south-china-sea-conundrum-perspective-the-us-20140926#sthash.Ace3x9Ds.dpuf

49. While the US navy conducts its Valiant Shield exercises, the focus in 2014 was 'Air Sea battle concept' which aims to overcome an enemy force's attempt to deny access and manoeuvrability within sea lanes and air space controversy was raised in China and its right leaning newspaper the global times reported the attempt by the United States to practise the scenario to blockade the Malacca Straits for more see: Erik Salvin. "Valiant Shield 2014: 18,000 service members gathering for Guam joint exercise" *Stars and Stripes* (Washington), 12th September, 2013 for more see: http://www. stripes.com/news/pacific/valiant-shield-2014-18-000-servicemembers-gather ing-for-guam-joint-exercise-1.302657http://www.stripes.com/news/pacific/valia |nt-shield-2014-18-000-servicemembers-gathering-for-guam-joint-exercise-1.302657, "US may block Strait of Malacca to contain China: Huanqiu" *Want China Times* (Taipei), 1st October, 2014 for more see: http:// www.wantchinatimes.com/news-subclass-cnt.aspx?id=20141001000001&cid =1101

Indo-US Relations in the Indian Ocean: Changing Chinese Perception

Vivek Mishra*

INTRODUCTION

The United States has been a resident power of this region since the 1960s ever since the British withdrew from the 'East of Suez'. By the late 1960s and the early 1970s the Indian Ocean witnessed one of the most dominant naval presences of the US, even as the Cold War peaked. By the early 1970s the Indian Ocean had the most number of submarines and subsequently it became one of the most nuclearised oceans of the world. So, in many ways, the Indian Ocean witnessed one of the fiercest clandestine iterations of the Cold War between the Soviet Union and the United States, played out in the maritime domain. The 1970s also saw the building of a military 'support facility' in the form of Diego Garcia in the Indian Ocean by the US. Since then, the United States has been dominantly present in this part of the world, sans a challenger. By basing itself in the Indian Ocean, the United States fulfilled a long standing desire of attaining a blue water navy in the true sense, even as it augmented its global reach by developing a military support facility in the heart of the Indian Ocean; Diego Garcia. The unilateral presence in the Indian Ocean allowed the US to be the only power with military and logistical capabilities having the capability for a time-bound implementation of its twin capabilities. In the post-Cold War period the United States continued its dominant presence, albeit with changed roles since the turn of the century.

Since the turn of the century, as opposed to the Cold War, today the Indian Ocean stands at the crossroads of world maritime trade. A yearly trade that passes from the Strait of Hormuz to the Strait of Malacca, has been estimated at a whopping US$18 trillion. With altered economic scenarios since the Cold War, today the Indian Ocean is sandwiched by India and China, the second and third largest, and the potential first and second largest economies of the world. The footprints of global powers

*Doctoral Candidate, US Studies Programme, School of International Studies Jawaharlal Nehru University, New Delhi.

have increased in the Indian Ocean, even as the Indian Ocean has come to become the new economic theatre of the world.

CHINA IN THE INDIAN OCEAN: NEW DELHI'S CONCERN

Although the quintessential Cold War rivalry has given way to economic competition of the 21st Century, great power competition still exists in the current global order. In many ways, the United States continues to be the number one power of the world today and China is the current number two. The international relations history of the world is replete with examples of an emerging power trying to challenge the established power. This is corroborated by the power transition theory as well. In this context, if the current game of power politics continues between the established Superpower, the US and the challenger, China, predictability of a war would not be far from reckoning. If one were to take an analogical leap and look at the current global order through the prism of A.F.K. Organski's Power Transition Theory, the United States and China would indeed appear to be two global powers separated by "4 degree" in so far as the possibility of a war is concerned. Furthermore, Organski's analyses would have it that the duration and the magnitude of war between an established power and a challenging power is the longest and most severe when a challenger to the dominant power enters into approximate parity with the dominant state and is dissatisfied with the existing system. This more or less defines the current state of relations between the US and China, where China has entered a level of parity with the US. In fact, China has already overtaken the US in Purchasing Power Parity (PPP) terms and is soon poised to overtake it in pure GDP terms. Hence, what comes to the fore is a fragile global order in so far as power politics is concerned.

Of late, the US-China geopolitical frictions have grown. 2013 saw the two geopolitical heavyweights slugging it out in the Asia-Pacific on many occasions. The United States seeks to re-establish its dominance in the Asia-Pacific, primarily enunciated through its "pivot-to-Asia" (now referred to as the Rebalance strategy). Concomitantly, China's consecutive three-decade rise has made it a powerful challenger to the US in this part of the world. The rise of China has been accompanied by its military modernization primarily depicted through its growing naval power. Beijing's growing power, at least in the last decade, has been invariably accompanied by growing assertion to territorial claims, sufficiently backed by naval power projection. Beijing meteoric rise in economic and military capabilities have thrown the zeal behind the US' Rebalance strategy in a tailspin. Washington's economic inter-dependence with Beijing is an Achilles' heel in the former's latent desire to contain the latter. As a result the US' strategy in Asia-Pacific has undergone a subtle change whereby it is willing to do two very important things; to diversify the area of operation and a willingness to work with other countries to achieve the desired balance of power in the region.

The limitations faced by the US in the Asia-Pacific in countering China despite having defence understandings with at least five countries in the region, compelled the US to think of the need of a regional heavyweight; India. Simultaneously, the idea to expand the scope of its Rebalance strategically was also mooted. However, the US did a very poor job of selling the concept to India. The tacit proposal by the US matches with India's own desire to create a regional balance of power architecture, gone awry due to an asymmetric rise of China together with its rising ambitions. For the past decade or so there has been a new found bonhomie between India and the US, the constant iteration of which has been in the maritime domain. Resultantly, the Indian Ocean has seen many activities reflective of cooperation and collaboration between India and the US. This has expectedly caused concern in China.

All these have together contributed in the opening up of a new strategic arena in world power politics; the Indian Ocean. Albeit the Indian Ocean is yet to see, or probably would never see, an iteration of the kind of great power politics being played during the Cold War years but it certainly is the new domain of the new kind of power politics that is dominated by subtle economics. As the bonhomie between New Delhi and Washington grows, the Indian Ocean has become the potential area where a comprehensive partnership between the two can undo the concern that emanates from China's rise depicting a regional-hegemon in the making. While there may be truth in the discourse that perceives China's rise as 'peaceful,' there is no denying the fact that China's asymmetric growth has created a power imbalance in Asia. This, together with Chinese desire to enter the Indian Ocean, has caused strategic concerns in India. Most recently, the Lombok Strait exercises that began on January 29 early this year signaled that Chinese intentions vis-à-vis the Indian Ocean may not be as benign as claimed by Beijing. The larger implications of such an exercise in the Indian Ocean has been summed in the following lines:

"The five-day exercise that began on Jan 29 this year showed a continuance in the pattern of Chinese maritime assertiveness; only this time, outside the 'Cow Tongue' area (China's claims in the South China Sea) representing traditional maritime Chinese sovereignty. The naval exercise was not an explicitly stated signal to India, but is an example of China's psychological moves. All such recent instances of China's assertive behaviour cannot be only coincidental or an absence of coordination in planning among the Chinese military hierarchy. These moves in fact reflect a clear strategy...... These exercises were neither 'routine' nor for 'patrol', they involved combat simulations...."

(Mishra, 2014)

Apart from the above concerns that India has vis-à-vis the Chinese presence in the Indian Ocean, there is a more immediate concern; that of rising clandestine activities by the People's Liberation Army Navy (PLA-N). In this regard the immediate reference is the concern in New Delhi regarding the Chinese submarine "Great Wall 0329" docked at the Chinese-funded Colombo International Container Terminal in Sri Lanka from 7 to 14 September, 2014, just before a one-day visit to the country by Chinese President Xi Jinping (Brown, 2014). Furthermore, a nuclear-powered People's Liberation Army Navy (PLAN) Type 093 Shang-class attack submarine was sighted cruising regional waters in 2013 (Holmes, 2014). Since the year 2012, more particularly, the PLA-N submarines have frequented the Indian Ocean more than ever before, raising New Delhi's strategic radars. With regards to this, Brown (2014) rightly argues that if the PLA-N continues with its tactics of sending Chinese submarines to the Indian Ocean, the regional strategic calculus will change. India will look to counter the Chinese under water moves by its own, setting in the region an unwanted submarine race.

What also concerns India is the timing of the Chinese submarine expeditions to the Indian Ocean. The PLA-N's capabilities are at an all time high and the Chinese military's experiment with submarines is a relatively new area. The Indian Ocean becomes an easy route for the Chinese submarines, as India's submarine as well as anti-submarine capabilities are at an all-time low. India's two important projects; Project 28 and Project 75I standing for anti-submarine and submarine capabilities, are currently underway. As such, the Chinese timing to frequent the Indian Ocean has been perfect. Since both these military projects are going to take some time (at least a year), India has little choice but to offset these concerns at the earliest. One of the ways in which it can do that is through frequent maritime cooperation with the US in the Indian Ocean.

INDO-US COOPERATION IN THE INDIAN OCEAN: ABATING CHINESE CONCERNS

Better relations with China is very Amidst these geopolitical and strategic concerns it is very essential that India abates the Chinese concerns that are emanating from its growing closeness with the US, particularly in the Indian Ocean. One of the foremost things that India needs to do is to explore the roots of the geo-strategic question; why is China concerned?

There are at least two reasons as to why the growing bonhomie between India and the US, particularly in the Indian Ocean has deeply concerned China; one is the presence of the US itself in its extended backyard, as if the presence of the US Asia-Pacific was not enough for China, the latter is concerned about growing maritime cooperation between Indian and the US. The second and a more important concern is the coming together of two countries which are not so friendly to China, to put it mildly.

Why should India cooperate with the US in the Indian Ocean? An important way forward for India, in so far as its cooperation with the US in the Indian Ocean is concerned, would be to let its relationship with the US take a natural course, particularly one that is shaped by mutual and bilateral interests. Simultaneously, India should also lay down its principles on the basis of which it wishes to cooperate with the US in the Indian Ocean in particular. These policy enunciations will go a long way in abating Chinese concerns emanating out of the India-US cooperation. In this context, there can be at least three broad objectives as part of policy enunciations on India's cooperation with the US.

Maintaining Systemic Stability of the Region by Sharing Global Commons

The asymmetric rise of China has changed the balance of power in Asia, to the extent that India as another important regional player feels the onus to restore the power balance, necessary for an equitable growth in Asia. India, all by itself, lacks the wherewithal and political will to maintain the systemic stability in the region. In the US, India finds a willing partner that has many common interests in the region. Therefore, both, from the perspective of an important as well as responsible regional player in South Asia, India should cooperate with the US in maintaining systemic stability of the region.

In the maintenance of systemic stability, two indispensable components are maintaining regional stability and sharing of global commons. The effort to maintain regional stability would require India to contribute significantly in providing security to the region, apart from occasionally playing the balancer in the region. With a different government at the helm in India, the question of political will can be put aside for a moment. India under Narendra Modi has shown the political willingness to expand India's regional security scope to the Indo-Pacific and beyond. The $100 million defence credit to Vietnam and training offered to Sukhoi 30-MKI fighter pilots in Vietnam (Karambelkar, 2014) are part of India's agenda to restore systemic balance in the region, which has of late been upset by Beijing's growing closeness with India's strategic neighbours. Although this runs the risk of a conflict between India and China, it is integral to maintaining systemic stability so that the players rise together and not disproportionately, least of all hegemonically. Therefore cooperation with the US to maintain systemic stability is an option that India is already weighing.

An important aspect of cooperation between major players in the Indian Ocean, which can mitigate the apprehensions arising out of the balance of power game between two out of the three players, is sharing of global commons in the region. Sea, as you would know, is a global common. Both India and China will stand to benefit immensely if the Indian Ocean, as much as the South China Sea, is used on a shared basis. To that extent, India will have to recognise the fact that China has legitimate interests in the Indian Ocean as much as China will have to live with growing India-Vietnam closeness. But as China also sees the Indian Ocean as a future strategic maritime domain, then in the interest of stability in the region, India should bolster its strategic deterrence through regional cooperative efforts.

Containing Transnational Threats

Terrorism and piracy have inflicted both India and China significantly in continental and maritime domains. Even as China looks forward to be the country with pan-Asian presence in the maritime domain, containing both piracy and terrorism should be a shared onus with India. Both the countries should cooperate in the Indian Ocean, as according to Krasik (2014), "the Indian Ocean hosts the world's most significant Sea Lanes of Communication (SLOCs) and as such plays a pivotal role in the global economy, particularly in the past 20 years." We don't realize, but piracy poses significant risks to goods transit in seas and security in general in the Indian Ocean, particularly off the Horn of Africa. Since the Indian Ocean is one of the busiest maritime routes, it begs security at high seas more than any other region. The US is the foremost navy of the world and China and India have very modern and capable navies to cooperate and contain the sea-piracy. India, China and Japan already have an understanding to cooperate in containing sea-piracy (Gokhale, 2012). Imagine the potential of counter-piracy efforts if the US is also roped in for this endeavour. The Indian Navy can learn a lot from the US Navy in both containing piracy and terrorism emanating from sea routes.

In so far as international terrorism is concerned, there could not be another region as severely afflicted by it as South Asia. As the region has witnessed (26/11 attacks on Mumbai), open seas can be a handy conduit to foster terrorism. International sea monitoring has the potential to significantly thwart maritime terrorism. Between India, China and the US, cooperation to contain maritime terrorism is an opportunity that awaits consensus. For India, it has announced globally through the platform of the United Nations (Prime Minister Modi's UN address) that it is very serious about a joint mechanism to fight terrorism, sea-borne or continental terrorism. It is the route that sees Prime Minister Modi's emphasis in his address to the UNSC about a globally concerted effort to contain terrorism could not be more timely. A serious effort towards cooperating to contain international terrorism can be initiated through the Indian Ocean, as all the three powers; the US, India and China have formidable naval capabilities.

Cooperation in Building Military Security

Building a strong military security in region for India, of which the Indian Ocean is an integral part, should be a pre-requisite for cooperating with China. India soon is going to take the Look East Policy Act hands on, for which a strong military security at home and in the region is required. Cooperation with the US will be required by India if it has plans to venture into the South China Sea and the East China Sea, as the US has defence cooperation with five countries in the Asia-Pacific apart from bases.

In the Indian Ocean, the Diego Garcia base has remained more like a military support facility than a military base. India is yet to see any substantive cooperative efforts with the US presence in the Diego Garcia, but that is an option for India, especially to improve logistics and disaster management. As India looks forward to augment its security and balancer role in Asia, logistics and disaster management are two important areas that need to be explored and, in there, with a cooperation of the US. India's building of the Andaman and Nicobar Islands as its strategic outpost should make the willingness to take logistical and disaster management responsibilities in the Indian Ocean, a more concrete idea. It will be an important step in the direction of a trilateral cooperation between India, China and the US and will go a long way in dispelling security concerns. A possibility to work with Beijing in the Indian Ocean should be explored by India, and non-security/non-strategic areas of cooperation could be the best beginning points of cooperation.

A clear enunciation of India's current and prospective cooperative principles with the US in the Indian Ocean is the only way forward to accommodate China as part of a regional symmetric growth in South Asia. A pragmatic cooperation between India and the US would also be a self-explanatory step to justify India's cooperation with the US, to the extent that China is cooperating with neighbours all around India, particularly Pakistan and of late Sri Lanka. Similarly, India's rising concerns about the presence of China in its backyard, needs to be abated too.

CHANGING PERCEPTIONS ABOUT INDIA-CHINA-US COOPERATION IN THE INDIAN OCEAN: A TWO WAY PROCESS

A very disturbing but common understanding that emanates from the yet unexplored India-China-US cooperation is the apprehension that the third country has vis-à-vis the cooperation between the other two of the troika. This mandates that the first requirement of the feasibility of such a trilateral cooperation in the Indian Ocean would necessarily ask for change of perceptions. There is as much a need for changing the Chinese perception about the Indo-US cooperation in the Indian Ocean as there is need to change perceptions back home here in India about growing Chinese presence in the Indian Ocean.

Now, how does India change the Chinese perception? As argued elsewhere in the paper, the Indo-US cooperation should be allowed to take its natural course based on mutual interests, while simultaneously evading such relations to be directed against China. While there is need to change the threat perception that China has out of the Indo-US cooperation in the Indian Ocean, any conscious effort from India will lead to appeasement of China. What India and the US therefore need to do is to move ahead in cooperation with their new found realism, despite concerns caused to China. If the bilateral relationship between India and China is sans hostility towards China, China as a pragmatic power of the 21ˢᵗ Century should take it in a positive stride. Thus, it is important to realise that any deliberate step to direct the cooperation against China will have detrimental effect on the stability of the Indian Ocean Region (IOR).

When one talks about changing perceptions as a two-way process, what one means is the fact that it is as important to change India's own perception of Chinese involvement in the Indian Ocean Region. India cannot own the Indian Ocean just because there is a titular resemblance between the country's name and the ocean. But certainly India can be more dominant, responsible and active in this region by taking a lead in maritime security, environmental concerns, disaster management and being more outgoing to the smaller nations across the Indian Ocean Region (IOR). It would also require India to be more proactive in cooperating with other countries which includes the US in this region. For that, India needs to lay its cards on the table and say that yes, it is going to cooperate with the US because the reality is that India is cooperating with the US in this part of the world and it is going to continue with that. A clear vision on India's cooperation with the US in the Indian Ocean will go a long way in removing the Chinese apprehensions in this regard

Another way in which there can be a substantial change in perceptions of each other between India, China and the US is by mooting a trilateral cooperation between the three countries in the Indian Ocean. A trilateral cooperation between India, Japan and the US is already being talked about and it would not be impossible to explore the inclusion of the Chinese along with India and the US. India should take the lead in mooting this geopolitical idea that will contribute significantly to the stability of the IOR in particular and Asia in general. If China is indeed serious about its 'legitimate interests' in the Indian Ocean, it should take the possibility of a trilateral cooperation in the Indian Ocean, along with India and the US, with both hands.

IS INDIA GETTING CO-OPTED?

Amidst the debate to cooperate with the US in the Indian Ocean, there is a parallel apprehension that many see as a possibility; India getting co-opted by the US in its agenda. Many would say that in the effort to cooperate with the US in the Indian Ocean, India runs the risk of getting co-opted in the US' Rebalance Policy which is still up and running. This paper would comprehensively negate any such strategically harmful outcomes for India, out of its cooperation with the US. Cooperation with the US in the Indian Ocean might require a few compromises, but that will be on either side of the bilateral relationship. A relationship formulated on the tenets of Non-Alignment Movement (NAM) might not be the ideal way to move forward for India, given considerably altered geopolitical realities. Once a country rises as an economic and, military power (as India has), co-option by even the strongest country is an absent possibility. There will be some costs for India in the process, and one that is most expected is a compromise with its Strategic autonomy principle.

CONCLUSION

Thus, cooperation between India and the US in the Indian Ocean is as essential as it is to change the Chinese perception about it. There are two clear ways in which India can dispel the apprehensions of China arising out India's cooperation with the US; to invite China to be a trilateral stakeholder in the Indian Ocean along with India and the US and more importantly, laying out broad policy principles on the basis of which India is looking forward to base its relationship with the US in general and more particularly in the Indian Ocean. Inviting China to be onboard this trilateral cooperation would not just be beneficial to India but a strategic grace that has the potential to catapult India into a responsible regional and global power. With India in between, the likelihood of US-China friction going out of hand is also limited, given India's moderate approach to global relations. The Indian Ocean can be the ground for the start of such a maritime diplomacy.

A realist and pragmatic assessment of the geopolitics in the maritime as well as continental domains around India will reveal that today, it is China that India has threat perceptions of and not the US. India clearly is not threatened today by the US. In fact, there is a significant perceptional change in the US about India from a struggling third world country to a country which has risen. The US perceives the India of today very differently. Today, unlike 1970s, the US would think twice before worsening relations with India, over Pakistan. The growing defence cooperation and its strategic partnership are pointers towards this attitudinal shift that has taken place in the US vis-à-vis India. The threat perception that we had of the US presence in the region pre-1990 has certainly dissipated.

India should realize that it is high time it stops piggybacking on the regional security provided by the US and that it has to let go off its deep faith in hegemonic stability theory. As a responsible and capable power of the region, the need of the hour for India is to take the mantle of regional security in the Indian Ocean in its own hands, albeit in its own limited capacity. If it means that India will have to cooperate with the US and run the risk of being co-opted, India should take that risk, rather than live with the nightmares of popping submarines in its backyard. It is time that India realises strategic autonomy is not unique to India and its also time India changes its strategic autonomy to strategic influence. India should look at its cooperation with the US as an opportunity to extend its maritime influence upto Australia and the Far East and benefit from its cooperation with other partners like Australia, Japan and more importantly Vietnam. The much ballyhooed triad of India, US and Japan is an unexplored area of cooperation and should be pursued. Therefore, if India can use its proximity to the US to deter China, it should. Strategic deterrence should always be a option on the table.

REFERENCES

1. 7-5700 RL33536 [Online] Accessed 07 Aug. 2013, URL: http://www.fas.org/sgp/crs/row/RL33536.pdf

2. Bajpaee, C (2012), "Factors Fuelling China's Expanding Maritime Operations", [Online: web] Accessed 08 Aug. 2013, URL: http://www.e-ir.info/2012/07/10/factors-fuelling-chinas-expanding-maritime-operations

3. Bhaskar, Uday (2013), "US-China-India Strategic Trinagle", [Online: web] Accessed 30 Jul. 2013, URL: http://post.jagran.com/uschinaindia-strategic-triangle-1352881628#sthash.yyhFc9wd.dpuf.

4. Booth, K. and Dowdy, W.L. (1985), *Structure and Strategy in Indian Ocean Naval Developments* (ed.) Dowdy, W.L. and Trood, R.B. (1985), The Indian Ocean: Perspectives on a Strategic Arena, Duke University Press: Durham.

5. Braun, Dieter (1983), *The Indian Ocean: Region of Conflict or 'Peace Zone'?* Oxford University Press: Delhi.

6. Brewster, D. (2014) "The Bay of Bengal: The Maritime Silk Route and China's Naval Ambitions" [Online: web] Accessed Dec 03, 2014. Available at: http://thediplomat.com/tag/china-in-the-indian-ocean/

7. Brown, J. (2014), Chinese Subs Lurk Under the Indian Ocean: Cause for Concern? [Onbline: web] Accessed Dec 02, 2014. Available at: http://nationalinterest.org/blog/the-buzz/chinese-subs-lurk-under-the-indian-ocean-cause-concern-11367.

8. Clinton, H. (2011), "America's Pacific Century", *Foreign Policy*, November.

9. Cole, J.M. (2013) "Red Star Over the Indian Ocean?" [Online: web] Accessed Dec 03, 2014. Available at: http://thediplomat.com/2013/04/red-star-over-the-indian-ocean

10. Full Text of PM Narendra Modi's Address at UN General Assembly [Online: web] Accessed Dec. 04, 2014. Available at: http://www.ndtv.com/article/india/full-text-of-pm-narendra-modi-s-address-at-un-general-assembly-598828

11. Ghoshal, B. (2010). *The Rise of China: View from India,* Journal of Indian Ocean Studies, Vol 18, No 2, August.

12. Gokhale, N. (2012). "India, China and the Pirates" [Online; web] Accessed on Dec 01, 2014. Available at: http://thediplomat.com/2012/03/india-china-and-the-pirates

13. Green, M.J. and Shearer, A. (2012). *Defining U.S. Indian Ocean Strategy,"* Washington Quarterly, Vol. 35, No. 2, Spring.

14. Holmes, J. (2014). Coming to the Indian Ocean, the Chinese Navy: How Should India Respond? [Online: web] Accessed Dec. 01, 2014. Available at: http://nationalinterest.org/feature/coming-the-indian-ocean-the-chinese-navy-how-should-india-11415

15. Jae-Hyung, L. (2002). *China's Expanding Maritime Ambitions in the Western Pacific and the Indian Ocean,* Contemporary Southeast Asia, Vol. 24, No. 3 December.

16. Karambelkar, A. (2014). "India, Vietnam and $100 Million in Defense Credit" [Online: web] Accessed Dec 03, 2014. Available at: http://thediplomat.com/2014/09/india-vietnam-and-100-million-in-defense-credit/

17. Kaushik, D. (1983). *The Indian Ocean: A strategic dimension,* Vikas Pub PVT LTD: Delhi.

18. Kondapalli, S. (2010). *Premier Wen Jiabao's Visit to India: Setting Terms for Engagement,* Journal of Indian Ocean Studies, Vol. 18, No. 2.

19. Krasik, T. (2014). "Why all eyes should be on the Indian Ocean" [Online: Web] Accessed Dec 01, 2014, URL: http://english.alarabiya.net/en/views/news/world/2014/01/09/Why-all-eyes-should-be-on-the-Indian-Ocean.html

20. Lawrence, S.V. (2013). *U.S.-China Relations: An Overview of Policy Issues,* Congressional Research Service 7-5700 R41108 [Online] Accessed 08 Aug. 2013, URL: http://www.fas.org/sgp/crs/row/R41108.pdf.

21. Chintamani, Mahapatra (2011). *Complex Cold Warriors: US-China Relations and Implications for India,* Journal of Defence Studies, Vol. 5 No. 3, July.

22. Mahapatra, C. (2011), *India-China-Pakistan Triangle: The US Factor,* Indian Foreign Affairs Journal, Vol. 6 No 4, December, pp. 404–421.

23. Mahbhubani, K. (2010). *Will China and India Grow Together or Grow Apart? Journal of Indian Ocean Studies,* Vol. 18, No. 2, August.

24. Maurice, P. and Oliver, G. (1994). *International Relations in the Indian Ocean,* Papers given during the International Symposium held in Saint-Denis, LA Reunion.

25. Medcalf, R. (2013). *"Whose Indo-Pacific? China, India and the United States in the Regional Maritime Security Order",* Paper presented at the Asia-Pacific

Centre for Security Studies Workshop on Maritime Cooperation in the Indo-Pacific Region: China, India and U.S. Perspectives, [Online] Accessed 05 Aug. 2013, URL: http://www.lowyinstitute.org/publications/whose-indo-pacific-china-india-and-united-states-regional-maritime-security-order.

26. Mishra, V. (2013). *Why does India shy away from Indian Ocean leadership?* [Online] Accessed 05 Aug. 2013, URL: http://southasiamonitor.org/detail. php?type=sl&nid=5113.

27. Mishra, V. (2014). China's Indian Ocean exercise: Beyond the obvious [Online: web] Accessed Dec 02, 2014. Available at: http://southasiamonitor. org/detail.php?type=sl&nid=7653

28. Osborn, K. (2014). "China's Submarine Fleet Takes Historic Steps Forward" [Online: web] Accessed Dec 03, 2014. Available at: http://defensetech. org/2014/10/29/chinas-submarine-fleet-takes-historic-steps-forward

29. Pai, N. (2009). "Indian submarine says an unfriendly hello to Chinese destroyers" [Online: web] Accessed Dec 03, 2014. Available at: http://acorn.nationalinterest.in/2009/02/04/indian-submarine-says-an-unfriendly-hello-to-chinese-destroyers

30. Panda, A. (2014). "Chinese Naval Exercise in Eastern Indian Ocean Sends Mixed Signals" [Online: web] Accessed Dec 03, 2014. Available at: http://thediplomat.com/2014/02/chinese-naval-exercise-in-eastern-indian-ocean-sends-mixed-signals

31. Panda, A. (2014). "Indian Naval Chief: Sea-Based Terrorism Is 'Huge'" [Online: web] Accessed Dec 03, 2014. Available at: http://thediplomat. com/2014/12/indian-naval-chief-sea-based-terrorism-is-huge/

32. Raja Mohan, C. 2011. "India, China and the United States: Asia's Emerging Strategic

33. Ranasinghe, D.S. (2014). "Why the Indian Ocean Matters" [Online: web] Accessed Dec 03, 2014. Available at: http://thediplomat.com/2011/03/why-the-indian-ocean-matters

34. Rao, P.V. (2001). Regional Cooperation in the Indian Ocean: Trends and Perspectives, South Asian Publishers: New Delhi.

35. Saunders, P.C. *et al.* (2011). *The Chinese Navy: Expanding Capabilities, Evolving Roles* (Published by National Defense University Press for the Center for the Study of Chinese Military Affairs, Institute for National Strategic Studies, Washington, D.C.

36. Scott, D. (2012). *Conflict Irresolution in the South China Sea, Asian Survey*, Vol. 52, No. 6 (November/December 2012), pp. 1019–1042.

37. Seth, S.P. (1975). *The Indian Ocean and Indo-American Relations*, Asian Survey, Vol. 15, No. 8, August.

38. Sharma, S.J. (2014). "The Indian Ocean in ASEAN's Future Maritime Discourse" [Online: web] Accessed Dec 03, 2014. Available at: http://the diplomat.com/2014/06/the-indian-ocean-in-aseans-future-maritime-discourse

39. Singh, A. (2014). "Rebalancing India's Maritime Posture in the Indo-Pacific" [Online: web] Accessed Dec 03, 2014. Available at: http://thediplomat. com/2014/09/rebalancing-indias-maritime-posture-in-the-indo-pacific

40. Singh, J. (ed.) (1994). *Indo-US Relations in a Changing World: Proceedings of the Indo-US Strategic Symposium*, Lancer Publishers: New Delhi.

41. Stanhope, M. (2010). *Royal Navy and the Maritime Security in the Indian Ocean, Speech to National Maritime Foundation, Delhi in the eminent lecture series, Journal of Indian Ocean Studies*, Vol. 18, No. 2, August.

42. The US in the Indian Ocean, Interview: Ray Mabus [Online: web] Accessed Dec 03, 2014. Available at: http://thediplomat.com/2013/12/ray-mabus

43. Triangle", *Strategic Snapshots, Snapshot 8, Asia Security project*, February, Lowy Institute for International Policy, [Online] Accessed 07 Aug. 2013, URL: http://apo.org.au/sites/default/files/Mohan,%20India_Snapshot8_web.pdf.

44. Zonyui, L. (2012). *The China-India-US Relationship: Where Will It Go?* [Online: web] Accessed 10 Aug. 2013. URL: http://www.futuredirections.org.au/publications/associate-papers/474-the-china-india-us-relationship.

Geopolitical Interests of China in the Indian Ocean Region: Security and Economic Implications for India

Durga Bhavani*

INDRODUCTION

Indian Ocean has acquired such significance in 21ˢᵗ century as never before. Indian Ocean Region (IOR) is the busiest trade region through which over one lakh vessels traverse annually. In the words of Robert D. Kaplan, "*The Indian Ocean area will be the true nexus of world powers and conflict in the coming years. It is here that the fight for democracy, energy independence and religious freedom will be lost or won*". The IOR is most sought after trade region as it contains 65% of oil reserves, 35% of natural gas, 80.7% of gold, 77.3% of natural rubber, 56.6% of tin, 28.5% of manganese and 25.2% of nickel.[1] Heavy traffic of petroleum products from the oil fields of the Persian Gulf and Indonesia pass through the International Sea Lanes (ISL)s and Sea Lanes of Communication (SLOC)s of the Indian Ocean to leading oil trading countries such as US and China. Annually, two-thirds of the world's seaborne trade in oil, 50 percent of the world's seaborne container traffic, one-third of the world's seaborne bulk cargo and the world's highest tonnage in the seaborne transportation of goods transit through the Indian Ocean and its adjacent waterways. Formation of regional trade blocs such as the SAARC, ASEAN and Indian Ocean Commission has led to tremendous increase in sea trade and development of new products.

No wonder, this is the period wherein most of the developed and developing economies are equally diverting their interests towards the third largest ocean on the earth. The trade and economic policies of these countries now include a definite 'Indian Ocean' policy. China is to be mentioned first and foremost in this context.

China now is not only a fastest growing economy due to its liberal policies but also an emerging regional power in terms of military,

*Researcher of International Relations. Member, Board of Studies, Andhra Mahila Sabha Arts and Science College for Women, Hyderabad.

particularly, navy. The economic boom within the country resulted in the increasing demand of raw materials and energy supplies and China began to feel the pressing need for looking beyond near seas for the same. As her dependence grew on her SLOCs, the protection of the same became imperative for China. The SLOCs of China extend from Malacca Strait in the east to Persian Gulf in the west passing through Indian Ocean. China laid focus on the South China Sea, Yellow Sea and now on Indian Ocean to protect her SLOCs. Over a period of time China began befriending various littoral members in the IOR and setting up naval bases, airstrips and harbours, metaphorically called 'String of Pearls', with their help. The consequence is that now there is an increased geo-political presence of China in the Indian Ocean.

This paper mainly studies the geo political interests of China in the Indian Ocean Region arising out of economic changes and development in the new millennium. The paper also studies the seaborne trade of India during the last decade and the implications of the rising China on the same apart from the security.

GEO-POLITICAL INTERESTS OF CHINA IN INDIAN OCEAN REGION

China has the distinction of becoming a very large trading nation. Till now, it stood second after US but reached the top slot in 2013 with trade volume of the Chinese mainland hitting a record high of US $4.16 trillion, overtaking the US $3.91 trillion.[2] This in spite of the fact that there is a decline in oil imports by around 9% than the 26.11 million tons of crude shipped last year and up around 2% from 23.28 million tons in June according to the Wall Street Journal's calculations.

Thus it is evident that China's dependence on Middle East for oil imports has reached new heights. This fact would undoubtedly impact the geopolitics of the region. Since its accession into the WTO in 2001, China's share in global trade has doubled—accounting for 10.38 percent of the world's merchandise trade exports and 9.3 percent of merchandise trade imports. From 2009–2011, its trade per capita was $ 2,413. As per the World Bank Data, the trade to GDP ratio of China during the period 2009–13 is about 47%. The primary imports are electrical and other machinery, oil and mineral fuels, optical and medical equipment, metal ores, motor vehicles, etc. The countries from where China primarily imports can be seen in Pic. 1. The major exports from China include electronic equipment, machinery, knit or crochet clothing, furniture, lighting, prefab buildings.

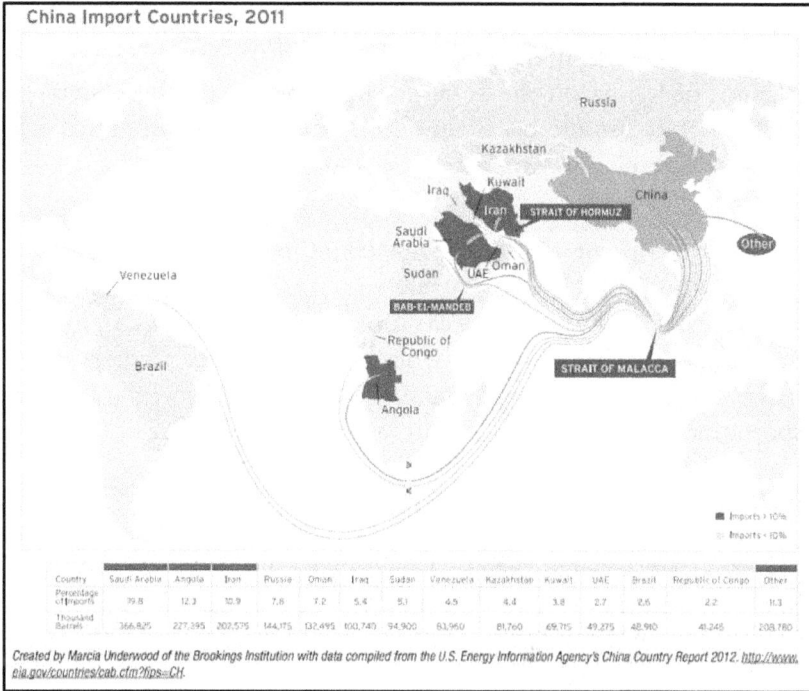

Pic. 1: Countries from China Imports

(*Source:* Created by Marcia Underwood of the Brookings Institution with data compiled from the US Energy Information Agency's China Country Report 2012. www.eia.gov)

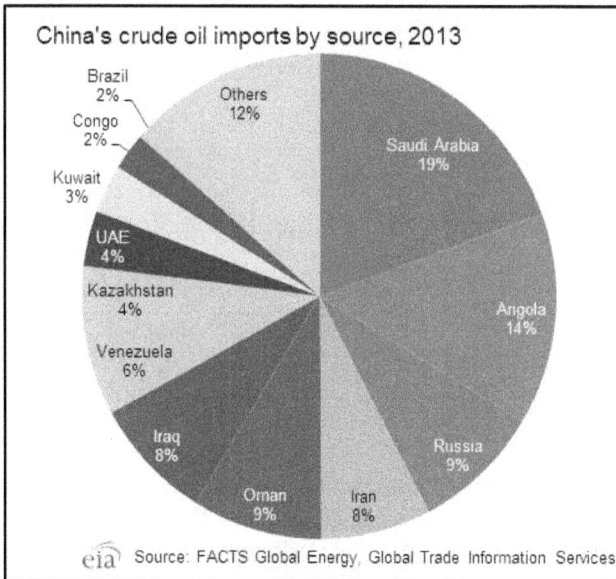

Pic. 2: Crude Oil Imports of China

(*Source:* FACTS Global Trade Information services)

The Pic. 2 shows the countries from where crude oil is being imported by China. As can be seen from the Pic. 1 and Pic. 2, there is a huge dependence of China on the IOR. A large portion of raw materials and energy for the economic boom in China must travel through the IOR. The most affected cargo would be of crude oil and dry bulk such as iron ore and coal.

As the dependence of China on the IOR grew, her sensitivity to the safety of her SLOC through the strategic choke points increased simultaneously. In the event of closure of the Southeast Asian strategic choke points, maritime traffic would have to sail farther south of Australia, placing increasing demands on vessel capacity, higher costs of transportation and disruption in both energy and material supply chains.

SIGNIFICANCE OF A CHOKE POINT

Owing to increasing growth of maritime circulation and global trade, choke points assumed considerable significance. Three vital characteristics determine the significance of a choke point. They are; *the Physical Characteristics, the Usage* and *the Access*. The *Physical Characteristics* are depth, width or navigability which might affect movement of vessels. *Usage* is the value of a choke point which is proportional to its degree of usage and availability of alternatives. *Access* to a choke point makes it a valuable resource for any maritime nation. To have access, some degree of control must be established to ensure that access like agreements, levying of tolls, etc.

CHOKE POINTS IN IOR

There are several choke points in the IOR which are shown in Pic. 3. The volume of the oil traffic through the choke points is given at Table 1.

Table 1: Volume of Oil Traffic through Choke Points in Million Barrels/Day

	2007	2008	2009	2010	2011
Babal Mandeb	4.6	4.5	2.9	2.7	3.4
Turkish Straits	2.7	2.7	2.8	2.9	N/A
Danish Straits	3.2	2.8	3.0	3.0	N/A
Strait of Hormuz	16.7	17.5	15.7	15.9	17.0
Strait of Malacca	13.8	NA	NA	NA	15.2

(*Source:* EIA estimates based on APEX Tanker Data (Lloyd's Maritime Intelligence Unit). Panama Canal Authority and Suez Canal Authority, converted with EIA conversion factors. (www.eia.gov/countries/regions-topics.cfm)

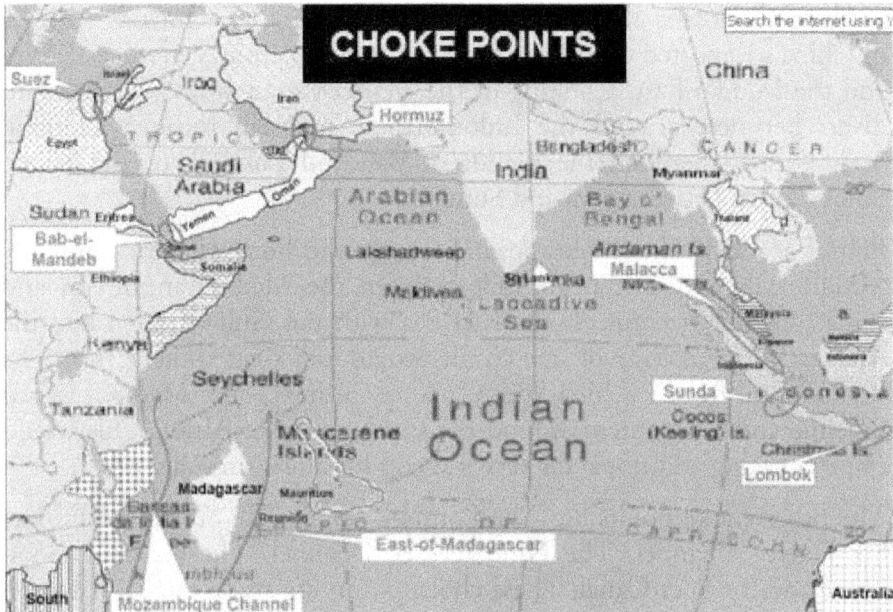

Pic. 3: Choke Points in Indian Ocean Region

(*Source:* Naveen Ahmed. *INS Chakra: A potential threat to Indian Ocean Stability.* OPINION MAKER. 16 April 2012.www.opinion-maker.org)

The sea lanes in the Indian Ocean are considered among the most strategically important in the world. According to Journal of Indian Ocean Region, more than 80% of world's seaborne trade in oil transits through Indian Ocean choke points, with 40% passing through the Strait of Hormuz, 35% through the Strait of Malacca and 8% through the Bab el-Mandab Strait. The ocean also contains an estimated 40% of the world's offshore oil production.

China imports 55% of its petroleum resources from the Persian Gulf with the majority of it passing through Strait of Hormuz. The significance of the Strait of Hormuz is that it is the only choke point which can come under a direct threat of closure by a nation within the chokepoint's region. If the Strait of Hormuz is closed, Chinese and other vessels would have to use longer alternate routes at increased transportation costs. Alternate routes include the 745 mile long Petroline, also known as the East-West Pipeline, across Saudi Arabia from Abqaiq to the Red Sea. From December 2011 to January 2012, some Iranian government officials openly threatened to close the Strait if sanctions are imposed on Iran's oil exports. This makes the threat perception of a vital choke point getting actually choked more than being hypothetical.

Strait of Malacca is another important choke point for China as 70-85% of China's imported oil passes through this Strait from Venezuela, Africa and the Middle East. Choking of the Malacca strait would cause her to divert her fleet around the Indonesian archipelago through Lombok Strait located between the islands of Bali and Lombok or the Sunda Strait located between Java and Sumatra.

Bab el-Mandeb is a choke point between the horn of Africa and the Middle East and a strategic link between the Mediterranean Sea and Indian Ocean. It connects the Red Sea with the Gulf of Aden and the Arabian Sea. Closure of the Strait would obstruct tankers from the Persian Gulf from reaching Suez Canal or Su-med (Suez-Mediterranean) Pipeline and divert them around the southern tip of Africa. This would cause engaging additional tankers and add to transit time and cost.

The other choke points are The Lombok Strait, The Sunda Strait, The Six Degree Channel, The Nine Degree Channel, The Cape of Good Hope and the Suez Canal. These choke points are also a cause of concern for China but of lesser significance than Straits of Hormuz, Malacca and Bab el-Mandeb.

GEO-POLITICAL INTERESTS OF INDIA IN IOR

India's maritime environment and geostrategic location makes it imperative that she takes effective steps in safeguarding her SLOCs in Indian Ocean. Total length of India's coastline is 7,516.6 kms including Lakshadweep and Andaman and Nicobar Islands. These islands together also form her island territories measuring 1,197 kms. A substantial amount of India's industrial and economic activity is located within 200 km of her coastline, including nuclear power stations. Her islands also have substantial economic potential. More than 90% of India's trade by volume and 77% by value are transported over the seas, and she being a considerably growing economy, these figures kept touching newer heights. According to a study conducted by ASSOCHAM, growing at a compounded annual growth rate (CAGR) of over 8%, the seaborne trade in India may cross 830 Million ton mark by 2016–17. This implies that India would require over ₹ 17,000 crore of investment to augment the port capacity by over 140 mt from the current level of about 690 mt.[3]

Pic. 4 shows India's various imports and exports and their relative importance. As can be seen from the picture, the major imports are petroleum crude, gold and silver and electronic goods. The major exports are the petroleum products and gems and jewellery. The major trading partners for the imports are China, UAE, Saudi Arabia, USA and Switzerland. Major exports from India are to USA and UAE.

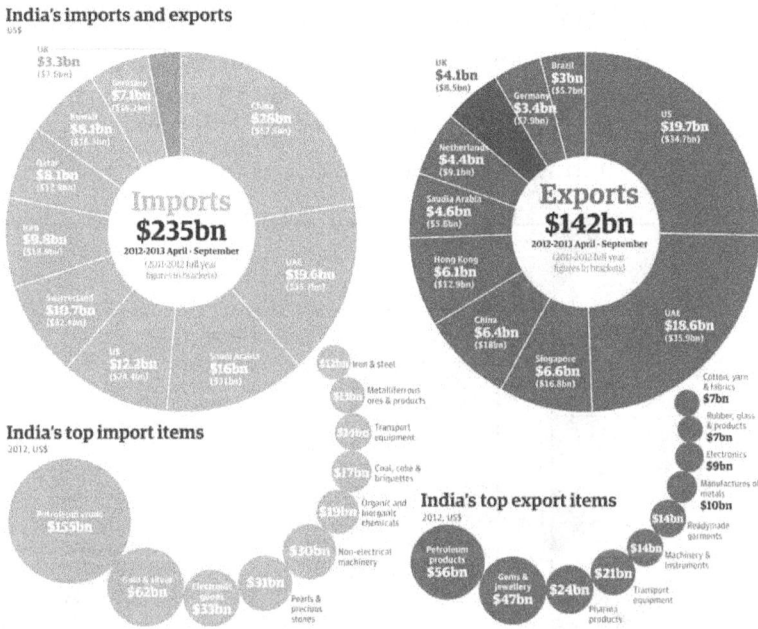

Pic. 4: India's Imports and Exports, 2012 in US $

(*Source:* India's trade: full list of exports, imports and partner countries. DATABLOG. www.theguardian.com)

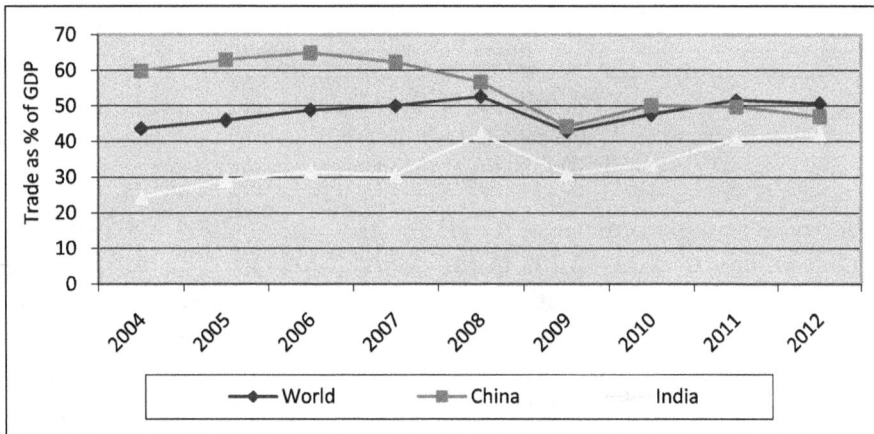

Pic. 5: Trade as % of GDP

India's merchandise trade increased exponentially in the 2000s decade from US$ 95.10 billion in 2000–01 to US$ 620.9 billion in 2010–11 and further to US$ 793.8 billion in 2011–12. India's share in global exports and imports also increased from 0.7% and 0.8% respectively in 2000 to 1.7% and 2.5% in 2011 as per the WTO. Its ranking in the leading exporters and importers improved from 31 and 26 in 2000 to 19 and 12 respectively in 2011. While India's total merchandise trade as a percentage of the gross domestic product (GDP) increased from 28.2% in 2004–5 to 43.2 per cent in 2011–12 as per provisional estimates, India's merchandise exports as a percentage of GDP increased from 11.8% to 16.5% during the same period.[4]

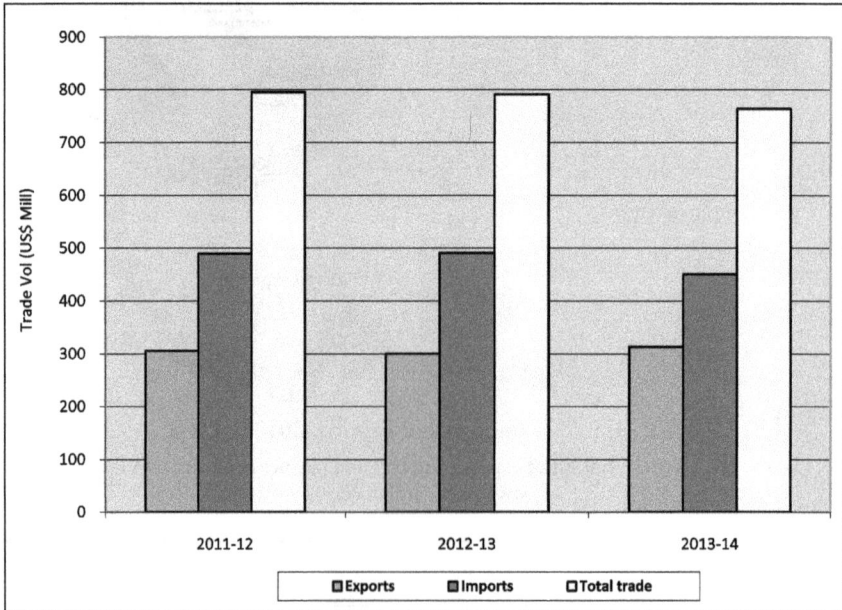

Pic. 6: Trend of Trade Volumes

(*Source:* Based on the data published in India Export Import Trade Statistics. INFODRIVEINDIA. www..infordriveindia.com)

The trade as a percentage of GDP for the period 2004–08 had been 40.8% while it rose to 42.1% in the period 2009–13. The trade volume of India for 2013 is estimated at US$ 779.3 billions. Pic. 5 shows the trends of the trade as a percentage of GDP of the World, China and India. It can be seen that the trend of India is gradually on the increase. Pic. 6 shows the trend in the trade volumes during the past three years which shows a steady state in both the imports and the exports. It can also be seen that there had been a slight increase in the exports while there is a marginal decrease in the imports during 2013–14.

Sea Resources: about 10–15 percent of population of India living in coastal areas are engaged in fishing as the sole means of livelihood. The security aspect of fishing entails safeguarding our EEZ against poaching, SAR cover and protection against use of fishing as a cover for inimical activities against the state, as seen in the 26/11 terrorist strikes in Mumbai in 2008.

Seabed Resources: presently India is depending mostly on imports for resources like nickel, cobalt and copper. With the International Seabed Authority ISA, according 'pioneer investor' status to India, and using advanced technology in deep sea mining, in future India may be able to harness, her own seabed resources.

Energy Security: India is the 4th largest energy consuming nation in the world after USA, China and Russia. Hence India needs assured supply of adequate energy resources to sustain its growth. While this includes oil, gas, coal etc, the requirement of hydrocarbon fields is part of energy security. The Persian Gulf and Africa are the major sources of India's oil and gas imports which are carried by the sea. Since India is also keen in investing hydrocarbon assets worldwide which need to be transported by sea lanes, security of energy will remain the prime concern. Incidentally, the choke points which are of significance to China are also of equal importance to India.

GEO-POLITICAL STRATEGIES AND INITIATIVES OF CHINA AND IMPLICATIONS FOR INDIA

Developing China into a strong maritime power has been a determination asserted from Mao to Xi Jinping. Delivering the political report to the eighteenth National Congress of Communist Party of China in 2012, General Secretary Hu Jintao declared "*We should enhance our capacity for exploiting marine resources and build China into a maritime power*". This was the first ever reference to 'maritime power'. To Liu Cigui, Director of State Oceanic Administration (SOA), building China into a maritime power is "an essential path on the way to the sustained development of the Chinese nation and [achievement of the status of a] global power".[5]

China's latest white paper on ocean policy, China's Ocean Development Report(2012), explains the relationship between strategy and policy and their respective scopes as "Ocean policy is a code of behaviour established for the state's strategy, course, development plans, and external relations concerning the seas.... It encompasses policies concerning development and use of the seas, including utilization of sea areas, development and protection of sea islands, protection of marine environment, marine science and technology, marine industry......".[6] Marine industry mainly includes among others, oil and gas development and manufacturing of engineering equipment and transportation.

China's Indian Ocean policy focuses, among others, on two important aspects. They are, (a) ensuring that China's national image is supported by a network of diplomatic relations with which to secure trade relations and influence; (b) ensuring that China's objectives are not jeopardised by India or the United States. Thus, China is quite clear about her India policy and very keen on protecting her SLOCs in the IOR.

CHINA'S PRESENCE IN INDIAN OCEAN

China's growing presence in and around the Indian Ocean Region begins with its submarine base in Hainan Island in the South China Sea. She has deployed submarines of Jin class in 2008 at a base near Sanya in the southern tip of Hainan which is just 1200 nautical miles from Malacca Strait and is its closest point to the Indian Ocean. This is a fact which definitely creates unrest in Indian circles. The base also has an underground facility that can hide the movement of submarines, making them difficult to detect. The strategic implication in this context is that this base includes access tunnels on the mouth of deep waters. With the aid of such presence, China could hamper shipping at the three crucial choke points in the Indian Ocean—Bab el Mandeb, the Strait of Hormuz and the Strait of Malacca.

In South China Sea, China has adopted a not so popular mechanism of 'naming' of thinly populated and uninhabited islands and thus gain a foot hold and assert her sovereignty. She has given names to 1,660 islands by 2012 and planned to name 1,664 more islands by 2013. The naming of smaller and weaker areas is a generally accepted procedure according to principles of International Law, says Jacques deLisle, a University of Pennsylvania law professor and expert on Chinese law. Harsh V. Pant says, "China's expansionist behaviour has, in fact long been evident. China has been acquiring naval facilities along the crucial choke-points in the Indian Ocean, not only to serve its economic interests but also to enhance its strategic presence in the region".[7]

According to Balaji Chandramohan, China seems to be adopting the strategy of "Island hopping"[8] in the Indian Ocean which involves capturing an island, building a base there and moving on toward its prime target. She is seeking to contain India in it, by forging alliances with island nations including Maldives, Mauritius, and Seychelles, and completing the chain of naval bases, popularly known as the' string of pearls'.

FOOTHTHOLDS OF CHINA: MILITARY AND OTHERWISE

Sitttwe Port a twin oil and gas pipeline was constructed linking west Arakan in Myanmar—Yunnan province. More than the pipeline, Sittwe is the site of the major Chinese-funded Kyakpu port which apart from being the starting point of the pipeline, is a vital access point to Southeast Asia and the Indian subcontinent. Minerals and other raw materials from Africa and oil from Middle East are shipped through this port to China. China offered to modernise Myanmar's naval facilities in return for the permission to use the Coco Islands. Implication of this for India is two-fold, being close to Indian border, the presence of China gives rise to concern of security. As Myanmar shares border with India, the threat of infiltration across the borders would increase; secondly, India's trade and energy security from Africa and Middle East could be challenged.

Coco Islands: The maritime reconnaissance and electronic intelligence station on Great Coco Island in the Bay of Bengal, some 300 km south of Myanmar's mainland, is the most important Chinese electronic Signals Intelligence (SIGINT) installation in Myanmar. The Chinese Army is also building a base on Small Coco Island in the Alexandra Channel between the Indian Ocean and the Andaman Sea, north of India's Andaman Islands. These two islands, located at a crucial point in traffic routes between the Bay of Bengal and the Strait of Malacca are an ideal location for monitoring Indian naval and missile launch facilities in Andaman and Nicobar Islands to the south, as those from ISRO at Sriharikota and DRDO at Chandipur on sea, and movements of the Indian Navy and other navies throughout the eastern Indian Ocean. This situation is certainly of concern to India.

Chittagong Port: Is the largest port in Bangladesh and is being funded heavily by China through which she could obtain container shipping facility. While it can be looked at as China's assistance to Bangladesh to developing infrastructure, but from a geo-strategic point it also indicates an expanding footprint in the IOR.

Hambantota Port: Hambantota port in Sri Lanka indicates China's expanding relations with strategically located member states in Indian Ocean. Though it is not considered as one of China's 'pearls', Chinese investment in the port suggests the country's wider naval ambitions in the region. They include extensive replenishment facilities that could be provided for Chinese warships submarines. The first phase was completed in 2011, and second phase expected to be completed in 2014. This port is strategically significant as it is located along east –west shipping route.

Gwadar Port: In Pakistan is also funded by China. It is close to the Pakistan-Iran border and the Strait of Hormuz, through which much of the Gulf's oil exports are carried by ship to international markets. Oil tankers from the Gulf bound for India's Vadinar Oil Terminal in the Gulf of Kutch generally pass about 40 nautical miles south of Gwadar port and would be vulnerable to interdiction by Pakistani or Chinese units based at Gwadar.

Maldives and Mauritius: China is also heavily investing in Maldives and Mauritius slowly getting them under her influence. India has a crucial strategic, military and economic interest in the Maldives as it has a naval and coast guard surveillance and maritime presence in the island nation, which is why she is closely watching China. Chinese investments in Mauritius gain strategic importance as the island nation facilitates key access to the former in her pursuance of economic objectives in Africa. Till now China invested around $700 million in a special economic zone in the Indian Ocean.

Seychelles: Is the latest addition to China's strategic presence in the Indian Ocean. China has been seriously involved in building a naval base in Seychelles which it claims would be purely to 'resupply and recuperate' other ships engaged in anti-piracy missions in the Gulf of Aden. She has been imparting military training to a batch of 50 soldiers in China as a part of a military cooperation agreement signed between the two countries in 2004. As a part of developing military ties, China gifted the Seychelles People's Defence Forces (SPDF) with two Y-12 aircraft for surveillance and anti-piracy duties.

On the other hand, while concerned about her own geopolitical interests in deep waters, China had been cautious about Indian vessels. China has expressed her disapproval regarding the presence of Indian oil companies in the South China Sea. India signed an agreement with Vietnam in October 2011 to expand and promote oil exploration in South China Sea and has since reconfirmed its decision to carry on despite the Chinese challenge to the legality of Indian presence. By accepting the Vietnamese invitation to explore oil and gas in Blocks 127 and 128, India's state-owned oil company ONGC Videsh Ltd(OVL), not only expressed New Delhi's desire to deepen its friendship with Vietnam, but ignore China's warning to stay away. After asking countries "outside the region" to stay away from the South China Sea, China issued a demarche to India in November 2011, underlining that Beijing's permission should be sought for exploration in Blocks 127 and 128 and, without it, OVL's activities would be considered illegal. India had decided to explore hydrocarbons with Vietnam, after an incident occurred in July 2011. It so happened that, an unidentified Chinese warship demanded that INS Airavat, an amphibious assault vessel, identify itself and explain its presence in the South China Sea after leaving Vietnamese waters. Completing a scheduled port call in Vietnam, the Indian warship was in international waters.

There is huge build-up of inventory by People's Liberation Army Navy (*PLAN*) including its modernisation. China has inducted her first Aircraft Carrier recently and had been planning to induct the second. There had been increased presence of *PLAN* in Indian Ocean through various forms like escorting the merchant ships, conducting of naval drills jointly with other countries etc. which increase threat perception due to war-preparedness in the process.

A document released by defence ministry of India, citing subsurface data shared by US forces, mentions that Indian navy has had 22 contacts with Chinese submarines, all in 2012.[9] Since it is believed that only two forces, those of India and the US are capable of operating in the IOR, Indian military concluded that the boats were very likely from the *PLAN*.

Very often, India's concerns about the likely disruption to her seaborne trade, security of her oil and energy supplies through the SLOCs of IOR, threat to security of her coast—are all rejected and considered baseless by China herself and some other states. However, when one considers the elevated status of China as a leading economic power, her ever growing presence, military or otherwise, in the IOR with some locations being within 500 or 300 nautical miles from India's coast, her expansion of military ties with some key members of the IORA etc, India's concerns cannot be totally rejected. "This is not a fear, this is a fact. When you put together all these jigsaw puzzles it becomes clear that Chinese focus in Indian Ocean is not just for trade.......It is a grand design for the 21st Century". says Professor Srikanth Kondapalli of Jawaharlal Nehru University-New Delhi.[10]

The bottom line is that today there is an increased presence of China in the Indian Ocean Region, due to which, Indian economy and security are facing a threat.

RESPONSE OF INDIA SO FAR

India's geostrategic location in the IOR connecting major routes of world trade, her own increasing dependence on these routes due to her rapidly growing economy, possessing the third largest army in the world—all these factors add to India's responsibility in maintaining the equilibrium, peace and security in the region. Today, Indian Navy is considered by many littoral countries as the right agency to facilitate regional maritime security in the IOR as a net security provider. To maintain peace, prevention of armed conflict becomes imperative. This quality is sufficiently exhibited by Indian navy during Kargil operations where it effectively achieved India's operational goals and more importantly, limited the scope of conflict. Thus, Indian navy's perspective plans are not just centred on building force structure, but capabilities to meet the identified and emerging challenges. India is not keen on competing with any other country in just increasing the numbers. "We are focused on creating capabilities and leveraging our strategic geography to assert and defend our sovereign interests in the maritime domain. With modern aircraft carriers, along with potent surface, sub-surface and air platforms, we have a balanced force capable of undertaking a range of operations, from the brown to the blue waters, and also contribute to regional security".[11]

India also undertakes bilateral coordinated patrols, or simply CORPAT, with Thailand and Indonesia, which address a range of maritime security issues. India is also a party to ReCAAP or Regional Cooperation Agreement on anti-piracy and Armed Robbery against Ships in Asia, a government to government agreement on anti-piracy and information sharing. Indian navy successfully sank four pirate mother ships in 2011. In fact, it has been actively participating in antipiracy operation in the Gulf of Aden since October 2008.

In the same year, India also pioneered the Indian Ocean Naval Symposium (IONS) comprising Indian Ocean navies. Today it has 35 member navies from the region. It led to establishing and promoting consultations and cooperation amongst various participants and is also facilitating evolution of common set of strategies to enhance regional maritime security.

Maritime security is central to overall development of Indian economy. Today, there is a need for a cooperative approach to security especially in maritime domain, where majority of global economic interests get intertwined and to which a majority of challenges such as proliferation of Weapons of Mass Destruction (WMD), piracy, terrorism and climate change confront all countries. Several regional economic groupings such as Association of Southeast Asian Nations (ASEAN), The Bay of Bengal Initiative for Multi-Sectoral Technical and Economic Cooperation (BIMSTEC), The South Asian Association for Regional Cooperation (SAARC), Indian Ocean Rim Association (IORA) and others have evolved over time in the IOR which work towards better cooperation among member states.

India has made significant regional agreements and bilateral naval exercises with France—VARUNA since 2002, the US—MALABAR first in 1992 and again regularly since 2002, Russia—INDRA since 2003, and the United Kingdom—KONKAN since 2004. India, Sri Lanka, Maldives signed tripartite maritime security pact for regional maritime cooperation in Indian Ocean in July 2013. Indian navy provides equipment and training to many Indian Ocean countries. It offered to train Sri Lankan navy officers through a bachelor's degree in technology, in 2013.

Indian navy conducts a biennial MILAN exercise since 1995. 15 ships manoeuvred in perfect harmony in Andaman Sea as a part of the MILAN 2014 biennial exercise of Navies at Port Blair, spread over 6 days. 17 nations, including India, had come together making it the biggest edition since its inception. It was the first time that countries from western IOR participated including two African nations viz. Kenya and Tanzania; island nations of Mauritius, Maldives and Seychelles. Philippines and Cambodia participated for the first time.

India, on her part, had been reaching out to littoral countries and extending helping hand. She had also been developing trading relationships and providing substantial aid and financial support for their development.

Andaman and Nicobar islands make for an extremely useful Indian listening post for the larger Indian Ocean region. However, the remoteness of these islands is the biggest insecurity, making them vulnerable to conventional and non-conventional threat. Considering China's maritime intentions in Indian Ocean, India has begun to step up military strength. Around these 572 islands Indian navy has begun to build a barrier of strength.

India unveiled her first indigenous aircraft carrier, INS Vikrant on August 12, 2013. This is a much needed step in modernising her navy to effectively deal with Chinese strength in the Indian Ocean. Indian navy now has an amphibious transport dock of Austin class, re-christened INS Jalashwa, and a fleet of landing ships. The navy currently operates nine guided-missile destroyers.

However, Indian navy presently is weakened by obsolete frontline warships and submarines falling prey to accidents like the explosions that destroyed INS Sindhurakshak kilo class submarine in August 2013. It is the same navy which successfully tackled Pakistan in 1971 in the maritime battle in the IOR. Today Indian navy is vulnerable with ageing fleet of warships and submarines. Today she is left with 20 major surface combatants such as INS Vikramaditya and INS Viraat aircraft carriers, destroyers and frigates, while her submarine fleet is down to just 13 vessels. The plan to have 24 submarines is delayed by a decade.[12]

CONCLUSION

It is quite evident that Indian Ocean Region is of paramount importance to China. She is bound to keep her presence vibrant to protect her economic interests. China is expected to continue augmentation of her inventory in *PLAN*, continue to befriend the littoral nations and strengthen its 'String of Pearls'. Initiatives taken by the Chinese leadership is ensuring that the growth of *PLAN* is in the direction of improving its capabilities of integrated offshore operations, strategic deterrence and strategic counter attacks. The extensive training to its manpower, rapid modernisation, increased self-reliance in building up its infrastructure is making it an organisation gearing up to meet the aspirations of China. Substantial build-up of inventory, both in terms of quality and quantity, is making the world wake up to the new challenge as they are capable of increased penetration with precision. The joint military exercises in far seas, setting out on sail for anti-piracy operations, conducting of escort missions etc. ensure their increased presence in the Indian Ocean Region. The continued raise in the budget outlay for defence till it became second only to USA and thrice that of India, is reinforcing the continued thrust on further build-up of the capabilities.

Given the resources that are built up strategically in the Indian Ocean Region, there is a vast potential for China to use the same for coercion. Since economy and security of India is highly dependent on Indian Ocean Region and preparation of herself to face any situation that arises out of the Chinese overtones anytime is an absolute necessity for India. While for China, it is an economic option for optimising its transportation for its imports and exports, it is a dire necessity for India for her survival.

India recognised these factors and started taking initiatives to strengthen her own naval inventory, missile strike capability, befriending littoral nations and immediate neighbours. But the pace and penetration of India is far less in comparison to that of China. The aggression with which China is pursuing her Indian Ocean objectives is yet to be matched by India. While China has the advantage of its political set up of the country, the task for India is more difficult as a democratic nation. It is needless to state that these issues be addressed beyond political short sightedness since the threat potential for the economic as well as security interests is huge.

Keeping in view the serious and negative implications for the security of India of the direction that geo-political scenario in IOR is taking, various initiatives can be taken by India in to minimise the impact on India's own interests. They include measures to improve bilateral relations, taking up of confidence building measures, developing Indian Navy world class and making use of various international platforms for increasing the say of India and addressing various issues of concern for India. Though the government is taking initiatives in each of these areas, the emphasis and thrust has to keep pace with the developments and initiatives being made by China.

REFERENCES

1. *Evolving Strategic Competition in the Indian Ocean.* STRATRISKS.18 April 2013.www.stratrisks.com, accessed on 28 September 2014.
2. *Follow the Money, China trade, imports and exports.* EW World Economy Team ECONOMY WATCH. 04 June 2013. www.economywatch.com/world_economy/china/export-import.html. Accessed 02 October 2014.
3. Das, Purba. *India's Seaborne Trade to cross 830 Million Tones Mark by FY17.* Business Insider. 7 October 2014.
   www.businessinsider.in. Accessed on 8 October 2014
4. Economic Survey 2012–13. International Trade Chapter 7.. 5 February 2013. www.indiabudget.nic.in. Accessed on 7 October 2014
5. Junichi, Tukeda. *China's Rise as a Maritime Power: Ocean Policy from Mao Zedong to Xi Jinping.* Review of Island Studies, 23 April 2014. www.islandstudies.oprf-info.org/research/a00011. Accessed on 8 October 2014
6. *China's Ocean Development Report.* China Institute for Marine Affairs. 2012. (China Ocean Press), p. 261.
7. Pant, Harsh V., "China's Naval Expansion in the Indian Ocean and India-China Rivalry", *The Asia-Pacific Journal: Japan Focus*, 03 May 2010, www.japanfocus.org/-Harsh_V_-Pant/3353, accessed on 10 October 2014.

8. Chandramohan, Balaji, "China Island Hopping in the Indian Ocean", *ATLANTICSENTINEL*. 23 December 2011, www.atlanticsentinel.com/author/balaji-chandramohan, accessed on 04 October 2014.

9. Singh, Rahul, "China's Submarines in Indian Ocean worry Indian Navy". *Hindustan Times*. New Delhi. 07 April 2013 www.hindustantimes.com/india-news/newdelhi. Accessed 22 September 2014.

10. "Is Chittagong one of China's String of Pearls". *Indian Defence Forum*. 24 May, 2010. www.defenceforumindia.com/forum/defence-strategic-issues/17032-. Accessed 04 October 2014.

11. Joshi, D.K., (Admiral), PVSM, AVSM, YSM, NM, ADC. [Chief of the Naval staff(CNS)] 05 March 2013. "Role of Indian Navy in Maintaining Peace in Indian Ocean Region". www.idsa.in/keyspeeches/ Roleof Indian Navyin Maintaining Peace in Indian Ocean Region_CNS. Accessed 11 October 2014.

12. Bipindra, N.C., "The Great Indian Ocean Game", *The New Indian Express*. 01 December 2013. www.newindianexpress.com/magazine/the-great-indian-ocean-game/2013/12. Accessed 11 October 2014.

A Chinese Observation: Indians' Perception of China and their "China Complex"

J.I.A. Haitao*

INTRODUCTION

The international community have treated China and India as a pair of counterparts or twin brothers for quite a long time, and described the Sino-Indian relations as competition or contest. Indians also like to compare or contrast India with China, and many people regard China as India's rival and feel jealous of it, however, some have quite positive attitude and advocate friendship with China. Thus, Indians' attitude towards China is complex, even contradictory, a sort of ambivalence. This is a "China Complex" or "Psychological China Knot". Although the Indians are very concerned about China, but their understanding of China is quite limited. With the deepening of mutual exchanges of diplomatic visits and dialogues the situation has changed and now a long-term friendship between the two nations is growing.

Some Western and Indian scholars view the relationship between India and China as competitors. It is believed that both countries with huge growth potential are running a neck-and-neck race in several sectors. Does this mentality of competition and contest prevail between China and India? Can the race be understood and the competition or contest be qualitatively and quantitatively analyzed from a positive perspective if it exists in certain degree between the two Asian giants? Can efforts be made to improve the bilateral relations of these two nations if the race with comparison goes to hostility and the competition turns unhealthy? This paper aims to investigate India's "competition and comparison psyche" vis-a-vis China and the root causes of it, as well put forward my opinions on the possibilities of reducing mutual misunderstanding and mistrust. The status quo of the Sino-Indian contemporary relationship will also be discussed, but the main focus will be on India's perception of China, the mindset in general and the 'psychological knot' of understanding China.

*Professor and Director of the Institute for Chindian Studies, Jinan University, Guangzhou, Chi.

THE COMPARISON AND COMPETITION
BETWEEN CHINA AND INDIA

The world's two most populous countries have since long been fascinated by the West and with comparing China and India in various aspects because there's a strong resemblance between the two countries. Both bear similarities or at least demonstrate potential for comparison in many aspects including history, population, international status, economic development, social condition, poverty and other social problems. As Stefen Cohen points out, "For Asians and Indians alike, Beijing is the measuring stick of India's 'emergence' as a great power"[1] and "India most closely resembles China in its current reemergence as major state, although it trails far behind in many respects".[2] However, he believes that the gap between China and India is far smaller than imagined and the former does not enjoy much advantage over the latter. He remarks, "Both India and China have domestic vulnerabilities, but here India may have the advantage."[3]

Admittedly, contemporary Indians always keep China in their mind and are obsessed about comparing with China. With China and India exercising increasing influence in international affairs and gaining momentum in economic development in the recent two decades, a growing number of international scholars, entrepreneurs, and politicians are keen of comparing Dragon and Elephant on various measures of development. Western academia and media even state that there exist "historical hatred and jealousy" between China and India.[4] Joseph Nye points out in his article published in the Singaporean leading Chinese newspaper *Lianhe Zaobao*, "Indian officials generally do not talk about India's relations with China in public, but privately they are very concerned", and he describes it as India's "anxiety".[5] A Chinese scholar, Hong Kong Phoenix TV host Qiu Zhenhai named this phenomenon as India's "China complex". As Qiu points out: "the 'China Complex' embedded in India's vision of Great India serves as the major obstacle haunting Indian diplomatic relations towards China. This sentiment indicates that India regards China as objective to compete or surpass in order to secure its great power status and it also has become one of the crucial external factors affecting the rise of India itself."[6] If his argument proved valid, then this sentiment had been in existence since India's independence, and deepened following the mutual hostility and antagonism after the 1962 Sino-Indian border war. The war has set Asia's two principal powers on a course of rivalry and deep mistrust, and the painful memory continues to torment both nations. The Indian elite class, to some extent has held certain degree of vigilance, jealousy, defiance and hostility towards China and the "Sino-Indian rivalry" has been a significant issue for discussion in India. On the other hand, we also witness many Indians who admire and appreciate the progress China has made and are eager to learn valuable lessons from this neighboring country. In regard to this, Mohan Malik once commented, "In India's policy makers circle and media, 'the China debate' is most active than at any time since the 1962 Sino-Indian War. How to deal with China plugs into wider debate in India—a debate about India's role in Asia and the world. For Indians, 'the China challenge' comes in four forms—enmity, envy, awe and emulation..."[7] In December 12, 2012, referring to the Indian External Affairs Minister, Salman Khurshed, Pakistan said that China has become India's 'main concern' over Pakistan.[8]

Inspired by international society and academic community, Chinese scholars lately have shown increasing interest in India and are continuously engaged in Sino-Indian comparative studies comprehensively or focusing on certain issues of prime importance to both the countries. It is worth pointing out that Chinese people have always been taking care of India's concerns without slightest resentment and jealousy, actively seeking possibility to revert bilateral relationship back to a long-standing condition of stability, enhancing mutual understanding and trust and boosting strategic cooperation. Therefore, the so-called "Sino-Indian hatred and jealousy" can only be originated from unilateral imagination of a very small group of Indians themselves or just the projection of the Western world. Of course, we cannot ignore the fact that many Indians genuinely demonstrate admiration, envy and appreciation of China's achievement without any negative or hostile sentiment. It is imperative for the Chinese to know India thoroughly and hold accurate and objective understanding of Indians' perception of China, otherwise, the Chinese will easily get trapped into some kind of misunderstanding and fixed mindset.

China and India share a lot of similarities, standing like a mirror image of each other and offering opportunities for mutual learning and emulating. In fact, as India and China continue to grow in prominence, each nation has certain advantages, but neither one is primed to have clear across-the-board competitive advantages over the other. A veteran in his field of journalism, a keen commentator on global economic movements for over two decades and a renowned entrepreneur in India, Raghav Bahl argued in his famous book *Super Power? The Amazing Race between China's Hare and India's Tortoise* maintains that the two Asian economic power houses India and China are almost behaving akin to the fabled hare and tortoise.

While China, almost hare like, leaps ahead and captures global attentions through its manufacturing juggernaut, India too in very sure steps is accelerating its way to set an economic pivot. From his perspective, China rises fast and but vulnerable and susceptible to chaos and social strife while India though appears to be far behind, its democratic and legal traditions and its strong entrepreneurial foundation make its model more robust, giving it a chance of overhauling China in the long run. Therefore, India and China have equal opportunity in establishing leadership within the final leg of this amazing superpower race. He believes, "Between India and China, the odds are fifty fifty. It's an amazing race between China's hare and India's tortoise—one that China need not automatically win, and India should not believe it is bound to lose."[9]

Actually, India may have edge over China in several aspects. Despite its slightly weaker comprehensive national strength to China, India has a better "brand" than China, thanks, largely to its successful display of soft power. As far as the safety and sustainability of development model is concerned, the Indian Model does not necessarily lag behind China Model. In other words, whether "China Model" or "India Model" can be hailed as the "role model" for development path to the entire developing world is difficult to predict. Consequently, it is crucial for the Chinese to carefully examine and analyze the development model of India, draw experiences from it thus to reduce their shortcomings.

In the recent years, in the international society and the international academic community, scholars and researchers tend to initiate certain comparisons (though often indirectly) between Chinese Diaspora and Indian Diaspora in playing a critical role in the economic growth of their country of origin. With regard to the similarity and comparability between China and India, the Chinese and Indian Diaspora also involve significant common characteristics. Nevertheless, the international influence and mutual competition between Chinese Diaspora and Indian Diaspora can only make sense or worth exploring within the broader context of the rise of China and India. The comparison of the two Diaspora groups is actually established against the comparison of the growth trajectories of China and India. Honestly speaking, there exists little value in comparing between Chinese Diaspora and Indian Diaspora without the general comparison of national development between China and India, giving the fact that there is no direct rivalry, connection or interaction between the two Diasporas. As a result, discussion on Chinese and Indian Diasporas should be put under the broader historical and contemporary background instead of being considered as an isolated phenomenon. To some extent, the development model, the level of development and the foreign relations of China and India determine the relationships and cooperation patterns of the two countries with their overseas migrants. This is a very important frame of reference for comparison between the two Asian giants in terms of their achievements and growth potential as well as their Diasporas.

India has the second largest Diaspora in the world after overseas Chinese. The overseas Indian community estimated at over 2.19 million is spread across every major region in the world.[10] The size and economic strength of the Indian Diaspora globally have increased dramatically and are well acknowledged. Cohen observes, "It also has a diaspora that constitutes a potential asset for the Indian state, as well as a new link with the United States."[11] He points out, "The Indian diaspora will play a greater role in key countries, especially the United States; it will develop closer links to India itself, and the Indian government will view it as a political and economic asset."[12]

Indian Diaspora retains a collective memory about their homeland and regards the ancestral homeland as their home, believing that they should be committed to the restoration of their homeland, and continuing relations with their homeland. They maintain communication to their roots and homeland through networks and interracial marriage and concern much about the cultural identity or "Indianness" of their children.[13] Moreover, Indian Diaspora, in the form of Non-resident Indian or Person of Indian Origin, persistently call for more opportunities to invest in India. They expect Indian government to set up constructive schemes or streamline investment procedures to facilitate Indian Diaspora's economic engagement with India. Makarand Paranjape, professor at the Jawaharlal Nehru University of India argues that Indian Diaspora is destined to have tremendous influence on India in every perspective. He has been calling for the emergence of a transnational Indian identity.[14] He further states that as a sovereign state, India's existence is not confined to its geographical or political territories but extends beyond national borders which gives birth to the notion of a "Greater India" including all Indian Diaspora.[15] The appeal from Indian media and intellectual community is well received by the Indian government. The Indian Diaspora wants to be regarded as Indian citizens while the Indian government wants to take advantage of the Diaspora network, resources and human capital to help drive the country's long-term economic growth. A fundamental transformation has been set in motion so far as policy towards Indian Diaspora is concerned among which the introduction of "Dual Citizenship" caught the largest attention. Nowadays, Indian Diaspora enjoy frequent and convenient interaction and integration economically and culturally with the motherland.

As an Asian powerhouse with a large population, abundant resources and high-skilled talent pool, India has registered fast and steady economic growth over the past decade. It is expected India has huge potential to overtake China as the fastest growing country mostly attractive for investment. In the next 20 years, the international influence and wealth possession of Indian Diaspora may be comparable to Chinese Diaspora and the comprehensive national strength of India, particularly the economic strength, may catch up with or even surpass China. To some extent, Indian Diaspora will play a significant role in boosting the future economic development of India and it is fair to say that the key to India's economic take-off lies in the harnessing of Indian Diaspora capabilities in the areas of capital, technology and talent. In recent years, Indian government has made major breakthroughs in policy and legislation considering leveraging the overseas Indians resources. Originally, India lagged far behind China in terms of Diaspora policy and the situation has changed radically attributed to the launch of these new policies.

Contribution of Chinese Diaspora to China's economic development is noticeable to the outside world and envied by the Indian government. Notwithstanding, with the deepening of China's reform and opening up and gaining in economic strength, the population, economic power and contribution to homeland of Chinese Diaspora will increase as well. However, much work still needs to be done on immigration policy, Diaspora policy and strengthening ties with Chinese Diaspora. There existed huge untapped strategic assets of Diaspora capital, knowledge, expertise and management know-how. The Indian government had once followed Chinese experience in Diaspora management with a much more radical policy and China in turn can learn from India's lessons carefully and proactively.

INDIA'S "CHINA COMPLEX"

One cannot fail to mention India's "Great Power Dream" when it comes to India's "China Complex" as referred by some Chinese observers. The former came into existence earlier and lasted longer and more intense than the latter. The emergence, frustration and revival of India's "Great Power Dream" might be related to China to some extent, which can be briefly summarized as India's "China Complex". This presents major challenge for the deepening and consolidating of Sino-Indian friendship and limits improvement in Sino-Indian relationships.

India has been dreaming of rising to the top of the heap of economically powerful nations and assumed a natural leadership role in South Asia by the virtue of its size, location and economic potential since its independence. In fact, India has established dominant status in the entire Indian Ocean Region once it claimed independence. However, India's ambition does not end here. Jawaharlal Nehru once addressed in a national speech arguing that India was destined to become the third or fourth most powerful nation in the world. He firmly believed that India's international status should not be compared with Pakistan and other South Asian countries, but with United States, the Soviet Union and China.[16] He once stated, "India constituted as she is, cannot play a secondary part in the world. She will either count for great deal or not count at all. No middle position attracted me. Nor did I think any intermediate position feasible".[17]

Once upon a time, India enjoyed high prestige in the newly independent former colonies or developing countries and exercised great influence in the international political arena. It not only played an important role in the course of the Korean armistice and the Vietnamese peaceful negotiations, but also became the dominant player in the Asian-African Conference in the 1950s as well as led the Non-Aligned Movement with countries such as Yugoslavia and Egypt. It once seemed to be the only developing country which reached equilibrium balanced between Western world and the Socialist camp as well as between developed and developing countries. However, India failed to realize the "Super Power" objective set by Nehru due to its economic backwardness and severely limited military strength. The international society even witnessed the fading of India's international influence during the 1960s to 1980s in the 20th century. However, some Indians, maybe small in group, did not reflect on India itself and instead blamed China for its decreasing international credibility and declining world status. The China's self-defense war against India in 1962 became the excuse for India's diplomatic failure, weakening international prestige and stagnant economic development which resulted in India's resentment towards China. Some ruling elites even explicitly or implicitly long considered China as its primary opponent. Some Indian government officials have repeatedly and openly talk about the so-called "China threat", paving the way for its nuclear policy. In 1998, India successfully launched its nuclear weapon test. Facing international condemnation and U.S. economic sanctions, on one hand, the Indian government maintained tough stance superficially; on the other hand, the then Indian Prime Minister Atal Bihari Vajpayee secretly wrote to the then US. President Bill Clinton explaining India's development and utilization of nuclear weapons were directed against China. He claimed that India shared the same strategic objective of "encircling China" as US and the development of nuclear capacity by India conformed to the national interest of the US. Vajpayee expressed in the letter with a view to seek support and understanding from the US. Unexpectedly, the U.S. government publicized this secret letter which embarrassed Vajpayee and the Indian government. Indian Defense Minister George Fernandes had publicly declared China as India's number one military threat which served as a perfect motive to achieve military expansion and develop nuclear weapons in India.[18]

All these episodes have given the Chinese a very deep impression. For the understanding of many people, both Vajpayee's secret letter and Fernandez's remark can largely represent the India government and elites' attitudes towards China. Quoted from former Chinese Ambassador to India Pei Yuanying, India has always perceived China with caution and apprehension, and the mainstream newspaper "Global Times" in China vividly described this sentiment as "Jealous Complex".[19]

India's jealousy of China, if it is there, maybe has a lot to do with the gap between India and China in terms of economic development and comprehensive national strength. India is gripped by a frenzy of catching up with China. In fact, once gained independence, India had no illusions in the short term to match the international position United States and the Soviet Union achieved, but strongly believed that it should have enjoyed the same international influence as China. To its disappointment, the defeat in the 1962 Sino-Indian border war made Indians realize the cruel truth: China walks far ahead of India in military might with overpowering superiority and comprehensive national strength. It also proved that India still painfully struggled for reaching major power status, let alone comparable with China. Therefore, some of the Indian elites are preoccupied with keeping up with its Chinese counterpart especially after the 1962 Sino-Indian clash on the Roof of the World. Indian Scholar Mohan Malik points out, "Since the 1962 war, [Indo-China] relations have been characterized by mutual antagonism, rivalry, distrust, and hostilities."[20] These are the summary of the Indians' unilateral feelings and policies. Indians' mixed sentiment of jealousy and vying joined with economic factors continue to rankle bilateral relations between China and India. That's the reason why India's "Super Power Dream" always entangled with China.

It seems that Indians share complex and ambivalent attitudes towards China. Professor Tan Zhong, a Chinese scholar who has long served as a teaching faculty at the Jawaharlal Nehru University in India (now retired) stated that: Indian elites' attitudes towards China can be generally classified into four categories: The first category is mainly made up of military and security strategic specialists who view China as a major security threat; The second is called "civilized faction" according to the former Indian Commerce Minister Jairam Ramesh with Amartya Sen, a Nobel laureate and a professor of Economics and Philosophy. This small group of people is deeply convinced that China and India can live in harmony and expect that in the foreseeable future that sense of brotherhood will return to the Sino-Indian relations; the majority of Indian elites constitute the third category who advocate the middle path: promote Sino-Indian friendship as well as defend Indian national interests with a realist approach; Indian leftist parties and the intellectuals compose the fourth category. Their official stand is pro-China based on socialist ideology.[21] However, India's stance or diplomatic policy towards China depends mostly on the Indian government or policy makers.

It is worth pointing out that tension remains between the two countries and problematic and hawkish attitude vis-à-vis China is most obvious in military and those who engage in strategic and military research. Due to the negative impact of these people, conflicts often arise during the process of Sino-Indian trade relations and even people-to-people contact. India is indeed prone to protectionist impulses and has repeatedly initiated anti-dumping or illegal employment investigations against China. Furthermore, India has prevented mainland China or Hong Kong companies from bidding for large infrastructure projects in India citing security risk.[22] Thus in the eyes of many Chinese and Indian people, the Sino-Indian relation is full of hurdles with negative future prospect. Some western media even sensationally visualizes a border dispute which could become the spark that launches China and India into a war in the future.[23]

Of course, we cannot ignore the fact that a certain amount of Indian people possess very positive attitude towards China and advocate benign relationships with China which help to restrain anti-China statements and activities in Indian society. Inspired by the "China View" of Nehru, Tagore and other eminent personalities of modern India, there exist a large number of Indian intellectuals who sincerely appreciate Chinese civilization and have a very good impression and high expectation of China. For example, the Indian scholar with Chinese origin-Professor Tan Zhong and his friend, the former Indian Commerce Minister Jairam Ramesh are iconic representatives while the latter coined the popular term of "Chinadia" and the former translated it as "Sino-Indian harmony". Nobel Prize-winner economist Amartya Sen who was born in India and spent most of his life working in US and UK is strongly in favor of Sino-Indian friendship and mutual learning. The intellectual dimensions of the India—China comparisons in aspects of historical culture and modernization and urbanization process have been extensively explored by Amartya Sen in his numerous publications on Indian development. In his books, Sen made several references to China and praised China for the economic achievements it has made. Sen firmly holds that China and India will undoubtedly benefit and progress from the mutual learning of each other. He maintains, "India and China learned a lot from each other in the first millennium, but the significance of that epistemic process has not dried up even at the beginning of the third millennium".[24]

Due to insufficient information and education, Chinese and Indian people share different perception and understanding of each other. Comparatively speaking, Chinese people are less hostile to India and view Sino-Indian relations with confidence and goodwill. In contrast, Indians hold a more negative attitude towards China.[25] The 1962 border war paved way for the speedy rise of a group of hawkish military generals, strategic experts and government officials who created and facilitated an anti-China public opinion by exaggerating the contradictions between China and India. The Indian hawkish personnel also took the centre stage and felt the need to act independently and defiantly against China which helped shape an uncompromising and tough stance by Indian policy makers towards China especially on border disputes. It is fair to say that eliminating the contradictions, problems and differences between China and India is no easy job and the hostility and misunderstanding rooted in some Indians' perception are much harder to remove. To some extent, there must exists certain rivalry relation between big powers, especially between two neighboring powers. As put by an Indian scholar, "To some extent, China and India are indeed destined by geography to be rivals".[26] India's "Super Power Dream" demonstrates that it's not reconciled to remain as a regional power. Moreover, India has always been wary of China because of troubled history and realistic reasons. Therefore, China cannot hold blind optimism or wishful thinking towards Sino-Indian relationship and cooperation. Of course, the existence of problems and contradictions between China and India does not exclude the possibility of mutual collaboration in various fields.

According to the analysis by Western media, India is neither an ordinary regional power nor a super power and is at the crossroads of status changing. Some analysts believe that three key issues dominate India's current military strategy: First, India's maritime ambition to ensure the safety of the Indian Ocean routes, making the vast Indian Ocean a truly Indian lake; Secondly, India antagonizes China from the perspective of military and economic competitiveness and the India's nuclear tests in 1998 as a deterrent against China is a clear evidence; Third, India antagonizes Pakistan by a number of historical and political issues. It is clear that India's military strategies will remain unchanged for a long time and affect India's foreign policies and its relations with China. In fact, it is evident that the three key military strategies have more or less involve China with the second one entirely directed against China. Of course, it is worth pointing out that sensitive issues such as military strategies and territorial disputes have been separated from economic cooperation in India's foreign policy towards China as a trend. This shows that through joint efforts, China and India can conduct collaboration or communication in the economic field first while political and military issues can be set aside temporarily. Currently, both sides have reached the consensus of make consolidating and growing economic ties the top priority.

THE EVOLUTION OF INDIANS' PERCEPTION OF CHINA AND ITS INFLUENCE ON SINO-INDIAN RELATIONS

Indians' perception of China determines India's foreign policies towards China and has a decisive influence on Sino-Indian relations. Indians' perception of China or the perspective on Sino-Indian comparison can be roughly divided into two phases: the pre-independence period and post-independence period. Otherwise, it can be divided into three stages: the pre-independence period, Sino-Indian friendship period and post Sino-Indian war period. To be more specific and precise, it can be further divided into four phases: the pre-independence period, Sino-Indian friendship period, from Sino-Indian war to the normalization of Sino-Indian relations period (symbolized by Rajiv Gandhi's visit to China) and the normalization of Sino-Indian relations period (since Rajiv Gandhi's visit to China until now). A systematic introduction of Indians' perception of China according to the four phases will be explored in the following paragraphs.

It is fair to state that before independence, Indians shared friendly, cordial and positive attitudes towards China. Both the people of India and China rendered support and sympathy to each other in their anti-imperialistic struggle as a challenge to the colonial order. Many Indians even wanted to seek assistance from China during its freedom movement in order to establish leadership and expand International influence. Stephen Cohen points out, "Nehru saw China as India's natural partner, and he hoped that together they would shape the destiny of Asia by challenging, and defeating, the Eurocentric world that had made India a colony and China a weak, semi-occupied state."[27]

It is noticeable to point out that Indian's first Prime Minster Jawaharlal Nehru was one of the early initiators and motivators to establish the tradition of pairing of China and India in modern India. China is referred to as "a highly civilized and mature state"[28] in his words. He once pointed out, "But nowhere else, apart from India and China, has there been a real continuity of civilization. In spite of all the changes and battles and invasions, the thread of the ancient civilizations has continued to run on in both these countries."[29] Nehru respected and admired Chinese civilization and considered Chinese culture being superior to Indian culture in many aspects historically. He argues that the flexibility and tolerance inherited in Chinese culture helped Chinese society build up a balance and an equilibrium which survived through many changes. From Nehru's viewpoint, China should be regarded as a role model for India to learn from. For a long time, Nehru's views on China laid the foundation for Sino-Indian friendship and represent the viewpoints of mainstream Indian public opinion and intellectuals as well as inspired contemporary Indian scholars. Nehru's predecessors, both India's contemporary spiritual mentor Rabindranath Tagore and Mahatma Gandhi, the preeminent leader and freedom fighter of Indian nationalism in British-ruled India also delivered a message of love and brotherhood to China symbolized the essence of the ties between the two countries.

Regretfully, China and India did not realize mutual support, respect and cooperation as expected by both leaders and did not ascent to a higher platform of strong brotherhood, fraternal partnership and strategic trust after each nation shook off the grips of the foreign imperialist countries. The early ten years of "honeymoon" in Sino-Indian relations was marked by a close warm friendship. The two sides shared a wide ranging consensus on many issues and cooperated in advocating world peace. However, bilateral relations deteriorated due to the unresolved border disputes and the Tibet issue. Ultimately Sino-Indian war broke out in 1962 and bilateral ties entered an "ice age" and remained in a deep freeze. Therefore, India's attitudes towards China changed from respect, appreciation and goodwill to jealousy, envy and caution. However, India has continuously attached greater attention to China during the twists and turns of Sino-Indian relations.

India's attitude towards China had changed several times from its independence to the outbreak of its border war with China. Of course, during the early years of Sino-Indian diplomatic relations establishment, Nehru and other Indian leaders continued to take an idealistic approach when dealing with China while some political forces of extreme nationalism in India started nurturing a different feeling and perspective towards it. Some people, although very small in number, took a hostile approach towards China resulted from purely selfish nationalism and chauvinism without morality and goodwill for international cooperation. They tried to take advantage of the chaotic Chinese domestic situation and deteriorating international environment in the late 1950s and the early years of the 1960s for their own benefits. In short, when dealing with China, a small number of Indians chose extreme nationalist approach with the purpose of maximizing India's national interest at the expense of China's. This is a serious impediment to the continuity and persistence of "Pro-China policy" insisted by Nehru and other politicians and influenced Nehru's China policy concerning negatively.

However, even during the "honey moon" 1949–1959 period, India's policies and perception towards China can be understood as the idealism and realism inextricably intertwined, even the balance and compromise of two different ideologies and forces within India. The conflict of these two ideas can even be noticed in Nehru himself. Many Indians criticized Nehru as being too idealistic in foreign policies and relations with China. In fact, this is a misunderstanding and underestimation of Nehru. One Indian scholar argues, "Those inclined to believe that idealism of Nehru outran realism ought to think again."[30] The pro-China stance and establishment of diplomatic relations with China by Nehru actually manifest his realistic value orientation. Contrary to the accusations of Nehru's being overly idealistic and romantic, He actually formulated a rational and wise policy after meticulously examining the situation and took into account of all the variables in the international environment.[31] His "China Policy" is no exception. Indian scholar Dutt believed that Nehru's foreign policy was based on the thinking of realism and driven by the fundamental Indian national interests.[32] Nehru's problem lied in being too realistic rather than idealistic on Sino-Indian relations in his later life and failed to hold on to the original aspirations.

The viewpoint of China's making use of Sino-Indian friendship in the 1950s was both lopsided and incorrect. During most time of Nehru's tenure as Indian prime minister, he treated Sino-Indian relations with sophistication, pragmatism and wisdom. His blunder occurred later when he was subject to the pressure of anti-China forces domestically with wavering stance towards China. This attitude shift brought great suffering not only to Nehru himself but also devastation to Sino-Indian relations. India's debacle at the hands of the Chinese in the 1962 border war shattered Nehru's image at home and abroad. Never before had Indians reviled him, or even railed against him, and at that time Nehru seemed to be the easy target of criticism and was under the pressure of voluntary resignation.[33] Nehru was a broken man, health began declining sharply. It is said that he never really recovered from the defeat of the Sino-Indian War and soon passed away.[34] This casted another shadow over the sky of Sino-Indian relations. Indians in general became highly skeptical of China and many Indians view the war as China's betrayal of both Nehru and India.[35] Nehru himself also justified his failures or blunders by blaming China for its "betrayal". This is probably one of the main reasons that the concept of "China betrayal" emerged. However, none of the above Indian arguments proved valid. There is no "China Betrayal".

Following the aftermath of Sino-Indian border conflict, India's overall attitude towards and perception of China have undergone a dramatic change and fell into a fixed pattern or stereotype. Since then, an irrational and hostile sentiment or attitude concerning China dominates and maintains in some Indians' minds. India's China policy has also gone through a structural change: unfriendly but remained realistic. The diplomatic relation did not break, but both sides carried forward the process of rapprochement slowly with little progress until Rajiv Gandhi's "ice-breaking" visit to China in 1988. During this period, the Indian news media and academia took a skeptical and even hostile stand against China. Hyped up by Indian media on border disputes with the cliché 'China Threat Theory', public opinions within India were quickly churned up into a roaring sea against China and the Chinese people, which imposed negative influence on the already volatile bilateral ties.

Rajiv Gandhi's visit to China in 1988 marked a new beginning in Sino-Indian relations and had brought Indo-China relations to the right track of rapprochement even without ostensible signs of reconciliation. The visit was judged a success by both sides and indicated both parties' willingness to increase cooperation and communication with each other on a range of international issues. Following his visit, Sino-Indian relation became more cordial. Although there still exist numerous disagreements and frictions between China and India especially concerning the territorial dispute, we also witnessed increasing people-to-people exchanges and high-level diplomatic negotiations and strategic meetings as well as cooperation in various aspects. Despite India's reluctance to put behind the historical grievance of China and the Sino-Indian bilateral ties having yet to unwind the border impasse, the normalization of the diplomatic relations has been basically achieved. India's foreign policy towards China has become more rational, mature, flexible, stable and practical. India has realized that a strong and mutually beneficial partnership between the two nations without confrontation and crisis would help India's growth both domestically and internationally. India is also aware of the need to enhance Sino-Indian comprehensive exchanges and cooperation concerning China's skyrocketed economic development. Indian media had recently argued that "India's greatest challenge is to learn how to get along with China".[36] Against this backdrop, the Indian perception of China has become complicated, but also more realistic, pragmatic and objective. On one hand, growing sentiment of competition, jealousy and envy about China have prevailed a great deal of Indians' minds; on the other hand the re-appreciation and rediscovery of China has gained momentum which is favorable for Sino-Indian bilateral cooperation and friendship.

In view of China's rapid rising after its reforming inward and opening outward and the popular trends of Sino-Indian economic exchanges, China and India have gradually found out how to keep on good terms through properly handling their differences and disputes and making commitments for common development and better bilateral relations. Indian government has behaved less hostile and friendlier towards China. In the 2012 BRICS summit, Indian Prime Minister Manmohan Singh's attitude toward China was extremely amicable, and expressed his desire to strengthen bilateral cooperation: "India-China relation is one of the most important bilateral relations in the 21st century".[37] Words can also be heard in India recently about taking a more realistic stance on Sino-Indian relations which encouraged Indian government to moderate its hard-nosed approach on border issues and highlighted that some give and take is necessary for ultimately settling territorial problems. The Governor of the so-called Arunachal Pradesh State, which belongs to the southern Tibet of China but illegally occupied by India, once stated that: "The settlement of the Sino-Indian border disagreement is important which requires certain concessions from both sides. India must change its non-negotiable stance on the border issues."[38] He also strongly condemned the rumors from irresponsible persons or organizations by stating that "Those futurists who predicted that China and India would fight a war in 2010, 2012 or 2020 were nonsense. India and China are competitors, not adversaries. Admittedly, these baseless assumptions will eventually declare their own bankruptcy when confronted with facts and with time gone by." His statement may barely represent personal opinion, but also likely to fly a kite in order to facilitate the Indian government's adjustment on its tough stance on border negotiations with China.

In October 2012, in commemoration of the 50th anniversary of the traumatic Sino-India war, one famous Indian critic advocated that "Now is the time for reconciliation".[39] He believed that if India really learned a lesson from the 1962 war, they should seek reconciliation with the Chinese gloriously, rather than boldly declaring how they should have won the war. On October 7, 2012, *The Times of India* published an article calling for Indians "Bury the ghost of 1962 and live peacefully with China".[40] On December 16, 2012, the former Indian Foreign Minister Salman Khurshid stressed to the media that China is especially important in India's global perspective and India will not participate in any strategy of containing China and has no intention to fall into any confrontation or to be trapped in quarrels with it."[41]

CONCLUSION

Overall, due to the complex and challenging nature of Sino-Indian relations, there is fewer government or people-to-people communications taking place and less mutual understanding of each country's citizens. Indian's growing attention to China stands in stark contrast to their limited knowledge about China. A handful of irresponsible Indian media institutions fabricated stories of China to incite anti-China sentiments among the Indian public. As a result, the dominant voice when it comes to China is antagonistic, identifying the country as a bully that covets Indian land. In contrast, one of the popular topics in Chinese media is comparing China and India with a view to building up national pride by highlighting India's inferiority with contempt. This is a dangerous attitude. If both countries attempt to adopt a positive attitude towards each other with goodwill, we can better understand, take care of each other's concerns and respect mutual interests. The key is to explore ways in which Indian and Chinese media people, talking heads and scholars could collaborate in presenting useful, yet critical, coverage in order to promote mutual understanding and awareness among Indians and Chinese. The benign and objective competition and comparison between two countries are common and conductive to mutual learning and progress while vicious rivalry between nations in the context of mutual misunderstanding and hostility is detrimental to bilateral relations. That China and India is vying for influence and power can hardly be defined as hostility or malice. Against the backdrop of growing demands for strengthening Sino-Indian government level and grassroot level communications from both sides, there is a bright and positive prospect of broader and deeper mutual understanding, gradual elimination of misgivings and tensions, more frequent interactions and enhancing brotherly friendship between China and India.

REFERENCES

1. Stephen P. Cohen, *India: Emerging Power* (New Delhi: Oxford University Press, 2001), p. 266.
2. Ibid, p. 8.
3. Ibid, p. 301.
4. "Rivals and Partners: Are India and China coming Together?", *The Economists Weekly*, Mar. 5, 2005.
5. Nye, Joseph, "Sino-Indian relations are iffy", *Lianhe Zaobao*, Jan. 17, 2011.
6. Qiu Zhenhai, "China-India's 'Non-enemy' Progress and Its Implication to China-Japan Relations", *Lianhe Zaobao*, April 8, 2005.
7. Mohan Malik: *China and India: Great Power Rivals* (Boulder and London: First Forum Press, 2011), p. 37.
8. Guo Xishan, Zhu Xiaolei, "India's Foreign Minister Says China Is the Main Object of Attention, But Don't Want to Be Trapped in Quarrels", *Global Times*, December 18, 2012.
9. Raghav Bahl, *Super Power? The Amazing Race between China's Hare and India's Tortoise* (New Delhi: Penguin Books India, 2010), p. xxx.
10. The Ministry of Overseas Indian Affairs: "Population of Non-resident Indians (NRIs): Country Wise", <http://moia.gov.in/writereaddata/pdf/NRISPIOS-Data (15-06-12)new.pdf>.
11. Opcit, p. 2.
12. Opcit, p. 126.
13. Venkatesan, V., "Partisan Citizenship", *Frontline*, January 31, 2003.
14. Paranjape, Makarand, preface, *In Diaspora Theories, Histories, Texts* (New Delhi: Indialog Publications), p. vi.
15. Paranjape, Makarand, "One Foot in Canda and a Couple of Toes in India; Diasporas and Homelands in South Asian Experience", in Makarand Paranjape, ed., *In Diaspora: Theories, Histories, Texts* (New Delhi Indialog Publications), pp. 161–170.

16. Hewitt, V.M., *The International Politics of South Asia* (Manchester University Press, 1991), p. 195.

17. Nehru, Jawaharlal, *The Discovery of India* (New Delhi: Penguin Books India, 2010), p. 48.

18. Feng, Qian, "Indian Defense Minister George Fernandes Began Rendering China Threat Theory", *People Daily* Online, March 10, 2001. <http://www.people.com.cn/GB/guoji/22/85/20010310/413351.html>.

19. Jintao, Wang, "An Interview with Ambasidor Pei Yuanying: 'Jealousy Complex' Troubled Sino-Indian Relations", *Global times,* April 9, 2012.

20. Malik, Mohan, op cit., p. 38.

21. Zhong, Tan, "Retrospect and Prospect of Sino-Indian relations", *Lianhezaobao,* Feb. 22, 2006.

22. Fangming, Han, "Why India Refused to Cooperate with Chinese Companies for Infrastructure Construction? ", *Lianhe Zaobao*, July 28, 2008.

23. Jiangyue, Shi, "Western Media Say That India Has Occupied Southern Tibetfor 50 Years and There Must be a War between China and India", *Shijiebao*, Mar. 21, 2012.

24. Sen, Amartya, *The Argumentative Indian* (London: Penguin Books Ltd, 2005), p. 190.

25. Zhu, Chen; Shuangchen, Ji; Duanfang, Tao; Mu, Qing; Yongzhen, Qiu; Yang, Liu; Yupeng, Liu and Xi, Wang, "Indian Media Talk about Indo-China War: A 32-Day-War Gave India a 50-Year-Nightmare", *Global Times*, October 22, 2012.

26. Narayanan, M.K., "Sino-Indian Relations: Need for a Balanced Approach", in S. Gopal, Nebeel A. Mancheri, *Rise of China: Indian Perspectives* (New Delhi: The Lancer International Inc, 2013), p. 7.

27. Stephen, P. Cohen, op cit., p. 25.

28. Nehru, Jawaharlal, *The Discovery of India* (New Delhi: Penguin Books, 2010), p. 204.

29. Nehru, Jawaharlal, *Glimpses of World History* (New Delhi: Penguin Books India: 2004), p. 15.

30. Inder Malhotra, "Introduction" to V.P. Dutt: *India and the World* (New Delhi: Sanchar Publishing House, 1990), p. xiii.

31. Dutt, V.P., *India and the World* (New Delhi: Sanchar Publishing House, 1990), p. 1.

32. Ibid, p. 19.

33. Ibid, p. 32.

34. Malhotra, Inder, "Introduction" to V.P. Dutt: *India and the World* (New Delhi: Sanchar Publishing House, 1990), p. xvi.

35. Dutt, V.P., opcit, p. 53.

36. Zhu, Chen; Shuangchen, Ji; Duanfang, Tao; Mu, Qing; Yongzhen, Qiu; Yang, Liu; Yupeng, liu and Xi, Wang, "Indian Media Talk about Indo-China War: A 32-Day-War Gave India a 50-Year-Nightmare", *Global Times*, October 22, 2012.

37. Qimin, Wu; Zhengjun, Miu and Lei, Wang, "Hu Jintao Meets Prime Minister Manmohan Singh", *People Daily*.

38. Xishan, Guo and Liangliang, Wang, "Indian High-ranking Official Suggests to Solve Boarder Dispute through Mutual Concessions and Condems it Nonsense for Predicting Another War between China and India". *Global Times*, April 19, 2012.

39. Zhu, Chen; Shuangchen, Ji; Duanfang, Tao; Mu, Qing; Yongzhen, Qiu; Yang, Liu; Yupeng, liu and Xi, Wang, "Indian Media Talk about Indo-China War: A 32-Day-War Gave India a 50-Year-Nightmare", *Global Times*, October 22, 2012.

40. Xishan, Guo, "Indian Media call India to Bury the Ghost of 1962 and Live Peacefully with China", *Global Times*, October 8, 2012.

41. Xishan, Guo and Xiaolei, Zhu, "India's Foreign Minister Says China Is the Main Object of Attention, But Don't Want to Be Trapped in Quarrels", *Global Times*, December 18, 2012.

BCIM Economic Corridor:
A Game Changer in India China Relations

India and China in the past few decades have witnessed significant economic growth. But a major challenge before both the countries was to address the economic imbalance between the coastal developed regions and the underdeveloped frontier regions. Given the mainland size of both, the interior regions have not benefited as much as the coastal regions that enjoy the geographical advantage of maritime connectivity. India and China view the BCIM (Bangladesh, China, India, Myanmar) project an important strategy to open up their landlocked frontier regions to the neighboring countries. India's development initiatives in the Mekong region and China's growing presence in South Asia converge in the BCIM region. The proposed area is the meeting point of the three markets of China, Southeast Asia and South Asia that is abundant of natural resources, labour and established international sea routes. The four countries are part of various regional and sub-regional groupings such as SAARC and SAFTA (Bangladesh and India), BIMSTEC (Bangladesh, Myanmar and India) and APTA (Bangladesh, India and China), none of which has been able to emulate the success of institutions such as ASEAN or NAFTA.[1] BCIM is simultaneously interregional [i.e. linking East Asia, South Asia and Southeast Asia], regional [linking adjacent countries within a region]; and sub-regional for prioritizing a sub region of China (Yunnan province and adjacent south western provinces), a sub-region of India (particularly, India's Northeast states and the eastern sea-board state of West Bengal), along with the two intervening countries, Myanmar and Bangladesh.[2]

China in recent times has been re-establishing ancient trade and cultural routes between China and South Asia as part of China's foreign policy. China has been aggressively pursuing building economic bases in South Asia through its 'maritime silk road' on the Indian Ocean as well as overland linkages. China has engaged in several infrastructure development projects such as deep-sea ports and railway lines in Myanmar and is in talks with Bangladesh for the same. Once connected, China's dependence on

*Assistant Professor of Political Science, UGC Centre for Indian Ocean Studies, Osmania University, Hyderabad.

the Malacca Straits will be drastically reduced and maritime trade costs and transportation time will be decreased significantly. While BCIM acts as an interconnection between China and the SAARC countries, the idea of the BCIM Economic Corridor aids China's Silk Road diplomacy and intra trade. The corridor retraces and revives much of the ancient "Southern Silk Road," dating from 200 BC, and the Ledo or Stilwell Road (see Map 1), a World War II-era road that supplied military equipment from Assam and British India to Chinese Nationalist forces fighting Japan.[3] In the 20th century, the frontier regions were closed in order to safeguard national security. International boundaries and border tensions divided and disunited theregion,though the people of the land, believe the region was one.

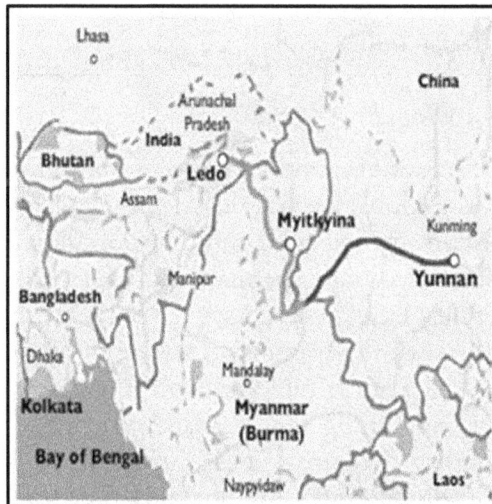

Map 1: The Bangladesh-China-India-Myanmar (BCIM) Corridor: Reopening and Reviving a Historic Cross-Border Transport Route
(*Source:* Asia Times (January 2011), with additions by Mustafa Ibraheem)

BCIM ECONOMIC CORRIDOR REGION

The 'BCIM' countries have huge potential, consisting of 9 per cent of the world's total area, 40 per cent of global population and 7.3 per cent of global gross domestic product. Intra-regional trade among BCIM member states amounted to 5 per cent of total BCIM trade in 2012, as opposed to ASEAN, where 35 per cent of total trade was intra-regional.[4] There is great potential as the historical connection and geographical proximity of these countries makes the region a natural economic zone and creates opportunities to develop a network through regional cooperation. The

Northeast region of India shares 1880-km border with Bangladesh and 1331 km border with Myanmar, making its borders with the neighbouring countries longer than with mainland India. Myanmar shares a 2192 km border with China in the north and northeast and 2699 km border with Bangladesh on the west. Bangladesh is surrounded by India from three sides while Myanmar shares a short border in the southeast.[5] The BCIM Corridor will allow all four countries to exploit existing complementarities in trade-in terms of both sectors and products. Myanmar is a primary goods exporter and has abundant cheap labour, India as a leading services exporter, China as the largest manufacturing exporter in the world, and Bangladesh has exporter of services and low-end manufactured goods. Further BCIM sub-regional cooperation can capitalize immensely on conventional and renewable energy resources in the region such as hydrocarbons in Bangladesh, hydro-electric and mineral resources in Northeast India, natural gas reserves in Myanmar, and coal reserves in East Indian states like Odisha, Chhattisgarh, Jharkhand and China's Yunnan province.[6]

Myanmmar after decades of isolation and economic sanctions, post 2010 elections entered the global economic system. It has the potential to emerge as an important natural trade and transportation hub for the entire region, with its established trade channels with Japan, Thailand, Malaysia, and Singapore.[7] The Yunnan province of China, shares a 4000 km international border with Myanmar, Laos and Vietnam. China has invested heavily in Yunnan in building highways such as the Kunming-Bangkok highway connecting to Thailand and the Kunming-Hanoi highway connecting to Vietnam. The 'Kunming to Kolkata' highway, as part of BCIM Corridor can open up not only the vast emerging market of South Asia to China but also gain access to ports along the Indian Ocean. Thus opening up, the relatively backward and landlocked western region of China to new markets and trade routes.[8] Bangladesh, with its own natural gas reserves and access to the Bay of Bengal, has potential to attract India and China's interest for infrastructure and port development projects. India has great strategic interest in Bangladesh for both restricting China's access to its territory and improving its own access to the Northeast region. The Northeast states of India constituting about 7.7 per cent of the India's territory is connected to the mainland through the narrow Siligurri Corridor popularly known as the 'chicken's neck', which is approximately 33 km on the eastern side and 21 km on the western side.[9] It restricts trade and transit with mainland India and is inadequate to support economic traffic, but this geographical barrier could be surmounted by transiting through Bangladesh and further linking to Southeast Asia and East Asia through Myanmar.

Thus the proposed BCIM Economic Corridor (BCIMEC) will cover 1.65 million square kilometres, encompassing an estimated 440 million people in China's Yunnan Province, Bangladesh, Myanmar and Bihar in Northern India through the combination of road, rail, water and air linkages in the region. This interconnectedness would facilitate the cross-border flow of people and goods, minimize overland trade obstacles, ensure greater market access and increase multilateral trade. Goods from China's landlocked Yunnan province will gain faster overland access to the Bay of Bengal. Meanwhile goods from India's northeast which now take seven days to move by road to the Kolkata port, and then another three to four weeks to move by sea to China; with the reopening of the Stilwell Road will allow them to reach Yunnan in less than two days, and reducing transport costs by about 30%.[10] Bangladesh also stands to benefit from the coastal shipping line as the movement of basic commodities would be much cheaper and faster.

The intra-BCIM trade in 2011 was US$ 90 billion, as opposed to only US$ 6 billion in 2001, out of which 77 per cent or US$ 70 billion of the total trade was driven by India and China.[11] Empirical studies suggest that improving transport infrastructure have a direct bearing on the social and economic development as it enables the region to emerge as a thriving economic belt that will promote social development of communities along the Corridor. Some scholars such as Rahman and Amin have predicted that, if the BCIM economic corridor is built, merchandise trade in the region would increase by US$ 5.7 billion, US$ 4.1 billion, and US$ 2.7 billion under full, moderate, and partial tariff liberalization, respectively. The welfare gain might be US$ 411 million, US$ 281 million and US$ 193 million under full, moderate, and partial tariff liberalization scenarios.[12] According to Rahman and Kim, common border, common language as well as regional trade agreement will have positive impact on trade flows among the four nations. Their study confirms that a large part of BCIM's trade potential has remained unrealized and the 'trade transaction cost' is one of the major barriers prohibiting the growth of BCIM intra-regional trade.[13] Building a common economic corridor would increase the capacity of the smaller countries, Bangladesh and Myanmar, and they would be able to have a greater participation in the regional trade and reap the benefits of providing overland transit and port services to the region. BCIM Economic Corridor might well be the game changer that the Indian Ocean Region needs, as it is proposed to become the land bridge connecting the Pacific Ocean with the Indian Ocean.

BCIM INITIATIVE: HISTORICAL BACKGROUND

The concept of economic cooperation within the BCIM region was first developed by Rehman Sobhan who advocated the 'multi-modal transport connectivity' and supported by other initiatives and infrastructure development could significantly reduce transaction costs, stimulate trade and investment and consequently accelerate growth and poverty alleviation in this region. The first meeting of the 'Kunming Initiative' was convened in 1999 in Kunming; presided by a number of representative organisations such as *The Centre for Policy Dialogue* (CPD) Bangladesh, *Centre for Policy Research* (CPR) India and *Yunnan Academy of Social Sciences in Kunming*, China, and Ministry of Trade, Myanmar.[14] The 'BCIM Initiative' initially termed as the 'Kunming Initiative', is a sub-regional grouping of Bangladesh, China, India and Myanmar. It started off as a 'Track 2' exercise as an offshoot of the conference on "Regional Cooperation and Development among Myanmar and Bangladesh".[15] The aims of the initiative included building a combination of road, rail, water and air linkages in the region to ensure greater market access tourism, investment and economic growth.

The 'Kunming Initiative' evolved into the "BCIM Forum for Regional Cooperation", with the objective to create a platform where major stakeholders could meet and discuss issues in the context of promoting economic growth and trade in the BCIM region; identify specific sectors and projects which would promote greater collaboration amongst the BCIM nations; and strengthen cooperation and institutional arrangements among the concerned key players and stakeholders to deepen BCIM ties.[16] Eleven successive BCIM Forums were held annually making a seminal contribution in raising awareness about the potential benefits accruing from the BCIM cooperation. The initial vision of the Kunming initiative was to gradually steer the endeavour from an essentially civil society (Track II) to an intergovernmental (Track I) one where political buy-in and intergovernmental ownership would be key to realising the vision and the objectives of the initiative.[17]

THE EVOLUTION OF THE BCIM FORUM

In the fourteen years since its inauguration, for China and Myanmar, the BCIM was always a Track I activity and Bangladesh has increasingly moved in that direction while retaining its Track II operations in parallel. The formal official recognition of the BCIM Forum by the Bangladesh government was incorporated in the Bangladesh-China Joint Communiqué, signed in April 2005 during the visit of Premier Wen Jiabao.[18] Support for BCIM was reiterated in the Joint Statement issued at the conclusion of Bangladesh Prime Minister, Sheikh Hasina's visit to China in March 2010. From the Indian side the BCIM remains ostensibly a Track II venture as Indians have had reservations regarding building overland linkages with China. There have been security concerns over Chinese support for militant groups in the Northeast, as well as economic reservations of allowing China's access to Indian Ocean Region.[19] The BCIM agenda has undergone evolution from the conceived form as a forum for regional *economic* cooperation. By a resolution the word 'economic' was dropped from the BCIM Forum's title at the Ninth forum meeting (Kunming, 2011), to create space for the elaboration of a broader 'social' agenda. Since the trans-border issues of drugs- and arms smuggling appear to fallen from the reckoning, the Sixth Forum (Delhi, 2006) saw an effort to introduce regional, social and human development issues on the agenda, including discussion of HIV/AIDS, which is endemic in this trans-national zone of high Injecting Drug Use (IDU).[20] But the priority items on the agenda of the successive BCIM meetings were the '3-T's' of Trade, Transport and Tourism. Environment, climate change and resource-sharing issues have increasingly been discussed as massive infrastructure projects began to impinge on the sensitive bio-diversity hotspots. Despite of the growing demand, during the Eleventh BCIM Forum (Dhaka, 2013), social, cultural and environmental issues found no place on the formal agenda. The 3-T's transmuted into Trade, Transport and Energy (TTE), dropping Tourism and focused on the new 'challenges and opportunities' created by the recent developments in Myanmar.[21] With new governments in Myanmar and Bangladesh the 'soft' social, cultural and environmental cooperation agendas and tourism promotion are seen as relatively peripheral to the hard core issues of trade, connectivity and energy cooperation. The BCIM Forum has so far failed to persuade the four governments to set up *quadrilateral* cooperative inter-governmental mechanisms to institutionalize the activities on the agenda though the respective governments showed interest to carry forward the hard core objectives.

After over a decade of parleys, in 2012–13 both from the political and geostrategic perspective the initiative received a new lease of life. In the 10th BCIM meeting, India's External Affairs Minister and Foreign

Secretary, respectively, stressed India's desire to re-engage with its eastern neighbours and emerge as 'a significant player in the strategic dynamics' of the region.[22] In February 2012, officials from the four countries approved initial plans to develop the 2,800 km highway connecting Kolkata to Kunming' highway.[23] Once completed it would be the first expressway connecting Southeast Asia with South Asia. In 2013, the then Prime Minister of India, Manmohan Singh, and Chinese Premier Li Keqian met in New Delhi (May) and Beijing (October) to discuss 'possible regional cooperation'.[24] In 2013, the historical 'BCIM Car Rally' was held to cover this proposed route from India to China.[25] Eighty participants from Bangladesh, China, India and Myanmar, covered 2,800 km in 20 cars from Kolkata to Kunming via Jessore, Dhaka, Sylhet, Silchar, Imphal, Ka Lay, Mandalay, Ruili, Tengchong, Erhai Lake, Dali. [See Map 2]

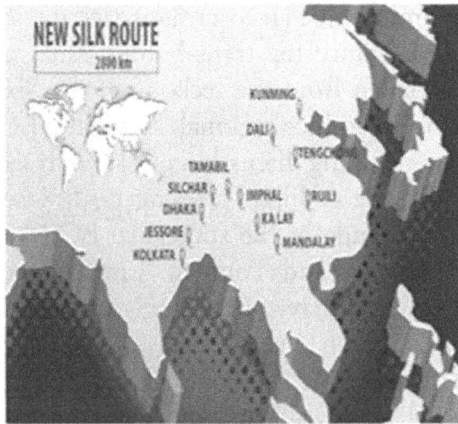

Map 2

Following the success of the car rally, the first joint working group meeting of the 'BCIM initiative' was held in Kunming in December 2013 that focused on quickly improving the physical connectivity in the region to advance the plans for economic corridor.[26] This marked the formal endorsement of the BCIM-EC by the four nations, whereby it was agreed that the corridor will run from Kunming to Kolkata, linking Mandalay in Myanmar as well as Dhaka and Chittagong in Bangladesh.[27] A first step in the planning and activation of the BCIM-EC project was the constitution of a four-country Joint Study Group (JSG). During its first meeting in Kunming (December 2013), the JSG resolved to prepare a comprehensive report or vision document to be presented to the four respective governments for consideration and action. It estimated the cost to be approximately $22 billion to build the proposed BCIM Economic

Corridor and about 55 percent of the fund is expected from various multilateral development partners, while the remaining might be borne by the four governments and the concerned private sectors. The trade potential of the corridor is estimated to be at $132 billion.[28] Thus for years caught between Track 2 and Track 1, the 'BCIM Initiative' has finally received official recognition from all the countries involved..

The 2013 Dhaka Forum also brought a new focus to the BCIM 'connectivity' agenda in the form of an expansion of the idea of 'multi-modal transportation'. Bangladesh, at this meeting, unfolded ambitious and strikingly costly plans for the construction of a new deep sea port (or ports), beyond the long-planned renovation of the old Chittagong and Mongla Ports. Several possible sites were mentioned, but the main emphasis was on Sonadia island, offshore from Cox's bazaar.[29] Though initially, Inter Water Transport (IWT) and port development projects and the promotion of coastal shipping may appear to be diversions from, or in contradiction to, the promotion of *'overland 'continental' links* by road and rail; the traditional trade routes and the infrastructure of colonial mercantilism were all associated with outlets to the Bay of Bengal.[30] They were further linked to maritime networks in the Indian Ocean. Their reactivation in the present, unlocking land-locked regions and backward regions of China and India would surely lead to greater and more prosperity in the BCIM region. In order to ensure inclusive prosperity and that no country dominates the Initiative, the four nations agreed to a partnership on the principles of mutual trust, respect and equitable sharing of benefits. A specific timetable for future projects agreed upon at the meeting was to be released by the end of 2014.

INDIA'S GEOPOLITICS: BCIM-EC A GAME CHANGE

In recent decades, regionalism has become a key transformative factor in international relations. India and China are among the fastest growing economies in the world and have the potential to guide the way for successful Asian regionalism and sub-regionalism. India's development initiatives in the Mekong region and China's growing interest in Indian Ocean Region converge in the BCIM region as intraregional trade between South Asia and Southeast and East Asia has grown significantly in recent years. In 2011, intraregional trade comprised around 52% of total trade in developing Asia.[31] Economic relations among the four BCIM countries are vastly different and most certainly have not been optimised. Unfortunately, various apprehensions such as security, both political and economic, have come in the way of realizing this objective.

But despite the so called 'trust deficit' between China-India the trade has increased enormously and China has emerged as India's biggest trading partner in the fiscal year 2012–13, replacing the UAE and pushing it to the third spot, after the United States, which is second. India's ties and trade with ASEAN has also improved due to its Look East Policy, but China-ASEAN trade in 2011 was four folds. China, besides trade and commerce, has been providing developmental assistance, grants and aid to woo the countries in the BCIM region. China has successfully secured natural gas exploration rights at Barakpuria, and gained naval access to Bangladesh's Chittagong port which India has been eyeing for a long time.[32]

The Chittagong sea port is important for India, as it is less than 200 km away from Agartala (Tripura capital), and is vital in connecting to its Northeast. China has been courting Bangladesh to build a deep-sea-port in Sonadia which is a small island in the Chittagong District, as well as a multi-lane tunnel under the Karnaphuli River in Chittagong. If completed, the Sonadia port would play a major role in regional seaborne trade. At present, cargo from Kunming in China has to travel about 1,800 km on land to the east to reach the nearest sea port in the China Sea from where it is transported by ships bound for Europe, traversing a sea distance of 18,300 km.[33] In future, the same shipment may reach Sonadia, thus reducing the distance. Not only China, even India would greatly benefit from this port as the same would apply to every shipment from the Northeast states of India travelling only 1,000 km to the west and then be transported to Europe traversing a sea distance of 15,100 km with a total net saving of 4,000 km.[34]

Further an upgrade of the 312 kilometre stretch of Stilwell Road, which connects Northeast India with Yunnan through northern Myanmar, could lower transportation costs between India and China by 30 per cent[35] and escalate already growing Sino-Indian trade through the BCIM Corridor. The BCIM corridor also creates potential trading opportunities for Myanmar and Bangladesh by integrating them into regional supply chain. The special and uniquely valuable feature of the BCIM economic corridor from the Indian perspective, is the complementarity of the goals of developing and opening up an economically backward and land-locked region of the country and engaging constructively with the China in its own parallel effort to unlock the potential of its relatively backward western regions and simultaneously providing opportunities for Bangladesh and Myanmar.

The shifting geopolitics of Asia are offering India new opportunities to strengthen integration with its eastern neighbors and developing its own poor northeastern region but India has been slow to embrace regional cooperation, and has been even slower to embrace sub-regional cooperation. India's domestic concerns about the BCIM Economic Corridor are mainly rooted in many factors. Given the unresolved China-India border disputes, the opening-up of the northeastern area may pose a threat to the region's defense security if conflicts were to break out. A number of rebel groups that share ethnic ties with people in Myanmar and China are causing turbulence and thus this may escalate regional frictions into international conflict. Secondly commodities from China and other Southeast Asian nations are in demand in the Indian market, which could change amid regional economic integration. Thirdly India is concerned that too much Chinese access to India's underdeveloped border states will limit the potential of the corridor as Yunnan is the most advanced in the cluster, India fears that it will become BCIM's economic centre, with the rest of the region reduced to its periphery. Fourthly the success for the BCIM corridor requires enormous changes in the political and economic environment of Northeast India. The region is a crucial starting point and link in the BCIM corridor, but suffers from weak infra-structure, 40–60% poverty levels and as many as 109 ethnic insurgencies.[36] China in future may show interest to connect the Mekgon-Ganga Cooperation Initiative (MGCI) making it imperative for the Indian analysts to grasp that the Silk Road, Southern Silk Road and Maritime Silk Road as interrelated through complementary policies that will leave a permanent Chinese footprint in the Indian Ocean region. China also hopes that its economy will integrate with those of the countries in the region thus strongly encompassing them into its fold through economic and strategic outreach.

China's drive for Maritime Silk Road in the Indian Ocean and BCIM in the overland Indian Ocean Region has been viewed cautiously by India. Inspite of sending positive signals for the BCIM initiative, India has a countercheck for the growing 'China presence' in the region has been insisting on the Bengal Initiative for Multi-Sectoral Technical and Economic Cooperation (BIMSTEC) comprising of Bangladesh, India, Myanmar, Sri Lanka, Thailand, Bhutan and Nepal. Launched in 1997, members states established a framework for a free trade agreement in 2004 and target completion by 2017. BIMSTEC is important as it acts as the bridge between ASEAN and SAARC, in linking the 'Look West Policy' of

Thailand and ASEAN with the' Look East Policy' of India and South Asia. This sub-regional framework was part of India's overall strategy of restoring its traditional links and integrating India with its immediate and extended neighbourhood besides responding positively to the imperatives of globalization. The vision of BIMSTEC is similar to BCIM i.e., to improve connectivity between India, Bangladesh, Myanmar, Thailand and other members through a network of multi-modal transport corridors. These networks would facilitate trade, exchange of energy through oil and gas pipelines, promotion of tourism and increase of communication links leading to what can be termed as a 'zone of co-prosperity'. The Trilateral Highway project under BIMSTEC that connects Moreh (in India) with Mae Sot (in Thailand) through Mandalay (in Myanmar) is an excellent initiative. BIMSTEC contains all major SAARC countries except Pakistan along with Myanmar and Thailand. Since SAARC has not made any progress due to troubleshooting of Pakistan, BIMSTEC is an alternative for India to garner South Asian countries under one umbrella to promote economic cooperation and The Ganga-Mekong Initiative to link countries of Mekong Basin (Myanmar, Thailand, Cambodia, Laos and Vietnam) with India.[37] Thus overlapping in the goals and objectives of a number of regional and sub-regional groupings, BIMSTEC is an important sub set of India's 'Look East Policy' It can balance any regional dominance by any one country and can act as a counterweight to the increasing Chinese presence in the Indian Ocean Region. The developments of BIMSTEC initiative exhibit the region's growing appetite for promoting regional economic cooperation. It also reveals India's assertive inclination to connect to east as a parallel to growing Chinese dominance in the Indian Ocean region while playing pro to the BCIM Economic Corridor.

CONCLUSION

The BCIM Economic Corridor could be a win-win arrangement if the opening of the borderlands brings about redistribution of social and economic interests. The border defense cooperation may help dispel both the countries national security concerns, as such cooperation ensures that the two sides will not resort to force when addressing their border controversies. Economic integration will not only inject vitality into the region, but also weaken popular support for the insurgents. China has already made impressive advances through various investment and infrastructure projects in Bangladesh and Myanmmar. India, despite holding apprehensions regarding China's growing presence in its neighbourhood, has opened up to the idea of deeper integration and the 'BCIM Initiative'. The 'BCIM Initiative' appears to lead the way for a potential sub-regional economic grouping, as political strategic skepticism is intertwined with possible economic cooperation. Bangladesh, China, India and Myanmar should utilize this regional economic integration in future as a mutually beneficial journey for stability and prosperity. Thus inspite of apprehensions, BCIM Economic Corridor has the potential of transforming a 'conflict zone' into a 'cooperation zone' in the Indian Ocean Region by unlocking land-locked regions and backward regions of India and China to greater and more prosperity through inclusive growth.

REFERENCES

1. Zaara Zain Hussain (2014). "Initiative for 'Southern Silk Route' Linking Bangladesh, China, India, and Myanmar" ISAS Working Paper No. 192–17 June http://www.isas.nus.edu.sg/Attachments/PublisherAttachment/ISAS_Working_Paper_No._192_-_Initiative_for_Southern_Silk_Route_17062014100358.pdf

2. Rana, Kishan S. (2013). "Sub-Regional Diplomacy: An Imperative of Our Time". Paper presented at the ICSSR-NERC Conference on 'India's Look East Policy and the North-Eastern Region: Strengthening the Continental Route." 'Shillong, 21–22 March, 2012; and Patricia Uberoi (2012). "India's North East States, the BCIM Forum and Regional Integration", Delhi: Institute of Chinese Studies, Monograph No 1.

3. Xiangming Chen "China and South Asia (2014): "Contention and Cooperation between Giant Neighbors" *East by South East;* July 18; http://www.eastbysoutheast.com/china-south-asia-contention-cooperation-giant-neighbors

4. Sahoo, Pravakar and Bhunia, Abhirup (2014). "BCIM Corridor a Game Changer for South Asian Trade," *Institute of Economic Growth",* 18 July 2014, http://www.eastasiaforum.org/2014/07/18/bcim-corridor-a-game-changer-for-south-asian-trade

5. Rahman, Mustafizur; Rahman, Habibur and Shadat, Wasel Bin (2007). "BCIM Economic Cooperation: Prospects and Challenges." Centre for Policy Dialogue (CPD) Available at http://www.cpd.org.bd/pub_attach/op64.pdf

6. Sahoo, Pravakar and Bhunia, Abhirup (2014). "BCIM Corridor a Game Changer for South Asian Trade", Institute of Economic Growth", 18 July 2014, http://www.eastasiaforum.org/2014/07/18/bcim-corridor-a-game-changer-for-south-asian-trade

7. Ferrarini, Benno (2013). "Myanmar's Trade and its Potential". Available at http://www.adb.org/sites/default/files/pub/2013/ewp-325.pdf

8. Thakur, Ambuj (2011). "The BCIM: China's Stakes for its Southwestern Region". *World Focus,* Vol. 381.

9. Hussai, Zaara Zain (2014). "Initiative for 'Southern Silk Route' Linking Bangladesh, China, India, and Myanmar" ISAS Working Paper No. 192–17 June, 014 http://www.isas.nus.edu.sg/Attachments/PublisherAttachment/ISAS_Working_Paper_No._192_-_Initiative_for_Southern_Silk_Route_17062014100358.pdf

10. Chen, Xiangming (2014) "China and South Asia: Contention and Cooperation between Giant Neighbors" *East by South East;* July 18, 2014; http://www. eastbysoutheast.com/china-south-asia-contention-cooperation-giant-neighbors; also see Briefing, Asia. "Bangladesh-China-India-Myanmar Economic Corridor Builds Steam". http://www.asiabriefing.com

11. Ahsan, Nazmul (February 8, 2014) "Bangladesh to Proceed with BCIM Economic Corridor Plan". Available athttp://www.newagebd.com/detail.php? date=2014-02-08&nid=83108#.UxWk-fm1ZKc.

12. Rahman, Md. Tariqur and Amin, Muhammad Al (2009). "Prospects of Economic Cooperation in the Bangladesh, China, India and Myanmar region: A Quantitative Assessment." *Asia-Pacific Research* and *Training Network on Trade Working* Paper Series, No. 73.

13. Rahman, Mohammad Masudur and Kim, Chanwahn (2012). "Trade and Investment Potential among BCIM Countries: Prospects for a Dynamic Growth Quadrangle". *Journal of International Trade Law and Policy,* Vol. 11 No. 2, pp. 163–190.

14. Rahman, Prof. Mustafizur (2014). "BCIM-economic Corridor: An Emerging Opportunity". www.thedailystar.net. Transcom Group. 9 June 2014 (Retrieved).

15. Rana, Kishan S. and Uberoi, Patricia (2012). "India's Northeast Region, The BCIM Forum and Regional Cooperation," Delhi: Institute of Chinese Studies, Monograph No. 1.

16. Barlow, Nathan (2013). "The Bangladesh-China-India-Myanmar Trade Corridor". Asia Briefing, June 7 http://www.asiabriefing.com/news/2013/06/ the-bangladesh-china-india-myanmar-trade-corridor

17. Rahman, Mustafizur (2014). "BCIM-Economic Corridor: An Emerging Opportunity". www.thedailystar.net. Transcom Group.

18. Uberoi, Patricia (2013). "The BCIM Forum: Retrospect and Prospect", Institute of Chinese Studies, paper 2013/11/1http://www.icsin.org/ICS/ WorkingpaperPdf/20.pdf

19. See George J. Gilboy, Eric Heginbotham (2012). *Chinese and Indian Strategic Behavior: Growing Power and Alarm.* New York: Cambridge University Press.

20. Uberoi, Patricia (2013). "The BCIM Forum: Retrospect and Prospect," Institute of Chinese Studies, paper 2013/11/1http://www.icsin.org/ICS/Working paperPdf/20.pdf

21. Ibid., See also Gonsalves, Eric. 2013. "Ten Years of BCIM." Presentation at the China South Asia Think Tank Forum, Kunming, 5–7 June 2013.

22. See speech of External Affairs Minister, SM Krishna, and Foreign Secretary, Ranjan Mathai at the Delhi Dialogue and BCIM Meeting, respectively, Available at http://www.hcidhaka.org/fortnight/20120229_eng.pdf. Accessed on 28 February 2014.

23. Shahiduzzaman Khan (24 November 2013) "BCIM bid to Build Economic Corridor Gathering Steam". Availableat http://www.thefinancialexpress-bd.com/ 2013/11/24/5439/print. Accessed on 31 January 2014.

24. For India-China Joint Satement of Cooperation, see Joint Statement—A Vision for Future Development of India-China Strategic and Cooperative Partnership.

Available at http://pib.nic.in/newsite/PrintRelease.aspx?relid=100198. Accessed on 30 January 2014.

25. Ranjan, Alok and Patricia Uberoi (2013). "Reviving the Southern Silk Road: Overland Odyssey from Kolkata to Kunming. BCIM Car Rally," 2013: A Handbook. Delhi: Institute of Chinese Studies.

26. See, Conference on Regional Cooperation among Bangladesh, China, India and Myanmar (BCIM). Dhaka, 23–24 February 2013. Available at http://www.cpd.org.bd/11_BCIM/Papers/Session%20IV_Institutional%20 Arrangements%20for%20Effective%20Cooperation/Debapriya%20Bhattach arya.pdf; see also Rashid, Harun Ur (12 Nov 2013). "BCIM Economic Corridor: A Giant Step towards Integration". Institute of Peace and Conflict Studies (4172).

27. Krishnan, Anant (21 Dec 2013). "BCIM Corridor Gets Push after First Official-level Talks in China". The *Hindu.*

28. (2014). "Harnessing Benefits from BCIM Initiatives", *The New Nation* 20 December http://thedailynewnation.com/news/36463/harnessing-benefits-from-bcim-initiatives.html

29. Dan Steinbock (November 4, 2013). "Bangladesh plays key role in China's re-balancing in Southeast Asia." http://www.scmp.com/comment/insight-opinion/article/1345375/bangladesh-plays-key-rolechinas-rebalancing-southeast-asia.

30. Yang, Bin. 2004. "Horses, Silver and Cowries: Yunnan in Global Perspective", *Journal of World History,* Vol. 15, 3, pp. 281–322.

31. PHD Chamber of Commerce at http://www.phdcci.in/admin/admin_logged/banner_images/1374650008.pdf

32. Sahoo, Pravakar (February 5, 2010) "China's Growing Presence in India's Neighbourhood;" http://www.eastasiaforum.org/2010/02/05/chinas-growing-presence-in-indias-neighbourhood.

33. Ibid. see also Pravakra Sahoo (2013). Economic Relations with Bangladesh: China's Ascent and India's Decline". South Asia Research Volume 33, p. 123.

34. Shafiqullah, K.M. (March 20, 2013). "Deep Sea Port in Sonadia: A Unique Opportunity for Bangladesh."; http://archive.thedailystar.net/beta2/news/deep-sea-port-in-sonadia-a-unique-opportunityfor-bangladesh.

35. See Sahoo, Pravakar and Bhunia, Abhirup (2014). "BCIM Corridor a Game Changer for South Asian Trade", Institute of Economic Growth, 18 July 2014, http://www.eastasiaforum.org/2014/07/18/bcim-corridor-a-game-changer-for-south-asian-trade; Ravi Bhoothalingam (May 2013) "China and its Peripheries: Beijing and the BCIM. "Issue brief # 216 http://www.ipcs.org/issue-brief/china/china-and-its-peripheries-beijing-and-the-bcim-216.html

36. Jinping, Xi, President of the People's Republic of China, Speech at the Indian Council of World Affairs, New Delhi, 18 September 2014.

37. See Anand, Brig Vinod (2014). "BIMSTEC and BICM: Two Competing Sub-Regional Frameworks?" 11 March 2014; http://www.vifindia.org/article/2014/march/11/bimstec-and-bicm-two-competing-sub-regional-frameworks

China-Myanmar Relations: A Study on Strategic and Economic Dimensions

Murali Manohar Gogulamudi*

INTRODUCTION

The Indian Ocean has become a key strategic arena in the 21st century. One reason is the growth of the Asian economies and their increased need for raw materials, including energy from the Middle East, to provide for their economic growth. Myanmar's strategic location at the junction of South Asia, South-East Asia and China is both economically and strategically significant: Myanmar offers China's landlocked inland provinces of Yunnan and Sichuan a trading outlet to the Indian Ocean and the possibility of a strategic presence there, thus escaping U.S. encirclement and containing Indian influence.

China and Myanmar share a 2,000-km border, and Myanmar is key to China's pursuit of regional and border stability and to fulfilling its need for natural resources. China today is Myanmar's most important trading partner and one of its most important investors. However, Myanmar's political transition has complicated a previously cozy arrangement between two authoritarian governments. Hostility to China at all levels of society and unresolved ethnic tensions in Myanmar have focused popular anger on Chinese investments, seen as symbols of the continuing power of Myanmar's military and its crony business partners. Tensions have resulted in a sharp drop in Chinese investment and have forced the Chinese government to demand more responsible behavior from its overseas companies. Myanmar's transition remains fragile and China's corporate behavior has important implications for both Myanmar's future and China's domestic policies (Isabel Hilton 2013). To understand China's economic and strategic interests in Myanmar we must look at Myanmar as its strategic position shares common borders with two super powers, India and China. Myanmar is struck between India on Northwest and China on the Northeast. It is a weak power with internal ethnic and political conflicts. As it succumbed to external pressures it loses its sovergenity and independence. It has become a part of China's sphere

---

*Department of Political Science, University of Hyderabad.

of influence as a result of its entente with China from 1989 onwards (J. Mohan Malik 1997: 52–73).

Not only geographical location but historical factors are also conditioning Myanmar's perception of external relations. Historically it was predicted that Myanmar will be a victim of expansionism of great powers. Myanmar was invaded by Mongols in 13th century, by British in 19th century and finally by Japanese in 20th century. Myanmar is not a strategic or economic pawn of China. Although China-Myanmar ties are uneven, asymmetrical but is never-the-less reciprocal and mutually beneficial. China-Myanmar relations since 1950 can be briefly divided into the following phases.

- First, ambivalent peaceful coexistence: 1949–1961;
- Second, temporary setback: 1962–1970;
- Third, improving relationship: 1971–1988;
- Fourth, closer entente since 1989–2002.

The last phase saw the most significant change in Myanmar's China policies that is from 'strategic neutrality' to 'strategic alignment' after the military coup, when the present Military Junta took over in 1988.

CHINA'S INTENSIONS IN MYANMAR

- Since 1979 China's Myanmar policy is to maintain stable external environment with neighboring countries with which it can develop its domestic modernization.
- Maintaining the spirit of Bandung's policy of peaceful co-existence with neighbors.
- Its geo economic dimension where Myanmar is very important for China for its land ridge, that is 'Southwest Silk Road' from Yunan to Myanmar and westward to Bangladesh, India and West. This route will help poor economies of south western part of China to have trade relations with South East Asia and India. (J. Mohan Malik 1997:57).
- China can form sub-regional group with Myanmar, Thailand and Laos for economic cooperation. With this, it can export cheaper goods to these countries. Myanmar is key for China's western development strategy. (Tian Xiaowen 2000). Its linking will help a lot to Kunming, in case of trade and investments. The sub-regional grouping with five mainland South Asian economies; Thailand, Vietnam, Laos, Cambodia, Myanmar with a market of 200 million people can be the outlets for goods and products for Kunming and other Southern Western provinces. This link between China's South Western provinces and the mainland Southeast Asian states can help to remove the economic

disparities between China's coastal and its poverty driven southwestern inland provinces.

CHINA'S STRATEGIC THINKING ON MYANMAR

Myanmar is geographically important for China's PLA (Peoples' Liberation Army) to reach Indian Ocean via the Myanmar controlled Coco Islands which is 30 Km away from North Andaman Islands. It is expected that China will achieve world class Blue Water Navy status by 2050 (Shee Poon Kim 1998: 369–387). Strategically Myanmar is very important for China to reach Pacific and the Indian Ocean. PLA can reduce 3000 KM journey of six days if they pass through Myanmar to reach Bay of Bengal. According to Japan, by 1994 China has developed radar and electronic surveillance facilities on Coco Islands which are under Chinese lease. There are also discussions that China and Myanmar are trying to have joint development of deep water port at Kuaukpyu on Ramree islands in the Bay of Bengal. Suspicion is also there about China's military installation at the Zadetkyi Island on Myanmar's southern tip which is close to Indonesia's Sabang Island. Thus China's thinking on Myanmar has serious security implications not only for Indonesia, Thailand and ASEAN, but also for India, Japan and US.

Yangon has closer military cooperation with China after 1988. A negotiation to purchase arms from China was held in 1989 in Beijing where the cost was US$1.4 billion and even China agreed to train Myanmar army (D.M. Seekins 1997:534). The intention of China here was to develop Myanmar's military capacity and to use them to suppress the minority separatist insurgencies. Army Chief General Maung Aue's visit in 1996 to China helped them to gain military and intelligence cooperation and China agreed to train 300 Myanmar air force and naval officers. China offered free loans and granting credit to Junta to purchase arms. It even helped Myanmar to develop its infrastructure with intentions to have the construction of strategic roads along the Irrawaddy river trade route linking Yunan province to Bay of Bengal.

China's intention to have strategic alignment and economic cooperation can be seen from Li Peng's visit to Yangon in 1994. Li Peng and General ThanShwe agreed to strengthen bilateral relations between the two countries to promote cooperation in economic, agricultural, environmental, cultural, tourism, forestry, education and scientific fields. As Yangon lacks political legitimacy and failing economy, China is now much concerned about Myanmar's long term political and social stability.

MYNMAR' INSIGHT AND RESPONSES

The killing of students in 1988 in Yangon and Tiananmen square in China, incident in 1989 received strong criticism. With these incidents western economies triggered of their sanctions towards these countries, thereby China started to enter into Myanmar and because of its necessity even Myanmar decided to move closer to China to get both military and economic assistance. Military of Myanmar never accepted external power to in its land because of their strong feeling of Sinophobia s well as Xenophobia. Myanmar is not willing to be a pawn of China. Its military clearly knows the dangers with Chinese existence. So Myanmar decided to adopt a 'counter hedging strategy' where it diversified its diplomacy and welcomed good relations with India, with ASEAN and friendship with Japan and other industrialized countries like Singapore and the EU to invest in Yangon. Besides this, it tried even to decrease its dependence on China, so it purchased 12 MIG 29 fighters from Russia in 2001 and it send 300 military personnel to Moscow to learn flying MIG. These relations with Russia helped Yangon to maintain balance between India and China. To reduce its economic dependence on China, the military regime had no choice but to accept political reform and accept democracy. These reforms can strengthen its free market economy.

ASEAN RESPONSE

China's growing influence over Myanmar has resulted in anxiety for the ASEAN (Association of Southeast Asian Nations) states. The suspicion over China's inroads into Myanmar has resulted—with the support of other ASEAN members—in Thailand's initiative to lobby for Myanmar to become a full-fledged member of ASEAN, which then finally led to accepting Myanmar as a member of ASEAN in 1997. To counter China's strategic inroads into Southeast Asia was one of the important considerations to accept Myanmar and Laos in 1997 and Cambodia in 1999. Thus ASEAN, especially Thailand changed its non-interference attitude to a pro-active 'constructive engagement' strategy to 'constructive intervention' policies towards Myanmar. ASEAN was worried and saw the danger of Myanmar's slow strategic, military and economic tilt towards China. Thus there appeared to be a need to adopt a common strategy to deal with a resurgent China. From Myanmar's perspective, joining ASEAN, the Bangladesh, India, Myanmar, Sri Lanka, Thailand Economic Cooperation (BIMSTEC), is a bridge network strategy to promote regional cooperation between South Asia, Southeast Asia and China and counter balance its over reliance on China.

ECONOMIC DIMENSIONS

There was a significant change in Myanmar's trade policy towards China in 1988. Its interest in promoting economic ties can be seen from the State Law and Order Councils (SLORC) which later changed to State Development and Peace Council (SDPC) in 1997 which liberated border trade in 1988. This resulted in not only border trade but also illegal trade and drug trafficking. China's Yunnan province emerged as potential target of China's long term strategic ambition. It transformed the whole region as part of a golden quadrangle regional trade zone involving Yunnan, Myanmar, Thailand and Laos (Mya Maung 1998:186). This zone can be China's land ridge to the Indian Ocean for its maritime trade. Yunnan provinces importance in China-Myanmar relations can be seen since 1989 when SLORC signed a multiple trade and economic agreement with Yunnan authorities which included geological surveys, television station, coal and tin mining. In 1989 China agreed to offer an interest free loan of Rmb 50 million to develop Rangoon Thanhyin rail and road bridge construction project (Liang Chi shad 1997: 81).

During 1961 to 1994 Myanmar has received Rmb 500 million aid from China and 18 out of 20 projects were completed by Chinese in Myanmar (Qiao Yiming 1996:87). Their economic ties can be understood from the trade volume between them. For example in 1988 the trade between China Myanmar reached US$9.51 million. In 1989 it jumped to US$76.03 million which is eight times greater than earlier year. From January to October 2012, two-way trade stood at 1.722 billion U.S. dollars, up 2.2 percent year on year.

ILLEGAL BORDER TRADE AND TRADE DEFICIT BETWEEN CHINA AND MYANMAR

According to Myanmar official statistics, the total value of China-Myanmar bilateral trade is 6.619 billion U.S. dollars in 2013, accounting for 28.4 percent of Myanmar's total foreign trade value which was 23.29 billion U.S. dollars during the year. Figures also show that China's investment in Myanmar has reached 14.251 billion U.S. dollars in 65 projects as of June 2014, accounting for 30.5 percent of the total and ranking first in Myanmar's foreign investment line-up (Xinhua 19 Aug 2014). If we take illegal contraband of opium, heroin and the jade trade along the border it will be very larger amount of trade and Myanmar is the biggest opium producer. This will have implication on military survival, economic and security interests. In 1995 alone it produced 2340 tons of opium of which

98% were for export (Mya Maung 1998:196). In 2010, the U.S. Congressional Research Service estimated the country's drug export trade to be worth between $1 billion and $2 billion per year. At the time, Myanmar's GDP was just over $50 billion, by the International Money Fund's estimation.

According to Mya Maung some of the top military leaders were involved in this illegal trade and the amount which they got from that trade is used to purchase arms from China (Mya Maung 1998: 205). As its illegal trade involves huge amount of money, the region of golden triangle became an area of 'politics of drugs'. There is so much power struggle between Myanmar military elite, ethnic Chinese warlords, ethnic separatist insurgencies and the local authorities of China and Thailand. The symbiotic cooperation for the drug trade among the relevant authorities was one of the main reasons for the success of the SLORC in averting international economic sanctions by the West. Hence, the SLORC, with the help of its partners, 'has been part of the problem not the solution' of the underground lucrative drug trafficking in Myanmar (Mya Maung 1998:197).

Myanmar recorded a trade deficit of 406.50 USD Million in July of 2014. Balance of Trade in Myanmar averaged -72.71 USD Million from 2010 until 2014, reaching an all-time high of 593.30 USD Million in August of 2011 and a record low of -854.60 USD Million in January of 2014 (Trading economics 2010–14). Foreign Direct Investment grew from US$1.9 billion in 2011/12 to US$2.7 billion in 2012/13. Most of this investment was in the energy sector, garment industry, information technology, and food and beverages. Following last year's record-breaking Foreign Direct Investment, which saw outside firms put US$3.5 billion into Burma, the first two months of the current 2014–15 fiscal year tallied more than $1.1 billion in FDI. Myanmar is one of the poorest states in Southeast Asia. As China is stronger than Myanmar it should purchase more from Myanmar than enjoy trade surplus with Yangon. Here we have to concentrate on structures of both the economies. Myanmar is a agrarian economy which can export only rice and teak to China. USDA (United States Department of Agriculture) estimates Myanmar's rice exports in 2014 to grow to around 1.3 million tons, up about 12% from the previous year's level of around 1.16 tons. The country's milled rice production is estimated at 11.96 million tons in 2013–14 (January 2014–December 2014) against a consumption of around 10.5 million tons. Unless and until Myanmar shifts its economy from agrarian to other sectors, trade deficit with China is likely to continue.

Myanmar is producing very few manufacturing items which can be exported to China. But the prices rate subjected to fluctuations in international markets and the rates are manipulated by big buyers. For neighboring states of Myanmar like Vietnam and Thailand Myanmar's market is cheaper when compared to other markets. China's largest exports are many household items to Myanmar such as electrical appliances, cosmetics, textiles, shoes, watches, medical products etc., and because of its size, China can produce cheaper goods at very low price. That's the reason, merchants of Myanmar used to get items from Chinas outposts and used to sell them at higher prices in Myanmar. It suffered structural weakness. From 1962 to 1988 under General Ne Win's leadership, the Burma Road to Socialism program highlighted the importance of equality and ideology rather than productivity and efficiency. Its policy of inward looking has led to poverty. Even military has not done so well to mobilize sufficient capital and investments.

There are signs that Myanmar's northeast may become an economic sphere of influence of China. The development of new roads, rails, bridges and the massive influx of Chinese into Myanmar's northern towns, point to signs that the northeast may become an economic sphere of influence of China. Since 1988, Chinese immigration to Myanmar, in particular from Yunnan, has been growing rapidly There is a tendency toward Sinicization of Mandalay not only in the economic but also in the cultural and social dimensions. China's inroads into Myanmar were also partly due to the success in its economic modernization since 1978. By the end of the 1990s, the dependency model or patron-client model had already taken shape in the economic and military ties between the two countries. After a decade of introducing a strategy of limited free market economy, the foundation of Myanmar's economy remains weak and shaky and it is unlikely that Myanmar can get out from its closer economic and military entente with China.

PROSPECTS OF MYANMAR—CHINA RELATIONS

Myanmar is in the hands of fire as it seeking close military cum strategic and economic ties with China. The relations may lead to anti-Chinese riots as China dominates Myanmar with its economy. The arms support to military leaders in Myanmar can be a hurdle to political reforms. China's entry may create some problem with the neighboring countries as its following the policy of neutrality (D.M seekins 1997: 539). In the long run Myanmar will become a colony of China because of China's influence from all sectors. Regarding China's strategic intentions towards the Indian Ocean, using Myanmar as a 'land ridge' for its maritime ambitions is evident.

CONCLUSION

There are many issues which have great impact on Myanmar's dependence on China. Their policies of 'positive strategic neutrality' to 'strategic isolationism' and finally temporary strategic alignment are results of internal political and economic needs and also external pressures. From many years Myanmar is facing so many problems of unstable ethnic insurgencies. Even it faced many challenges from its people who are aspiring changes. As ideological shift has taken place in China after 1978 with the entry of Deng Xiaoping, its policies towards Myanmar were mainly motivated by economic and long term strategic cum security considerations. The extent of China's friendliness or hostility towards Myanmar depended on the extent of Yangon friendliness or hostility. China's friendliness or hostility towards Myanmar in particular and other Southeast Asian states in general, depended on China's favorable or unfavorable perception of the strategic and security situation on the southern flank of its border. China reacted positively when Myanmar did not join the Southeast Asian Treaty Organization (SEATO) and refrained from endorsing the Manila Pact in the 1950s. China was also pleased when Myanmar did not join the Soviet camp in the 1970s. Myanmar will be safe till it did not join hands with other super power US, against China. Beijing is interested to have cordial relationship with Myanmar irrespective of the ideology of the respective governments.

China reacted negatively against Myanmar while receiving aid from the West, and when Myanmar did not actively support China's 'Bleed Vietnam White Policy' in the 1980s. When Ne Win adopted a hardline policy towards the ethnic Chinese in 1967, China condemned the Ne Win government as 'fascist'. All these examples serve to prove that China's Myanmar policy was mainly shaped by Yangon's China policy. From the year 2000 onwards, China's Myanmar policy can be assessed in the context of China's growing interests in promoting an East Asian Free Trade Area (EAFTA) and economic integration with ASEAN within the framework of ASEAN plus China and eventually ASEAN plus China, Japan and Korea.

Myanmar is not a strategic pawn nor an economic pivot of China, Myanmar's strategic location on a tri junction between South Asia, Southeast Asia and China is nevertheless economically and strategically significant. Economically, Myanmar is important for China as a trading outlet to the Indian Ocean for its landlocked inland provinces of Yunnan and Sichuan. Strategically, Myanmar is potentially important for China to achieve its strategic presence in the Indian Ocean and its long-term 'two-ocean' objective. Furthermore, a China-Myanmar nexus is strategically useful for China to contain India's influence in Southeast Asia. Finally, Myanmar is part and parcel of China's grand strategic design to achieve its goal of becoming a great power in the 21st century. Despite growing Chinese influence over Myanmar, it is unlikely that Yangon will become a strategic satellite base for China. Myanmar's strong sense of nationalism, its past ability to successfully deal with foreign powers, and its determination to preserve its independence and cultural identity, will likely make Myanmar withstand most odds.

REFERENCES

1. Seekins, Donald M. (1997). 'Burma-China relations: playing with fire'. *Asian survey,* Vol. 37, Number 6.

2. Hilton, Isabel (October 2013). 'China in Myanmar: implications of the future'. NOREF, *Norwegian Peacebuilding recourse centre,* report.

3. Shad, Liang Chi (1997). *Burma's relations with the People's Republic of China: from delicate friendship to genuine cooperation,* in Peter Carey. ed., *Burma, the Challenge of Change in a Divided Society.* London. MacMillian press.

4. Malik, J. Mohan (June 1997). 'Myanmar's role in regional security: Pawn or Pivot? *Contemporary southeast Asia,* Vol.19, Number 1, Singapore.

5. Maung, Mya (1998). *The Burma Road to capitalism, economic growth versus democracy.* Connecticut. Praeger publishers.

6. Myanmar Balance of Trade 2010–2014 http://www.tradingeconomics.com/ Myanmar/balance-of-trade (accessed on 27 Sep 2014).

7. Myanmar implements central economic zone in border town with China. Aug 19, 2014. http://shanghaidaily.com/article/article_xinhua.aspx?id=236136 (accessed on 12 Sep. 2014)

8. Yiming, Qiao (January 1996). 'China and Burma: political and economic relations'. *Mainland China studies.* Taipei, Vol. 39, Number 1.

9. Kim, Shee Poon (March 1998). 'The south China sea in China's strategic thinking'. *Contemporary southeast sia,* Vol. 19, Number 4, Singapore.

10. Xiawen, Tian (28 Sep. 2000) 'China's drive to develop its western region (I): why turn to this region now? *EAI background brief.* No. 71. East Asian Institute, National university of Singapore.

India's Role in the Revival of the Indian Ocean Rim Association

Sukalpa Chakrabarti*

INTRODUCTION

The rapid rise of the Asian economies, renewed interest in Africa and the crises in Iraq and Afghanistan have put the spotlight on the Indian Ocean region (IOR) pitching it to be the main theatre for 21st century global politics. The Indian Ocean is the world's third largest Ocean. It carries half of the world's container ships, one third of the bulk cargo traffic, two-thirds of the world's oil shipments. It is a lifeline of international trade and economy. The region is woven together by trade routes and commands control of the major sea-lanes. The Indian Ocean Rim constitutes between a quarter and a third of the world's population (close to two billion) which makes it a massive market. It is rich in strategic and precious minerals and metals and other natural resources, valuable marine resources ranging from food fisheries to raw material and energy for industries. It has abundant agricultural wealth in terms of the variety and mass of arable land and has significant human resources and technological capabilities. Many countries of the Rim are becoming globally competitive and are developing new capacities, which can be jointly harnessed through regional co-operation efforts. The IOR is also a region wherein instability and conflict can be quick to spark off over border disputes, internal conflicts, resource security, piracy, terrorism, environmental security issues, economic exploitation of the oceanic resources and conflicting national interests. A highly diverse political, demographic, economic, environmental and strategic agglomeration, the IOR raises debate over the nature of any regional security regime that might be constructed to effectively counter the military and non-military threats.

China has viewed US presence in the region as an effort to ensure the stability of friendly regimes and primarily a control over oil prices. While the earlier inclination of India's foreign policy was to keep extra-regional powers out of her sphere of influence, the wariness about China's rise has

*Associate Professor (IR and Public Policy) Deputy Director, Symbiosis School of Economics, Symbiosis International University, Pune.

persuaded India to encourage external involvement in the Indian Ocean such as—Japan and USA. Added to this are future energy concerns and vital stake in proposed pipeline projects and on-going deep-sea oil drilling and gas wells within the Indian Ocean region. Given the growing geopolitical significance of the region, this paper will seek to analyze Indian imperatives vis-a-vis that of China and thereby attempt a better understanding of the shaping of relationships between major regional and extra-regional powers in the IOR. The paper will also examine the potential of the existing regional organization, viz. the Indian Ocean Rim Association (IORA) and its revival as a key player. The paper proceeds to argue that instead of devising a new security arrangement, it would be prudent to put to use the existing IORA framework while incorporating pertinent changes to respond to changing nature of security challenges in the zone. This would entail a need to enhance IORA's scope beyond economic matters to incorporate a range of non-traditional security issues that require policy attention and development, through collectivized action of all stakeholders. As the countries of the Rim become globally competitive and generate new capacities, regional co-operation efforts should focus on a collaborative approach to nurture and promote the same.

The rapid rise of the Asian economies, renewed interest in Africa and the crises in Iraq and Afghanistan have put the spotlight on the Indian Ocean Region (IOR) pitching it to be the main theatre for 21st century global politics. The Indian Ocean, which links Europe with Asia, as the new global center of trade and energy flows has become critical in determining the eclectic geopolitics, maritime order, and balance of power in Asia and beyond. The Indian Ocean is the world's third largest Ocean. It carries half of the world's container ships, one third of the bulk cargo traffic, two-thirds of the world's oil shipments. It is a lifeline of international trade and economy. The region is woven together by trade routes and commands control of the major sea-lanes. The Indian Ocean Rim constitutes between a quarter and a third of the world's population (close to two billion) which makes it a massive market. It is rich in strategic and precious minerals and metals and other natural resources, valuable marine resources ranging from food fisheries to raw material and energy for industries. It has abundant agricultural wealth in terms of the variety and mass of arable land and has significant human resources and technological capabilities. Many countries of the Rim are becoming globally competitive and are developing new capacities, which can be jointly harnessed through regional co-operation efforts.[1] The IOR is also a region wherein instability and conflict can be quick to spark off over border disputes, internal conflicts, resource security, piracy, terrorism, environmental security issues, economic exploitation of the oceanic resources and conflicting national interests. A highly diverse political, demographic, economic, environmental and strategic agglomeration, the IOR raises debate over the nature of any regional security regime that might be constructed to effectively counter the military and non-military threats.

EXTRA—REGIONAL POWERS IN THE IOR

The instability in oil rich West Asia and power vacuum in the IOR has resulted in the sizeable presence of extra regional powers. Because of Indian Ocean's growing importance to global trade and energy flows, extra-regional powers too have sought to build maritime security by forging strategic partnerships with key littoral states in the Indian Ocean Rim. Emergence of both China as a major maritime and economic power has posed a challenge to USA's traditional hegemony. In response, USA is also enhancing its naval presence in the region. The US strategy has been to leverage the naval power of its closest allies—India in the Indian Ocean and Japan in the western Pacific—to set limits on China's expansion; as is evinced through the "Asia pivot" strategic shift. The 2010 US Quadrennial Defense Review talked of India's positive role as a "net security provider in the Indian Ocean and beyond." India's "Look East-Act East" policy, which envisions high-level engagement with nations in Asia that are traditionally perceived to be China-wary, is in perfect sync with the US policy. The other emerging power of the Indian Ocean with control of the most critical Strait of Hormuz is Iran. The Hormuz transit route is responsible for the supply of oil to most of the world. It is an effective tool in the hands of Iran to bargain with USA and its allies over the thorny nuclear issues. This has been clearly indicated in the Iranian response to the European Union's oil embargo with a defiant show of military strength and renewed threats to close the Strait of Hormuz. Parallely, preserving the security in the Strait of Hormuz is a priority of Iran's defensive deterrence strategy in the Persian Gulf. Meanwhile, Europe too has robust economic and security interests in the Indian Ocean. The UK and France hold territories and military bases in the Indian Ocean and provide support to counter terrorism and counter piracy operations through NATO, the EU and Combined Maritime Forces. European countries are working to obtain rights to mine the seabed of the Indian Ocean for valuable metals, with some foreseeing a rush in deep-sea exploration in the coming years. Japan and South Korea are highly dependent on imported oil and gas that transit the Indian Ocean. Both nations have companies that are undertaking exploration activities in the Bay of Bengal and western Indian Ocean, while their navies have conducted escort operations in the Gulf of Aden. Japan also built a counter piracy base in Djibouti in 2011. Also as the other Asian economies grow and their energy requirements increase, their interest in IOR is going to get intensified.

SINO-INIDAN STAKES IN THE IOR AND SECURITY ISSUES

Indian Ocean has assumed a central place in the strategies of the major powers of the world and the regional powers as well. Therefore, in the enhanced competition of power between these nations, India must not lose sight of her own strategic and security interests. Among the Indian Ocean littorals, it is a fact that the Indian navy is the most powerful and with the new government, the rhetoric about maritime security, interests and influence in the Indian Ocean region has significantly changed. It is a historical fact that all major powers have also been great sea powers. This was reiterated by India's first Prime Minister Shri Jawaharlal Nehru in the following lines "to be secure on land we must be supreme at sea." The Indian Navy's 2004 Maritime Doctrine also argues that, "Control of the choke points could be useful as a bargaining chip in the international power game, where the currency of military power remains a stark reality." A rising share of India's growing military budget is being passed to the Indian navy, amounting to $6.2 billion,[2] or nearly a fifth of total military spending. India is also the founding member of the Indian Ocean Naval Symposium as well as Contact Group on Piracy, as well as a signatory to the tripartite maritime security pact with Srilanka and Maldives emphasizing on joint cooperation on exclusive economic zone surveillance and anti-piracy efforts. India has also engaged with USA in the maritime drills, popularly known as the Malabar exercises. Wariness about China's rising influence has led India to encourage USA and Japan's involvement in the IOR. This marks a major shift in India's foreign policy directive which was previously aimed at keeping extra regional powers out. China views the American presence in the region as an effort to ensure the stability of friendly regimes and primarily a control over oil prices. It harbours the suspicion that USA is trying to contain People's Republic of China by roping in Indian Ocean littorals within an Indo Pacific littoral. The January 2014 naval drill by China on Lombok

Strait near Indonesia is seen as a signal that maritime security interests have come to dominate Chinese thinking on IOR. The Chinese government is also envisaging a canal across the Isthmus of Kra, in Thailand, to link the Indian Ocean to China's Pacific coast—a project that could further tilt Asia's balance of power in China's favor by giving China's flourishing navy and commercial maritime fleet easy access to a vast oceanic continuum stretching all the way from East Africa to Japan and the Korean Peninsula.[3] Parallely, China is also cultivating its relations with the countries of the region through aid, trade and defense agreements. With China rapidly increasing its naval and strategic might in the Indian Ocean, India is also looking for ways to counter the threats in what she considers to be her backyard. India has forged close defense ties with almost all important countries in the region such as Mauritius, Maldives, Singapore, Seychelles, Sri Lanka, Vietnam, Malaysia and Oman. At the same time India is anxious to preempt any suspicion of maritime power projection. The Ministry of Defence's annual reports seek to project Indian navy's presence in the Indian Ocean as a catalyst for peace, tranquility and stability. All these developments seem to reinforce, noted American journalist and writer, Robert D. Kaplan's observation that "The Indian Ocean area will be the true nexus of world powers and conflict in the coming years. It is here that the fight for democracy, energy independence and religious freedom will be lost or won." In an essay in Foreign Affairs, entitled "Center Stage for the 21st Century: Power Plays in the Indian Ocean,"[4] Kaplan hypothesized the scenario of a maritime Great Game in the Indian Ocean between India and China. A summary of his views reads: "Already the world's preeminent energy and trade interstate seaway, the Indian Ocean will matter even more as India and China enter into a dynamic great-power rivalry in these waters."

Security considerations aside, commercial concerns are equally important determinants of India's foreign policy prerogatives for the region. Added to this are future energy concerns and vital stake in proposed pipeline projects and on-going deep-sea oil drilling and gas wells within the Indian Ocean region. In what is being dubbed as a rapid ascent into the geo-energy era, questions of energy security would entail a re-configuration of world power hierarchy and thereby condition inter-state relations. Simply put, energy security will play decisive role in creating conflict and co-operation situations. The fact that oil is shipped from the Persian Gulf to almost entire world via the Indian Ocean, and through the Straits of Malacca to China, Korea, and Japan, helps one realize the importance for state powers to dominate the Indian Ocean Region. China's strategic imperative in the Indian Ocean is to protect its sea lines of communication (SLOCs), especially the transport of energy to China through the Malacca Strait. Faced with this "Malaccan Dilemma" i.e. China's over dependence on the Malacca strait and conversely USA's objective to control this strait politically to manipulate China's energy needs, China needs new avenue to consolidate its energy supplies. The Straits of Malacca is undoubtedly a critical sea route that will enable the United States to seize geopolitical superiority, restrict the rise of major powers, and control the flow of the world's energy. Therein the IOR gains in strategic significance as a viable alternative for China to partially bypass the Malacca strait by transporting oil and other energy products via roads and pipelines from ports on the Indian Ocean into the heart of China.

The maritime arc stretching from the Gulf through the Straits of Malacca to the Sea of Japan holds promise of a trade bloc worth more than US $ 2000 bn. Indian Ocean ports handle 30% of global trade[5] with the important choke points of Malacca, Hormus, Bab-el-Mandeb straits. India being located strategically in the middle of the north west of sea borne energy and trade in the IOR astride critical sea lanes of communication has a great stake. China too attaches vital importance to IOR, especially in view of its 18000 km coastline. Chinese President, Xi Jinping has been open in proposing a new maritime silk road (MSR) similar to ancient Chinese trading route to accelerate economies of the region, and has even proposed setting up of a China-ASEAN Maritime Cooperation Fund. This strategy helps China dispel the notion of "string of pearls"[6] theory, legitimizing its involvement in the maritime infrastructure projects along the maritime silk route. It extends from its naval base in Hainan Island (South China Sea) to Bagamayo in Tanzania, Africa, with several of the ports encircling mainland India. Hambantota (Sri Lanka), Gwadar (Pakistan), Chittagong (Bangladesh) and Marao Atoll (Maldives) are the ports being built by China as per the initiative. The larger Chinese interest in the region is that it needs ASEAN resources and its markets. The tricky territorial dispute issues in the South China Sea that vexes China in its relations with Vietnam, Philippines, Malaysia and Brunei, also connected with energy security issue, needs a peaceful solution. Any act of assertiveness by China can push these countries closer to extra regional powers like Japan or USA. Possibly therefore, China is trying to cement peaceful relations by taking the initiative to share its development dividend; the maritime silk route being one such technique. The Indian

Government's response has been to launch 'Project Mausam' for countering Beijing's growing influence in the Indian Ocean region. This transnational program is aimed at restoring India's ancient maritime routes and cultural links with republics in the region. The project purposes to determine the Indian Ocean "world"—expanding from East Africa, the Arabian Peninsula, the Indian subcontinent and Sri Lanka to the Southeast Asian archipelago. Therefore the IOR, comprising of 56 littoral and hinterland states, is where India is looking, to take on the high stake power play. India is seeking to enhance its involvement in the region, in a bid to expand her sphere of influence from the Plateau of Iran to the Gulf of Thailand. India is also set to become the world's fourth-largest energy consumer, after the USA, China, and Japan. In this, she is dependent on oil for roughly 33 percent of the energy needs, 65 percent of which is imported; and 90 percent of the oil imports could soon come from the Persian Gulf. Another reason is India's "Hormuz dilemma" -her dependence on imports passing through the strait, close to the shores of Pakistan's Makran coast, where the Chinese are helping the Pakistanis develop deep-water ports. In response, India is enlarging its navy to establish strategic autonomy in the IOR. Thus we see that, both China and India continue to vie for similar strategic space in the IOR. While China's commercial influence in the region has increased, India meanwhile has called for a common maritime security regime in the IOR. This move is seen as a calculated regional cooperative approach to maritime security, in a bid to counter China's overtures.

EXPANDING THE ROLE OF IORA

Despite maritime bonding, the IOR has unfortunately not seen the emergence of a vibrant trans-oceanic community. India's geo strategic location and power can serve to organize the states of the Indian Ocean littoral.

The Indian Ocean Rim Association (IORA), formerly known as the Indian Ocean Rim Initiative and Indian Ocean Rim Association for Regional Cooperation (IOR-ARC), is an international organization consisting of coastal states bordering the Indian Ocean. The IORA is a regional forum, tripartite in nature, bringing together representatives of Government, Business and Academia, for promoting co-operation and closer interaction among them. It is based on the principles of Open Regionalism for strengthening economic cooperation particularly on trade facilitation and investment, promotion as well as social development of the region. The organization was first established as Indian Ocean Rim Initiative in Mauritius on March 1995 and formally launched on 6–7 March 1997 by the conclusion of a multilateral treaty known as the Charter of the Indian Ocean Rim Association for Regional Co-operation.

Though dormant for many years, the Indian Ocean Rim Association (IORA) would be the right forum for the negotiations to take place. The expansiveness of the themes that are addressed at the forum has been pointed out by critiques to be unwieldy and resulting in the non-performance for over fifteen years. However, this very weakness could also turn out to be its strength, for it cannot be identified either as a militarized monolithic unit, or as a bloc of revisionist powers. What unite this remarkable diversity are the common bond of an ocean and a common commitment to the prosperity and sustainable economic growth of the region. As global economic power increasingly shifts to the east, maintaining prosperity and stability across the Indian Ocean region becomes more important than ever.[7] True the IORA has suffered from a lack of leadership, but with Australia as the chair and Indonesia as the next in line and India stepping up an active Look East policy, there is renewed interest in the organization.

IOR-ARC, a regional cooperation initiative of the Indian Ocean Rim countries, was established in Mauritius in March 1997 with the aim of promoting economic and technical cooperation. IOR-ARC is the only pan-Indian ocean grouping that brings together countries from three continents having different sizes, economic strengths, and a wide diversity of languages, cultures. It aims to create a platform for trade, socio-economic and cultural cooperation in the Indian Ocean rim area, which constitutes a population of about two billion people. The Indian Ocean Rim is rich in strategic and precious minerals, metals and other natural resources, marine resources and energy, all of which can be sourced from Exclusive Economic Zones (EEZ), continental shelves and the deep seabed. The 13th meeting of the Council of Ministers of the Indian Ocean Rim Association for Regional Cooperation (IOR-ARC) was held on November 1, 2013 in Perth, Australia's Indian Ocean capital. At this meeting, Australia took over as Chair of the Association from India, which has been Chair since 2011. Indonesia became the new Vice-Chair. A new name for the Association was agreed upon—the Indian Ocean Rim Association (IORA) as well as directions for the further development of cooperation. IORA comprises of 20 members viz., Bangladesh, India, Indonesia, Iran, Malaysia, Oman, Singapore, Sri Lanka, Thailand, United Arab Emirates and Yemen, Comoros, Kenya, Madagascar, Mauritius,

Mozambique, Seychelles, South Africa, Tanzania, and Australia. China, Japan, Egypt, France, the UK and the USA are the six dialogue partners. Indian Ocean Organization and Indian Ocean Research Group are the two observer organizations. The six priority areas for co-operation identified by the organization are: include maritime security and safety, trade and investment, fisheries management, disaster and risk management, science and technology, academic co-operation and tourism. The IORA declaration issued in Perth, dubbed as Perth Principles,[8] seeks to take forward co-operation in these areas. It recommends stronger control at ports, collaboration in disaster response and risk management, fisheries, science and technology and maritime security and oceanic research. The Perth Communiqué highlights IORA's work on maritime security, safety and disaster management; however, it falls short of developing a framework for security co-operation. Instead of devising a new security arrangement for the region, it would be prudent to put to use the existing pan Indian Ocean economic grouping framework of the IORA. This would entail a need to enhance IORA's scope beyond economic matters to incorporate a range of non-traditional security issues that require policy attention through collectivized action of all stake holders. While maritime interests would include energy security, fisheries and mining, equally varied would be the complex maritime security threats and challenges that span from terrorism and piracy to drug trafficking, illegal immigration, movement of contraband etc.

CONCLUSION AND RECOMMENDATIONS

Therefore the maritime-security challenges in the Indian Ocean need to be addressed in a holistic strategic framework. IORA therefore needs to be well equipped to deter conflict in the region-both military and non-military. Also in the IORA, while China is a dialogue partner, India is a member. This is where India can take lead by focusing on cementing multilateral relationship through the four Cs of Collective diplomacy, Commerce, Communication and Culture. Given the enhanced interest of regional and extra regional powers in the IOR, India would have to proactively work towards developing strategic security architecture within the IORA so that her status as a predominant power in the region is recognized. This would call for a policy of cooperative engagement to: (a) create and maintain regional balance (b) continue improving maritime governance and transport and (c) enhance security architecture through information sharing and surveillance. In short, good governance through sustained interstate cooperation and collaboration should be the goal.

Some recommendations that India should work towards execution through the IORA are as follows. First, we need to adopt a strategic cross sectorial approach to security encompassing all partners in the context of law enforcement, border control, customs and environmental vigilance, fisheries and mining control, research and development and so on. Therefore we must promote a synergetic and coordinated approach to maritime trade and security. Secondly, rule based good governance at sea, in line with the existing treaties and legislations (UNCLOS—United Nation's Convention on Law of the Sea) must be enforced. Thirdly, instead of seeking to create a new structure, programme or legislation, we need to build upon and strengthen existing achievements, be it joint contingency planning, risk management, conflict prevention or crisis response and management. Fourthly, in order to establish stronghold in the IOR, India needs to chalk out comprehensive development plan for the strategically located Andaman and Nicobar Islands as a security and trade zone. In the words of Admiral Sureesh Mehta, former Chief of Naval Staff, India—"we need to project power and show presence; catalyze partnerships through our maritime capability; build trust and create interoperability through joint operations and international maritime assistance."[9] It is only through sustained engagement with the IOR states and translating the proposals into actions for collective good, that India can successfully position herself as a credible, reliable and effective partner in the maritime domain, ready and able to take on her international responsibility. While looking through the traditional security analysis lens, one may naturally conclude great-power rivalry in the IOR, but there is a greater likelihood that the Indian Ocean may become the theatre where great powers can end up acting together to address transnational security challenges in the spirit of harmony and collaboration.

FOOT NOTES

1. http://www.iora.net/about-us/background.aspx
2. http://www.economist.com/news/asia/21617000-india-eyes-strategic-opportun ity-bay-bengal-outpost-springboard
3. http://orientalreview.org/2013/04/19/evolving-strategic-competition-in-the-ind ian-ocean/
4. http://www.foreignaffairs.com/articles/64832/robert-d-kaplan/center-stage-for-the-21st-century
5. http://www.galledialogue.lk/assets/Research_Papers/2012/rear_admiral_rc_wije gunarathne.pdf
6. The "String of Pearls" describes the manifestation of China's rising geopolitical influence through efforts to increase access to ports and airfields,

develop special diplomatic relationships, and modernize military forces that extend from the South China Sea through the Strait of Malacca, across the Indian Ocean, and on to the Arabian Gulf. Each "pearl" in the "String of Pearls" is a nexus of Chinese geopolitical influence or military presence. Hainan Island, with upgraded military facilities, is a "pearl". An upgraded airstrip on Woody Island, located in the Paracel archipelago 300 nautical miles east of Vietnam, is a "pearl." A container shipping facility in Chittagong, Bangladesh, is a "pearl." Construction of a deep water port in Sittwe, Myanmar, is a "pearl," as is the construction of a navy base in Gwadar, Pakistan. Port and airfield construction projects, diplomatic ties, and force modernization form the essence of China's "String of Pearls." The "pearls" extend from the coast of mainland China through the littorals of the South China Sea, the Strait of Malacca, across the Indian Ocean, and on to the littorals of the Arabian Sea and Persian Gulf. China is building strategic relationships and developing a capability to establish a forward presence along the sea lines of communication (SLOCs) that connect China to the Middle East.

7. http://www.thehindu.com/opinion/op-ed/putting-out-to-sea-a-new-vision/article5305845.ece

8. https://www.dfat.gov.au/geo/indian-ocean/perth-communique-2013.html

9. Admiral Sureesh Mehta, Chief of Naval Staff, India at the Indian National Defence College, November 2005.

REFERENCES

1. Barber, N., Coe, K., Steffes, V. and Winter, J., "China in the Indian Ocean: Impacts, Prospects, Opportunities", (Robert M. Lafollette School of Public Affairs, University of Wisconsin-Madison, Spring 2011).

2. Lou, Chunhao, US-India-China Relations in the Indian Ocean: A Chinese Perspective, IDSA, Volume: 36, Issue: 4, Article July 2012; http://www.idsa.in/strategicanalysis/36_4/USIndiaChinaRelationsintheIndianOcean_LouChunhao.html (Accessed on Aug 2014).

3. Selig S., Harrison ed. Super Power Rivalry in the Indian Ocean: Indian and American Perspectives (New York: Oxford University Press, 1989).

4. Robert D., Kaplan, "Center Stage for the Twenty-First Century", (Foreign Affairs, March/April,2009)http://www.foreignaffairs.com/articles/64832/robert-d-kaplan/center-stage-for-the-21st-century (Accessed April 5, 2013).

5. Robert D., Kaplan, China's Unfolding Indian Ocean Strategy-Analysis, February 11, 2014 http://www.cnas.org/content/china%E2%80%99s-unfolding-indian-ocean-strategy-%E2%80%93-analysis#.VLZqT9KUf84 (Accessed Aug. 2014).

6. David, Michel and Russell, Sticklor, ed., Indian Ocean Rising: Maritime Security and Policy Challenges, July 2012, Stimson; http://www.stimson.org/images/uploads/research-pdfs/Book_IOR_2.pdf (Accessed August 2014).

7. Rajan, D.S., China in the Indian Ocean: Competing Priorities, http://www.ipcs.org/article/india/china-in-the-indian-ocean-competing-priorities-4302.html (Accessed on Sept 2014).

8. Ryou, J.H., South China Sea and the Indian Ocean, http://orfonline.org/cms/export/orfonline/modules/analysis/attachments/South%20China%20Sea_1249644687106.pdf (Accessed on Sept. 2014).

9. Africa-Asia Confidential, "The battle for the Indian Ocean." May 2009. http://www.africa-asia-confidential.com/article-preview/id/234/The-battle-for-the-Indian-Ocean (Accessed Sept. 2014).

10. www.mea.gov.in/Portal/ForeignRelation/IORARC.pdf (Accessed Aug. 2014).

11. Quadrennial Defence Review Report, February 2010, Department of Defence: Washington DC. www.defense.gov/qdr/images/QDR_as_of_12Feb.10_1000.pdf (Accessed Aug 2014).

The Rising Tide of China in the Indian Ocean Region and India: Strategic Interests and Security Concerns

Amrita Jash*

INTRODUCTION

With the dawn of the twenty-first century, the axis of geopolitical influence of the world has shifted into a new centre of gravity—from the continent to the maritime sphere. The Oceans dominate the twenty-first century power politics, as new and old economic powers struggle to dominate the maritime routes—which carries 90 per cent of global trade, and where the quest for security is expressed in the increasing naval postures—to showcase their political and military might of the great powers. In addition, the interest in the oceans is also equated with the need to procure minerals and other reserves under the sea that cover two-thirds of the globe.

In the changing nature of geopolitics, the new pivot of international politics lies in the oceans and more specifically, the Indian Ocean. Where, the international focus has further shifted from the dominant Atlantic-Pacific to that of the Indian Ocean—which has rapidly emerged as the strategic geographical nexus of global economic and security issues. Indian Ocean, third largest ocean in the world tactically placed between the Arabian Sea and the Bay of Bengal, has surpassed the Atlantic and Pacific Oceans and has become the most important strategically significant trade corridor—a converging point of energy security and geopolitics.

The importance of the Indian Ocean Region (IOR) in the present global politics can be assessed in the prophetic words of maritime strategist Rear Admiral Alfred Thayer Mahan, who once famously stated: "Whoever attains maritime supremacy in the Indian Ocean would be a prominent player on the international scene. Whoever controls the Indian Ocean dominates Asia. This Ocean is the key to the seven seas in the twenty-first century, the destiny of the world will be decided in these waters." It is viewed as an "active ocean", which many perceive as the emerging centre of gravity in the strategic world.

*Doctoral Research Scholar, Chinese Division of Centre for East Asian Studies, School of International Studies, Jawaharlal Nehru University, New Delhi.

Today, IOR has become an area of crucial geostrategic importance, chiefly owing from as Robert Kaplan notes—the growing impact in world affairs of Persian Gulf oil and the Indian Ocean's Sea Lanes of Communications (SLOCs) and choke points as well as the fickle regional socio-political environment (militarisation, power politics, social and economic challenges), America's heavy military involvement, China's advent on the regional chessboard and India's ascent as a real Indian

Ocean great power.[1] Thereby, in assessing this vital paradigmatic shift in international politics, Robert Kaplan rightly pointed that Indian Ocean forms the 'Centre Stage for the Twenty-first Century',[2] where the new great game of power politics will be played out, in addition to, conflicts over energy security, clashes between Islam and the West and rivalry between a rising China and India.

In this context, the Indian Ocean Region (IOR) has become the key strategic arena of international politics due to its increasing importance in the area of global economic trade and security. Keeping this context, the People's Republic of China seem to 'Look West' in the IOR—shifting its policy from the Atlantic-Pacific to that of the Indo-Pacific as a key route for international trade and energy flows through the international Sea Lanes of Communications (SLOCs), thereby, making the stakes very high. This maritime policy is driven by a surging quest for great power status fuelled by a booming economy equated with its rising national power and expanding interests.

This growing Chinese influence in the IOR creates a discord for India, as the IOR is of vital importance for its strategic value in the national security calculus. India faces a severe challenge in its guarded sphere of influence as China's expanding naval presence in India's strategic backyard is seen as an encirclement policy aimed to counter-balance India in the IOR. This is reflected in the increased Chinese activities in the IOR—by investing in local states, building ports and infrastructure, military modernization and acquiring energy resources. Therefore, given their size and growing dependence on the sea lanes for energy supplies and trade, there is an emerging 'great game' of rivalry between India and China in the IOR.

Thus, keeping this context, the present paper attempts to focus on the strategic objective behind China's entry in the IOR. It would seek to analyse the impact of the growing Chinese presence in the IOR—in the overall regional stability and most, importantly, on India's strategic maritime and security interests.

INDIAN OCEAN REGION—THE PIVOT OF GLOBAL POLITICS

Historically, Indian Ocean as the third largest ocean in the world has always been a vital crossroad for different cultures, civilizations, armies and trade, and an important connecting link between the east and the west. But the Ocean's relevance witnessed a significant decline till the twentieth century as the pivot of global politics anchored in the Atlantic and the Pacific Oceans.[3] But with the turn of the century, Indian Ocean has returned to its erstwhile centre stage as the rise of the former great powers— China and India and the gradual decline of the US influence in the region has significantly changed the nature of geopolitics in the Indian Ocean Region (IOR). Thereby, what makes the IOR a strategic landscape in the present times, is its significance as a key linkage between maritime power and energy supply. To which, Lee Cordner argues that "maritime security in the Indian Ocean is fundamental to energy security and, more broadly, the global trading system".[4]

The vitality of the Indian Ocean in international politics lies in the linkage between the growing insatiable demand for energy security and maritime trade across the IOR and the national interest of the states. This can be understood in terms of the unusual geography of the region which imparts vulnerability to the most significant geopolitical corridor. The Indian Ocean Region[5] is surrounded by Africa, Asia and Australia serving as a maritime highway linking transcontinental human and economic relationships. And most importantly, as a global thoroughfare, the Indian Ocean is "home to important SLCOs and maritime choke points",[6] which are narrow entry and exit points to and from adjacent waters. These include the Strait of Hormuz which joins the Indian Ocean with the Persian Gulf and the Strait of Malacca, which is the primary exit/entrance between the Indian and the Pacific oceans. While the other vital chokepoints include the Bab el-Mandab, the narrow strait that links the Indian Ocean with the Red Sea and the Mediterranean, and the Mozambique Channel/Cape of Good Hope, which is the gateway between the Indian and South Atlantic oceans—which form the vital routes for trade and energy (oil and gas) supplies.[7] Together these carry over 50 per cent of the world's container traffic and over 80 per cent of the world's seaborne oil trade travels through this maritime corridor of the Indian Ocean.

Of which, the two most significant chokepoints are:[8] first, the Strait of Hormuz, located at the head of the Persian Gulf between Iran and Oman, is the world's most important oil chokepoint—moving around

35 per cent of the world's seaborne trade in oil, largely destined for Asia, Europe and the United States. And, the second major chokepoint is the Strait of Malacca, between Indonesia and Malaysia, which is the major trading route between the Indian Ocean and the Pacific Ocean. This trade route carries almost one-third of global trade with energy supplies, transported from the Middle East to East Asia. Thereby, any disruption to the sea lanes has severe security impediments which directly affects the economic development of the nations.

Owing to the strategic importance of the IOR in looking the "Mahanian Way", it is widely believed that the country which holds paramount position in the Indian Ocean will control the flow of global trade and energy supplies. At present, USA is the dominant player in the IOR but there is a gradual rise of China in the region which earlier focused in the Pacific Ocean. China's emergence in the IOR is seen as an act of balance against US power dominance in the region in order to protect its interests with regard to its growing economy and energy needs. The growing Chinese activities in the region have risen concerns for dominant regional players, particularly India, which has been a natural major player in the region. It has become the hub of political, strategic and economic activities between the major powers and potential regional powers Thereby, the unfolding phenomenon of China's rise and India's role vis-a-vis the Indian Ocean has further exacerbated the strategic importance of the Indian Ocean in twenty-first century—making it the new hotspot of global power politics.

CHINA'S RISE IN THE INDIAN OCEAN REGION

The People's Republic of China (PRC), under its 'Reform and Opening Up' (*Gaize Kaifeng*) Policy initiated by Deng Xiaoping in 1978 has surpassed the US in its economic performance achieving an exponential growth. At present, China has net assets of $2.3 trillion compared to US debt of $2.5 trillion. Chinese exports surpassed U.S. exports in 2007 and Chinese fixed capital investment overtook US investment in 2009. Similarly, manufacturing output and energy consumption exceeded US levels in 2010. It is anticipated that Chinese imports will be greater than the US and that Chinese stock market capitalisation will be greater than the US by 2020.[9] Chinese defence expenditure will surpass the US in absolute terms by 2025. And above all, China has become 'World's Second Largest Economy' in 2010 overtaking Japan and is estimated to surpass the US by 2027, as suggested by Goldman Sachs Group Inc. chief economist Jim O'Neil.[10] Thereby, fuelled by a booming economy, China's ambition also lies in attaining political weight and supra-regional influence.

Traditionally, China's maritime focus has mainly centered on the Pacific but with the changing international status-quo, supremacy over Asia's maritime sphere, specifically over the waters between the IOR and the South China Sea, has become Beijing's one of the primary strategic goals. This is because China's national security is heavily dependent on the safety and protection of the sea routes in order to sustain its rapid economic development and increasing power projection. This quest for security can be understood in the context that more than 70 percent of China's imported energy supplies are transported through shipping lanes in the Indian Ocean Region (IOR), with major strategic checkpoints at the Malacca Strait. And that for PRC, internal peace acts as the key determinant of its international behaviour. Whereby, the emerging social needs rely heavily upon energy to underpin necessary growth rates, which enable the success of government policies and programmes aimed at improving the living standards of China's population. With a plan to urbanise 400 million people before 2030 China energy demand is seen to rise about three and a half times more than if this population remained in rural areas. A rapidly increasing energy supply is fundamental to China's future.[11]

Hence, to secure its strategic goals, China is expanding its military posture and naval modernisation in the Indian Ocean.[12] The exemplary to China's unfolding Indian Ocean strategy is its recent January 2014 naval drill conducted by a three-ship Chinese navy squadron—where the largest amphibious Chinese landing ship—*Changbaishan*—along with two destroyers—*Wuhan* and *Haikou* took part.[13] The choice of Lombok Strait near Indonesia as the drill location has been a strategic choice—which demonstrates to the Indo-Pacific region that China's combat reach now extends to the eastern Indian Ocean.[14] Srikanth Kondapalli notes that with this "China could be testing the waters in the eastern Indian Ocean, including its ability to operate some distance away from its bases in the region".[15] Above all, the principle driver behind China's strategic gaze into the Indian Ocean can be understood in its aspiration for great power status fuelled by a booming economy which is primarily guided by the quest for economic and energy security. It is therefore, important to assess China's strategic interests and policies of being a potential maritime player in the Indian Ocean.

CHINA'S STRATEGIC INTERESTS IN THE IOR

China's strategic interests in the IOR are motivated by two key factors: a) energy security and b) aspirations of becoming an active player in the region.

Energy Security

The quest to procure and secure energy has been the paramount concern for China that has driven its interests in the Indian Ocean. To this, Maharaja Krishna Rasgotra, a former Indian Foreign Secretary interprets as an interest "to safeguard the supplies of much-needed energy and material sources from Middle East and Africa".[16] With a booming economy, China's energy use has more than doubled over the two decades, increasing the dependency on energy imports. As a result of the increasing demand, China has become a net importer of crude oil in 1993 from being a net exporter, being the world's sixth largest oil producer. According to the US Energy Information Administration, China is the world's second largest consumer of oil after the United States and the second largest net importer of oil. According to a report by RAND Corporation, it is estimated that China's oil demand is projected to grow at an "average annual rate of 3.8 percent during the period 1996–2020, increasing consumption from 3.5 million barrels per day (mb/d) to 8.8 mb/d".[17]

But with an increasing energy demand, China faces a grave oil supply crisis. China has proven oil reserves of 24 billion barrels (bb), which constitute just 2.3 percent of the world total for a country with 22 percent of the world's population.[18] China's oil crisis is also resultant of the fact that the major oil fields in eastern China, which account for about 90 percent of total crude production, have peaked and are in decline.[19] And that its efforts to develop both offshore reserves and the Tarim Basin in Xinjiang Uighur Autonomous Region have failed to produce adequate reserves and are not cost-effective as that of the onshore wells.[20]

Though China's oil production is projected to grow somewhat over the next two decades, increasing from 3.1 mb/d in 1996 to 3.6 mb/d in 2020, but it will not be able to keep pace with consumption, which is projected to increase from 3.5 mb/d to 8.8 mb/d over the same period.[21] Currently, importing 48 per cent of its oil, China perceives heavy energy shortages from a constricted global market as one of its gravest threat.[22]

This increasing energy demand has created a domestic political pressure on China to ensure an uninterrupted flow of energy. To meet the demand, China has sought oil and gas supplies from the Persian Gulf and Horn of

Africa. Therefore, this quest for energy has compelled Beijing to "cast anxious eyes on the Sea Lines of Communication" whereby the "security of the waterways stretching from China's coastlines to the Indian Ocean has taken on special policy importance for Beijing"[23]—asIndian Ocean is the geographic centre of global oil market.

Therefore, to fulfil its interest of energy security, the primary concern for China lies in securing the SLOCs that spread from the Persian Gulf to the South China Sea. As to pursue a 'well-off society', a rapidly increasing energy supply is fundamental to China's future.

Aspirations to Become an 'Active Actor' in the IOR

This strategic interest of China in the Indian Ocean is driven by its deep seated security dilemma which drives its ambition in building an ocean capacity to become an active player in the region. Rasgotra views this interest to be motivated by a desire "to project power in the Indian Ocean in rivalry not only with India but primarily with the U.S."[24] This is primarily driven by the need to secure freedom of navigation in the Indian Ocean whereby China faces a 'Malacca Dilemma'[25]—as 80 per cent of its petroleum imports pass through the Indian Ocean into the Straits of Malacca, which face obstacles from US and India.

China's security dilemma vis-à-vis US is posed by the US Navy's dominance of the high seas stretching from the Persian Gulf to the Indian Ocean to the South China Sea. Here, China's strategic thinking in the Indian Ocean is guided by a fear of US containment of PRC—"by roping in Indian Ocean littorals within an 'Indo-Pacific' framework"[26] and of America's prowess in holding of China's sea-dependent economy hostage in times of crisis, mainly the Malacca Straits[27]—which is the maritime portal for virtually all of China's Persian Gulf oil.

In connection to China's Malacca Dilemma towards US, Shi Hongtao states that: "From the perspective of international strategy, the Straits of Malacca is without question a crucial sea route that will enable the United States to seize geopolitical superiority, restrict the rise of major powers, and control the flow of the world's energy [...] It is no exaggeration to say that whoever controls the Strait of Malacca will also have a stranglehold on the energy route of China. Excessive reliance on this strait has brought an important potential threat to China's energy security".[28]

Apart from the US security threat, China's interest in the Indian Ocean is also guided by the dominant presence of India in the region. As India, by virtue of its geographic location and, given its potential to be a great power together with its aspirations runs antagonistic to a rising China's quest to gain strategic and hegemonic space in an off-shore region. As Zhu Fenggang notes that New Delhi's maritime strategy aims to: "control of the waters adjacent to neighbouring littoral states and, unfettered control of the seas stretching from the Hormuz Strait to the Malacca Strait in peacetime, and the capacity to blockade these chokepoints effectively in wartime".[29]

Furthermore, China recognises India's requirement for energy security, which it anticipates as another challenge to its own energy procurement.[30] This external influence to China's Indian Ocean seems apparent in the official statements and observations of authoritative scholars, including the remarks in the 'Blue Book of Chinese Academy of Social Sciences' published in 2013, which confirm China's dominant thinking on the Indian Ocean—which is majorly driven by the presence of two dominant powers, the US and India.[31] Hence, China's strategic interest in the IOR is to safeguard the expanding national interests—trade and energy, by securing an uninhibited access to the high seas as there is an inherent paranoia of 'Malacca Dilemma'.[32]

CHINA'S STRATEGIC POLICIES IN THE IOR AND CONCERNS FOR INDIA

China'sresponses to its energy vulnerabilities and quest for great power in the Indian Ocean vis-à-vis India and US is seen as a soft power policy with a long term aim to secure a strong maritime position. But China's Indian Ocean Strategy in terms of its military presence in the IOR has raised concerns among the regional players, particularly for India. India sees China's policy as a counter-balance strategy in the region. China's strategies in the IOR are as follows:

China's Naval Activities in the IOR

The People's Liberation Army Navy (PLAN) been expanding itself and reconfiguring its role in view of changing circumstances and the growing importance of the Indian Ocean. PLANs growing operations in the Indian Ocean reflect China's desire to improve its ability to combat perceived threats to sea routes vital to its economic development—to "break through" the First Island Chain to operate in China's "distant seas".[33] As it is argued by the PLA strategists and academics that the United States uses the First Island Chain to "encircle" or "contain" China and prevent the PLA Navy from operating freely beyond China's immediate periphery.[34]

The PLA Navy has progressively increased its maritime influence by transforming itself from a coastal defence navy to a force capable of sustained open-ocean operations, which is reasonably commensurate with China's super-power status.[35] Of which, the most recent activity (January 2014), is observed in the forays of the PLA Navy through the Lombok Strait near Indonesia into the Western Pacific—a navy drill conducted by a three-ship Chinese navy squadron, where the largest amphibious Chinese landing ship—*Changbaishan*—along with two destroyers—*Wuhan* and *Haikou*.

Apart from this, China has deployed submarines in the Indian Ocean that has raised concerns for the Indian Navy. For example, China has deployed its Jin class submarines in 2008 at a submarine base near Sanya in the southern tip of Hainan, raising alarm in India as the base is merely 1200 nautical miles from the Malacca Strait and is its closest access point to the Indian Ocean.[36] While it is also reported that the Chinese Navy appears to be building "expeditionary maritime capabilities" and could use nuclear-powered submarines and area denial weapons such as the DF-21D anti-ship ballistic missile to threaten India within the region.[37] To this Chinese strategy, You Ji, a Chinese origin expert on the PLA Navy, says, "China's current strategy (in the Indian Ocean) is... to make its presence felt through building a credible naval strength. Submarines, at present, give China a short-run relief".[38]

China's "String of Pearls" Strategy

This Indian Ocean strategy of China is aimed at growing naval bases in and around the Indian Ocean region to serve its economic interests but also to enhance its strategic presence in the region. China realizes that its maritime strength will give it the strategic leverage it needs to emerge as the regional hegemon and a potential superpower. It is reported that this policy is mainly centered around reported fears of an oil blockade of one or more key choke points for shipping at the straits of Hormuz, Malacca, Luzon and Taiwan.[39]

India sees this as China's "Encirclement Policy". This strategy as argued is seen as an attempt of Beijing to establish a series of naval outposts in the Indian Ocean, with the presumed aim of keeping the Indian Navy from consolidating its influence over its own strategic backyard (to use the same logic that Beijing applies to the South China Sea).[40] The pearls are: Gwadar in Pakistan, the Hambantota port in Sri Lanka, Chittagong in Bangladesh, and Sittwe and Coco Island in Myanmar.

According to Indian claims, the "string of pearls" strategy apart from the strategic ports also include electronic intelligence gathering facilities on islands in the Bay of Bengal, funding construction of a canal across the Kra Isthmus in Thailand, a military agreement with Cambodia and building up of forces in the South China Sea. These "pearls" are to help build strategic ties with several countries along the sea lanes from the Middle East to the South China Sea.[41]

China's "Maritime Silk Road" Strategy

Apart from the hard power policies, Chinese President Xi Jinping in October 2013 floated the policy of a 'Maritime Silk Road'. Under this plan, China announced 10 billion Yuan ($1.6 bn) fund to build ports and to boost maritime connectivity with Southeast Asian and Indian Ocean littoral countries, in support of infrastructure projects under the 'silk road plan'. In the Indian Ocean, China is cooperating with littoral states in building the China-Pakistan Economic Corridor and China-India-Myanmar-Bangladesh Economic Corridor. With these mega-projects and heavy investment, China intends to mitigate the security concerns in the Maritime Silk Road, ranging from territorial disputes in the South China Sea to transnational threats such as piracy, armed robbery and terrorism.[42] This initiative, which intends to deepen Chinese economic and maritime links with both South-East Asia and Indian Ocean Region countries, is also perceived as an attempt to reframe the regional anxieties about China's growing military and naval presence amid a number of disputes—which Zhou Bo calls as a response to the "String of Pearls" theory.[43]

Therefore, China's Indian Ocean policies which aim to protect and enhance its interests in the region, are in turn generating apprehensions in Indian strategic circles, thereby engendering a classic security dilemma between the two Asian giants. And it is India's fears and perceptions of China's growing naval prowess in the Indian Ocean that is driving Indian naval posture.

CONCLUSION

In an overall assessment, it can be rightly stated that the Indian Ocean has become the centre of gravity for twenty-first century power politics. With the strategic shifts in global politics, China has directed its attention towards the Indian Ocean from the Pacific Oceans. China's Indian Ocean policy is driven by its motivations to secure its increasing energy demand amidst a supply crisis and also to manoeuvre its great power status in the region. But China's unfolding posture in the Indian Ocean have raised concerns in the regional sphere, especially for India, which has been a natural player in the IOR for its strategic geography. China's gradual rise in the IOR is indicative of the fact that it is inclined to create its sphere of influence in the most strategic geopolitical landscape of twenty-first century. It is a strategic move on China's part which is aimed to avert the 'Malacca Dilemma' and secure its 'peaceful rise' by safeguarding the national strategy of economic development. Thus, the overlapping of interest have made the Indian Ocean a new bone of contention between China and India.

REFERENCES

1. Quoted in Sidra Tariq, 'India and China in the Indian Ocean: A Complex Interplay of Geopolitics', Spotlight, Institute of Regional Studies, Islamabad, January-February 2014, p. 4, at http://www.irs.org.pk/spjf14.pdf.

2. Kaplan, Robert D., 'Centre Stage for the 21st Century: Power Plays in the Indian Ocean', *Foreign Affairs*, March/April 2009, Vol. 88, No. 2, pp. 16–29.

3. The historical importance of the Indian Ocean can be traced in terms of the fact that—the Ocean has served as the cradle of great powers like the Mughal Empire. It had become a vital sea lane with China's legendary Admiral Zheng He's dispatch of seven large Indian Ocean diplomatic naval expeditions where he sailed as far as the Persian Gulf, the Red Sea and East Africa. Similarly, the Ottomans, Persians and Mughals also developed navies in their respective regions, which were responsible for protecting the east-west trade route across the IOR. The Ocean also acted as the spice route particularly for cinnamon trade between the East and West since the foundation of the Dutch East India Company in 1600. That is to say, until 1700, the Indian Ocean hosted the world's largest thriving sea borne trade, with Muslim, Indian and Chinese traders sailing its waters. While in the 19th century, the Indian Ocean became the key trade corridor for opium transport from India to China, carried out by subsidiaries of the East India Company which led to two colonial wars and marked the irreversible decline of the Chinese Empire. See, Pettigiani Claudio Angelo, 'Chinese and Indian interest in the Indian Ocean and driving forces behind naval modernisation', Asia-Pacific Youth Organization, February 7, 2012, http://apyo.org/articles/2012/chinese-and-indian-interests-in-the-indian-ocean-and-driving-forces-behind-naval-mode rnisation/. For further elaboration see, Sergei Desilva-Ranasinghe, 'The Indian Ocean Through the Ages', *Journal of the Australian Naval Institute*, Issue 140, 2011, pp. 20–25.

4. Quoted in Captain Jamie Hatcher, 'China's growing Indian Ocean Maritime interest—sowing the seeds of conflict?', Dissertation, Royal College of Defence Studies: Seaford House Paper, July 2012, p. 5.

5. The Indian Ocean Region is composed of the Indian Ocean itself, comprising of all the tributary water bodies (such as the Persian Gulf, Red Sea, the

Andaman Sea and the Malacca Straits), 38 coastal states and 13 landlocked states which are dependent on the Indian Ocean for transit to and from the sea. On the whole, this region covers an area close to 102,000,000 sq Km (2/3 of sea and 1/3 of land)—representing 20 per cent of the entire globe's surface, inhabited by 40 percent of world's population.

6. Ghosh, P.K., 'Maritime Security Challenges in South Asia and the Indian Ocean: Response Strategies', Paper prepared for the Centre for Strategic and International Studies—American-Pacific Sea Lanes Security Institute Conference on Maritime Security in Asia, Honolulu-Hawaii, January 18–20, 2004, at http://tamilnation.co/intframe/indian_ocean/pk_ghosh.pdf (Accessed September 6, 2014).

7. Brewster, David, *India's Ocean: The Story of India's Bid for regional Leadership*, Routledge: Oxon, 2014, p. 2.

8. Ibid, pp. 2–3.

9. Captain Jamie Hatcher, p. 9.

10. Quoted in 'China overtakes Japan as World's Second-Biggest Economy', *Bloomberg News*, August 16, 2010, at http://www.bloomberg.com/news/2010-08-16/china-economy-passes-japan-s-in-second-quarter-capping-three-decade-rise.html (Accessed September 30, 2014).

11. Captain Jamie Hatcher, p. 10.

12. 'China's Navy Extends its Combat Reach to the Indian Ocean', US-China Economic and Security Review Commission Staff Report, March 14, 2014, at http://origin.www.uscc.gov/sites/default/files/Research/Staff%20Report_China%27s%20Navy%20Extends%20its%20Combat%20Reach%20to%20the%20Indian%20Ocean.pdf (Accessed 7 September 7, 2014).

13. HouQiang, 'China Navy Starts West Pacific Drill', *Xinhua*, February 3, 2014, at http://news.xinhuanet.com/english/china/2014-02/03/c_133091282.htm (Accessed September 7, 2014).

14. 'Chinese fleet wraps up open sea control', *Xinhua*, February 11, 2014, at http://english.peopledaily.com.cn/90785/8533237.html (Accessed September 7, 2014).

15. Quoted in Ankit Panda, 'Chinese Naval Exercise in Eastern Indian Ocean Sends Mixed Signals', *The Diplomat*, February 7, 2014, at http://thediplomat.com/2014/02/chinese-naval-exercise-in-eastern-indian-ocean-sends-mixed-signals/ (Accessed September 7, 2014).

16. Quoted in Stanley Weiss, 'China's Indian Ocean Strategy Not a Danger—Yet', *The World Post*, July 7, 2013, at http://www.huffingtonpost.com/stanley-weiss/chinas-indian-ocean-strat_b_3561582.html (Accessed September 7, 2014).

17. 'Energy Demand and Supply in China', Chapter 2, *RAND Report*, p. 5, at http://www.rand.org/content/dam/rand/pubs/monograph_reports/MR1244/MR1244.ch2.pdf (Accessed October 1, 2014).

18. Ibid, p. 6.

19. Ibid, p. 7.

20. Ibid.

21. Ibid.

22. Barber, Nathaniel *et al.*, 'China in the Indian Ocean: Impacts, Prospects, Opportunities', Workshop in International Public Affairs, Robert M. La Follette School of Public Affairs, University of Wisconsin-Madison, Spring 2011, p. 18.

23. Holmes, James R. *et al.* (eds.), *Indian Naval Strategy in the Twenty-First Century*, Routledge, Oxon, 2009, p. 129.

24. Stanley Weiss.

25. China's 'Malacca Dilemma' is a resultant of its geostrategic position, which is vulnerable along with the requirement of the heavy use of the Malacca-Strait in the Southeast Asia—a significant strategic choke point where SLOCs travel through.

26. Rajan, D.S., 'China in the Indian Ocean: Competing Priorities', IPCS Article# 4302, February 10, 2014, at http://www.ipcs.org/article/india/china-in-the-indian-ocean-competing-priorities-4302.html (Accessed September7, 2014).

27. 'Chinese Strategy in the Indian Ocean History Essay', at http://www.ukessays.com/essays/history/chinas-strategy-in-the-indian-ocean-history essay.php#ftn15#ixzz3CbpkQ53E (Accessed 7 September 2014).

28. Quoted in Sidra Tariq, p. 26.

29. Quoted in Sidra Tariq, p. 24.

30. Hughes, Lindsay, 'China's "String of Pearls" Indian Ocean Policy and India's Responses: Potential for Conflict?', Paper presented at the annual meeting of the International Studies Association Annual Conference "Global Governance: Political Authority in Transition", Montreal-Canada, March 16, 2011, p. 12, at http://citation.allacademic.com/meta/p_mla_apa_research_citation/5/0/1/0/6/pages501066/p501066-1.php (Accessed September 7, 2014).

31. Rajan, D.S.

32. Jash, Amrita, 'Is China Looking the "Mahanian Way": The Quest for a Blue-Water Navy', China Focus—21ˢᵗ Century China, at http://chinafocus.us/2014/07/14/china-looking-mahanian-way-quest-blue-water-navy/ (Accessed September 6, 2014).

33. 'China's Navy Extends its Combat Reach to the Indian Ocean', US-China Economic and Security Review Commission Staff Report, March 14, 2014, at http://origin.www.uscc.gov/sites/default/files/Research/Staff%20Report_China%27s%20Navy%20Extends%20its%20Combat%20Reach%20to%20the%20Indian%20Ocean.pdf (Accessed 7 September 7, 2014).

34. Ibid, p. 7.

35. 'Evolving Strategic Competition in the Indian Ocean', Phantom Report, at http://www.phantomreport.com/evolving-strategic-competition-in-the-indian-ocean (Accessed October 1, 2014).

36. Pant, Harsh V., 'China's Naval Expansion in the Indian Ocean and India-China Rivalry', The Asia-Pacific Journal, 18-4-10, May 3, 2010, at

http://www.japanfocus.org/-Harsh_V_-Pant/3353 (Accessed September 10, 2014).

37. Cole, Michael, 'Red Star over the Indian Ocean?', *The Diplomat*, April 9, 2013.

38. Quoted in Gurpreet Gurpreet S. Khurana, 'China's 'String of Pearls' in the Indian Ocean and Its Security Implications', *Strategic Analysis*, Vol. 32, No. 1, February 2008, p. 3.

39. Barber, Nathaniel *et al.*, p. 17.

40. Fillingham, Zachary, 'China-India Relations: Cooperation and Conflict', *Geopolitical Monitor*, April 7, 2013, at http://www.geopoliticalmonitor. com/china-india-relations-cooperation-and-conflict-4798/ (Accessed September 7, 2014).

41. Quoted in Sidra Tariq, pp. 29–30.

42. Bo, Zhou, 'The String of Pearls and the Maritime Silk Road', *China-US Focus*, February 11, 2014, at http://www.chinausfocus.com/foreign-policy/ the-string-of-pearls-and-the-maritime-silk-road/ (Accessed September 7, 2014).

43. Krishnan, Ananth, 'China 'Silk Road' plan to push Indian Ocean ports, trade zones', The Hindu, April 17, 2014.

Acronyms

ADIZ	Air Defence Identification
AII	Australia India Institute
APTTA	Afghanistan-Pakistan Transit Trade Agreement
ASEAN	Association of Southeast Asian Nations
BIMST	Bangladesh, India, Myanmar, Sri Lanka and Thailand
CAGR	Compounded Annual Growth Rate
CCP	Chinese Communist Party
CNOOC	China National Offshore Oil Corporation
CPD	The Centre for Policy Dialogue from Bangladesh,
CPR	Centre for Policy Research
CTF	Combined Task Force
EAS	East Asia Summit
EEZ	Exclusive Economic Zone
EIA	Energy Information Administration
ETIM	East Turkmenistan Islamic Movement
GWOT	Global War on Terror
IDU	Injecting Drug Use
IMDEX	International Maritime Defense Exhibition
INCH	India and China
IOC	Indian Oil Company
IOMAC	Indian Ocean Marine Affairs Cooperation
IONS	Indian Ocean Naval Symposium
IOR	Indian Ocean Region
IORA	Indian Ocean Rim Association
IORAG	Indian Ocean Rim Academic Group
IOR-ARC	Indian Ocean Rim Association for Regional Cooperation
IORBF	Indian Ocean Rim Business Forum
IOZOP	Indian Ocean as a Zone of peace

IRTC	International Recommended Transit Corridor
LLDC	Land-Linked Developing Countries
LNG	Liquefied Natural Gas
MGCI	Mekgon-Ganga Cooperation Initiative
MILES	Millennium of Exceptional Synergy
MSR	Maritime Silk Road
NAM	Non-Alignment Movement
NM	Nautical Miles
OPEC	Organization of Petroleum Exporting Countries
PLA	People Liberation Army's
PLAN	People Liberation Army-Navy
POK	Pakistan-Occupied Kashmir
PPP	Purchasing Power Parity
PSI	Proliferation Security Initiative
QDR	Quadrennial Defense Review
RMSI	Regional Maritime Security Initiative
SAFTA	South Asian Free Trade Agreement
SAGIA	Saudi Arabian General Investment Authority
SAPTA	South Asian Preferential Trade Agreement
SCS	South China Sea
SLOCs	Sea Lines of Communication
SLORC	State Law and Order Councils
SPDF	Seychelles People's Defence Forces
TAC	Treaty of Amity and Cooperation
TPP	Trans Pacific Partnership
UAE	United Arab Emirates
UNODC	United Nations Office on Drugs and Crime
VLCC	Very Large Crude Carriers
WMD	Weapons of Mass Destruction
ZOPFAN	Zone of Peace, Freedom and Neutrality